Forest Brothers

lv. Lt Christmas 1947
ret. Oct 3/4 1950
killed Sept. 4, 1951

Forest Brothers

The Account of an Anti-Soviet Lithuanian Freedom Fighter 1944–1948

by
Juozas Lukša

Translated and with
an Introduction by
Laima Vincė

Central European University Press
Budapest – New York

Published in 2009 by Central European University Press

An imprint of the
Central European University Share Company
Nádor utca 11, H-1051 Budapest, Hungary
Tel: +36-1-327-3138 or 327-3000
Fax: +36-1-327-3183
E-mail: ceupress@ceu.hu
Website: www.ceupress.com

400 West 59th Street, New York NY 10019, USA
Tel: +1-212-547-6932
Fax: +1-646-557-2416
E-mail: mgreenwald@sorosny.org

We gratefully acknowledge the following organizations and individuals for providing the photographs: Museum of Genocide Victims, Vilnius; Lithuanian National Museum; Centre for Research of the Ukrainian Liberation Movement; Nijolė Bražėnaitė-Paronetto; Laima Vincė Sruoginis; Jonas Öhman.

ISBN 978-963-9776-58-6 paperback

Library of Congress Cataloging-in-Publication Data

Daumantas, Juozas, 1921-1951.
[Partizanai. English]
Forest brothers: the account of an anti-Soviet Lithuanian freedom fighter, 1944–1948 / by Juozas Lukša ; translated by Laima Vince.
p. cm.
Includes bibliographical references.
ISBN 978-9639776371 (cloth : alk. paper)
1. Daumantas, Juozas, 1921-1951. 2. World War, 1939-1945--Underground movements--Lithuania. 3. World War, 1939-1945--Personal narratives, Lithuanian. 4. Guerrillas--Lithuania--Biography. 5. Lithuania--Politics and government--1918-1945. 6. Insurgency--Lithuania--History--20th century.
I. Title.
D802.L5D313 2009
940.53'4793092--dc22
[B]
2009002744

Printed in Hungary by Akaprint Kft.

Contents

Introduction

Part III.
On the Partisan Road, January 1946–May 1947

The Invisible Front

Lithuania's Armed Resistance Against the Soviet Union

Laima Vincė

The Unknown War

By 1945 World War II had ended, but in Lithuania the war against the Soviet Union had only just begun. One of the bloodiest battles of the Lithuanian armed resistance, the battle of Kalniškės, was fought only days after VE day.

Lithuanian farmers, school teachers, university professors, university and high school students, and a small number of remaining non-commissioned officers and lower ranking officers from independent Lithuania's military, organized themselves into a partisan movement that at its peak was roughly 30,000 strong. Many of these same men and women had opposed the Nazis during World War II. Most of these partisan fighters had little or no formal military experience or training.

For half a century the Soviet Union kept this war a secret. Its participants were hunted down, tortured, and exiled to prison camps in Siberia. Its survivors learned to keep quiet. Of the three Baltic States, Lithuania fought the hardest and the longest. Nonetheless, they were forgotten by the outside world. As the vastly outnumbered and undersupplied Lithuanians continued to resist their Soviet occupiers for nearly a decade after World War II had ended, America and Western Europe moved on to reconstruct a peaceful and prosperous post-war Europe.

In February 1945, at the Yalta Conference American President Franklin D. Roosevelt "let it slip that the United States would not protest if the Soviet Union attempted to annex the three Baltic States."[1] After Yalta, the three Baltic States and much of Central Europe was left in Stalin's control.

---

1 "The Yalta Conference." *The Latin Library*, [URL:http://www.thelatinlibrary.com/imperialism/notes/yalta.html] accessed June 30, 2008

Pre-War independent Lithuania's Consuls and Ambassadors in the United States and in Western Europe refused to close down their embassies and continued to function in exile as representatives of independent Lithuania's pre-war government. Because of their efforts, the United States and a few other countries did not legally recognize the incorporation of Lithuania into the Soviet Union. In essence, the United States was playing both sides by appeasing Baltic émigrés in the United States on the one hand by not *de jure* recognizing the Soviet occupation of Lithuania, while on the other playing a political game by handing over the Baltic States and Central Europe to a ruthless dictator and a totalitarian regime.

Despite the West's politics, the resistance continued to fight for freedom, hoping for support from the outside world. That support never came. The men and women of Lithuania resisted the Soviets for nearly a decade, outnumbered and undersupplied, refusing to accept that Eastern Europe could be left in the grips of a totalitarian regime. Behind the Iron Curtain they waged a desperate guerilla war, dubbed by Soviet Interior Forces as "The Invisible Front."

The armed resistance came about as the result of three foreign occupations that occurred within the span of four years. Lithuania was first occupied by the Soviets on June 15, 1940. As part of the territorial agreement between the Soviet Union and Nazi Germany—commonly referred to as the Molotov–Ribbentrop pact—the Soviets invaded the three independent Baltic nations: Estonia, Latvia, and Lithuania. On October 10, 1939, Lithuania's Minister of Foreign Affairs, Juozas Urbšys, signed an agreement with Stalin allowing the Soviet Union to station Soviet troops on Lithuanian soil. Urbšys writes in his memoir, published in 1988:

> The choice facing the Lithuanian government was as follows:
> 1. Either sign the mutual assistance treaty as demanded, thereby according the Soviet Union the right to establish a set number of military bases at specific locations on Lithuanian territory, and regain Vilnius and part of its territory;
> 2. Or, refuse to sign the treaty, forsake Vilnius, and enter into a ruinous conflict with the Soviet Union. A graphic example of the form which such a conflict could take was the Finnish experience which I have alluded to earlier.
>
> Understandably, the government of Lithuania chose the first alternative.[2]

---

[2] Juozas Urbšys, "Lithuania and the Soviet Union 1939–1940: The Fateful Year, Memoirs by Juozas Urbšys," Translated and edited by Sigita Naujokaitis, *Lithuanian Quarterly Journal of Arts and Sciences*, Volume 34, No. 2, (Summer 1989).

The Lithuanian government ordered the Lithuanian army not to resist. Lithuania's president, Antanas Smetona, fled across the border to Germany. The decision not to resist enraged the Lithuanian populace at the time and was popularly considered to be a mistake. However, this decision was made in part because of conclusions drawn from the war in Finland, 1939–1940. This conflict was closely monitored by the Baltic countries. Although the Finns ultimately defended themselves from the Soviets, that war displayed Stalin's ruthlessness and his willingness to sacrifice troops in order to achieve his objectives. Independent Lithuania's government feared that there would be a massive blood bath in Lithuania if the tiny country were to attempt to resist. Another factor influencing the decision not to resist was the lack of allies and supporters who would have been willing and able to come to Lithuania's aid to backup the Lithuanian army—an army the fraction of the size of the Red Army.

After the Soviets entered Lithuania in 1940, they employed a few covert political maneuvers and rigged an election, incorporating Lithuania into the Soviet Union. The Soviets quickly introduced radical social and economic changes, nationalizing private property and centralizing farming. These measures were accompanied by strict control measures and various means of oppression and acts of terror. Urbšys himself was arrested along with his wife on July 16, 1940 and deported to Siberia. June 15–22, 1941, just before the Germans attacked the Soviet Union, the Soviets organized the arrest and deportation of Lithuania's national elite: the country's politicians, military officers, school teachers, businessmen and wealthy farmers. Three thousand Lithuanians were deported at this time.[3] They were deported to the far reaches of Siberia, some wearing just their summer clothing, and with no supplies or provisions. After being left in areas as remote as the mouth of the Lena River, the exiles were ordered to build their own barracks from whatever materials they could scrounge and to "fish for the state"[4] in Lake Baikal or the Laptev Sea or to build railroads or work in mines. Most of the exiles from 1941 died of starvation, exposure, and disease.

The Nazis invaded in the summer of 1941 and imposed their own brand of terror from 1941 through 1944. They conscripted young Lithuanian men into the German army or into forced labor and sent thousands of Lithuanians to work as unpaid slave laborers in Hitler's war industry in Germany. The Nazis annihilated Lithuania's Jewish population, which had roots in Lithuania dating back to two

---

3 "Lithuania in 1940–1941: The Persecutions Start," Museum of Genocide Victims, Vilnius, Lithuania, 2008.

4 Dalia Grinkevičiūtė, *Lietuviai prie Laptevo Jūros* (Lithuanians by the Laptev Sea), Vilnius: Pergalė, 1988.

major migrations, one that took place in the eighth century and the other in the twelfth century. Vilnius was an important Jewish cultural center, often referred to as a "second Jerusalem." The loss of Lithuania's Jews was a traumatic blow to the Lithuanian nation.

The German Army retreated from Lithuania in the summer of 1944 when the Soviet Red Army occupied the country a second time as their troops pushed forwards towards Berlin. The Soviet Red Army remained on Lithuanian soil until 1991, one year after the country declared its independence March 11, 1990.

In 1944, the Soviets immediately initiated efforts to integrate Lithuania into the Soviet Union. They forcibly conscripted young men for service in the Red Army on the push to defeat the Germans. Individuals who were perceived as potentially dangerous or who were accused of collaborating with the Germans were arrested and sentenced without trial. These measures caused large groups of people to go into hiding. It did not take much to appear suspicious to the Soviet Security.

As the Germans retreated, a number of Lithuanians who had been forced into service under the Germans took the opportunity to desert, taking their weapons and equipment with them. These groups spontaneously formed guerilla units, calling themselves *partizanai* (partisans) or *miškiniai* (the forest brotherhood). Men and women hiding from the Soviets joined their ranks.

According to the Lithuanian scholar, Arūnas Bubnys,[5] up to five percent of the partisans may have cooperated with the Germans. However, most of the partisans had no such connections. They sought independence from any occupation forces. A large number of the partisans in 1944 were very young, the average age being 20, making them too young to have collaborated with the Germans during the German occupation.

The Deportations to Siberia

On Stalin's orders the Soviets carried out a program of genocide in 1941, 1944, 1948, and throughout the 1950's, with the goal of subduing the local population and integrating it into the Soviet Union. Those who resisted or who were perceived as bourgeois were disposed of by being transported via cattle cars to hard labor camps in Siberia or to exile in remote areas of the Soviet Union.

During these years the Soviets deported about 130,000 people from Lithuania to the outlying areas of the Soviet Union. There were several waves of mass deportations aimed at annihilating specific groups of the population, conducted

5 Arūnas Bubnys, *Nazi Resistance Movement in Lithuania 1941–1944*, Vilnius: Vaga, 2003.

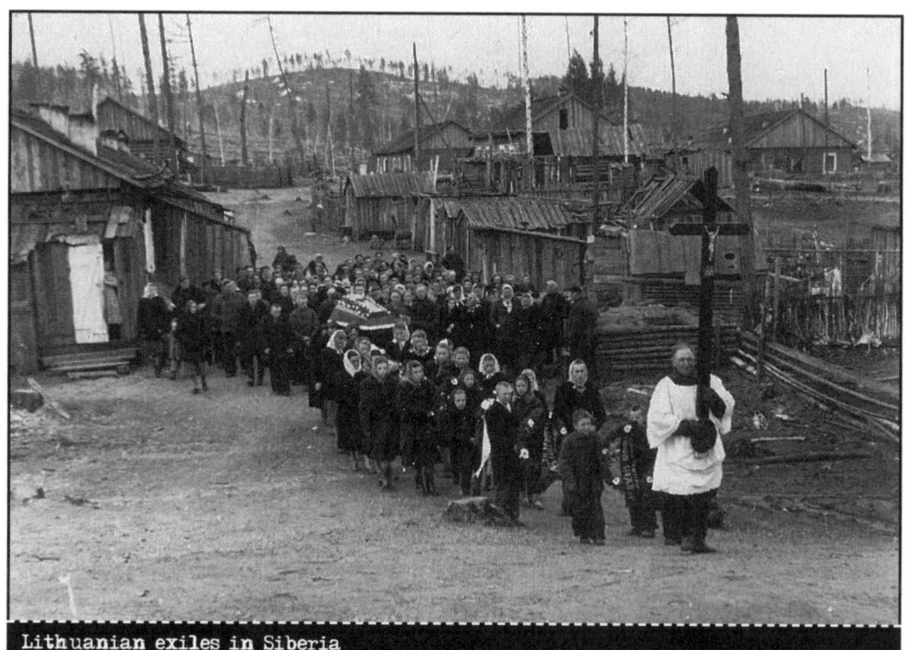

Lithuanian exiles in Siberia

in defiance of international law on the protection of civilians during an occupation. The highest echelons of power in the Soviet Union and the Lithuanian Soviet Socialist Republic organized and gave out instructions to carry out the deportations. The direct perpetrators were the heads of the Communist Party and the repressive agencies of administrative units, the chairmen of executive committees, secretaries of the Communist Party, the heads and ordinary officers of the NKGB (MGB) and the NVKD (MVD) of the Lithuanian Soviet Socialist Republic as well as local Soviet activists who were in charge of carrying out the deportations. In total, about 250,000 Lithuanians were deported or imprisoned during 1944–1951.[6] Lithuania's Center for Genocide and Resistance estimates that approximately 118,599 Lithuanians died in Siberia. Roughly 50,000 Lithuanians fled to the West to avoid deportation and Soviet repressions.

A document from the Lithuanian Special Archive of the Lithuanian Center for Genocide and Resistance reveals that in 1944 at a war council meeting of the 3rd Byelorussian and 1st Baltic Fronts a proposal was seriously considered to deport *all* Lithuanian residents to Siberia "as had been the case in other Soviet

[6] A. Anušauskas, *Fiziniai genocido padariniai//Lietuvo sunaikinimas ir tautos kova.–V.* (The Consequences of Genocide//The Destruction of the Lithuanian Nation and Resistance), 1999, pp. 577–578.

Lithuanian prisoners building a railroad in Siberia

republics." Only, the members present at the meeting failed to come to an agreement on whether to deport them all at once as was done in the Caucasus, or to deport them in stages.[7] The Russian Communist ideologue Mikhail Suslov had joked that "Lithuania is beautiful without the Lithuanians." His remark put in the context of these discussions is rather macabre.

There Was No Alternative

A major reason why the armed resistance was organized in 1944 was because the traumatic experience of the Soviet occupation of 1940–1941 was still fresh in many Lithuanians' minds. The return of the Soviets in 1944 created a sense of desperation in Lithuania. Many felt they had no alternative but to join the underground.

When the Soviets returned in 1944, Juozas Lukša, a twenty-three-year old student of Architecture at Kaunas University, went into hiding along with his three brothers, Jurgis, Stanislovas, and Antanas. All four eventually joined the Tauras Military District partisans and quickly rose in partisan ranks.

Juozas Lukša was born in the village of Juodbūdis in the Marijampolė district August 10, 1921. He was the son of a farmer, Simonas Lukša. Juozas Lukša had

---

[7] Pranas Morkus, *Resistance to the Occupation of Lithuania: 1944–1990: Call to Arms (1944–1953)*, Vilnius: The Genocide and Resistance Research Center, 2002.

two elder stepsisters, Marija (born 1898) and Angelė (1900–1930) and an elder stepbrother, Vincas (born 1905) from his father's previous marriage and three brothers: Jurgis (born 1922), Antanas (born 1923) and Stanislovas (born 1926). According to Lithuanian tradition at the time, the eldest stepbrother, Vincas, was to inherit the family farm. Therefore, Juozas and his three brothers were sent to study at Kaunas University.[8] They represented the pre-World War II generation that was making the cultural shift from an agricultural life to a professional urban life.

Lukša as a student of Architecture at Kaunas University

The Lukša family were wealthy farmers who owned 33 hectares of land. Marija married Pranas Tūtlys from the neighboring village and Vincas managed the farm. All the Lukša brothers divided their time between their studies in Kaunas and work on the farm. Juozas studied Architecture; Jurgis studied Mechanics; Antanas studied Geodesy; and Stasys studied handicrafts, then later Chemistry at Vilnius University. When the second Soviet occupation began, it was clear that because of the brothers' activities in the resistance against the first Soviet occupation and against the Nazis, that would need to join the underground. They were monitored by the MGB (precursor to the KGB) and eventually joined the partisans. All four brothers went down on their knees before their mother, Ona Lukšienė. She put her hands on their heads and said these words: "I give you my blessing as you set out on this holy battle. May the Lord God protect you. Swear that you will never allow yourselves to be taken alive."

The first of the Lukša brothers to die was Jurgis (Piršlys). He died on June 13, 1947 when Soviet Security forces surrounded the Lukša farm. Simonas Lukša, who was 84 at the time, was dragged over to view the remains of his son. The sight drove him mad. He died a few months later on October 13th, 1947. Ona Lukšienė was arrested by the MGB and was interrogated, kicked, and beaten. The remains of Jurgis Lukša were brought to the town of Veiveriai where they were defiled by Soviet Security soldiers. At the time Jurgis was engaged to a young local woman

[8] Interview with Antanas Lukša, Kaunas, Lithuania, May 25, 2008. Interview conducted by Laima Sruoginis.

named Kazytė. She was arrested and tortured, beaten, and held prisoner in a cellar in MGB headquarters in Veiveriai. After several days of torture, what was left of Jurgis's corpse, burned and badly deformed, was brought in by two Russians and dumped on Kazytė's lap. "Now, make love!" the Russians said, standing over Kazytė and the corpse of her fiancée.

On that same day, Antanas Lukša (Arūnas) was betrayed and arrested. He was badly beaten, tortured, and interrogated. He was sentenced to 25 years hard labor in Siberia. He was imprisoned throughout the Soviet gulag, in Komia, Irkusk, Taishet, Magadan, and Kolmia. After serving fifteen years, Antanas returned to Lithuania. He said to his mother, upon seeing her for the first time: "Forgive me for breaking my vow and remaining alive."[9]

Vincas Lukša was arrested for "harboring bandits" and was sentenced to ten year's hard labor in Vorkuta. He returned to Lithuania in 1955. Vincas Lukša died in Lithuania in 1993.

Stasys died covering his fellow partisans in battle August 12, 1947 in the forests of Kazlų Rūda.

Ona Lukšienė lived in hiding until Stalin's death, finding shelter with various friends and relatives. She died October 6, 1966 of cancer.

The tragic fate of the Lukša family was not unusual. Many families lost all or most of their members during the post-war resistance. The main reason young men and women joined the resistance was the ruthless behavior of the Soviets, who crushed and oppressed any expression of dissatisfaction with the Soviet system. Arrests, imprisonments, brutal interrogation methods, executions, abductions, and deportations created fear among the populace as well as hatred, desperation, and a decisiveness to resist. Many surviving partisans testify that they were motivated to join the resistance because of atrocities committed against their families or to avoid deportation or conscription.[10]

On a practical level, the loss of independence meant the loss of personal opportunity, property, and wealth. The collectivization of the countryside was perceived as one of the most crucial changes of societal structure forced onto the local populace by the Soviets. Many farm boys saw their inheritance and their way of life being expropriated and saw no other alternative than to join the resistance.

---

9 Interview with Antanas Lukša, Kaunas, Lithuania, May 25, 2008. Interview conducted by Laima Sruoginis.

10 Kadžionis's entire family was deported to Siberia in May 1948. He escaped deportation by joining the partisans. After living in hiding in an underground bunker for five years, Kadžionis and his wife were arrested and deported to hard labor in Siberia. Kadžionis survived twenty-five years hard labor. Interview conducted by Jonas Öhman and Rytas Narvydas.

The backbone of the armed resistance consisted of farm boys, who for one reason or another withdrew to the forest and joined the guerillas. These boys were born in the independent Lithuania between the wars. This photo shows an unknown young partisan, partly dressed in Lithuanian pre-war uniform.

Every volunteer was required to take an oath of loyalty. A few underground guerilla training sessions were organized in the forests, but volunteers mainly learned to fight first hand by participating in battles and skirmishes. Lukša's descriptions in this memoir of the course for non-commissioned officers held in 1947 is remarkable because it describes the decisiveness to develop and improve the resistance.

Almost no high ranking military officers participated in the resistance. At the end of the war in 1944, most of the remaining officers who had survived the liquidation of Lithuania's military officers in 1941, escaped to the West.[11] A number of Lithuania's high ranking military officers had been arrested and killed during the first Soviet occupation of Lithuania. The leaders of the resistance who did have military experience were of low or middle rank. The well-known chief commanders, Jonas Žemaitis and Adolfas Ramanauskas, had been an artillery captain and a reserve lieutenant respectively in independent Lithuania's army. Juozas Lukša, who was a university student at the beginning of the conflict, was eventually promoted to the rank of major by partisan command.

11 Kęstutis Girnius, *Partizanų kovos Lietuvoje* (The Partisan War in Lithuania), Vilnius: Mokslas, 1990, p. 100.

Youth in the Žemaičiai area in northern Lithuania are sworn into the resistance. The young girls were used for liaison and supply tasks. Of the more than 20,000 resistance participants killed during the conflict about half were between the ages of 16–21.

It is difficult for historians to determine the exact number of participants in Lithuania's post-war armed resistance for obvious reasons: It was nearly impossible at the time, under the circumstances, to maintain accurate records. Possibly up to 100,000[12] individuals may have either actively participated in the resistance or supported it in some way. Available statistics indicate that between 40,000–50,000[13] individuals were under arms at one point or another during 1944–1953. At its peak in the spring of 1945 the partisan movement was about 30,000 strong. This number diminished after the end of World War II as a result of amnesties[14]

12 This number is still being debated.

13 In his book *Partizanų kovos Lietuvoje* (The Partisan War in Lithuania), Girnius elaborates on a definition of "partisan years" or the number of total years served by a partisan, meaning one individual's service could be counted for several years. Girnius establishes his numbers at 50,000. The historian N. Gaškaitė, in her book *Pasipriešinimo istorija* (The History of Resistance), provides an estimation in which she counts each year separately, coming up with a total number of participants in the resistance at 56,000–57,000. Bearing in mind, as Girnius notes, that many partisans were active for several years and therefore included in the count more than once, it is reasonable to suggest that 40,000 to 50,000 partisans participated in total in the resistance. However, all of these numbers are estimations. Not counted are the number of reservists among the civilian populace who were prepared to be mobilized as partisans and who participated in partisan operations without officially joining or belonging to a single partisan unit.

14 J. Starkauskas, *Čekistinė kariuomenė Lietuvoje 1944–1953* (The Soviet Interior Forces in Lithuania 1944–1953), Vilnius: Genocide and Resistance Research Center, 1998, p. 9.

and because supply problems made it difficult to maintain such large numbers of resistance fighters in the forests. Increasing pressure from the Soviets further forced the partisans to change their tactics to smaller, less vulnerable groups. By the end of the 1940s, as the armed resistance movement was winding down, the active partisan movement consisted of only several thousand individuals.

However, the partisans continued to recruit people into the resistance throughout the late 1940s. The armed resistance strove to set up a plan for general mobilization to provide support to Western armed forces in the event of a major conflict.[15]

Historians at the Center for Genocide and Resistance in Vilnius, Lithuania, argue that archives reveal that around 250 women were active fighters in the armed resistance between 1944 and 1953. Married women made up 72% of the fighters and unmarried women 28%. The wives of partisans often had no other choice than to join the resistance because they were subject to arrest and interrogation.

In addition to the men and women who fought in the armed resistance, a significant number of men and women in the Lithuanian countryside supported the resistance by providing food, shelter, supplies and medicine, and by acting as liaisons. One of the main reasons the resistance endured for so many years in Lithuania despite massive attacks and oppressive measures employed by the NKVD was because of this support. Several tens of thousands of families and individuals actively provided the partisans with food, clothing, shelter, liaison and moral support.

The endurance of the resistance, despite an almost total lack of support from abroad, can only be explained by the considerable loyal support from parts of the population in the countryside. This support is one of the reasons why the

15 Intelligence report on the Lithuanian resistance by the Swedish Intelligence Agency (T-kontoret), July 1947, Swedish War Archives, No. 80. II.4.10/4.

resistance in Lithuania was about ten times as intensive, and more difficult to stamp out, than in the two other Soviet-occupied republics, Latvia and Estonia.

Extensive civilian support was one of the main reasons why large numbers of Lithuanians were imprisoned and deported in the years after World War II. In May 1948 more than 40,000 Lithuanians were deported to Siberia, accounting for 50% of all deportations that took place within the entire Soviet Union that year.[16]

An unidentified partisan poses for a photograph beside his mother. Often entire families supported the armed resistance and as a result often entire families perished

In order to act as combat squads and for the squads to feel like units and for the units to be organized into districts that made up an army that defended its homeland, communication was necessary. The post office, radio, and telephone system were taken over by the Soviets. Therefore, the partisans had to rely on messengers, or liaisons. An intricate network of liaisons maintained connections, provided supplies, and conveyed information between the civilian society and the partisans.[17] Many of these liaisons were teenage village girls who would travel unarmed between units and squads conveying messages and delivering supplies. If they were caught, they were interrogated and tortured as harshly as the partisan fighters. They were also sent to hard labor concentration camps in Siberia. These little-known women remain the unsung heroes of the resistance.

16 The International Commission for the Evaluation of the Crimes of Nazi and Soviet Occupation Regimes in Lithuania/Conclusions ratified June 20, 2005. Regarding deportations of inhabitants of Lithuania 1944–1953, conclusion No. 10.

17 Interview with Leonora Grigalavičiūtė (code name Vida), one of the liaisons of the last commander-in-chief of the resistance, Jonas Žemaitis, Jūrmala, Latvia, April 2008.

When men joined the armed resistance, often their wives joined as well. Women fought side by side with men, tended to the wounded, and operated as liaisons. Here a husband and wife partisan couple frolic in the snow. They are wearing "snow camouflage"-often sewn from white linen tablecloths

From the beginning, the resistance fighters were outnumbered, undersupplied, and lacked proper weaponry and ammunition. However, they had the advantage of knowing the local terrain, were accustomed to a life outdoors, and had the trust and practical support of the local populace. They were also deeply commit-

In many families the different family members contributed in various ways to the resistance. In this picture company commander Povilas Grumbinas–codename Ąžuolas (Oaktree) greets his sister, the liaison girl Domicele Grumbinaitė–codename Žibuoklė (Liverwort).

Among the ranks of partisans there were several women who contributed to the resistance in several ways. Here Sofija Budėnaitė–codename Ramunė (Daisy) –receives a medal for bravery in April 1948. The medal is awarded by the commander of the military district Adolfas Ramanauskas–codename Vanagas (Hawk). The motivation for the award is read by Lionginas Balukevičius–codename Dzūkas (The man from Dzukija). These were, besides Juozas Lukša and some others, some of the most well known resistance leaders. Both of the men on the picture wrote accounts of their lives as partisans, which were published posthumously.

ted to their cause. The generation that fled to the forests to defend their nation had been born into an independent Lithuania (1918–1939). This generation had been educated during a period of great idealism and patriotism[18] as the fledgling nation enthusiastically threw itself into a period of reconstruction and rebirth following several centuries of serfdom under the yoke of the tsars of Russia.

The Catholic faith also provided a strong source of moral consciousness to the Lithuanian armed resistance and served as an alternative to the overbearing ideological incentives forced on the populace by the Soviet system. Lukša's memoir emphasizes the importance of Catholicism and religious tradition, especially among the partisan leadership.

Altogether roughly 21,500[19] Lithuanian partisan men and women died in Lithuania's forests or bunkers or as a result of torture or by execution after being

[18] Interview with Nijolė-Braženaitė-Lukšienė-Paronetto, June 15, 2007, New York, USA. Interview conducted by Laima Vincė Sruoginis.

[19] This figure is the official number provided by the Center for Genocide and Resistance in Vilnius, Lithuania. In fact, other Lithuanian historians argue that the number is too low, that actually roughly 30,000 men and women died in the resistance. These numbers are the subject of intense debate among historians in Lithuania.

captured by the Soviets. The majority of these men and women were about twenty years of age. Most of their bodies were tossed into unmarked graves by the Soviets. To this day many of them are still missing.

The typical partisan was a farm boy with limited understanding of discipline and military life, but who was familiar with life in the outdoors and who had intimate contacts with people in the provinces. Soviet propaganda spread the myth that the partisans were rich people who were involved in a class struggle against the "People's Government" that meant to protect the interests of the poor. In fact, statistically most of the partisans were poor villagers and farmers. Lukša writes in *Forest Brothers* about how at one guerilla training session as he stood observing the men, he was struck by how the partisan life was truly democratic as it brought the poor farmer and the university student together to fight side by side for a single cause:

"I opened the tent flap and saw the faces of these men.... It would be very difficult to find one man among these forty who was not marked by battle and who had not shed his own blood for his beloved country. ... The backgrounds of the soldiers were very diverse. Among them were University students, high school students, farmers and laborers. Also among them were priests, older intellectuals, even officers from Independent Lithuania's army. Here you could also find volunteers from the fight for Lithuania's last independence. They were all united with one and the same sense of duty towards their native land and a duty to protect their brothers and sisters from the terror of the Russian barbarian invaders. They felt they had to defend freedom and humanity. They understood perfectly well that to defend their country and their people they would have to sacrifice their own personal lives. That they had only their strength and their alertness to go on. All the while they secretly held onto the hope that finally those who so recently had talked about how to set up life after the War will feel a responsibility towards generations to come and will condemn barbarism, terror, and slavery—the barbarism, terror, and slavery that had taken over the larger part of Europe and Asia. ... These sentiments made blood brothers of the farmer with the student."

A Military Structure

The partisan commanders strove to maintain a military structure as a continuation of the pre-war Lithuanian army and subsequently as representatives of an independent state. The command of partisan units was modeled on the regular army. Military uniforms, insignia and badges were introduced and military regulations were modified to accommodate the non-conventional conditions. Court procedures were set up to punish any behavior that disgraced the name and reputation of the partisans. Punishments for betrayal were also established.

Many of the names of partisan units were from the names of units in the former Lithuanian army. Efforts were undertaken to create and maintain a formal military structure with military districts and subordinated units. Indeed, the entire resistance, which had arose organically in separate regions throughout Lithuania, was briefly unified into one structure in 1949. The partisan command made a declaration that the partisan movement should be perceived as the only legal government of Lithuania.[20]

Sadly, these goals were reached by the partisans just as they were losing their civilian support because of the mass deportations and the collectivization of farms. Surviving partisans claim that they received significant support from the civil population up until 1949. After 1949 that support began to decrease, due to the massive deportations of civilian supporters, the collectivization of private farms into collective farms, and infiltration by elaborate networks of agents and informers.[21]

When the Soviet Union occupied Lithuania, the society was still a largely agrarian society. Compared with neighboring Estonia and Latvia, the process of urbanization was far less advanced in Lithuania and the proportion of the population living in the countryside was much larger. The social networks in the countryside were often very tight and provided strong incentives to support the local partisans.

Also, compared with the other two Baltic republics, Lithuania had implemented agrarian reforms during the period of independence, 1918–1940, and for this reason farms were located at relatively remote distances from each other. Geographically this provided an excellent opportunity for the resistance to elude the Soviets and to reach the farms and use them as bases of operation. By comparison, in the Ukraine, where farms were located close to each other, forming village complexes in the center of expansive fields, the Soviet interior forces had an easier task controlling the countryside. [22]

---

20 A. Anušauskas, *The Anti-Soviet Resistance in the Baltic States*, Vilnius: Akreta, 2002, p. 81.

21 Interview with former partisan Jonas Kadžionis, Bebrūnai village, Lithuania, May 2008. Interview conducted by Jonas Öhman and Rytas Narvydas.

22 Interview with former NKVD Officer Gennadiy Gusev (served in the Ukraine 1946–1948 and in Lithuania 1951–1954), Volgograd, June 2004. Interview conducted by Jonas Öhman.

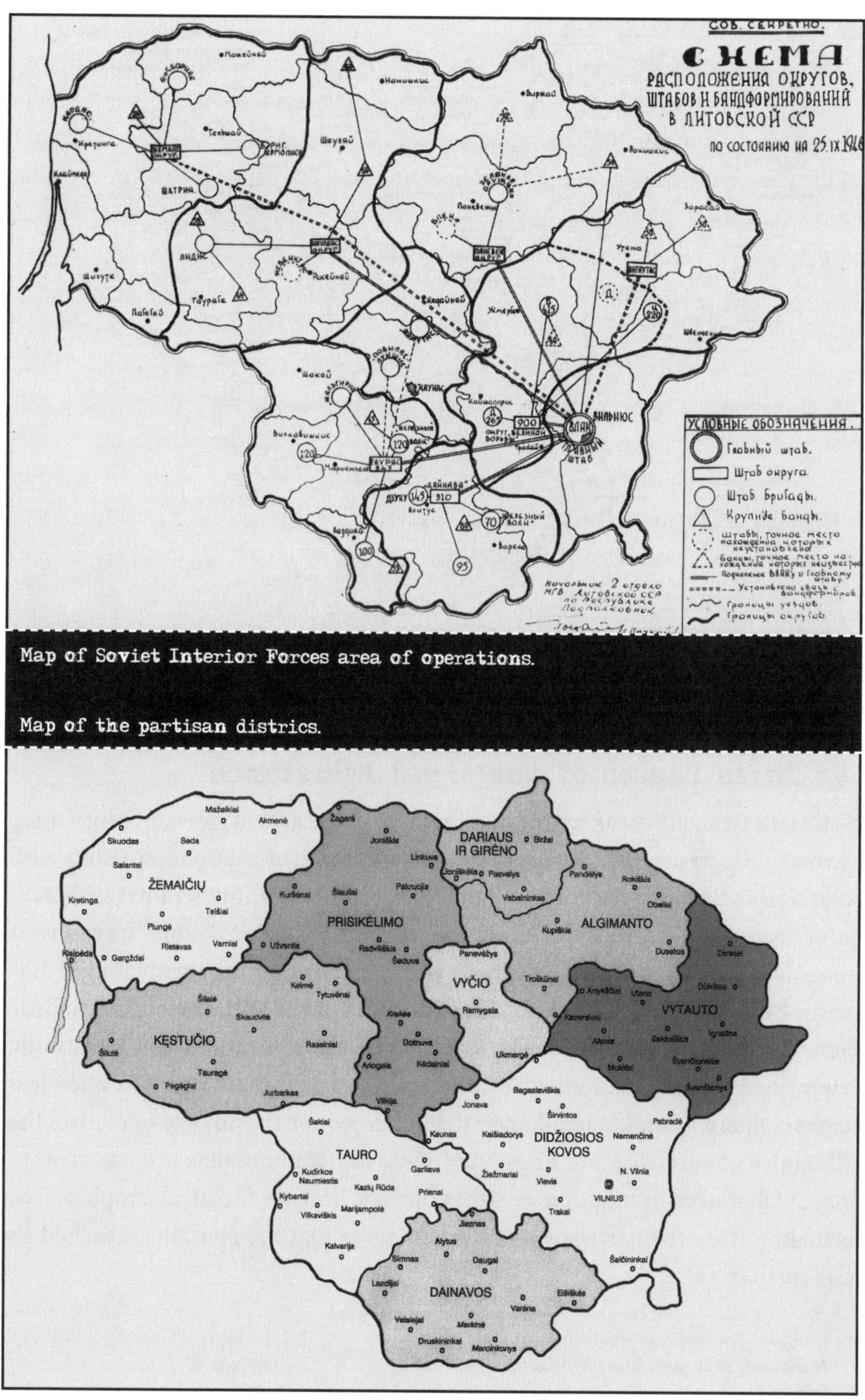

Map of Soviet Interior Forces area of operations.

Map of the partisan districs.

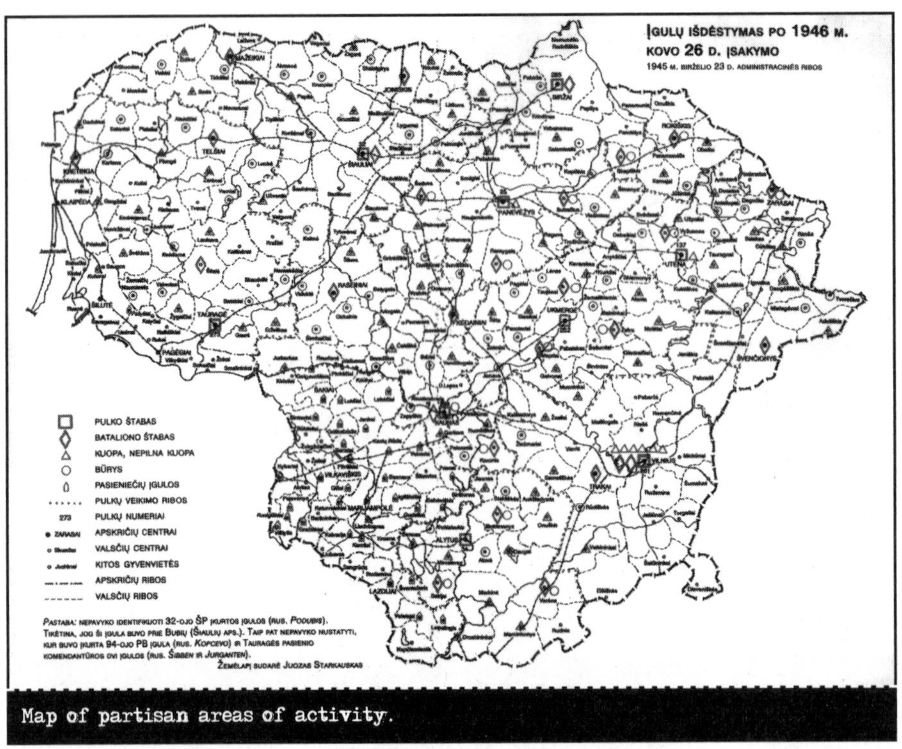

Map of partisan areas of activity.

The Three Phases of the Armed Resistance

Historians typically break up the development of the armed resistance into three phases.[23] The first phase, 1944–1945 took the form of a public uprising with open clashes between the partisans and Soviet troops. The Soviet Interior Forces on occasion had to call in artillery and aircraft for help. Despite huge losses (roughly 3,500 Soviets died in the early weeks of fighting) the enemy fought diligently. Beria put out a decree to "clear Lithuania of the anti-Soviet nationalistic element within two to three weeks." Meanwhile, the resistance was idealistically determined to fight the Red Army and overestimated their strength: they lost 10,000 fighters. It took much longer than planned for the Soviets to control the Lithuanian countryside. For a few years it was nearly impossible in some areas to find collaborators to function as Soviet officials because the local people feared retaliation from the partisans.[24] Historians agree that the resistance reached its peak in 1945.

---

[23] Anušauskas et al., *Anti-Soviet Resistance*, p. 28.

[24] *Ibid.*, p. 53.

Moscow soon realized that the Lithuanian resistance needed to be seriously dealt with. Moscow ordered Soviet Security officers to employ all means necessary. One of the most hard-core Communist officials, Mikhail Suslov, who was responsible for the deportations of the Chechnyans in 1944, was appointed by the Kremlin to "liquidate" the "bandits" in the Baltics. Twelve NKVD-regiments, or Soviet Interior Forces, about 15,000–20,000 troops, were deployed to Lithuania for operations aimed at subduing the resistance.[25] A local Soviet militia was set up. Collaborators were recruited from the local populace to serve in the Soviet militia.[26] These security agencies at once established a network of agents and informers to infiltrate the ranks of the insurgents.[27]

The local Soviet militia, or *Stribai,* are remembered with the most bitterness by survivors. These people were home grown traitors who agreed to collaborate with the Communists to make up deportation lists and to infiltrate the partisan ranks. They terrorized the local people and were emboldened by the strength of the Soviet Interior Forces who they reported to. Most of these people were the dregs of society—the local village drunks or outcasts or bullies who were looking to empower themselves by joining ranks with the enemy. Their low social status made them vulnerable[28] to manipulation by the occupiers. The *Stribai* often took advantage of their mandate from the authorities in order to harass and steal from the local population at will. In total, during the post-war period roughly 8,000 *Stribai* operated in Lithuania together with 7,000 Lithuanian Communist party members.

Relying on a method that was successful in crushing the resistance in Ukraine, the Soviets developed a system of using secret agents, or *Smogikai,* recruited from former partisans taken alive who had agreed under torture to collaborate, and to infiltrate Partisan units. These agents would return to their former comrades-in-arms in uniform and would execute them or deliver them into the hands of the NKVD. Another Soviet tactic was to send Soviet agents dressed as partisans into the countryside to seek liaison with remaining partisans.

The second phase of the resistance lasted from 1946–1949 and was characterized by a deadly game of hide-and-seek where the Soviets employed huge resources to hunt down the remaining partisans. After 1946, having suffering heavy losses and with the increased pressure from Soviet Interior Forces, the par-

---

25 Ignatavičius I. "Naikintojų karinės pajėgos"//Lietuvos naikinimas ir tautos kova 1940–1998.-V., 1999. p. 117.

26 Anušauskas et al., *Anti-Soviet Resistance,* p. 61.

27 *Lietuvių nacionalistų kenkėjiška veikla ir kova su ja* (The Activities of the Lithuanan Nationalists and the Battle Against Them), Lithuanian KGB special issue, Moscow, 1986, pp. 49–50.

28 Juozas Starkauskas, *Stribai,* Genocide and Resistance Research Center of Lithuania, Vilnius, 2001, p. 434.

tisans changed their tactics. They avoided direct combat and no longer convened in large camps in the forests. Instead, they set up small mobile squads that were suitable for ambushes and quick strikes on the occupier's administration. The idea of a unified military command now became an urgent necessity. Squads were organized together into units that were organized into territorial formations made up of districts. In the beginning, seven military districts were set up.

At this time the partisans rarely engaged in actions directly aimed at the Soviet Interior Forces or other military structures. The number of casualties from the Interior Forces was relatively low. The vast superiority of the Soviets in terms of numbers, equipment, training, liaison and intelligence made such efforts very dangerous. The local Soviet militia units, or *Stribai*, set up by the Soviet authorities sometimes got involved in skirmishes with the partisans.

After the shift towards guerilla tactics, the number of casualties stabilized. However, by the end of the forties only several thousand partisans remained.

When losses were suffered, the ranks would immediately be replenished. The annual deportations, the horror of the forced collectivization of farms, the persecution of the Catholic Church, and the expropriation of land, homes, and property left many with no choice but to join the resistance.

Over time the aggressive tactics, the continuous search parties in the forests and villages, the deportations of supporters, and an increasingly efficient use of agents coupled with the diminishing hope of a war between the Soviet Union and the West, a lack of support from abroad, and other factors forced the resistance literally underground. Thousands of bunkers and hideouts were built and the fighting took the form of raids and ambushes. Many farmers allowed the partisans to build their hideouts inside or under or adjacent to their farm houses.[29]

By the late forties and early fifties the partisans were concerned for their own survival. The Soviet authorities would not relent as long as one partisan remained alive. Because Lithuania lacks natural hiding places—mountains or caves—the Lithuanian partisans had to dig bunkers deep into the ground. The earliest bunkers resembled pits. Later, the partisans began constructing bunkers where several fighters could live for long periods of time. These bunkers contained plank beds, a small work desk, ventilation pipes and stoves, fire exits, and toilet facilities. The entrances to the bunkers were camouflaged to match the natural surroundings and were opened only at night. During the day the partisans lived as though buried alive in their bunkers, tensely listening for footsteps or dogs. During the

[29] Kęstutis Girnius, *Partizanų*, p. 310.

winter, after the snow fell, the partisans could not leave the bunker for months, because of the danger of leaving tracks. Partisans also hid underground in villagers' houses, in barns, in wells, beside rivers and in the forests.

During the third phase of the resistance, 1949–1953, the last remnants of the partisans were infiltrated and hunted down by Soviet Interior Forces. Historians have come to an agreement that 1953 marks the official end of the armed resistance because that was the year the organizational structure of the movement collapsed. However, individual partisans were hunted down and executed as late as 1962 and 1965. The last two active partisans, Antanas Kraujelis and Pranas Končius, were killed in 1965.

Moscow's Effort to Suppress the Armed Resistance

Moscow put considerable effort into suppressing the well-organized partisans. At its peak, 12 regiments of the security interior forces were dispatched to Lithuania and were commanded directly from the Kremlin. Documents found in the Special Archives of the Center for Genocide and Resistance reveal that at times up to 1,000 interior troops would be called in to hunt down a group of two or three partisans. On average, 30 Interior Ministry soldiers and armed supporters of the regime were assigned to each individual partisan. Together with the guerilla war in western Ukraine, the resistance in Lithuania is considered the fiercest among the countries occupied by Soviet Russia. In total, about 13,000 Soviet Russians were killed in the conflict with the partisans in Lithuania.

According to available records from Soviet Security archives, about 20,000 men and women who had actively participated or had supported the resistance were killed in action.[30] Of the more than 250,000 individuals who were imprisoned in concentration camps or deported to Siberia a third allegedly had some connections with the resistance, or were family members. Soviet Security archives state that 4,000 individuals were killed on the Soviet side during the conflict. Of this number, roughly 1,500 were military, mainly soldiers from the interior troops. Roughly 2,500 were Soviet local militia, police officers, and armed Communist officials.[31] The partisans are reported to have killed or executed at least 12,000 individuals, including Soviet troops and various collaborators. These estimates provide a sense of the dynamics of the conflict.

---

30 A. Anušauskas, "Fiziniai genocido padariniai//Lietuvos sunaikinimas ir tautos kova," (The Results of Physical Genocide//The Destruction of Lithuania and the Nation's Battle) V., 1999, p. 577.

31 J. Starkauskas, *Čekistinė kariuomenė Lietuvoje 1944–1953* (The Soviet Interior Forces in Lithuania 1944–1953), 1998, p. 390.

Lithuania's geographical and climatic features put it at a disadvantage in a guerilla war. Winters are cold and harsh and summers are short and rainy. The country is almost completely flat with few forests. The minefields and barriers of barbed wire that stretched across Lithuania's border with Soviet-controlled Poland ensured Lithuania's political isolation from the outside world.

An Ideological War

Even after the resistance in Lithuania was squashed, it remained a source of irritation and worry to the Soviet authorities. The fact of the existence of a resistance movement encouraged a sense of defiance among the population. This sense of defiance could cause great problems in the event of a major war. This was a risk that could not be ignored during the Cold War.

The Soviets waged an ideological war against Lithuania. Soviet authorities burned all the books in Lithuania's public libraries that were considered to "advocate reactionary bourgeois ideology and religious ideas." In total, 600,000 books were burned in Lithuania.[32] Radios were confiscated, leaving only a few hundred radio sets in the country. To replace access to international news, loudspeakers were installed in the streets that blared radio transmissions of propaganda from Moscow.

After February 16, 1952 *The Voice of America* began to transmit informational programs over shortwave radio to Lithuania. These were jammed by the Soviets. At the same time a few little known radio stations began to broadcast continual promises from the United States, promising the beginning of an East–West conflict that would begin "after Easter," "before Christmas," "in a week's time" and so on.[33] These broadcasts raised the partisans' hopes that help was on its way from America.

The Soviets began an information blockade that remained in place until the loosening of censorship with Mikhail Gorbachev's *perestroika*. The resistance defied the information blockade by publishing 54 underground periodicals and 18 occasional publications, including even a Russian-language newspaper for Russian soldiers called *Svobodnoe Slovo* (The Free Word). Printing was done by typewriter and by rotary press. There were several small printing houses hidden in bunkers throughout Lithuania. Circulation was 500 copies. Collections of poetry, partisan songs, and works of fiction and memoir were also

---

32 *Resistance to the Occupation of Lithuania: 1944–1990: Call to Arms (1944–1953)*, Pranas Morkus, Vilnius: The Genocide and Resistance Research Center, 2002.

33 *Ibid.*

published. The fighters were mostly religious and wrote partisan prayers and religious texts.

The aim of these underground publications was to provide local people with reliable international news. This news was gathered by listening to short wave radio broadcasts from abroad. They also provided editorials and discussion boards. Explanations of the underground army's regulations were provided, as were analyses of prospects. The underground press provided significant moral support for a society that was divided by the information vacuum and by relentless and conflicting rumors. The sophisticated level of the writing in these publications shows that they were written and edited by educated intellectuals.

Even though the impact of the underground press was rather limited, this source of alternative information made it a threat to Soviet Security agencies, who spent vast amounts of time and resources hunting down the publishing structures. The underground press continued to exist in Lithuania throughout the Soviet period up until independence in 1991.

Only Photographs Remain

A number of authentic black and white photographs of partisans remain. They were amassed by the Soviet Security and used to identify and locate partisan fighters. The partisans themselves took these photos. They took them as keepsakes for their families, knowing that death was a certainty for them. During the early years of the resistance the photos show rows of disciplined young people with bright, idealistic faces. By the 1950s the partisans in the photographs no longer show strict rows of men and women with bright smiles. The partisans in these photos wear casual clothes, beards and have shoulder-length hair. They gaze into the camera with cold, stubborn faces.

Historians estimate that the average lifespan of a partisan was two to three years. The partisans died in battle or were taken unawares in the bunkers. If ambushed or trapped, the partisans would avoid being taken alive at all costs. Some would hold a grenade close to their face and blow themselves up so that later the enemy could not identify them and implicate their family and friends. The author of this book, Juozas Lukša, is remarkable in that he eluded the Soviets for an unusually long period of time. Lukša often relied on intuition and an inner voice that guided him until he was betrayed by his close friend and comrade, Jonas Kukauskas, in 1951.

The remains of every single murdered leader of the resistance have disappeared without a trace. According to Lithuanian customs and traditions, surviving family members cannot be at peace until the remains of lost loved ones are laid to rest properly in the Catholic tradition. The missing remains of the partisan fighters and the leaders of the resistance are particularly painful not just to the families of these men and women, but to the Lithuanian nation. Since independence in 1991 efforts have been made to recover the lost remains of the partisans, to exhume them, and to provide a proper burial. Recently, efforts were made to locate the remains of Juozas Lukša. However, to this date, Lukša's remains, and the remains of other leaders of the resistance, have not yet been found and properly laid to rest.

Juozas Lukša Breaks Through the Iron Curtain

In December, 1947, the Lithuanian partisan leadership appointed Juozas Lukša as a special representative to the West for the armed resistance in Lithuania. A few days before Christmas Eve, 1947, Lukša and a few comrades broke through the Iron Curtain in a border zone between the postwar Russian Kaliningrad enclave and Poland.[34] Lukša's mission was to meet with contacts in Western Europe in order to describe Lithuania's fight against Soviet oppression and plead with the West to intervene and stop the mass deportations of Lithuanians to Siberia. His mission was to find out the answer to two questions: Can the Lithuanian Resistance expect a conflict between the Soviet Union and the free world in the near future? And, is the free world committed to coming to the aid of the occupied nations left behind the Iron Curtain after the Yalta conference?

Lukša carried with him a number of documents and testimonials, including a letter written in French to the United Nations and a letter written in Latin to Pope Pius XII describing the mass deportations and asking for the support of the Catholic Church. Although this letter, written in desperation by Lithuanian Catholics and addressed to Pope Pius XII, was translated into many European languages and requested only "compassion and a soothing word," it was met with no response.

The answer to both Lukša's questions and the reaction to documents and testimonials he brought with him was overwhelmingly clear. That answer came from a variety of sources, ranging from Lithuanian politicians in exile to representatives of various governments in the West. That answer was, No, the West was not preparing to come to the aid of the oppressed nations left behind the Iron Curtain, nor were they planning on waging a war against the Soviet Union.

---

34 The term "Iron Curtain" is used here based on a different understanding than in the West. For people in the Soviet Union the border with Poland was considered the Iron Curtain.

The Soviet authorities deported large numbers of people during the post-war years. There were two main objectives. The first was to break the opposition against the collectivization of agriculture, by deporting farmers opposing this idea and their families. The second was to remove the base of support to the armed resistance. Among the deported about two thirds were women and children. The deported were used for all kinds of labor tasks. The picture was taken at Trofimovsk, by the river Lena at a fishing camp.

The answer flew in the face of the Lithuanian's rather literal belief in the Atlantic Charter, signed August 14, 1941 between the President of the United States of America, Franklin Delano Roosevelt, and the Prime Minister, Mr. Winston Churchill, of the United Kingdom. The resistance fighters took the Atlantic Charter literally. They believed it was only a matter of time before the West would intervene in their cause. They particularly believed in the second, third, and the sixth points of the Atlantic Charter. These points stated that the President of the United States of America and the Prime Minister, Mr. Churchill, of the United Kingdom, "desire to see no territorial changes that do not accord with the freely expressed wishes of the peoples concerned" and that "they respect the right of all peoples to choose the form of government under which they will live; and they wish to see sovereign rights and self government restored to those who have been forcibly deprived of them." The sixth point stated that "after the final destruction of Nazi tyranny, they hope to see established a peace which will afford to all nations the means of dwelling in safety within their own boundaries, and which will afford assurance that all the men in all lands may live out their lives in freedom from fear and want."

At the same time the mass deportations of Lithuanians continued. By the beginning of 1954 massacres, arrests, and deportations had affected more than a quarter of a million people in a country with a population of three million. Lukša quickly adapted to the situation and began working on structuring a new tactical strategy for the resistance. Since Lithuania could not expect military intervention and could look forward only to a long period of occupation, the dwindling numbers of members of the resistance would need to make the shift from armed resistance to small pockets of internal leaders of the resistance who would use their influence to preserve the Lithuanian culture and the Lithuanian nation by working directly with the people.[35] These pockets of this intellectual resistance would answer to a very strong central leadership. The central leadership would maintain strong ties with the West and would rely on the West for both moral and material support in the fight against the occupier. The pockets of resistance would be made up of individuals who were well prepared and had a firm moral ideology in place, and were prepared not only to physically defend themselves and others but to inform the public on internal and external affairs and take care that the nation would not give up the fight for independence. These cells of the resistance would need to have a very strong communications network that could not easily be cracked from the outside and to reassure the nation that there still were individuals who protected them from Russification, from Communist tyranny, from colonization, from deportations, arrests, and so on. A strong and reliable flow of information between the occupied nation and the West would prove to be more dangerous than any military revolt, which only could have an impact at the appropriate time and under the appropriate circumstances.

Lukša Receives Espionage Training from the CIA

Lukša turned to various intelligence organizations in Western Europe, seeking support. Eventually, he was approached by the CIA and invited to participate in special espionage training sessions taking place in the West German town of Kaufbeuren. Lukša accepted the CIA's offer and during 1950 received espionage training. At the time the United States was preparing to enter the Korean War.

35 Kestutis Kasparas, and Vidmantas Vitkauskas, *Sugrįžimas: Partizanai* (The Return) (Lietuvos Politinių Kalinių ir Tremtinių Sąjunga ir Lietuvos Gyventojų Genocido ir Rezistencijos Tyrimo Centras, Kaunas, 2005).

Juozas Lukša at his desk writing Forest Brothers, Paris, 1949.

The CIA training camp, part of a CIA-sponsored Cold War espionage effort, was designed to train former East European resistance fighters to infiltrate the Soviet Union on information-gathering missions. During 1950–1951 secret CIA-trained East European operatives were flown back into the Soviet Union with C-47 Dakotas manned by former RAF Czech pilots. Several such air-drops were completed in the Baltics and in the Ukraine. These operations in the end were only moderately successful, mainly because of infiltrations by Soviet counter-intelligence.

Lukša was parachuted into Soviet-occupied Lithuania on the night of October 3–4, 1950. The return of Juozas Lukša from the West in 1950 caused a panic. Vast efforts were employed to hunt him down.[36] Among other tactics, the Soviet Security set up special units, made up of former partisans, to counter the attempts by infiltration from the West. Juozas Lukša was lured into an ambush and killed by members of such a special unit in September 4, 1951.[37]

36 Anušauskas, *Anti-Soviet Resistance*, p. 43.

37 Report by MGB captain Nikolay Sokolov to the Security Minister of the Lithuanian Soviet Republic, general-major Kapralov, December 27, 1951. Lithuanian Special Archives (LYA), F. K-1, ap., b.304, 1 56-60.

Lukša Writes his Memoir

While living in Paris, over the course of three years, between French Intelligence and CIA training sessions, Lukša began writing a memoir in which he carefully documented the battles, skirmishes, strategy, and military organization of the armed resistance. In his memoir he detailed his own transformation from a farmer's son and student of Architecture at Kaunas University to a leader of the resistance. Lukša's memoir *Partizanai Už Geležinės Uždangos* (Partisans Behind the Iron Curtain) would become one of the single most reliable accounts of the post-war armed resistance in Lithuania and a source of inspiration to Lithuanians left behind the Iron Curtain and those living as émigrés abroad.

Lukša's memoir remains one of the few reliable eye-witness accounts of the *Invisible Front* and is still one of the primary sources of accurate historical information about the Lithuanian resistance against the Soviets, giving detailed information about battles and strategies and the inner workings of partisan military structures. It also was a source of inspiration to several generations of Lithuanians living in exile who did not forget the plight of their people behind the Iron Curtain. Lithuanians living under Soviet occupation managed to read and pass on underground publications of the book smuggled over the border.

Because the memoir was written at a time when the armed resistance was still being fought, Juozas Lukša used one of his code names "Daumantas" as a pen name. Daumantas was the name of a 13th-century Lithuanian grand duke and the name of a legendary figure who smuggled books written in Lithuania across the border from Latvia during the 19th century when the Tsar of Russia banned the Latin alphabet in Lithuania (at that time a province of Russia).

The armed resistance fighters hid their identities behind code names. These code names were often the names of birds, animals or trees: Vanagas (Hawk), Lokys (Bear), Uosis (Ash). Other times they were the names of historical or mythological figures: Vytautas (a grand duke), Juodis (the spirit of a dead soldier), Vampyras (Vampire). To protect the partisans who might still be alive in Lithuania or in exile in Siberia, Lukša sometimes deliberately confused the code names or used several code names for one individual. Lukša left behind a secret code, revealing the true identities of most of the individuals depicted in his memoir. The actual names of the partisans are provided in the footnotes.

Lukša drew on his experience as managing editor and journalist for two of the partisan underground resistance newspapers while writing. He describes the process of Sovietization and genocide taking place in Lithuania. He documents the brutal practices of the Soviets that drove farmers to drop their plows and students to drop their pens and join the guerillas fighting in the forests.

It is important to remember that Lukša was not a writer, but a guerilla leader. In places his writing is fragmented and in others it lacks coherency and events are depicted out of chronological order. Also, Lukša purposefully obscured names, dates, and locations because at the time the book was being written the war in Lithuania was still being fought.

It is important for the reader to understand the structure of this book. Lukša tells the story of how he joined the partisans, moved up the partisan ranks, and describes his various duties and the battles he participated in. Additionally, drawing on oral testimonies and written accounts, he also retells the stories of battles, skirmishes, and operations in which he did not participate without giving a clear indication to the reader that a break in his narrative has occurred.

Despite structural problems with the narrative, *Forest Brothers* is a good read. Lukša possessed that specific brand of East European survival humor. He managed to show humor in the most unlikely scenarios. For example, on one occasion the NKVD has local populace rounded up and interrogated one by one. Lukša describes the scene of a simple-minded villager being interrogated by the NKVD. The farmer is asked, "Do you know Saulė (the sun)?" The villager eagerly leads the interrogator outside and points up at the sky. Saulė was a partisan code name. Because the Russian interrogator does not speak Lithuanian, he does not know that the code name literally means "the sun" in Lithuanian. The interrogator explodes in a burst of rage. The situation is tragic and comic at the same time and shows the cruelty and absurdity of this little-known period in European post-war history.

Lukša was also a keen observer. His description of war-torn East Prussia and the deadly silence that prevailed in that no-man's land region after the war is chilling. He also describes the rhythms of archaic agrarian traditions as they are vanishing under the yoke of Soviet occupation. In one of the early scenes in the memoir the Lukša family celebrates Christmas Eve together with the partisans in the traditional manner with Lithuanian foods, songs, and prayer. In the final scene of the memoir Lukša and his comrades spend Christmas Eve huddled in the straw in a barn in Poland, hunted by both Soviet and Polish border patrols.

After Juozas Lukša returned to Lithuania in 1950, the Lithuanian writer Dr. Antanas Vaičiulaitis took possession of Lukša's manuscript and made efforts to publish it for the Lithuanian émigré community in the West. The first edition of *Partizanai už geležinės uždangos* (Partisans Behind the Iron Curtain) was published in 1950 by the Lithuanian Catholic Press Organization. The print run was

500. The book was widely read and was often quoted in the émigré press. Information about the resistance and genocide in Lithuania taken from the book was used in international conferences and meetings.

The memoir was published a second time by the émigré press in 1962 with the title shortened to *Partizanai* (Partisans). *Partizanai* was published a third time in 1984 by an émigré organization in Chicago, The Freedom Fund. The second and third print runs were 500.

During the Soviet occupation the book was banned in Lithuania; however, a few copies did make it into the country through the underground and were secretly retyped, reproduced, bound and distributed throughout the country.

In 1990, when Lithuania declared its independence from the Soviet Union, but was still not yet internationally recognized as an independent country, the Lithuanian publisher VAGA published 100,000 copies of *Partizanai* (Partisans) in paperback. The book quickly became a best seller. The proceeds from the sale of the book were donated to Lithuania's Organization for Political Prisoners and Exiles who used the funds to exhume the remains of Lithuanian exiles buried in mass graves in Siberia and give them a proper reburial in Lithuania. In 2005, a fifth edition of the book was published by the Lithuanian Organization for Political Prisoners and Exiles and the Center for Genocide and Resistance. This edition contains considerable thoroughly researched notes and supporting scholarly articles. Notes from this edition of *Partizanai* were used to create the footnotes for this edition.

Partisans in Translation

Partizanai was translated from an abridged version of the Lithuanian into English by E. J. Harrison and published in the United States by Manyland Books in 1975 with the title *Fighters for Freedom*. In 2004 *Partisans* was translated into Swedish by Jonas Öhman and published by Bäckströms Förlag with a print run of 13,000 under the title *Skogsbröder* (Forest Brothers).

This translation is the first unabridged translation of *Partizanai* into English. It follows the original with few omissions.

The Armed Resistance Today has Symbolic Value

Although the direct military consequences of the Lithuanian resistance were rather limited, the resistance has an important symbolic value to the Lithuanian nation and has served to help create a national post-Soviet identity in Lithuania. The conflict has also been the subject of intense debate in post-Soviet Lithuania. Some contemporary Lithuanians question whether it was justifiable or even responsible to wage an unequal battle against an enemy as powerful as the Soviet Union—a battle in which tens of thousands sacrificed their lives. Others argue that at the time, Lithuanians had little choice because the populace was faced with genocide and conscription into the Red Army. In other words, the sentiment was that it was better to die fighting rather than to die passively. Surviving partisans say that they were driven by a sense of idealism and firm moral values that would not have allowed them to act otherwise.[38]

In Soviet Russia the Lithuanians were always considered "different" and were treated with respect because they had resisted Sovietization.[39] As a result of the armed resistance, Lithuania was the least colonized of the three Baltic states and the most successful in retaining its ethnic heritage. The collectivization of farms was delayed in post-war Lithuania. The partisans sometimes attacked and temporarily controlled smaller cities, successfully interrupted the Communist elections in 1946, kept people informed about international events through their underground press, and tried to maintain order and morale in the rural areas of Lithuania.

Even today the armed anti-Soviet resistance still has an impact on the political relationship between contemporary Lithuania and contemporary Russia. Lithuania has expressed solidarity and sympathy for Chechnya and for Georgia, based on its historical experience.

Whatever position one might take in this debate, the idealism and sacrifice of the partisans serves as a reminder that freedom, independence, and human rights are precious commodities worth fighting for and worth dying for. Juozas Lukša's memoir can be understood as a memorial to all people who sacrificed their lives so that future generations may live in freedom.

Laima Vincė
Fulbright Lecturer, Vilnius University
Vilnius, Lithuania

---

38 Interview with Antanas Lukša, May 25, 2008, Kaunas, Lithuania. Interview conducted by Laima Vincė Sruoginis.

39 Morkus, *Resistance to the Occupation.*

Works Cited

Interview with Antanas Lukša, Kaunas, Lithuania, May 25, 2008. Interview conducted by Laima Sruoginis.

Interview with former partisan Jonas Kadžionis, Bebrūnai village, Lithuania, May, 2008. Interview conducted by Jonas Öhman and Rytas Narvydas.

Interview with Leonora Grigalavičiūtė (code name Vida), April, 2008, Jūrmala, Latvia. Interview conducted by Jonas Öhman and Rytas Narvydas.

Interview with Nijolė Bražėnaitė-Lukšienė-Parronetto, New York, U.S.A. June 15, 2007. Interview conducted by Laima Sruoginis.

Interview with former NKVD Officer Gennadiy Gusev (served in the Ukraine 1946–1948 and in Lithuania 1951–1954), June, 2004, Volgograd. Interview conducted by Jonas Öhman.

Anušauskas, A. *Fiziniai genocido padariniai//Lietuvos sunaikinimas ir tautos kova,* (The Results of Physical Genocide/The Destruction of Lithuania and the Nation's Battle). Vilnius: The Genocide and Resistance Research Center, 1999.

Anušauskas, A. *The Anti-Soviet Resistance in the Baltic States.* Vilnius, Akreta, 2002.

Bubnys, Arūnas. *Nazi Resistance Movement in Lithuania 1941–1944.* Vilnius: Vaga, 2003.

Girnius, Kęstutis. *Partizanų kovos Lietuvoje* (The Partisan War in Lithuania). Vilnius: Mokslas, 1990.

Grinkevičiūtė, Dalia. "Lithuanians by the Laptev Sea: The Siberian Memoirs of Dalia Grinkevičiūtė," *The Earth Remains.* Edited and translated by Laima Sruoginis, East European Monographs, Columbia University Press: New York, 2004.

Intelligence report on the Lithuanian resistance by the Swedish Intelligence Agency (T-kontoret), July 1947, Swedish War Archives, No. 80.II.4.10/4.

Kasparas, Kestutis and Vidmantas Vitkauskas. *Sugrįžimas: Partizanai* (The Return). Lietuvos Politinių Kalinių ir Tremtinių Sąjunga ir Lietuvos Gyventojų Genocido ir Rezistencijos Tyrimo Centras, Kaunas, 2005.

Museum of Genocide Victims exhibit, "Lithuania in 1940–1941: The Persecutions Start," Vilnius, Lithuania.

Morkus, Pranas. *Resistance to the Occupation of Lithuania: 1944–1990: Call to Arms (1944–1953),* Vilnius: The Genocide and Resistance Research Center, 2002.

Pečiokaitė-Adomėnienė, Birutė. *Likviduoti Skirmantą* (Liquidating Skirmantas), Kaunas: Atmintis, 2002.

Starkauskas, J. *Čekistinė kariuomenė Lietuvoje 1944–1953* (The Soviet Interior Forces in Lithuania 1944–1953), 1998.

Urbšys, Juozas. "*Lithuania and the Soviet Union 1939-1940: The Fateful Year: Memoirs* by *Juozas Urbšys,*" Translated and edited by Sigita Naujokaitis. *Lithuanian Quarterly Journal of Arts and Sciences,* Volume 34, No. 2–Summer 1989.

Report by MGB captain Nikolay Sokolov to the Security Minister of the Lithuanian Soviet Republic, general-major Kapralov, December 27, 1951. Lithuanian Special Archives (LYA), F. K-1, ap., b.304, 1 56-60.

The International Commission for the Evaluation of the Crimes of Nazi and Soviet Occupation Regimes in Lithuania/Conclusions ratified June 20, 2005. Regarding deportations of inhabitants of Lithuania 1944–1953, conclusion No. 10.

"The Yalta Conference." *The Latin Library.* [URL:http://www.thelatinlibrary.com/imperialism/notes/yalta.html] accessed June 30, 2008.

Voverienė, Ona. *Žymiosios XX amžiaus Lietuvos Moterys: Partizanės, ryšininkės, tremtinės, kovotojos* (The Most Significant Lithuanian Women of the Twentieth Century: Partisans, Liaison Women, Exiles, Fighters). Kaunas: Naujasis Amžius, 2005.

I

The Decision to Stay on Our Native Land

July 1944–July 1945

Between Home and Kaunas

The Occupiers Change

It was a Sunday afternoon at the end of July, 1944. We sat at the dinner table in our usual places: Father at the head of the table; Mother to his right; our maid, Marytė, beside Mother. My brothers Jurgis,[1] Vincas,[2] Stasys,[3] Antanas,[4] and I sat along both sides of the table. It was lunchtime. Father ate his borsch quietly. The rest of us followed suit. None of us had any appetite.

Mortars flew overhead, crisscrossing in several directions. Whenever they connected with their targets, they rattled our cottage windows. It was humid. Our faces were lined with worry. We waited for the inevitable. A sense of unease filled the cottage. The air was full with it.

We heard the heavy boots of soldiers on the porch. A group of Germans pushed their way inside. We read exhaustion in their faces, and hunger, and that same sense of uneasiness.

"Essen," one of them gasped and sat down at the table.

None of the others waited for an invitation. We stood up from our seats and backed away from the table. They quickly finished what remained of our lunch.

---

1 Jurgis Lukša, (1920–1947), was a student at Kaunas University. He joined the Iron Wolf Regiment partisans sometime in 1946. He was killed by Soviet Interior Forces June 13, 1947 when he returned to his family farm to visit his sick father and his mother.

2 Vincas Lukša, (1905–1993), the eldest Lukša brother and step-brother to Juozas, Jurgis, Stasys and Antanas, was an active supporter of the partisans. He was arrested when Jurgis was killed and brought to the Kaunas Prison where he was tortured and interrogated and then deported to Vorkuta. He was given a ten-year sentence in a concentration camp in Siberia. He was allowed to return to Lithuania in 1955. He died in 1993.

3 Stasys Lukša, (1926–1947) the youngest Lukša brother, joined the partisans together with Juozas in 1946. He was killed in battle August 12, 1947.

4 Antanas Lukša (1923–) is the only surviving Lukša brother. He was a teacher at the Veiveriai School. He joined the partisans in 1946 as a liaison man and later fought as a partisan. He was arrested in an ambush set up by partisan infiltrators, or *Smogikai*, June 12, 1947. He was particularly cruelly tortured in the Kaunas Prison, using the most barbaric methods. His interrogation transcript reveals that he did not betray a single partisan, liaison person, or supporter. He was sentenced to twenty-five years of hard labor in a Siberian concentration camp. He was released June 27, 1956 and returned to Lithuania. Today he is an active member of the Lithuanian Union of Political Prisoners and Exiles.

Ona Luksiene, mother of Juozas, Jurgis, Antanas, and Stasys (1966).

One young blond soldier was not satisfied with what he found on the table. He pulled out his submachine gun and pointed it at Mother.

"Mutter, speck," he said and shoved her out of the kitchen and into the larder. A short while later the German returned to the table. Instead of his submachine gun, he now held a hunk of ham in his hand.

At the head of the table, in Father's place, sat the oldest soldier. Half of his beard was shaved off.

"It's a good thing the damn Russians gave me enough time to shave at least half of my beard," he said cheerfully. "Today they're hot on our heels." Then he waved his hand and said, "It's all over for us anyway, for us and for Deutschland."

Those were the last words spoken by the last German soldier to set foot in Lithuania.

Suddenly, outside it was quiet. There were no more whistling mortars.

We could see the silhouettes of the last German soldiers, spread out across the fields, heading West. Here and there we heard occasional gunfire, answered by enemy machine gunfire.

The first Red Army soldier appeared at the rear end of our barn on the back of a tired, old nag. A pair of old pants slung over the nag's back served as a saddle and stirrups. He had a tattered Russian tent strapped over his shoulders. His clothing was filthy. He looked as though he had not bathed in ages. This Russian looked more like the Grim Reaper than an advance army scout.

"Hello Comrades," he said in Russian, "are the Germans gone? You've probably grown tired of waiting for us to come liberate you."

He shook our hands and asked, "Do you have anything to drink?"

Marytė brought him some milk. The Russian drank it greedily, tossing his head back as he emptied the pitcher. He extended the empty pitcher towards her, hardly able to contain his surprise. "You can still find milk around here?" he said.

Stasys Lukša

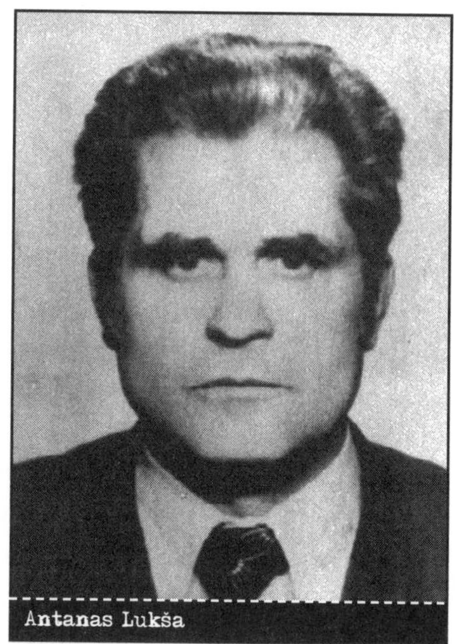
Antanas Lukša

He thanked us, kicked his heels into the nag's ribs, and moved on.

From the rye field we heard other lost soldiers calling out to each other:

"Aleksy, Aleksy, did you see where our cannon went?"

Slowly, with resignation, we relaxed. Finally, it had come.

It had happened. Against our will. The "Red Horror" had returned to our land.

It had returned slowly, creeping across the land, marking its trail with fires and ruins, leaving people with a sinking sense of horror. A month ago the first of our farms to the east were reduced to piles of ash. A battle between two giants was waged in the fields of our three million farmers. It was a battle that had brought with it an equal amount of devastation from the East and from the West. As this war was waged in our furrows, we could do nothing, but stand by and watch. At this moment, for three million Lithuanians, only two alternatives remained: to stay on our land and to continue with determination and whatever means we had at our disposal the fight we had begun four years ago, or to retreat from the trenches with the hope of reaching asylum in the democracies of the West.

There had been enough time to choose, but it had been a hard choice. Because most people hesitated, they became victims of circumstance. Afterwards, they could do no more than accept their fate.

Our family decided to stay even when the front stabilized on the banks of the Nemunas River. It was not easy. We had no objective information to go on or advice to follow. The underground press that had operated so prolifically during the Nazi occupation had stopped publishing a while ago. The links with the centers of resistance had broken down. Many of our friends were overcome with the panic to escape.

A few weeks back I had gone to Kaunas, hoping to find one of my friends. It turned out they were all gone. The streets were thronged with retreating German soldiers and civilians laden with suitcases. Outside the shop doors there were long lines of people waiting to buy whatever food and necessities they could get. However, the lines were not moving because German soldiers and local civilian government representatives were pouring out of the shops' back doors laden with armloads of goods. Signs hung on the shop windows warning the Lithuanian civilian government representatives and the Germans that they could not use weapons and that they were required to evacuate. There were also signs posted that read: "Looters will be shot."

I returned home not knowing anything more than when I had started out.

Along the way there were units of the German army everywhere. A large percentage of them were not German. They were Ukrainians, Byelorussians, Cossacks, and other nationalities. These soldiers had no discipline whatsoever and looted wherever they could get away with it. They took possession of livestock, farm tools, and clothing as if it were their own, and not the property of civilians. Only those areas that were lucky enough to have Lithuanian self-defense partisan units[5] escaped. They were the only protectors of our lives and of our possessions. The thinking of the leaders of these units was not to retreat deep into Germany, but to try to take advantage of the current situation and to leave behind as many guns as possible. Various battalions' soldiers decided to desert and returned home to their farms and villages with wagons filled with loot. In this way many divisions "disappeared" into the forests with large munitions and weapons supplies.[6]

When the Soviet troops reached our region of Suvalkija, they encountered a natural barrier, the Nemunas River. The front was momentarily stabilized.

The Bolsheviks were pushing forward quickly. The Germans lost a few kettle tank fights near Minsk and now lacked the reserves to fill in the holes in the lines

---

5 These partisan self-defense units collaborated with the German occupiers; however, they were not ideologically loyal to the Germans. They saw collaboration with one occupier against another as a means of securing eventual independence for Lithuania from both occupiers. They secured railroads, they hunted down "Red Partisans," and they fought against the Red Army, mainly in southern Latvia in 1944.

6 These weapons and ammunition were used to later arm the partisans.

that the Russians made. In our region, Prienai-Kaunas and Pakuonis-Kaunas, the German forces were quite weak. They had a few anti-aircraft units, a few tanks, and a few machine gun squads.

After a few days, the Bolsheviks were able to build themselves a pontoon bridge near the village of Rumšiškės. The first Bolshevik infantry and tank units managed to cross before the Germans destroyed the bridge. The Bolshevik troops that had reached the other side engaged the Germans in a fierce battle in which the Bolshevik tanks were destroyed by the German "Tigers." However, the Red Army infantry proved themselves to be unusually brave; they would attack the tanks on foot in squads of several dozen men armed with grenades, shouting, "Forward, hurrah!" The Bolsheviks managed to take over the Pociūnas airport. One of the Russian units even managed to reach the Bačkininkų heath field. Here the Germans surrounded them and wiped them out with flamethrowers. That is how the Germans eliminated the Bolshevik units that had managed to cross the first bridge.

The Bolsheviks were able to bring rocket artillery to the right bank of the Nemunas and force the Germans out of their positions near the river. We could tell that the Germans were preparing to abandon these positions. At this point their carnage knew no bounds. Without any provocation or warning they turned their flame-throwers on people's abandoned farms and burned them down. The tanks rolled over fences, trees, and destroyed the orchards by pushing over the fruit trees, bushes, and bee hives. These actions had nothing to do with honorable warfare, but were more like acts of unrestrained revenge.

Whatever they had not managed to steal over their three years of occupation, they hurried now to destroy on the spot because they did not have the resources to remove it and take it with them. Entire fields were filled with pigs that the Germans had slaughtered and left behind to rot. For some reason, the only food they now took from people were shanks of ham. All the other meat they left behind for the Russian divisions because it would only rot anyway.

On July 24th, the Bolsheviks managed to build another pontoon bridge across the Nemunas. This time they constructed it several dozen centimeters under the waterline, so that enemy planes could not take it out. On July 25th, the Bolsheviks prepared to cross the Nemunas again. At about ten o'clock in the morning, a squadron of German planes made their way towards the Nemunas. They were greeted by heavy Russian anti-aircraft artillery backed up by Russian fighter planes. The German squadron lost two planes and did not reach the new bridge, but had to retreat. The Bolshevik bombers attacked the German "Tigers." After an hour of heavy fighting, the Germans began retreating. The Russians continued attacking them from the air. The Bolsheviks began crossing the Nemunas in large numbers—by boat and by bridge, some of them crossing by clinging to logs. Because they were in such a rush, many of them drowned without even having a single shot fired at them. The first lines of men were half-drunk, shabby, dirty, and armed as frequently with German weapons as with Russian weapons. They had no kitchen division, so they fed themselves with whatever the Germans had left behind. Among them there were women who had lost all appearance of femininity. They cursed and looted and knew no shame just like the rest of the Red Army soldiers. At the same time the Russians seemed elated with their recent victory.

* * *

The Germans prepared to retreat from Kaunas. They blew up the buildings where they had housed their units or which had some sort of military designation. The University's Physics and Chemistry Institute in the Aleksotas neighborhood was included on this unfortunate list of bombed buildings. Also bombed were the Damijonaitis School (on Darius and Girėnas Street), a convent close by, buildings belonging to the train station, the central electrical station, the Vailokas home next door, the telegraph station, the train station warehouses, the Petrašiūnas electrical station and many other less important buildings. The food production factory was also set on fire. Huge clouds of smoke hung over Kaunas; the best buildings were turned to ash, bearing witness to the final ravages of the German occupier.

Rumors criss-crossed the country, telling us that the Bolshevik terror had already started. One set of rumors surpassed the next. Some people said that any civilians who had followed German orders were being shot on the spot. Others said that any men who had not joined the Red Partisans[7] divisions would be shot. A third group argued reasonably that only those who had served the German occupying government directly would be shot or exiled to Siberia. Citizens took risks, sneaking across the front just to find out which rumors were true. They would return and tell people that the Russian soldiers were not so terrible after all, that they were actually rather friendly, though battle-weary. But even after those reports the people remained wary about the Russians. Saturday night, when it seemed that one group of "liberators" was likely to replace the other, the entire

7 The Red Partisans were Soviet selected and partially local volunteer underground groups that were used to interfere and sabotage German-occupied areas of Lithuania.

populace went into hiding, burying their valuables in the ground, emptying their cottages, sleeping in ditches or in temporary bunkers.

We passed that restless Sunday afternoon with these recent events on our mind.

We Go into Hiding

A cavalry platoon of thirty horsemen stayed in our village during the early days of the "liberation." They all looked exhausted. Most likely they had spent a long time on the front lines. Not a single one of them knew a thing about hygiene or cleanliness. They washed by bathing in the soiled water from the duck and goose pond and spent their free time lounging around the pig pen. All of the units lacked kitchens. The kitchens could not keep up with front lines, they told us. They would feed themselves by yanking up vegetables from the fields along the way, whether they were ripe or not. They would eat green apples and steal honey from bee hives at night. All of them, without exception, drank. To get vodka they would trade a variety of stolen goods with the local populace: shoes, sheets, saddles, tents. Often, you could get a horse for a bucket of vodka. However, the joy over the bargain soon dissipated when the horse's real owner showed up to reclaim his horse from a farm a few kilometers away. Their superiors banned their trading, especially when the trade involved bread or meat. Yet, all the warnings and punishments could not stop them from bartering and trading. These platoons seemed better off than we had expected from our first scouting missions. They all wore epaulettes. None of them wore the typical Russian soldier's forage cap.

The Red Army prisoners of war, who had lived with local farmers during the German occupation, joined up with the platoons passing through. Their first assignment was to report on the local sentiments and on the amount of collaboration with the Germans (however, this information was often misinterpreted). They reported on the lack of loyalty to the Bolsheviks during the German occupation. They knew who had relatives who'd fled to the West and who had relatives already living in the West.

All the village elders were immediately arrested, incarcerated, and interrogated without any proof of their guilt—only on the basis of the fact that they had been elders.

The Russians did not conduct an investigation on how they had fulfilled their duties as elders. People tallied their personal fall-outs with their neighbors and took advantage of the situation to get revenge. The criminal element came out of the woodwork and was able to operate unchecked, spilling a lot of blood unnecessarily. Many innocent people, fearing the Red Army's "helpfulness," went into hiding from the very first day.

It was harvest time. The ripe heads of rye weighed down towards the ground, as though begging to be harvested. But the farmers, while knowing they were late for the harvest, would walk lazily through their fields. They had no equipment and no help, and so they were not able to start any work.

Vincas asked me to go see Farmer Luokys[8] about the harvest. Luokys paced from corner to corner of his cottage, frustrated that he was unable to begin any work. When it was time for me to go home, he walked with me across the entire field. At the end of the field we ran into Šalčiūnas.[9]

"Looking to harvest?" Luokys asked, dispensing with all customary greetings.

"Yes, I'd like to harvest, but tell me, neighbor, how? They've trampled the fields; they've torn them apart. They act as though the fields were their training grounds. Why couldn't those fools go around the fields?"

"When has a soldier ever looked out for someone else's property? He goes wherever he feels like going, where it's safer. He doesn't stop and think about how those fields will feed him."

"What are you thinking about doing this year with regarding the work exchange? There's no one around to hire and there's nothing to hire them for. We don't even know what the currency will be. It might be rubles again. It looks as though we ought to pay in grain, but you don't know if they'll confiscate it all and not even leave you with a handful."

"It's a real problem. Remember how it was? We neighbors would join forces and we'd do one field one day, another field the next day. The work went quickly, and it was convenient. But this year we're all on our own. What has life come to, neighbor. We raised wonderful sons and we thought, 'Now we can relax and live.' But that damn mobilization has chased them all out of our homes. All three of mine have left home. They went to work for the railroad because they say they won't conscript them from there."

"Yours are doing alright. Two of mine are hiding with relatives. The other two ran off to Kaunas. They're not going to join forces with those vagabonds. What for? As though we don't see what's going on here day and night. All we hear is that

---

8 This farmer was either the Lukša family's neighbor Pranas Tūtlys or Antanas Čarneckis.

9 Šalčiūnas: Juozas Šalčius.

this one disappeared and that one. Yesterday Mykolaitis[10] was arrested with his son. Last night they took away Šalčiukas[11] and Degėsys.[12]"

"It's still a good thing that they didn't finish them off on the spot. You probably haven't heard what happened last night in Čibirkiai. Those devils showed up in a car at Grybauskas's[13] place, broke down his door, ripped the entire family naked out of their beds, shoved them naked into the kitchen, and as one of them guarded the family, the other one emptied the place. The man lost his equipment, and his clothing, and his food. The eldest son jumped out the window and ran. One of them shot him down before he could even raise the alarm. He was such a good man! May he rest in peace. Real 'liberators' they are."

"I keep telling my wife that she shouldn't argue with them so much. Damn it, just let them take what they want. Just keep yourself alive. No matter what we do, they'll leave us naked and without so much as a crust of bread. Did you hear that they've set up a government in the county?"

"I heard, how could I not? They say the bum who stayed with the Černiauskas's got in there. He can't even sign his own name, but he wants to be among the county's elite. They say they even set up new punishments. Meanwhile, the two of us are standing here thinking about how to harvest our fields. I think the first session takes place in five days."

"And you actually believed that they'll wait longer. You can see that everyone's starving. Nothing will come of their terms, they can go hang themselves. Let them give us our children back and then set their dates."

"What does the work mean to those who can't do it? You know, they don't accept any kinds of explanations. If you don't fulfill their terms, you'll end up behind bars. Don't you remember what it was like three years ago? And now they're even hungrier. These aren't the Prussians. It's not going to be like last year, when we wrote two zeros on the receipt, and things were taken care of."

"Oh, neighbor, we're about to see things the likes of which we've never seen before. The last time at least we didn't see Russians out here in the countryside, but now there's quite a few around. They're saying that the boss is going to be a Russian. The day before yesterday I the saw one with a big wart. He's probably the

---

10 Jonas Mykolaitis was arrested and given five years hard labor in Siberia. The family farm was dismantled. The remaining three brothers Kazys, Vytas, and Kostas joined the partisans. All three were killed in battle July 30, 1947.

11 Povilas Šalčius. His farm abutted the Lukša farm. He provided food and supplies to the partisans. He was betrayed, arrested and tried July 18, 1947.

12 Degutis. He was arrested December 31, 1944 and exiled to Komi.

13 Jonas Grybauskas, a farmer. He and his family were exiled May 1948 to Sibirsk, Usoly region in Irkusk.

one. So tell me now, have you really decided to take down the harvest on your own? It's time for lunch. My wife will be angry at me for talking for so long."

"I'll have to do it alone. I have no other choice."

They shook hands and we all hurried off in different directions.

Luokys, and Šalčiūnas, and the other neighbors cut down their rye on their own, without any help. We did not feel the traditional excitement of the harvest, the celebrations that overshadowed the rest of the summer's work. In the fields one elderly couple swayed, struggling as they worked. Almost no one used any machinery because the Germans had destroyed it. We also lacked horses trained for the work.

My brother Jurgis and I decided to lie low for a while because the arrests in the provinces were becoming more and more frequent. Jurgis was afraid because he had been a member of the student council. I was apprehensive because in 1941 I had been a Soviet political prisoner.[14] Although we were on very good terms with the local populace and did not expect any of them would turn us in, it was better to be careful. We left home and went to live with our friend Lupaitis.[15] There we built a hiding place, so if the need arose, we would have a place to go. There was certainly no time for boredom. The passing fronts had wiped out all of his farm buildings. He introduced us to his closest neighbors as hired hands. We spent our days digging through the ashes of the burned buildings, throwing out the garbage and the broken ceramic tiles. We picked whatever usable hardware we could find out of the ashes, and cleaned out the area in order to start reconstruction of the buildings. We took the opportunity to "borrow" necessary building materials from the forest. Our work was constantly interrupted by the women's and children's warnings:

"The Russians are coming! Hide!"

Within seconds we would be crouching in our hole, waiting until the danger was past. Lupaitis's four-year-old son was the most eager volunteer to run and inform us when the danger was past.

"Come on out, the Russians have come and gone," he would say, skipping happily around the entrance to our hole. He would help us climb out as best he could.

---

14 On July 6, 1941 Juozas Lukša was arrested for his participation in the underground. He was held prisoner in the jail in Kaunas until the Nazis invaded Lithuania. The prisoners escaped from the prison when the occupation changed. Lukša was 20 years old at the time.

15 Antanas Vilkas, a farmer from the Mogiškis village in the Prienai district. On May 22, 1948 he was exiled to Krasnojarsk. All his wealth was confiscated. His farm was taken away from the family. His house was leveled to the ground. His wife Petronėlė and their son Antanas hid. He was released from exile in 1955. He died in 1959.

The minute we were out, he would pop down into our hiding place. Then, he would emerge, prattling away happily:

"See, how fast I can get in? When I grow up the Russians really won't be able to catch me," little Vytukas announced joyfully, dreaming of his future. "Only I don't know who will be here to warn me that the Russians are coming? Mama will be old and slow already, and it's so hot down there, you could suffocate..."

We stayed with Lupaitis about two weeks. After that my brother, Antanas, came to visit us and told us that we needed to quickly get to Kaunas. The University was opening up again and its leadership was hurrying to create jobs for its professors and for university seniors. They had promised that the people they took in to work would be exempt from conscription. We were determined not to let this opportunity pass, although we worried about the University walls closing in on us.

With Antanas we returned home to our farm. There we found Vosily waiting for Jurgis. He had come to thank him for saving his life.

Vosily's Warning

In the summer of 1943 Jurgis was plowing the field along the forest. At twilight a ragged figure crawled out of the forest, approached Jurgis, greeted him in Russian, and seated himself on the furrow. He told Jurgis he was a Russian and that his name was Vosily,[16] and that he was a prisoner of war who had run away from Prussia. He was only nineteen. He carried an empty little tin cup in his hand. His clothing was in tatters, torn almost all over. He was barefoot. There were deep wrinkles in his adolescent face. Without hesitation, he asked for food. Jurgis told Vosily to take over the plowing while he ran home with the tin cup to get him some milk. Luckily, it was evening. Mama was home cooking pancakes. Mama heaped on a double portion for Vosily. When Jurgis got back to his assistant plowhand he was in for a good laugh. Vosily, unable to control the plow, had been plowing in a zig zag, dripping with sweat. They both sat down to eat.

Vosily told Jurgis his story about how he had managed to stay alive. He would hang around the edges of forests with his tin cup and wait until he saw women coming to milk the cows. Then he would creep out of the bushes and beg the women for some milk. He had kept himself alive like that for five weeks already. Now he asked Jurgis if he would take him in as a laborer. He thought it would not be worth it to go beyond Lithuania because he would never reach his home town that way. He had grown up not far from Moscow. Besides that, he did not believe

[16] Vosily Aleksander Osokin. Russian prisoner of war during the German occupation.

he would be treated as well by strangers in his own country as he was treated in Lithuania. Jurgis agreed to take care of him. And in that way, hiding with one local farmer after the other, Vosily survived the German occupation and lived to be reunited with the Red Army.

Today Vosily was waiting for us at our farm with a jug of honey and a bottle of home brew. He was on his way to join up with a unit in the Red Army, where he had managed to register a few days earlier. We commemorated our parting appropriately. When taking his leave from us, Vosily offered Jurgis an affidavit written in his own hand in which he explained what had happened to him, confirming that Jurgis, despite the German laws and the risks involved, had taken care of him during the entire German occupation and had saved his life, risking his own life. Jurgis did not want to take the document, but Vosily insisted. He told him a time would come when he would be thankful he had. He pointed out that already a number of people from our village had been arrested simply because they could not prove their loyalty to the Bolsheviks. It was not enough to be able to prove your innocence to avoid arrest, he explained. Vosily, who had been born and raised in the hell the Bolsheviks had created in Russia, knew all the Reds' destructive methods well, and that was why he insisted that Jurgis take the document. We shook hands affectionately and vowed to each other not to forget our friendship, which had formed under such strange circumstances—a friendship between a Russian collective farm peasant and Lithuanian students.

Burning Personal Files in the Crematorium

Jurgis and I, we set off for Kaunas, mindful of the fact that we had no guarantee of finding ourselves within University walls. We could just as well end up in a Red Army platoon. We chose bicycles as our mode of transportation to make our first trip under Stalin's "liberated" sky.

We reached the Marijampolė-Kaunas highway. This road was now very important. It was the main artery of movement to East Prussia. Every few hundred meters the road side was adorned with placards shouting out various slogans in Russian: "Long live the Red Army," "Long live All-Mighty General Secretary Stalin," "Long live the Communist Party," "Glory to the Heroes," "Vilnius is ours, Kaunas is ours, forwards to Berlin, where we'll fight the fascist animal in his own den, death to German fascists" and so on. After a while the same slogans began to repeat themselves. All the slogans were painted onto red-painted panel boards a few meters off the ground. Every few kilometers we would come across cut-out panel figures of Stalin or Lenin about three or four meters high with crudely painted faces. The crossroads were guarded by pathetic ragged Russians. We soon grew weary of all the slogans and figures. The only thing that caught my interest was the caricatures. The favorite theme of the caricature drawings was a fascist animal being crushed under the shoe of an Ivan[17] wearing a burlap jacket. The closer we got to Kaunas, the redder the slogans got.

The work at the University had only just begun. The University governance was forming with Professor A. Purėnas[18] and Professor Mošinskis[19] (senior) at its helm. First of all, we had to reclaim and organize the University buildings and move in the necessary supplies. During the German occupation what had been left of the University had crowded into the School of Medicine alone. All the offices had been set up there. It turned out not to be difficult to get the University buildings back, because the Russians were trying to do everything opposite of the Germans. When their antagonism coincided with our interests, we won them over without exerting much effort. Of course, while taking care of matters, we never forgot to remind our "Bosses" that Stalin's constitution guaranteed everyone an education and liberation from the German fascists. We found that if we managed to repeat one of the slogans we had read a thousand times out on the highway at the end of our sentences, then things easily went our way. Without much trouble at all, we were able to reclaim the Main Hall of the University, the first year quarters, the *Ateitininkų* Club[20] facilities, and the *Neolituanus* Club[21] facilities. We reclaimed Mažylio House on Kęstutis Street, Savanorių Prospektas Number 77 (formerly Ukmergė Road) and part of the women's dorms on Trakų Street.

We began cleaning up. The first thing we did was create a student space by carrying the files from the Department of Medicine to the Main Hall. The leadership even provided us with transportation in the form of a new truck.

Professor Mošinskis took it upon himself to defend us in the conscription commissariat. With our student identifications we went to the gymnasium to a desk that had been assigned to take care of our affairs. The officer at the war table issued a resolution deeming "excused" those who had been assigned identifications (diploma students and seniors). This took care of our military obligations,

---

17 Lithuanian slang name for Russians.

18 Antanas Purėnas (1881–1962) was a professor of Chemistry. He was a social democrat during the period of independence. For his leftist views he was appointed the Kaunas University rector in 1940–1941 and in 1944–1946.

19 Vytautas Mušinskis (1876–1955), an engineer.

20 A Lithuanian Catholic Youth Club.

21 A Lithuanian Patriotic Club.

but we were still obligated to assist in the preparatory work, since the academic year was about to begin.

We were curious about the chaos in the Department of Medicine. Student and teaching staff files were strewn about the corridors along with surveys and other archival papers. We were most concerned over the surveys. Students and teaching staff and office workers had filled them out during the German occupation. These surveys showed who had resisted the first Bolshevik occupation by belonging to the Activist Front.[22] They also showed who belonged to cultural organizations during the period of independence. After a good deal of effort, we managed to find our own files. Our hair stood on end. There was enough material there to have us executed on the spot. We hurried to find the files of our friends who had not escaped to the West. In the end we decided that it would be faster and our consciences would rest more easily if we simply burned all the files. And, that is what we did. We carted them over to the crematorium oven and turned all those documented sins into smoke.

Besides these files, we destroyed a number of files on teaching staff, who had traveled to the West to study. It was likely that these dusty papers would have brought about the cruel deaths of a few hundred people. We burned the files in the nick of time because the very next day Soviet Security Officers took control of similar documents, confiscating whatever was left.

After spending a few days in the city, we had to turn around and go home to our father to get some bread because it was impossible to get any food in Kaunas. The ruble had come into currency, but its buying power was very weak. A kilogram of butter or lard cost 400 rubles and a kilogram of bread cost around 50 rubles. One liter of vodka could cost up to 400 rubles. That price went up because of the constant demand by our "liberators." People in the city got their food from the surrounding villages by trading clothing and other valuables.

Our Friendship with the Red Army Soldiers

Having "liberated" Marijampolė, the front paused for a while. The Germans had put up some resistance before the Russians were able to break into their territory. The Bolsheviks, blinded by their recent victories, pushed their troops forwards with enthusiasm, straining to reach Hitler's hideout faster. All of the Red Army was bragging that it would not take longer than two months before they would be marching through the streets of Berlin as conquerors.

---

22 A Lithuanian resistance organization.

On the Aleksotas Road we asked a Red Army soldier to drive us in the direction of Marijampolė. There were three of us. Unfortunately, in the town of Garliava the soldiers directing traffic made us get out because the car was overcrowded. Here we had to join up with a large crowd that was hanging around for a few hours. The trains were not running because the rail lines that had been bombed by the Germans had not been rebuilt yet. After waiting around for an hour, we started out on foot. We had gone half a kilometer down the road when an American jeep with three Red Army soldiers inside it caught up to us. When they saw us turning around and looking at them, they stopped.

"Where you going?" their leader asked from behind the wheel.

"To our parents' farm," Jurgis answered, "where else?"

The leader offered to drive us if we provided him with a bottle of home brew. We promised him food on top of that.

"Wonderful," the leader said, gesticulating for us to hop in, "now we'll eat and drink too."

His two friends, one of them a captain and the other a senior lieutenant, did not participate in the barter, but they too seemed pleased with the deal. We reached our destination. Because our farm was a few kilometers away from the main road, we offered to pay our friends back right here, at our aunt's house, near the road. We explained to them that we had not reached our father's farm yet, and to do that we would have to bounce over very bad roads for a few kilometers more to the south. They all seemed very friendly, especially the senior lieutenant. He stubbornly insisted on driving us the entire way home no matter what the roads were like. We too liked their suggestion, since we preferred not to put our aunt in a difficult position. The jeep took the rutted road beautifully, drawing a chorus of praise from the Russians for American technology.

Our frightened mother met us at the gates.

"Good evening, Mama, don't worry, we found a couple of 'slaves' who agreed to bring us home to father in exchange for a couple of bottles of home brew."

As we climbed out of the jeep, Mama happily exclaimed, "Thank God that's what it is. I thought your days were over."

We sat our guests down in our living room, but not in the parlor. Mama and Marytė quickly put together some food in the kitchen. Jurgis went out to the stack yard and returned with our "payment," which was several times bigger than what we had promised them. I took on the role of footman, bringing in platters of food and taking away the empty bowls. In the kitchen I took the opportunity to tease our maid, Marytė.

"So Marytė, you see, I brought you home some men. Maybe you'll get lucky. You know how they're all after Lithuanian girls."

"You call those creatures men? They are bums, not men. First they should air themselves out so they wouldn't smell like herring," Marytė retorted. Then she slapped herself on her backside and added, "That's for your men."

As we ate, we talked about the new life that was now starting in Lithuania. We talked about the German occupation and about independent Lithuania. It was difficult to convince the Russians that it was actually true that during independence every Lithuanian farmer had his own independently run farm with his own farm animals and other wealth.

We sat at the table for about two hours. During that time Vincas, Antanas, and Stasys finished their work out in the fields. They joined us. The leader's wish had been fulfilled. His hunger had been satisfied and his thirst had been quenched. We granted him his request and made up a bed for him in the barn, but only after we had locked up all the storage closets. Not long afterwards the captain also passed out. Five of us were left at the table: four brothers and our lieutenant, who, after finishing off his sixth bottle, grew talkative.

"I'm jealous of your family for this evening. I can't believe it. Are there many families like yours here, where all the members of the family can come together often, like you did tonight?"

"And why not? In almost every cottage in this village entire families raised by one father come together," Antanas explained.

"You are incredibly lucky people. You know where your brothers are. You recognize your mothers. Us, they tear us away from our mothers when we're still infants. We have no feelings for our brothers, for our parents, because most of the time we can't even remember them. I would like to experience the kind of family togetherness I felt here tonight with you. I'd like to be among my brothers, to share my troubles with people close to me. Those troubles are hundreds of times worse in our land than here in yours. We would like to live like people every once in a while," the lieutenant said. His eyes filled with tears. He looked around him and continued:

"When we fought at Minsk, at Ilmen, they kept lying to us, telling us we were going to liberate the proletariat. It's been a month already that I've been traveling around Lithuania, and for the first time in my life I see their lies for what they are. I haven't yet found the exploiter, nor have I seen the exploited. All I found was all the people's collected hatred towards us, the Red Army. They see us as people who've taken away their freedom. I curse this Red Army uniform of mine, this uniform that makes you feel that hatred, for me this uniform that has brought slavery to your land!"

The lieutenant clutched his hand to his chest and ripped off half the medals hanging there. He tossed them into the corner with disgust. The medals clanged loudly against the floor, frightening the cats, who dashed out from under the table. The Red Army soldier looked around angrily and said, "My parents' bones rotted in a prison camp in Siberia. Now, with my victories, I contribute towards taking away the freedom of new millions. They are going to bring in the *Kolkhoz*[23] system. They're going to make beggars out of the farmers here. They purposefully spread rumors that in the Soviet Union *kolhozniks*[24] will be given their own plots of land to work. They do it only so they'd fight believing it and then die in battle happily. The *kolhozniks* have already seen the position of the world's workers. They know their standard of living is so much lower compared to that of other nations.

"You'll never find a single *kolhoznik* anywhere in the Soviet Union who could fill his table with such a variety of dishes for his guests or for his enemies the way you have set the table before us tonight," he continued, "but if the Soviet system is applied to your land, within a few years you will be as hungry and poor as we are—hungry and wearing rags. Today the people in our country are starving all the way from Leningrad to Staliningrad. We didn't have much to begin with, but the damn Germans leveled what we did have. Your country, even after having been destroyed several times over, looks like a small America to us. That's because here everyone works out of love, and not by force or out of fear. The farmer works for his own future and for his family's future, and that's something we don't even have the right to dream about."

We felt rather uncomfortable. We were afraid, to be honest, that he was trying to provoke us. After his anger ran through him, the Russian began to calm down. Jurgis collected his medals, rattled them in his cupped hands, and returned them to him.

"Take them back. Believe us that we understand their value just as you do. Pin them back where they were. Let's leave these unpleasant topics behind and go take a look at the farm."

Reluctantly, the lieutenant agreed. Jurgis, Antanas, and the lieutenant left.

They did not come back until the middle of the following morning. The Captain gave them hell because at twelve noon they were supposed to be at the front

---

[23] Russian term for Collective Farm.

[24] Collective farm workers.

in their unit's headquarters. They ate their breakfast quickly and hurried off, promising to stop by again in about a month.

After they had left, I assessed the situation and realized that besides the food, their visit had cost me my wristwatch. Their commander must have stolen it, since I had slept in the same end of the barn with him. How could a Red Army soldier resist such technology? I was surprised by his nimbleness. Needless to say, this theft was probably the reason why we never saw them again.

The Red Army Ransacks the Villages

Now the front line was beyond Marijampolė. Soviet Interior Forces came in behind the front lines. They were purging the local populace. Every day we heard about new civilian arrests. They had already managed to arrest every single village elder and all the members of the local police, even though almost every one of those individuals had opposed the Germans.

Families never knew where their relatives were detained. The arrested were interrogated and held in bunkers dug into the ground in the homes of private citizens. Later it turned out that these prisoners, most of them from our region, were being brought to territories within occupied Prussia. Only after the war had ended, were they granted permission to write letters home.

The local citizens who were forced to house the Interior Forces were better off than their neighbors because they were not subjected to looting. Guards were stationed day and night and not a single soldier from other units had the right to enter the family's yard. Only, the women were very unhappy about the arrangement because the units had no field kitchens and therefore their cooks used the families' kitchens.

All the local villagers had been looted several times over. Rank-and-file soldiers, officers, and even government officials looted day and night. An administrative unit for the county and for the region had attached itself to a Red Army division. These official administrators would visit the farmers, who hated them bitterly, during the day in their cars, often accompanied by soldiers, and would take as much food as they needed. When the farmers asked them for a receipt for food or feed that had been "requisitioned" for the war effort, they would always find some excuse not to give it to them. The farmers who lived closer to the road and could be easily reached by car were wiped out completely. But even more dangerous than these official thefts by the units and "agencies" were individual thefts by Red Army soldiers.

On September 24 I was witness to one of those events.

The oldest and the youngest brothers in our family had been summoned to dig ditches. Antanas was hiding from recruitment. Father asked me and Jurgis to leave the University for a short while and return home to sow the winter crop.

I was preparing the field for planting one afternoon when I heard our mother calling: "Help, get him, save me... They've robbed me... They're getting away..."

Three Red Army soldiers burst out of the end of the barn and were running along the potato patch towards the forest. There were two men and one woman. They were carrying sacks tossed over their backs. They turned and opened up at our screaming mother, only their aim was not very good.

I jumped off the harrow. Waving a whip over my head, I chased after them. Our neighbor approached from the opposite side. The Russian woman got scared. She tossed her sack into the potato patch and took off, disentangling her submachine gun from around her neck. The other two soldiers were more nimble than her. They clutched their sacks with one hand and their guns with the other. When our neighbor and I got too close they wailed: "Don't come any closer or we'll shoot!"

Knowing they might just keep their word, we stopped chasing them. We were all the more cautious because they reloaded their guns. I was furious that my submachine gun was hidden too deep down in the hay for me to get to it quickly. This would have been the perfect opportunity to teach them that the Bolshevik slogan "What's yours is mine" does not always apply. While they still had not yet disappeared into the forest, I hoped that maybe there was some partisan in this part of the forest who would arrive and could appropriately take care of the "liberators." But no. Without facing any resistance, they were able to slink away into the forest. The three of us who had participated in the "operation" gathered together. Mama told us what happened in detail. She had left the cottage door open and had gone out to bring leaves to the pigsty. Not even half an hour had gone by before she heard the little shepherdess calling: "Auntie, Auntie, the Russians are here!"

She ran home and found one "liberator" in the kitchen. He had put his submachine gun on the table, and had set a sack near the corner hutch. He was in the process of turning the "lords" of the house into proletariats. The last object from the corner hutch to be stuffed into the Ivan's sack, was the alarm clock. After he took that, the Ivan pointed his gun at Mama as though it were nothing at all and "asked:"

"Are there any bandits around?"

"You're the bandit," Mama said.

The "liberator" grabbed the sack with one hand and tossed it over his shoulder. With his other hand he shoved Mama out of the way. She lunged for the sack. He ran out the front hallway and warned his friends:

"Arkady, Marusia, there's a devil of a woman in there. Let's go. We got enough loot."

Two more "liberators" tumbled out of the parlor straight into the front hallway. That day they "liberated" our family from three suits, two pairs of shoes, four dresses, and a large quantity of women's clothing. They broke down the door to the parlor. The clothing they did not want was strewn about the room. All the ransacked closets were left with their doors wide open and drawers emptied.

Mama had not even finished telling us about our losses when our other neighbor ran inside. He too had been the victim of the "liberation mission." His wife had lost almost all of her good clothing and all her lingerie. He had lost his last suit. Their daughter had lost her shoes. In addition to that, they had lost their very last sausage, good only for garnishing borsch. It turned out that the "liberation mission" had begun at the north end of the village and had ended at our farm.

We found the sack the woman had tossed in the potato patch. There was mostly women's clothing in it. Women from four different farms found their belongings in that sack.

The robberies became more frequent. At night they came in trucks: they took cows, sheep, pigs, farm machinery. During the day they robbed on foot and took mostly food. There was no one to complain to. If anyone even tried to complain, they would be robbed even more. First they would call the victim a fascist, and then they would accuse him of slandering the Red Army and would punish him by taking even more of his belongings away from him. The bravest people who came forward ended up behind bars. In that way the Soviet leadership did not take any action. This approval of looting was one of the incentives for the Red Army to press on enthusiastically into the West. Meanwhile, the local citizenry met each night with real fear and anxiety because they did not know if during the looting they would have to part with their own lives as well.

Forced Labor Digging Ditches and Building Airports

At this time the local population that lived closest to the front was mobilized to dig ditches and to prepare a field airport. Anyone who could lift a shovel was mobilized. Despite the fact that the Russians kept pushing forwards without needing to retreat significantly, they played it safe by preparing trenches for the infantry as far as 100 kilometers behind their lines.

In the area around my native village this mobilization for forced labor had swept up all the physically able workers. My brother Vincas was sent out with the horses and Stasys and Marytė were sent out with shovels. The ditches were dug deep and were stabilized with thin metal rods. The work was overseen by divisions of the Red Army. Each worker was given a quota for the day. He could not leave before he fulfilled his quota. The workers had a big problem getting food. Often their assigned work areas were 20 kilometers away from home, and some times even three times more than that. The Russians gave them no food whatsoever. The workers were expected to provide their own food from home. They were only free at night, when they should have been resting, to go home and procure food. Workers who lived far away cooperated. One of them would travel home to bring back food for everyone and the others would fulfill his work quota. This lasted throughout autumn because the Germans held their ground and the Bolsheviks were not sure whether they would break through the front.

At the same time the forced laborers were obligated to repair the roads. Here too the local populace was put to work. They fixed the roads in a unique way. On a somewhat uneven road they would line up layered tree trunks to create a surface. This kind of road work required a lot of timber from the forests. But they did not repair all the roads, only the ones that were necessary to them.

The third type of work, the work most hated by the local populace, were the preparations to build field airports. That autumn about 150 field airports were built in Lithuania. To build them, the Russians confiscated local people's land. The work consisted of draining the confiscated plots, leveling them out, and building temporary facilities. Most of them were designed for small airplanes. To do the work they brought in people from the surrounding areas at gunpoint.

Because of the heavy work load piled onto the village workers, most of the local populace was not able to sow their winter crop, dig their potatoes, or complete other necessary work.

It was also unfortunate that in Lithuania that particular autumn was very wet.

Recruitment for the Front

Recruitment did not take place at the same time all across Lithuania. While western Lithuania was still in the hands of the Germans, eastern Lithuania was under the control of the Bolsheviks. The Red Army was mobilizing Lithuanian men with a vengeance. Every citizen was convinced that the new occupiers did not have the right to recruit from the local citizenry. Every one's stance was clear—ignore the Red Army mobilization, just like they had ignored the mobilization during the German occupation. However, the Russian occupiers proved themselves to be much more persistent than the Germans. They instituted their plans by any means possible. The men were supposed to report to the registration centers the same day they were called up for recruitment. Massive numbers of Soviet Interior Forces arrived in the provinces and combed the forests and villages, searching for recruits. This action showed that it was obvious to the Red Army that the locals were not going to show up at their registration points voluntarily. When the villagers saw the first group of arrested men, they fled for the forests. Soldiers shot at every running man without warning. In those few days Lithuania lost several thousand men. A large number of recruits hid in barns and granaries, crawling in among the feed or grain. The Soviet Interior Forces searched those areas by firing a round of gunfire into the haylofts and granaries. They shot up every barn. Some of the men were patient and would not crawl out of their hiding places even if they were injured. Others were betrayed by their screams of pain. Near my farm, in the forest near one of the villages, 18 men died on one of those "recruitment" days. All of them were simple laborers. They were all killed unarmed.

Travel Documents

This atmosphere caused me to lose faith in the documents I had. I did not wait to test them. I returned to Kaunas. Near the food processing plant a patrol stopped me and began rifling through my papers. As it turned out, our student papers lacked a military seal. Immediately, a narrow-eyed Mongol, a Central Asian, noticed that there was no seal on my papers (he probably could not read the text). "Hey you," he said, "your papers are out of order. Let's go see the boss." He pressed his submachine gun into my back and shoved me towards a kiosk where his "boss" had set up shop.

That was where the questions started. The boss (I think he was a lieutenant) was concerned. He asked me why there was no a seal on my documents. What reason did I, a student, have to leave Kaunas? How could I, a student, be traveling to the provinces to help my father with the harvest? And so on. It took a lot of patience to explain everything, mainly because his questions had the tone of childlike petulance to them. My explanation that it was not my fault, but the fault of the head of the military authorities, that the papers lacked seals did not help the situation. The boss's conclusion was that I had to be lying. He gave the guard the command to take me and many others like me to the conscription office. The guard clicked his heels together and shoved his submachine gun into my back once again and directed me towards a ditch where 15 of my colleagues sat. I chose a comfortable spot for myself and sat down. We all started complaining. We could not believe that we would now all be sent off to attack Berlin. Just then one more of my colleagues arrived on a bicycle. The patrol ripped him off his bicycle and was about to drag him in to see the boss. As it turned out, he was a lot smarter than we were. Instead of obediently going where he was told, he grabbed the Mongol under the arm and dragged him aside. The Mongol was immediately alarmed and raised his gun, but he soon understood what was up and allowed himself to be led aside. Our colleague pulled something wrapped in paper out of his briefcase and shoved it into the Ivan's hands. The Ivan smiled broadly and in a generous tone of voice said, "Everything's in order. You may pass." Our colleague got back on his bicycle and rode off. As he passed us he smirked and said:

"Are you out of ham? Is that why you're down and out here? See how quickly he took it."

Our Mongol came back to us with eyes happier than a dog's. Soon our ranks were filled to twenty. Then more Russians showed up. They divided us up into groups of five and sent us off to the Third Conscription Office on Gediminas Street. Here they handed us over to the official on duty as deserters. They started calling us one by one out of the heavily guarded hall to see the boss. Some of the men disappeared after that. It was clear that those were the ones who would have to go fight or dig coal in the Komi region in Russia.

A few, beet red, were led through the door and let free. While I waited that woeful hour, two more men were brought in. The official on duty immediately and ceremoniously registered them. They were from the town of Pakuonis. One of the guards, hearing the name of their town, approached the official and began whispering something in his ear. I overheard them talking about yesterday's incident in Pakuonis. Some men (the Russians referred to them as "bandits") had attacked the forced labor division in Pakuonis, killed the guards, and released all the forced laborers. The man telling the story kept turning around and looking fearfully at the men from Pakuonis.

My turn came to see the boss. They called out my surname and shoved me through the door towards the boss. A humanoid with matted hair and a bloated face sat behind a large table covered with a red table cloth. He was their boss. I made a move to step closer towards him, but the guard yanked me back. From a distance, the boss began the usual litany: surname, name, patronymic... Then he added, "You've heard, we're going to fight. You didn't have the chance to be a Red Partisan, but now you'll have the chance not to get left behind by the other great Red Army soldiers and participate in the final blow against that monster, Hitler."

I listened with wide eyes while at the same time searching my mind for arguments to wiggle my way out of his great offer to "restore my honor." When he was finished, I began explaining to him that it was not our place here to discuss these questions, and that we only had to fulfill the commissar's council decisions. They know better than we do who is meant to go and fight with a gun and who is meant to work in production. If I were taken from my duties without good reason, well, if I were to act differently than the commissar's council saw fit, then that behavior would be along the lines of treason. The boss had no choice, but to give in to my reasoning. He agreed that I was right, but he still assigned a guard to escort me to the Military Commissary for University Affairs. That office did not detain me for very long because we found the right official there, the one who was supposed to place a seal on my documents in the first place. He also should have been placing seals on all the documents of the other detained university students.

First News of the Partisans

Once I made it outside without my escorts, I felt much better. I hurried off to the Main Hall of the University. There I got the details about what had happened in Pakuonis. This was our first report of partisan activities. On the first day of the mobilization the Bolshevik divisions had captured a number of men. They crammed them into a bunker set up in the Bajoraitis home. Two men, Tigras (Tiger)[25] and Šarūnas,[26] were determined to rescue them. They took a box of grenades and a gun each. In the evening they snuck back to Pakuonis. Carefully, they crept up to the guard posts. They took stock of their targets and unscrewed their grenades. Simultaneously, they began tossing grenades at the guard post and at the bunker itself. In seconds the guards and the relief guards were blown to bits. They had not even had a chance to fire a bullet. The partisans broke down the door to the bunker and released everyone held inside. Within moments they all disappeared, leaving behind a landscape torn up by grenades and littered with the bodies of the guards.

I learned from my friends that the partisans were already making frequent appearances throughout Lithuania. A few days earlier, near the town of Prienai, Dešinys (Right)[27] and his organized group had blocked Soviet Security vehicles carrying prisoners at Nuotakų Hill. They shot all the Soviet Security guards on

---

25 Kazimieras Pyplys, 1923–1947. Pyplys participated in 18 battles and was wounded four times. He was betrayed, surrounded, and killed in a partisan bunker August 23, 1947.

26 Vytautas Juodis, 1922–1947. He was betrayed and killed in a bunker July 17, 1947.

27 Kazimieras Pinkvata, 1919–1949. He was betrayed and killed June 6, 1949.

the spot and released the prisoners. They doused all the cars, American Studebakers, with gasoline and burned them.

Events like these were taking place every week. The ranks of the partisans filled rapidly as the Bolsheviks continued making arrests, murdering, looting, brutally recruiting men, confiscating land and wealth. The partisans took action against the most active Bolshevik collaborators, against the most active administrative officials, and against Soviet Security agents. Day after day, here and there, collaborators began to disappear. The populace developed a vocabulary for these disappearances: the fox took him away; he went out to hunt rabbits; he went fishing, and so on. People's morale improved. Day and night the partisans and their couriers were on guard. Their goal was to stop the looting Russian soldiers and to stop the work of provincial collaborators or Soviet Security officers who had come to Lithuania to make arrests. Collaborators with the Bolsheviks, seeing their fellows disappearing before their very eyes, thought twice before using the situation to their personal advantage. Fueled by the outrage of their local traitors, the Bolsheviks intensified their terror. Rapidly the ranks of the partisans swelled like wildfire across the entire country, spreading throughout all social and economic classes.

A few days later I met my friend who went by the code name of Uosis (Ash Tree).[28] He was already a partisan. He had come to Kaunas to retrieve a printing press. When the mobilization began, the partisans had acquired a printing press to produce fabricated documents. Now they wanted to transport the press to the provinces and leave it in the command of the Iron Wolf partisan division. Uosis explained that he had no other choice but to join the partisans after he had not been accepted into the University. They would not let him study because his father was a volunteer in Independent Lithuania's army, a commander of the Vytis Cross[29]. He immediately offered me a few of his fabricated documents. He asked if I knew of any men without documents who were crouching in cellars, freezing, terrified of being shot or impaled by the Russians. He was confidant that their fabricated documents were as good as the enemy's. He bragged that with those documents he had passed through three control points that very day.

A few weeks previously, before he had acquired his documents, he had almost ended up having to go to the front himself. He had some business to take care of at the Iron Wolf headquarters. He was passing through Rutkiškės. He was

---

[28] Algirdas Varkala, 1927–1948. March 18, 1948 he was retreating from the enemy when he was shot in the leg. He shot himself to avoid being taken prisoner.

[29] The Lithuanian Coat of Arms. The Vytis symbol is a white stallion and mount on a red background.

dressed as a shepherd to avoid being identified as a partisan. He had rolled up his pants, was barefoot, had an empty sack slung over his left arm, and had hung a shepherd's horn on his belt. While crossing the road by the town of A., four Russians came from Rimas's farm with a wagon full of straw. Two jumped out of the straw and demanded to see his documents. Uosis explained that he was still very young and did not have any documents, that he only had a birth certificate his parents were holding onto for safekeeping. Those explanations were not good enough for the Russians. They demanded he take them to his parents' house to check. They pulled Uosis up onto the straw and drove him towards Dambrava. They seated him between two Russians armed to the teeth. Two others sat with their backs towards him, holding submachine guns. At the Deltuva crossroads Uosis tried explaining that his farm was in Daržavietė, which was only reachable by foot. He was trying to cut back the number of his guards, because he knew it would have been difficult to handle four of them at once. The Russians realized that the farm Uosis was taking them to would be rather shabby. It consisted of nothing more than two dilapidated shacks. So, they let him go, not expecting to be able to get anything good there. And so, Uosis never did get his chance to go fight on the front.

In the Student Dorms

When I arrived in Kaunas I needed to find a place where I could settle for a longer time. I learned from my friends that a lot of students were living in a student dorm in the Mažylis home at Kęstutis Street #24. I was tempted to take advantage of the accommodations. I asked the student committee, which was only just forming at the time, about the housing situation. They said I could move in on the condition that I helped with the renovations. They asked me to be a dorm monitor. We got a unit together—my brother Jurgis, Vilius, Julius,[30] and I. We were a little late, so the better apartments were already taken. We ended up on the top floor. The apartment we selected, like all the others, had been previously occupied by men enlisted in the German Army. When the Germans were expelled, Russian divisions had been housed here. The Red Army did not like the cleanliness and order of the Germans. They shredded the mattresses the Germans had left behind, pulling out the shavings and tossing them all over the floor. Apparently, some sort of a

---

30 Vytautas Kasparavičius, 1922–, was arrested January 24, 1945 for participation in underground organizations. On May 27 he was tried and given a sentence of 10 years hard labor and 5 years in exile. He was imprisoned in Vorkutlag, Komi. From 1954–1960 he lived in exile in Vorkuta. In 1960, he returned to Lithuania.

search had taken place. They had destroyed the cabinets, beds, tables, and chairs. Among the garbage on the floor there was trampled food as well as the remains of wine and other alcoholic drinks. The parquet was mottled in a variety of colors. The plaster on the walls was filled with nails. None of the windows had glass in them. Some did not even have frames. The doors had no locks, no door handles even. It was the same with the electrical installation.

We began our renovation by hanging a sign on the outside door that read in both Lithuanian and Russian: "Occupied. Please do not disturb." After sweating half a day, we began to see results: we burned all the garbage, building a bonfire from the shattered furniture. We had the hardest time with the washing. Water had to be carried up from the basement. Sometimes, when the tap was shut off, we would have to haul it all the way from the Nemunas River. Then we had to carry the dirty water back down to the basement because the pipes were clogged somewhere down the line. The kitchen and bathroom were the worst. After we had removed the trash, washed everything, and covered the windows with plywood, we installed locks on the doors.

The Fate of Property Left Behind

The existing University leadership received permission from the newly formed Education Commissariat to take possession of educational materials, tools, and other necessary University items that had belonged to professors who had fled to the West. The University leadership passed on a good amount of furniture to the student dorms. A number of books and materials disappeared without a trace because of the lack of accountability and because of the dishonesty of those transporting the materials.

We carried the furniture to the dorms ourselves. As seniors we had the right to chose first. Our dorm administrator, Ruzgys,[31] under the command of the University leadership regulations, required that a card with the name of the former owner be attached to each piece of furniture in an unobtrusive place.

That is how the professorships' apartments were disposed of. They had been repossessed quickly. Other émigrés were less fortunate because the University had not acted fast enough to protect their belongings. All sorts of street bums took advantage of the situation to get rich quick. Often they would break into

---

[31] Algimantas Ruzgys, 1924–, was active in the underground. In September 1945 he was arrested and released when he agreed to inform for the Soviet Security. However, he warned his friends and disappeared into hiding. August 23, 1947 he was arrested, tried and sentenced to 10 years hard labor and 5 years exile without rights. He returned to Lithuania in 1955.

abandoned apartments and loot them. Usually, the Red Army assisted them with the break-ins. The Bolsheviks always had a excuse handy. They had to inspect the former residences of "enemies of the state." It was not easy for the people who had been left behind to guard the property. Immediately, the guard would be labeled a fascist or a fascist collaborator and would be dealt a certain punishment. Even when we arrived with papers from the University Rector instructing us to take over the goods of people who had gone abroad, we ended up in a conflict with either the Red Army soldiers milling around in the street waiting for a chance to break in or with local "sons of the proletariat" who slunk around waiting to grab whatever they could. The Reds would say to us, "We from the front lines don't give a damn about your Rector." We couldn't get by without some shoving and fighting. We felt a lot braver when we brought a member of the Communist Youth along with us. In those cases, we knew responsibility would fall on him, so we did not hold back from slamming down a Billy club on the back of a proletariat's head to bring home the point of who the possessions belonged to. In this way most of the possessions left behind by those who fled to the West were saved in the sense that they were appropriated by the University.

At this time I was offered the position of assistant to a University department administrator.[32] It did not seem as though I would be able to work towards earning my diploma any time soon,[33] judging by the current situation, so I accepted, expecting that at least I could participate in restoring order.

At that time the University received permission to take the Kaušakis Villa on Mickevičius Street into its possession. With a group of University volunteers I went there to work on renovations. I was met with a horrific sight. What had once been a modern villa now was a death trap. None of the doors, from the garage doors to the bathroom door, were in place. They had been used as firewood. The inner walls were covered in dirt and graffiti and the plaster was smashed off the walls. The electrical fuses, switches, meters, had been torn out. The lamps were smashed. The cupboards had been torn out of the walls. The kitchen appliances had been torn out of the basement walls and their metal parts were scattered. The porcelain sinks and toilets were shattered. The wind blew in through the smashed out windows and scattered the shavings from the mattresses across the floor, mixing them with dirty papers and other garbage. In addition to other filth, in two

32 Lukša was assistant to Bronius Barzdžiukas, Director of University Maintenance, October 1944–March 1945.

33 Juozas Lukša had completed his course work in Architecture and needed only to defend his bachelor's project: blueprints to construct the "Lithuania" hotel opposite the Įgula Church in Kaunas.

corners we found human excrement—the Red Army's signature form of cultural expression. In the western corner of the first floor we found a hastily cordoned-off cell built from bricks about four deep. The cell was dark and about a meter and a half by a meter and twenty centimeters. This cell was evidence that recently the building had been occupied by some Interior unit. On the walls of the cells the prisoner's writing and signatures had been partially erased. Near the floor, where the Security Officers were too lazy to rub off the writing, one sentence read: "I remained silent—Father." A blackened spot of blood was pressed into the wall beneath the sentence. Numerous cells like this one had been set up all over Kaunas. In them there were the marks of torture, bearing witness to the suffering of innocent people.

During this period the Bolsheviks were trying to organize "property that belonged to the people," in other words, the wealth of those who had fled to the West. Most people had left more valuable items in the trust of people left behind. The Bolsheviks knew that people were trying to hide belongings in this manner. A massive campaign had started to claim the wealth and pass it into the hands of the "liberators."

Feeding and Heating the University

The work at the University was not progressing in the slightest. We did not even have the most basic utilities. The entire city had no electricity. The only exception was the soldiers' barracks, which were lit and powered by American generators. It was impossible to work by kerosene lamp, especially for students working in technical fields. Besides that, the students and faculty alike spent most of their time working in forced work brigades or waiting on food lines. All working people had ration cards of various types. The more money a worker earned, the better his card. The exception was the Soviet Security and other Communist Party members, who not only received special privileged ration cards, but who had the privilege of purchasing goods at special separate shops very much like the shops the Germans had created during the Nazi occupation. Those shops had large signs out front that had read: For Germans Only.

The working masses received ration cards that were very limited. They received only bread, sunflower seed oil, American powdered eggs, and millet grain. The other foods marked on their ration cards, foods like meat, butter, sugar, were not available because they were scarce. Different employers and institutions began organizing private shops to ease the workers "shopping" according to their assigned ration cards, at least to the extent that they could provide items that were still available. In this manner, a private shop appeared in the basement of the Main Hall of the University. Here we received the foods I mentioned earlier. We used work brigades to deliver the goods. We got our bread from the former "Parama" factory. (The factory had survived and only one of the large ovens had been damaged by a grenade detonated by the Germans.) We brought back the bread by pushing the carts across town ourselves.

We brought in the other food in the same manner. Once we had brought in the bread and other food the entire basement would fill up with lines of people, four deep, pushing and shoving to get that day's rations. The professors and office staff shoved and pushed their way through the lines together with the students. Often students spent more time waiting in line for bread than they did sitting in lectures.

The approaching winter promised more problems. We could not foresee any means of acquiring coal. A few students took the initiative to organize work brigades to bring back peat from the peat bogs in Raudonplynė and Gaižiūnai. The University planned to exchange the peat with a Kaunas factory for coal, since all the central heating systems in the University were designed to burn higher grade fuels. There was a lot of dedication and suffering involved, but in the end nothing came of our efforts. The Raudonplynė peat had not dried enough and it was loaded in the rain, which caused it to be saturated with water and therefore useless.

The Student Council

At this time the Communist Youth Čepinskas[34] (a medical student) was encouraged by someone to start a student committee that would be similar to the former student council. The existence of the Committee was nothing more than a propaganda ploy and an attempt to imitate former legitimate student organizations.

For some reason Čepinskas, who did not know the students very well, asked my friend Simas[35] to help select candidates to the proposed committee. He chose Simas because of his ability to successfully initiate work brigades and because of his social status as the son of a small farmer from Aukštaityja. At the time of the offer it appeared to us that Čepinskas considered him "trustworthy" and that was very useful to us. One evening Simas came to see us and told us that he had been asked to put together a list. I thought it over for half an hour and then

---

34 Čepinskis, a medical student, later the director of the Kaunas Red Cross Hospital.

35 Stasys Šinkūnas, 1918–1984.

hand picked the student committee. Between every few names we would insert the name of a Communist Youth to cover up for the other names on the list—all of them true patriots. Soon the list was presented to the rector, who approved it, ensuring that the balance of patriots and Reds would remain as we had rigged it. This type of student "vote" was typical of Bolshevik democracy and was typical in the University. The Communist Party did not plan to create such a committee out of Communist Youth alone. They most likely would not have had enough warm bodies to fill the seats. At the time, out of several thousand Kaunas University students, only a few dozen belonged to the Communist Youth. Besides, the Student Committee had about zero right to change student affairs and so it was not worth the trouble to let its "democratic elections" suffer by assigning all its seats exclusively to Communist Youth members.

During committee meetings not a single non-Communist member dared to speak the way he would have liked. The Communist Youth representatives would set up the meetings' agendas and show up with ready-made projects and decrees that the other members voted in favor of without asking any questions or suggesting any changes. The positive result of this Committee was that it managed to acquire two farms for the University. The importance of this acquisition could be felt in the student cafeteria when milk and potatoes became available.

Student Arrests Begin

In late autumn arrests of students and professors became more frequent. Until now the University had not experienced as many arrests as elsewhere in Lithuania. The reason for this relative peace could have been that during the German occupation our intelligentsia had massively and actively resisted the Nazis. The result being that, for a certain period, we were tolerated because we were perceived as being loyal to the Bolsheviks.

When the arrests began, the Bolsheviks organized a spy ring of Soviet Security agents and Soviet Security Ministry agents within the student ranks. Often one or another of our colleagues would disappear. Some were released after a few days in prison. Others were transported to Russia. The Bolsheviks selected people for arrest who had low moral values or a follower's mentality. They were accused of being "enemies of the people." Not a single one of them could defend himself, because no one even knew what an "enemy of the people" was. After these "accusations," the arrested would be forced to sign a paper stating that he or she would collaborate with the Soviet Security Ministry. Then they were released. Collaboration was interpreted as reporting on their friends' political opinions, moods, attitude towards the West, their loyalty to the Soviet Union, and so on. A portion of those arrested chose to die in Siberia rather than to betray their friends. Others, often not grasping and not foreseeing the results of their collaboration, signed and bought their freedom at this horrific price. One group of students who had acquired their freedom in such a manner immediately went to their closest friends and warned them never to say anything against the Soviet Union in their presence. That kind of warning was necessary because in every discussion group there could be someone who was working for the Bolsheviks in earnest and who would report back to his comrades. In this manner it could come out that someone who had signed was not a loyal follower and that would be enough reason to convict him on the grounds that he had not upheld his "voluntary" commitment.

We were lucky in our dorm. We were all friends, all of us trusting one another. We did not have to restrain ourselves in front of each other. In our stairwell, there were three stories of six apartments each, housing about thirty students who all knew each other very well after several years of study together. Often, in the evenings we would gather in smaller or larger groups and, besides discussing our studies, we talked about the resistance against the first Bolshevik occupation and the resistance against the Germans. We didn't miss any opportunity to discuss our current occupation, which was strangling us more and more and obliterating our few remaining basic human rights and our freedom.

We analyzed and attempted to predict the course of international politics in the near future. We did not believe for an instant that the West would allow the Red Asian Horror to destroy the nations of Eastern and Central Europe, who, after the Nazi occupation, had fallen into the grasp of Communist slavery. We believed that freedom and human rights and the rights of nations would not be violated, as declared in the Atlantic Charter.[36] This same principle was repeated again and again later in many various ceremonies and conferences. We could not believe that the continuing fight for freedom and human principles and human rights would be abandoned. It was a fight in which already many of the West's

---

[36] August 14, 1941, the United States and Great Britain signed the Atlantic Charter. This document expressed the coalition's position against Hitler and laid out a plan for a peaceful, coexisting post-war Europe. In this document the coalition expressed their desire to reinstate the independence of nations that lost their sovereignty during World War Two. Later, other nations signed the Atlantic Charter, among them the Soviet Union. This document was of extreme importance to Lithuanians because they believed it legally validated their right to the reinstatement of Lithuania's independence. The partisans interpreted the Atlantic Charter literally and fought in a war where they were greatly outnumbered because they believed that they only had to hold their own until forces from America and Western Europe arrived to aid them in their struggle and to undoubtedly reinstate Lithuania's independence.

most honorable had died. We refused to believe that the West would shamefully close its eyes as entire nations were left to die. We did not believe that Westerners could be that naive, or blind, or unable to see past the Bolsheviks' true motives and manufactured lies. We believed freedom would dawn once more, a freedom that would take the place of an inhumane Bolshevik slave system, one that was even more horrific than the previous Nazi enslavement.

The spirit of the fight was in us. We were hungering to join the fight against the world's new destroyer of the freedom of sovereign nations. It was the same spirit to fight that had led to the revolt in 1941. The same spirit to fight that over the course of a few years had driven out the German occupiers. That same spirit to fight had already pushed quite a few of our friends into joining up with the fight's most obvious expression of the fight for freedom—the partisan movement.

Lithuanian Soldiers are Deported to Siberia

At the beginning of 1945, the Bolsheviks were rushing to prepare for a new offensive to finally bring Germany to its knees. Because of that the mobilization units were working double time to conscript all available resources and people. However, the Lithuanians, just like a few months earlier, ignored all the Bolsheviks repeated demands that they register at their appointed recruitment centers and did not show up of their own free will. Throughout the entire country massive manhunts intensified. The captured men, guarded by heavily armed units, were herded to the closest recruitment centers. From here some were dressed in Red Army uniforms and formed into units while others were sent to jail. These so-called "Lithuanian units" were led by Russian officers and Russian was the only language used for orders and commands.

These hastily thrown-together units were sent to the front without any military training. Often soldiers lacked even a personal weapon. The Soviet viewpoint was that unarmed soldiers had to find their own weapons on the battlefield by taking them either from their killed comrades or from the enemy. Such thinking about recruitment from a Western perspective was horrific and unbelievable, but it was perfectly natural to the Russians. They did not worry about losing people because they had so many of them.

Moreover, they worried little about losing people from the occupied territories where people had a strong sense of nationhood and a vivid memory of life in a free and democratic nation. The recruitment was the perfect opportunity to liquidate this disloyal mass of people.

Because of the predominant anti-Bolshevik mood among their ranks, the units put together by force had no loyalty whatsoever to the Russians. Dubbed "pseudo-Americans" by the Russians, the Lithuanians took every opportunity available to run for the green forest complete with their entire Red Army uniform to join up with local partisan units.

If we are destined to die, then we will die on our native soil, defending our freedom, and not somewhere far away, scattering our bones in the name of a new form of slavery was the decision of Lithuania's farm boys, who had grown up close to the earth on their native land.

Because of the Lithuanian nation's firm, unbreakable resistance, the larger number of captured Lithuanian men were taken away not to the front, but into the depths of Siberia. Many of them were destined never to see their native land again.

At the end of January, while supervising a University work brigade of several dozen students, who were loading peat into the wagons at the Gaižiūnas Station, I became a witness to one of those "deployments" to the East. For some time I had been uneasily observing several dozen American cattle cars. Inside each car there were double bunks. The small windows were twisted with thick barbed wire. From the bunks I had guessed that these cars were set up to transport soldiers. But why then were the windows covered in barbed wire? They reminded me of the deportation cars I had seen so many times before.

On the occasion of the anniversary of Lenin's death this line of trains was pushed by steam engine towards the ramp. A large group of local people were congregating around the train station building. Every single one of them was carrying a bundle and looking around as though searching for someone. The atmosphere was calm. There was no anxiety in the air.

At a command and prompted at gun point, the men slowly climbed into the wagons, glancing through the barbed wire windows, straining to see the faces of their loved ones for one last time.

An armed Russian stood guard beside each filled wagon—they were Interior troops. The people waiting with the bundles began pushing their way through the thick lines of soldiers not paying any heed to their threats, searching for their family members. Mostly these people were women of various ages and old men. Wailing mothers searched for their sons, girls searched for their brothers and lovers, desperate to look in their eyes for one last time and to give them some food to take with them on this trip into the unknown. The Russian brigade's shouting competed with the women's wailing.

I heard the resounding, shrill sound of the train whistle. The officers standing near the wagons threatened the women with their weapons and slammed the wagon doors shut, fastening the latches with barbed wire. People who had not found their loved ones now stood beside the wagon closest to them and rushed to open up their bundles. They crammed food into the hands shoved out from in between the barbed wire. From inside voices called out for water. Between the loaves of bread, people shoved fistfuls of snow inside the windows. Out of nowhere an old, bent-over woman appeared beside the nearest wagon. She was the village beggar. Setting down her well-worn baskets on the snow, she began unpacking, calling for help.

"People, come help me give them my share. My hands are too weak and tired. I can't reach the windows. I've collected this food from those that might have been their parents or relatives. I'll collect more food if God gives me the strength. Now these poor souls are going to see more hunger than I ever will." The woman wiped away tears as she spoke.

No. It was too much for me. I had to turn away to hide my tears. I did not want to let the occupiers have the satisfaction of seeing a man cry.

Soon we heard the piercing whistle and the train, starting and halting convulsively a few times, began its trip east. Slowly the American wagons rolled away. The eyes of men who had lost their freedom burned through the barbed wire windows and we could hear their sad song: "Good-bye Lithuania, I was happy to live on your land…"

That was their last farewell to their lost freedom and to their native land. Most of them never set foot on this land again.

The steel clanged a few more times and the train turned around the bend, taking with it the sad, heart wrenching sounds of their songs. For some time I stood in the station watching the Interior troops take their leave along with the tearful mob. Not far away from me I heard a voice say hoarsely through his teeth:

"And once again, more bones for the Siberian dogs."

I swung around and saw one of my brigade workers, the janitor in charge of the University's coal stoves. These words of truth came from the mouth of the proletariat, supposedly dedicated to the "liberators of the worker." I wanted to add a few words of my own, but I bit my tongue, remembering that this man need not know my opinion because he could easily tell the difference between the liberators and the slaves.

My Brother's Turn Came

All night long I was tormented by nightmares. One of them was so vivid and so awful that it forced me awake. I dreamt I was in the student dorms. Suddenly a tornado rose above the city, carrying with it bloody red sheets, hitting the boarded-up dorm windows so hard that even the walls shattered. Frightened, I quickly ran down the stairs to the basement to hide. Along the way I tripped over three blanched corpses. I recognized the corpses as those of my friends Julius[37] and Vilius[38] and my brother Jurgis. The sight in the dream disturbed me so deeply that I started awake from my sleep.

I wiped off my hot, sweaty face and thought about what my dream could mean. In my thoughts I considered my surroundings, but I could not come up with any interpretation. Finally, I came to the conclusion that most likely the dream was my reaction to seeing the soldiers being exiled to Siberia.

The tired workers snored in the dark room. I could see ice frozen over the barbed wire beyond the window. I tossed from side to side for awhile and finally, overcome with emptiness, fell asleep.

After three weeks of work we were finished loading peat at Gaižiūniai. The results of our work was poor. We were only able to load a tenth of the amount we had planned on taking because first the wagons did not arrive on time and second because the peat was wet. Now the peat had frozen into one massive brick. We were only able to hack apart the congealed piles with axes. We did not have enough wheelbarrows to carry the peat from the piles to the wagons. Once we were finished we returned to Kaunas.

There I said good-bye to the workers, walked down Vytautas Prospect, and turned into Donėlaitis Street. I walked along deep in thought. I barely noticed where I was going until I came upon my good friend Stasys.[39]

"Where are you going, walking around carelessly, so close to Laisvės 6?"[40] he asked.

"I'm heading to my dorm. I just got back," I said. The moment I said it I read surprise in his face. His expression was not comforting.

"Are you crazy? Don't you know that your roommates and your brother are already behind bars?" Stasys said.

---

37 Jonas Kunigonis.

38 Vytautas Kasparavičius.

39 Antanas Kedys, 1923–, was a student in the Construction Department. In September 1945 he was arrested and imprisoned in Kaunas. In November he was exiled to Vorkutlaga and later to Komi. He was released February 11, 1947.

40 The Soviet Security Internal Prison. Officially, the prison could hold 100 prisoners.

When I told him I had no idea, he stumbled over his words in the rush to tell me what had happened over the past few days.

It turned out that on the night I had dreamt of the corpses, a red tornado really had swept through our dorm. All of my apartment roommates had been arrested: Julius, Vilius, and my brother Jurgis. In addition to them, a number of other students had also been arrested: Antanas,[41] Juozas K., P.,[42] and others. Stasys did not know if the Soviet Security was interested in me or not, but he advised me to play it safe and not return to my dorm.

"If they took the three of them, they'll come back for the fourth," Stasys said. "You know how the Soviet system works."

I, however, confident of my own innocence and refusing to accept that the NKVD would be looking for me so intensely, assured myself that I could return to the dorm for at least a while. I was one of the most active members of the University administration and at the time I did not yet have any ties with the illegal underground anti-Soviet resistance. Therefore, paying no heed to Stasys's warning, I returned to the dorm.

I found Julius's sister[43] staying in the room. From her I learned all the details of the arrests. On Saturday Julius, Jurgis, and Vilius had gone out somewhere for the evening. They returned on Sunday, after a party, just as the rooster was crowing. In the apartment they were met by the Soviet Security police, who demanded they hold up their hands. After a careful body search, they shoved them all into the end room and did a thorough search of the apartment. After that they interrogated them.

The Soviet Security had spent the entire day in our apartment and arrested every single person who stopped by. The students had their share of fun too. Around six Jokubas[44] stopped by, quite drunk. As he stepped over the threshold, one of the Soviet Security police, dressed as a civilian, confronted him and demanded he raise his arms above his head. Jokubas, thinking it was a bad joke,

---

41 Albinas Naujokas, 1919–, arrested January 24, 1945, for belonging to the student underground. On May 27, he was sentenced to 10 years hard labor and five years in exile. He was imprisoned in Dubrovlage, Mordova. From 1955, he lived in exile in Irkustsk. On March 10, 1956, he was released and returned to Lithuania.

42 Unknown.

43 Albina Kunigonytė, a medical student. After two semesters she left the university and joined the partisan movement. She was Juozas Lukša's liaison-woman. To avoid arrest she left Vilnius and went to work as a teacher in the village of Veivariai. On September 20, 1951, she was arrested along with her parents and brother and brother's wife and exiled to Irkustsk. The Soviets had no pretext for the arrest of the family, and so they tried them as relatives of the accused.

44 Medical student Jonas Gylys.

grabbed the officer by the collar with his strong arms, kicked him very hard in the backside and told him that if every shepherd boy starts demanding to know his last name he might as well not even get up out of bed in the morning. A group of Soviet Security ran in and beat him, forcing poor Jokubas to submit, finally holding him down on the ground.

I asked the girl if the Soviet Security had been looking for me too, but she had no answer for me. She was also of the opinion that it would be dangerous for me to linger at the dorm for any longer period of time. And so, after changing my clothes and making arrangements as to how to stay in touch, I rushed off into the city, to find my good friend.

I decided to leave Kaunas until the situation was resolved. I had decided to run only in the event that I found conclusive evidence that my days of freedom were numbered, although, according to Stasys, many people who had been just as fearless had found themselves at Laisvės 6. It was sad to leave the University and my surroundings. To avoid being branded by the local agent network as a fugitive fleeing the law, I asked my boss for three weeks' vacation.

My biggest concern was to find out the real reason my brother and my friends had been arrested. To that end for the next few weeks I met with a group of my friends and discussed the situation with them. We came to the conclusion that most of the students had been arrested for no reason at all, simply so that they could be bribed. We came to this conclusion because the NKVD were not able to find any ties that would prove their connection to the existing underground. Even here the Bolsheviks stuck to their principle: it is better to kill several thousand innocent people than to let one guilty one live.

After a few days the "red tornado" continued onwards, arresting people from all the student dorms and even the ones who were housed privately. Every night they took away men and women. From one day to the next the arrests grew more and more frequent. The reports we received showed that the situation was the same all over the country. I decided to leave Kaunas and to stay in the provinces until the fever of arrests died down.

Mardi Gras

It was early afternoon during the Mardi Gras. I had shut myself in the woodshed and was splitting firewood. I lazily chopped the frozen logs, in my mind mulling over my present situation. My legal vacation had ended.

Suddenly, I heard a woman scream. The scream came from the direction of my neighbor's and rang across the snow-covered fields. I tossed down my ax and ran outside. Sticking close to the wood pile, I looked towards my neighbor's farm. I saw some gray human-like figures, some of whom were chasing my neighbor's wife.

The Ivans are at it again, I thought. I was not mistaken.

Three hundred yards away from the house, the Russian caught up to my breathless neighbor and after kicking her thoroughly, yanked something out of her hands. Leaving the panting woman rolling in the snow, the Russian hurried back to where his comrades were waiting, ready to leave. In a second their sledge flew out of the neighbor's yard and turned in the direction of our farm. They whipped the mare mercilessly and within moments burst through our gates. Four sloppily dressed Russians were hunched down in the sledge, surrounded by piles of stolen goods. Three of them tumbled out of the sledge, holding Nagan revolvers in their hands. They began making themselves at home in our house. The Captain confronted me and demanded: "Who are you? Hand over your documents immediately." He added a choice Russian curse for emphasis.

I told him my documents were in my room and invited him inside.

"Of course we'll come inside, but not at your invitation," the Captain cut me off, pointing towards our cottage with his revolver.

Once we were inside, I found my wallet and asked him:

"And what documents interest you, Comrade Captain? Will you honor me by telling me who you are exactly and why you need my documents?"

"This is who we are," the Captain said, shoving the revolver in my face and at the same time tearing my wallet out of my hands.

I refrained from resisting because the Captain could barely stand on his own two feet. As he was rifling through my papers, I looked out the window at the Russians out in the yard. Two lieutenants were laughing loudly and watching a third drunken soldier retching beside the overfilled sledge. The drunk soldier managed to sputter out a litany of curses between each gag.

I smiled slightly to myself, though managed to pull together a serious expression for the Captain. He had already found his way around my wallet. In one hand he held my money, which he slowly stuffed into his overcoat pocket, while with his other hand he held out my documents, demanding that I make sense of them because some of the writing was in Lithuanian.

Acting as if I had not noticed that he had just stolen my money, I pulled out my passport, my military documents, my work identification, my travel papers, my union card, and my permission for time off. Meanwhile, the two lieutenants slunk into the room. Now the Captain did not even bother to look at my documents anymore. Instead, he pressed them together in his hands, blue from the cold and from drinking, and began interrogating me:

"Name, surname, patronymic, place of birth, date of birth, employment and so on."

Not even waiting for me to answer all his questions, he grew drowsy and drifted off, shoving my documents towards one of the lieutenants. This one was somewhat sober. He found my papers to be more than in order. He grew quite polite, all the more because through the window he spotted two more men walking towards the farm. It was my brother and my neighbor. Once they were inside, we began to treat them the way drunk Russians are meant to be treated. The soldiers' eyes often wandered to the room's corners, assessing our property. The revolver slipped away from the sleeping Captain's chest. The thud of the revolver hitting the floor woke him up. Sliding off the bench twice, the captain somehow managed to grab hold of the revolver's muzzle, and place it right beside his nose. He demanded: "Vodka and food." A stream of Russian curses followed his demand.

When he realized that we were equally matched, three on three, he emphasized that Arkady would be arriving soon.

Vincas brought in a bottle of home brew. Mama provided some food she had prepared for the Mardi Gras. I went to get Arkady. He was freezing, sleeping deeply, clutching that day's loot with both arms. The sledge and the bag were quite soiled from his vomit, which had frozen stiff. I yanked his sleeve a few times and woke him. I told him that Comrade Captain had commanded him to go indoors. He cursed the Captain and his mother a few times and then agreed to come indoors.

The Captain took a long swig and immediately collapsed, sliding beneath the table. His friends did not do anything for him, so I tried to pick him up or at least make him more comfortable, but one of the lieutenants waved me away, telling me not to bother because the Comrade Captain always got sober by lying under the table. He only asked that I chase the cats out of the room.

Arkady began to get worse after I brought him inside. He cursed twice in a row and after his fourth glass asked me to go get him sauerkraut juice to sober him up. I took a glass and headed for the pantry, but Arkady did not trust me. He followed me as soon as I stood up from the table.

"Wait, let's go together. The devil only knows what kind of juice you'll come back with if I let you go off alone."

After drinking three glasses of sauerkraut juice my comrade recovered enough to become concerned with my documents.

"Do you have your documents?"

"How could I not," I said. "All three of your friends have already checked them."

The Russian was displeased with my answer and pestered me with questions about my work. When I admitted that my actual profession was architecture, he grew concerned:

"Where's your weapon?"

"I have no weapon. What do I need a weapon for?"

"How can you not have a weapon? Here in the Soviet Union all architects are armed," Arkady said, trying to intimidate me.

I realized that he understood so little about architecture that he thought it was some official organ of the Soviet Security Ministry. I told him to go and ask his friends to explain to him what architecture was. He agreed, adding:

"And if I'm right, then I'll yank your weapon up out your throat," Arkady could barely get his tongue together to form the words.

We returned to the table. Arkady immediately jumped at the lieutenant seated closest to him and said, "That bastard is trying to tell me that in the Soviet Union not all architects carry guns. He doesn't want to show me his weapon."

"You idiot," the lieutenant shouted back at Arkady, "Where did you hear such nonsense."

"Motherfucker," Arkady cursed and sniffled. Furious, he sat down to eat Mother's Mardi Gras biscuits.

Finally, they had all had their fill. It was already evening. They all rose to leave. They dragged the Captain out. They tossed the heavier part of his body into the sledge, leaving his legs dangling over the side. His legs swung back and forth like a pendulum as they drove off.

Before they left they had to chase the dogs off. The dogs had taken advantage of the Russians' absence to tear open the sack left in the sledge and to drag out part of the sausage and dried meat inside it and had proceeded to calmly feed on it. There was nothing left of the sausage and the dried meat was fairly chewed. The lieutenant shoved the dried meat back inside the sack, honoring Brownie with a chorus of curses. Brownie just stood there, licking his chops, pleased that he had won himself a nice Mardi Gras meal.

It turned out that my brother already knew these "guests." They were the leadership of the local regional Meat Acceptance Point. They had set out on their party from M.'s farm. They had taken the mare and the sledge from P. They'd continued on their way, looting for meat and home brew. Their methods were crude and simple: when they came upon women or the elderly home alone, they would force them into a corner. One of them would search the room, the second would empty the cupboards, wardrobes, and trunks, and the third would load everything into sacks. The fourth would hunt for vodka. When they came upon men at home, they would satisfy themselves with a bottle or two of home brew and some food to go with it.

Our neighbor J. had suffered the most today. She was home alone with her daughter and granddaughter. After finishing their operation, the Captain could not resist shooting at the holy pictures hanging on her walls. He shot at least one hole into each of the pictures with his Nagan revolver.

"Oh, if only I'd known where the partisans were today," our neighbor said to us through her tears, "they would have shown those cowards what it means to beat old women and loot their pantries."

And she had reason to cry. She was the owner of only two thirds of a hectare. She never had much beef on hand. She had a hard time fattening her livestock. This robbery was the third that year and it had left the family destitute.

Hours and Days Spent Outside the Kaunas Jail

My vacation on my father's farm had ended. As I had not received any news about the University, I cautiously returned to Kaunas. Carefully considering the situation, I learned that I had not been drawn into the accusations against Julius, Jurgis, Antanas, and the others. For the moment, the NKVD was not interested in me. However, for the sake of caution I slept each night in a different location.

I often took turns with my brother Stasys waiting outside the prison doors, trying to pass on food and clean clothing to my brother and friends held under arrest. They had recently been transferred from Laisvės 6 to Mickevičius 9, to Prison #1. This prison was well known to me. I had experienced Bolshevik "justice" there myself in 1941 when I had been arrested. Now it was bursting with prisoners. The number of prisoners held in each cell was more than double the number held there in 1941. During independence these cells housed just a few criminals. Now fifty to sixty prisoners were crammed into the same space. In the mornings the stench and the humidity and sweat steamed out of the cells' broken windows into the street as though they were bathhouses and not prison cells. Each of the windows only opened up to a corner of the sky because they were nailed over with boards. At night there was not enough room for the prisoners to stretch out and rest. Usually the prisoners "rested" by curling up against each other, clutching the food they had to their chests because the Russian prisoners took advantage of the darkness to steal. When the infirm were brought back from torture sessions or dragged in prostrate after interrogation, their friends made room for them to stretch out and rest on the floor by spending the night standing up. There were Russian criminals mixed in with the political prisoners. The food rations in the prison were very limited, so those who did not receive food packages from friends or family were forced to steal from others to stave off starvation. There were also quite a few Soviet citizens of uncertain background who were added to the mix as provocateurs whose purpose it was to elicit information from the prisoners that could not be obtained during interrogation and torture.

It was very difficult to pass food onto the prisoners because the official in charge often would not give his permission. Most often permission depended on the "success" of the case. Among other methods, the Bolsheviks considered starvation a good means of loosening the tongue. There were no set rules on how food parcels were to be accepted. Relatives of a prisoner could spend weeks waiting with food parcels in the waiting room and never get anywhere, whereas someone who had their wits about them would figure out a way of getting to the food acceptance window. Every day there would be a few hundred people waiting to pass on food, but only about several dozen managed to get their food parcels through. If you wanted to make it into that lucky category, you had to take advantage of whatever tricks you had at your disposal or you had to give a bribe. Whoever did not have those "qualities" spent days and nights in vain standing out in the cold with their battered food parcels. Whenever I passed the prison around six o'clock in the evening when the food acceptance window was already closed, I would find elderly men and women leaning against the fence crying. When I asked them why they were crying, they would answer, "Again I didn't get my parcel past the window."

Food parcels were accepted in the following manner. The doors to the hall where food was passed on through the food acceptance window was about thirty meters from the prison gates. Every individual who wanted to deliver a food parcel had to fight his or her way through the throngs of people into the hall and then to the window to submit a request to deliver the parcel. The request had to be written in both Russian and Lithuanian and addressed to the prison boss. The request had to list what food was being delivered and who was delivering it. Once the request was delivered, the individual would have to stand around and wait to find out if his or her request to deliver the food parcel would be granted and whether his or her family member was still being held in this prison. Once the answer was received, the family member would shove the food parcel through the window and then stand around and wait until the empty sack was returned along with the copy of the request written in Lithuanian, signed by the prisoner.

The relatives of prisoners would line up outside the prison gates the night before, especially if they were coming from the provinces. All night they would wait, shivering outside the gates. At dawn they would all rush the prison gates, trying to arrange themselves into orderly queues. Often when there were arguments, the queues broke up, and confusion reigned. That was when the fights would start. Everyone would push and shove to get closer to the prison gates or at least to hold onto their established place in line. About a half hour before the doors opened the patrol guards would arrive and threaten the crowds with their guns, pushing them back from the doors. One of the guards would collect three rubles from each person in line; the other would hand out numbers. After they had made their money, the guards would leave. Not even a few minutes later the remainder of the crowd would lose their place in line and again there would be a confused shuffle. The doors would open just before nine.

I only was successful in passing on my food parcel after three days of shoving and crowding. When my sack was returned to me, I was overjoyed to see my brother's signature. It was a sign of life from him.

The best opportunity to get a good place in line at the window was when they led a group of prisoners out of the prison. Then someone standing outside would call out, "They're going!" Almost everyone inside the hall would repeat the cry. The crowd would hurry outside, abandoning their place in line, each of them hoping to catch a glimpse of their loved ones or friends.

Every month 3000 prisoners would be deported from the central prison in Kaunas or Vilnius to Siberia. After each wave of deportations the prison would be filled with new prisoners brought in from various parts of Lithuania, from temporary prison cellars, bunkers, and underground facilities.

The prisoners were brought in from the provinces by truck or train. They were forced to kneel on the ground in the backs of trucks. Armed guards stood in all four corners. When the trucks stopped at the prison gates, the prisoners were forced to kneel on the cobblestone with their heads down and turned towards the prison gates. This was done so that they could not see where they were and so that their loved ones could not identify or recognize their faces.

Prisoners from Kaunas or the surrounding suburbs were forced to walk to the prison. They too were forced to perform this enforced "worship" of hell's gates. They had to kneel with their stiff legs on the cold cobblestone and wait with their heads down for the gates to open.

These scenes of humiliation affected the entire crowd. People cried for their relatives or friends and their anger towards the enemy grew. It was even more tragic to watch when a woman would recognize her husband or son and cry out and run towards the prisoner only to be beaten down onto the cobblestone by the butt of a submachine gun.

Many of the prisoners looked as though they were starving. Their friends would prop them up by holding them up under their armpits.

These scenes of starving and physically tortured prisoners justified the relatives' shoving at the parcel window. Every single one of them felt responsible for their loved one who had been arrested, who might be starving behind those prison walls, and who might be cursing his relatives on the outside, thinking they had forgotten him and had left him to starve.

The luckier prisoners were the ones with relatives in Kaunas or close by. City dwellers tended to be better connected and sharper. They quickly found unofficial ways of getting food to their loved ones—through bribes.

In the cells the Lithuanian prisoners threw their fate together into small close-knit circles. They would form their own area in a corner of the cell and combine their food resources and whatever else they had. They shared their misfortunes and their "joys." The food any one of them received from their relatives was divided among all of them. Sometimes their free relatives outside managed to find out who was in a group together and joined forces with the other prisoners' relatives. Mostly they found out from the dirty laundry. When they collected the laundry, relatives would hunt for messages sewn into the fabric with important "announcements." If relatives on the outside were lucky enough to decipher the members of a group, they could work together, worry together, and solve problems as a group. These kinds of groups were especially important when it came time to collect money for a bribe to pass on a food parcel, since the price of a bribe was so high it was difficult for one individual to come up with the necessary sum.

My brother Jurgis formed a group with Pranas Liautukas,[45] Doctor Liudvikas Bieliukas,[46] Julius, and Zubeliauskas. We, their relatives who were still free,

[45] Pranas Liautukas, 1876–1945, was a graduate of the Tsarist Military School. He served in the infantry in Latvia and Russia. He was a company commander during World War I. He was wounded three times. He received many medals from the Russian army. In 1917 he was made a general. In 1918 he joined the newly formed Lithuanian army after Lithuania's independence from tsarist Russia. He was arrested January 30, 1945. He was imprisoned in Kaunas and Vilnius. He died September 2, 1945, in Lukiškis Jail from the results of prolonged torture.

[46] Liudvikas Bieliukas, 1901–date of death unknown. Bieliukas was an economist. He was arrested February 11, 1945. On August 9, 1945, he was sentenced to 10 years hard labor and five years exile. He was imprisoned in Archangelsk.

figured it out pretty quickly. Me, Julius's sister, Zubeliauskas's sister, Pranas Liautukas's daughter, and Doctor Bieliukas's wife assembled ourselves into a tight crew.

Unfortunately, in mid-April they would not allow food parcels into our group's entire cell because of a quarantine. We had to quickly find means of having the quarantine lifted because on most days Pranas Liautukas and Liudvikas Bieliukas could not get up from the floor themselves. Liudvikas Bieliukas was afflicted with tuberculosis. Pranas Liautukas was tortured so severely during interrogations that he would be brought back to the cell unconscious. All the members of our group were of the opinion that nothing was going to get accomplished without the help of a bribe. It was imperative that we get close to the boss of the food distribution department. Unanimously, it was decided that I should be the one to approach him, since I was the only man in the group. Not a single one of the women dared go near the mean-faced Ivan.

We already had confirmation that the boss took bribes. We only needed to think of a method, a format, and a means of giving him the bribe. The women left it up to me to decide.

I found out from a few sources that he lived on Donėlaitis Street, not far from the Main Hall of the University. He always went directly home after work. But there was no point for me to pursue him because a number of women always tried to do the same. Some of them tried to accomplish their goal by crying, while others, the more practical ones, gave bribes. The second method seemed to be much more effective than the first.

However, in my opinion, that moment was inopportune for bribery. Even the biggest giver of bribes tried to hide from the public's eyes. Besides, I wanted to establish a more long-term friendship with him, so that I could guarantee a more long-term arrangement until we were finished with the prison.

Comrade "Boss" took Mondays off because on Mondays they did not accept food parcels. It seemed to me that Mondays were his "bribe days." I too chose a Monday for my purposes. I did not think it was a good idea to go directly to his apartment. Instead, I decided to catch him on the street and make it seem as though we had accidentally run into each other. At twelve, I positioned myself on the stairs of the Main Hall of the University. From there I had a good view of his apartment building's front doors. We knew that the boss took 700 rubles for every unofficially delivered food parcel. I raised the sum to 1000. I wanted to guarantee our success. I arranged the 1000 in such a way that I could easily and quickly pull it out and put it into his hands without being seen.

After a few restless hours of waiting, someone appeared in the doorway. I recognized him—it was the boss. When he went out the door he paused for a few moments in plain view, as though waiting for anyone who was looking out for him to notice his presence. Then he turned slowly and with his polished shoes walked at a leisurely pace in the direction of the University. I thought it would be best to run into him "casually" on the corner of Donėlaitis Street and Gediminas Street. Slowly, I walked down the stairs. I knew already that I would have to speak to him in Russian, since he had only learned a few words of Lithuanian—the few words necessary to communicate with old women from the provinces and accept their bribes. I counted my footsteps, so that we would "run into" each other on the corner.

"Hello, Comrade Boss," I said in Russian, taking off my hat.

"Hello, hello," he answered. He smiled carefully, as though sensing why I had greeted him.

"You must remember me, Comrade Boss," I said, emboldened by the smile.

"A little."

"Yesterday I wanted to pass a food parcel on to my brother, but you didn't take it. You said there was a quarantine," I said, trying to get a conversation going.

"Yes, yes, I remember, they can't get packages now... It's not possible..." he drew out his final words to make it seem as though he himself doubted the veracity of the quarantine. I liked how things had started off. Now I had to be careful to make sure things ended well.

I asked him how long he thought the quarantine might last. I praised his new system in which every day a few letters were announced and only parcels for prisoners with names starting with those few letters were accepted. It cut back on the crowding around the prison. I stressed that this type of efficient system could only have been established by someone like him who had the characteristics of order and humanism. I also pretended that I had information from the quota boss that my brother would be soon released because he had not been found guilty of anything and because he had only ended up in prison due to a false denunciation from an Enemy of the State.

As we talked, we passed the Militia Station and Įgula Cathedral and turned onto Freedom Avenue (now renamed Stalin Prospect), and kept walking towards City Hall. I began complaining that because I was the Department Head of the Administrative Department of the University, I was very busy and standing for hours in line outside of the prison prevented me from getting my work done. I asked him to help me find a way to pass on my food parcels more quickly so that I would have more time to fulfill my duties at the University and not only satisfy the one-year economic plan, but to do better than that and do more than my fair share for the good of the Soviet State. Adopting this theme and several other tactics, I tried to depict myself as a true enthusiast of Stalin's five-year economic plan and the most loyal servant of the Soviet State. I lied without blinking my eyes, just like all good Soviet officials. At the end of my talk, I did not forget to mention that once my brother was free he would come and thank him himself. I reminded him of his power to remove the quarantine with a wave of his hand; it was all up to him, after all, whether there was quarantine or not. Then we came upon a café.

"Let's go inside and warm up, Comrade Boss. You might feel uncomfortable standing around outside with me," I added carefully.

"I don't see why we shouldn't," the Russian said. "Things ought to go smoothly enough," he said, pulling open the café doors.

I selected a table in a far away dark corner and ordered a few hundred grams of vodka for each of us, a few bottles of beer, donuts, and the American cigarettes "Airline." We drank our first hundred grams without a toast. We didn't coax each other to drink. I offered some food. My companion had a big appetite—he could swallow a donut in two bites. He polished off the first plate, so I ordered another. And then two more shots of vodka. I offered a cigarette.

The Comrade Boss praised the quality of the cigarettes. He picked up the pack from the table. His eyes bored into the label that had been glued onto the box: "To the Soviet heroes from the United States of America." Whether he was inspired by the greeting on the box or whether the vodka had taken effect on him I couldn't tell. But the Russian leaned back in his chair, rested his hand against the corner of the table, and with a meditative expression on his face gazed into the darkened window. He began telling me about the heroism of the Soviet people and of their endurance. He had been a front soldier. Twice he had been seriously wounded. He was a good storyteller and he took a long time telling his war stories, most likely mixing other soldiers' war stories in together with his own. He recounted his memories of 1942 spent near Moscow and Tver, when he and the other soldiers in the fox holes lived on boiled wheat and could not even dare dream of ever eating anything better. They would go into battle with their joints swollen from starvation. Then they started winning battles and they pushed forwards, living through unforgettable days when they had all they could eat and wanted for free.

Yes, those were the stories of a warrior from the winning side. There was everything in his stories: vulgar humor, sentimental suffering, heroic adventures. All Red Army soldiers told the same stories. They were boring to listen to after you had heard them a few times.

I wanted to cut him off and get to my point more quickly, so I lifted my second shot of vodka and offered a toast to the "heroic" Soviet Union. My friend liked the toast. He had probably already drunk at least ten buckets of vodka to that toast. He did not hesitate to toss back his shot this time either. I conscientiously did the same. After that we had beer, donuts, and then more beer. Only then did I dare bring up the topic that concerned me.

"How could we get that quarantine taken off? The sooner the better, Comrade, isn't there any way we could get rid of it?"

My "friend" smiled lightly. Tapping the beer splattered table, he said the magic words:

"Don't worry about it. It's already been lifted. From this minute onwards I've lifted it."

So, I had already reached my goal. I was ecstatic, but I didn't show it. Now all I had to worry about were the technical logistics of handing over the food parcel and getting through the food line quickly tomorrow.

As I had mentioned earlier, my "friend" had recently instituted a new system of delivering food. Now he bragged to me that he had developed this system especially so that he could better assist his "friends." I was surprised at how the boss had out-witted the pushing and shoving crowd in the hall. He had fooled even me. He was only taking parcels from those who had paid him bribes already.

The first letter of my last name had gone by only two days ago. Therefore, according to the system my turn would come up again only in two or three weeks. The boss solved this problem very quickly.

"Come to the window at ten o'clock tomorrow and ask the women which letter is being accepted. If I remember correctly, they'll say "P." Then you tell them that you're so sorry that your last name begins with "O" and you're so sad that you've only just missed it. You'll know perfectly well that it's all arranged ahead of time. The women will say they're so sorry about you having missed your day and they'll suggest you appeal to me personally. And you will. The stupid women will never even realize that we have set this up ahead of time. I won't need to check, but for the sake of saving face in front of the women, I'll wait a while and then I'll call your name. But listen carefully because I will call out a fake name that will start with the letter "O." If the women don't want to let you in, then I will try to accept your request from a distance, and if that doesn't work, I'll ask a soldier to come and shove the women aside, then you run directly for the window and as soon as you can, pass the package to me and I'll take care of everything."

Once I comprehended how it was all going to work, I thanked him sincerely from my heart and encouraged him to drink another shot with me. He did not need any encouragement. He tossed back his one shot and wiped his face from ear to ear. Then he started telling me his war stories all over again. He was getting tiresome, all the more because his Russian loquaciousness was now slowed by alcohol. Without meaning to, I began to see before my eyes the last victory of that glorious army, which had taken place under their flag of "liberation." I remembered events when the Red Army soldiers, led by their desire to drink or out of hunger, had committed a number of humiliating and cruel acts. Remembering their foolishness, I could hardly keep from laughing while my "friend" recounted his heroic tales of the Red Army.

We staggered out of the café barely able to see. From Freedom Avenue we turned onto Mickevičius Street. We paused at Kęstutis Street to say goodbye. The Ivan reeled to one side and caught his foot on an empty tin can. He kicked it aside and began pontificating, again praising the Soviet Union.

"You see my friend, the damn Americans, they're forced to produce tins to hold canned foods produced by the Soviets," the Ivan rambled on. He had found two Russian words pasted over the English label. They read: pork conserves. "The Soviet Union produces so much canned food that they can't produce the cans fast enough," he continued. "They need to import tins from America," the Soviet official blathered on, most likely not even believing his own words.

I wanted to end our conversation as quickly as possible, so I pulled out the money I had prepared and pushed it into my "friend's" hands and said good-bye.

"See you tomorrow," the Russian said and slipped the money into his overcoat pocket. He walked off towards the prison.

I walked away, thinking about my new acquaintance and my new impressions. A woman hurried to catch up to me from behind and broke my concentration.

"Excuse me Sir, but I saw you were talking with the boss. I recognized you from the day before yesterday. We stood in line together in the prison hall. Tell me, can anything be done with him. My husband has been in prison three months already and I haven't been able to get a single parcel to him," the poor woman cried.

I took a good look at this woman and I remembered her as well. Her villager's modesty had set her apart from the others in the hall. It was no wonder that she had not gotten any food past the acceptance window in three months. Even now I can still see that deep pain in her eyes. She had none of the aggressiveness and cleverness that was necessary if you wanted to keep your loved ones from dying of starvation. It was very difficult for me to give her any kind of advice because

I could see that besides cleverness she also lacked money. The only thing that I could give her was the comfort of knowing that all of the Lithuanian prisoners were equally hungry and equally fed because all of the packages were shared. I told her that if she could not get her food parcels past the window, she should give the contents to someone who could because the prisoners divide everything up amongst themselves anyway.

The following day I was preoccupied with our agreement. I arrived at the prison at the agreed upon time. I made my way into the food acceptance hall and found out that the last of the "Ps" were standing at the window. I began complaining to the women at the window that I was also a "P," only I had been late getting there. I needed to get some of the "P" women on my side. To my great fortune, not only did they not ask me to fill out any special request form, but told me to hurry and get in line so that they could take my package along with the other "P's."

A few minutes later the window opened and Comrade Boss gave me a look. I extended my request form towards the window. Although I was fifth in line, my request form was accepted second. He gave me a slight nod. I was incredibly pleased because I could already see the results of yesterday's conversation. I jumped out of line and rushed over to pick up my food parcel. This day had not been a good one for the crowd. Often people's requests were denied because they were told that the prisoners they were sending parcels to were no longer being held in this prison. The prisoners' relatives had no way of finding out where their loved ones were. They used the food parcels to find out if their family members actually were being held at the prison, because the prison administration never told the families if their prisoner was being held in this prison or not.

Soon I heard the person at the parcel window calling out my surname, only with a different first letter. To insure that I recognized it was my name being called, the boss winked at me.

I rushed over and pushed my food parcel through the window and then sat down to wait for the empty sack. The boss's face appeared in the window again. He repeated my surname. I ran to the window expecting to be handed the empty sack. But I was wrong. The boss began telling me that my brother had refused to sign because not everything listed in the request was in the sack. I understood that the guards had stolen part of the food. It was obvious to the boss that we had been robbed. I quickly realized that there was no point in me causing a fuss because this food was being delivered through a bribe and that the thieves themselves could call attention to the fact that I was handing over food not on my assigned day. There was also the danger of getting the boss in trouble. So, I took the request and wrote that the food my brother had not found in the sack had really not been there after all. It was my mistake, I wrote. My brother would have acted differently if he had known that this time the food was being handed over through a bribe. In the corner I wrote:

1) 1.5 kilograms of lard missing
2) 1 kilogram of sausage missing

I signed underneath.

The boss was happy with my decision. Before leaving the window he thanked me for saving him from an unpleasant situation.

I waited an hour and a half until finally I was handed my empty sack. I found my brother's signature, demonstrating the fact that he had received the food. It appeared that he had come to terms with what had happened. I took the empty sack and rushed out of the food parcel hall to go tell Mrs. Bieliukiene that today our cell would be very happy.

Looting the Middle Class Families of Prisoners

After a week Antanas and I took action to find out the particulars of the cases against Jurgis and our friends. With the help of a bribe Antanas managed to get close to the interrogator Nachman Dushansky,[47] a Lithuanian-Jew. After a few meetings I realized that even though Comrade Dushansky was part of the mechanism set-up to destroy our nation, he still had a conscience of sorts, meaning, he

---

47 Nachman Dushansky (1919–2008) was imprisoned 1936–1940 for Communist activities directed against the Lithuanian state. When the Soviet Union occupied Lithuania in 1940 he was made the head of the Secret Police in his native city of Šiauliai. From November 1941–April 1942 he was the Soviet Interior Forces director for the GULAG system. Later he completed the Soviet Security College and worked as an interrogator in areas of Russia that had been occupied by the Germans. In 1944 he was assigned to the Soviet Security in Kaunas where his duties were to infiltrate and persecute youth organizations. In 1945 his duties were to fight the underground resistance in Kaunas. Dushansky is suspected of participating in the 1941 massacre of local unarmed civilians in the town of Rainiai. He is also known to have arranged for the deportation of thousands Lithuanians to Siberia. He arrested thousands of Lithuanians, interrogated, and persecuted them. He did not only persecute Lithuanians, but Jews as well. In the city of Telšiai he arrested and deported a Jewish family, the Volpertas family, to Siberia. He oversaw the arrest of 25 young Lithuanians who wore tricolor armbands in protest. He organized the arrest of Antanas Lukša and actively participated in the hunt for Juozas Lukša. He was personally involved in the killing of Juozas Lukša. In 1956 he actively participated in the arrest, torture, castration, and later murder of the partisan leader Adolfas Ramanauskas-Vanagas. He fled to Israel in 1989, before Lithuania formally reestablished its independence from the Soviet Union. In June 2002 Lithuanian prosecutor Rimvydas Valentukevičius sent Israel's Minister of Justice, Meir Sheetrit, a letter in which he demanded that Dushansky be released to the Lithuanian judicial process. Sheetrit refused to hand over Dushansky, claiming that according to Israel's law an individual who has committed human rights abuses more than twenty years ago can no longer be held accountable for those crimes. Sheetrit further stated that the request for Dushansky's extradition was merely an attack on his religion. Dushansky died in Israel February 23, 2008, never having been held accountable for his war crimes and human rights abuses.

would help me as long as I could pay him well for his trouble. We didn't mind paying him because we learned a lot from him.

I had a harder time with our other contact. With the help of an acquaintance I was able to get close to someone named Valatka, who held some mysterious post in the complicated Soviet Security apparatus. He turned out to be a real traitor. He demanded 500 rubles immediately at our first meeting before even saying ten words to me. After I had paid him the money, he asked for my brother's and friends' dates of birth, surnames, names, and so on. He told me to return in a week, promising me that he would find out how their cases were progressing. He also told me to bring a larger sum of money with me next time because he thought he would be able to steal my brother's interrogation records. Stealing the records would enable Jurgis to be freed as innocent. The money was necessary to bribe people who were closer to the records.

I arrived at the agreed upon time and found Valatka completely drunk. That did not surprise me because I expected as much. Alcohol had been the Gestapo's best friend, but it was an even better friend to the Red Army and to the Soviet Security. One and the other used alcohol to numb their consciences over the masses of people they had murdered.

My contact told me to sit down on the couch. He seated himself besides me. He began telling me about my brother's case, recounting the "real" reasons for his arrest. As far as he knew, Julius and my brother were being held for harboring weapons. They were arrested allegedly after three neighbors complained. From Valatka's "facts" I formed the opinion that he was either lying or he had not read my brother's case or he hadn't heard anything about it. After he finished delivering his "facts," he expressed the hope that if everything went as well in the future as it had up until now, then he expected to "rescue" my brother within a few weeks. Only, for now he needed another 500 rubles. I could barely control my anger. I used his own methods on him. I told him to wait a few hours until I could get him the money. I did not come back.

The information I had received from the interrogator Dushansky had been accurate. My brother was being accused of having seen a proclamation from the underground and not having reported seeing it to the Soviet Security Ministry. My brother explained that he did not know what had been written on that leaflet and he did not believe the writing to be counterrevolutionary. He emphasized that he could not, after all, inspect every piece of paper that his friend left lying around the apartment. Jurgis explained that common manners and decency would not allow him to behave that way. This explanation did not satisfy the interrogator because Vilius had talked about the proclamation.

After some time I went to see the "Lawyer's College" where I expected to be able to secure a lawyer for the upcoming trial. But here I learned from the chairman that, according to the Soviet system, lawyers were only available for criminal or civil cases.

"We don't have a single 'licensed' lawyer for political cases," the chairman said, ending our conversation.

There was nothing left for me to do but to thank him for the information.

A few days later I met Mrs. L., I told her about my attempts to help my brother and about all my obstacles. My failure was clear and understandable to her from experience. It turned out that the aforementioned Valatka had already managed to get 700 rubles out of her. All of her efforts did not help her husband at all. She was not able to even find out the status of her husband's case.

My experience told me there were many individuals like Valatka, who had been given the directive from the Soviet Security Ministry to impoverish the prisoner's families by coming up with ways of wheedling their entire savings out of them, forcing them to sell off their better clothing, furniture, dishes, and other valuables.

Besides these "legal" methods of impoverishing families, through this means the Soviet Security was able to obtain missing information needed to build their cases. That would happen when the relatives of the accused were too open or even trusted them enough to consider them friends, or at least people who were on their side. The agents were clever enough to manipulate less sophisticated people and in this manner matters would become even worse for the accused.

The families were robbed yet again when the interrogator could not find any blame within the spectrum of Soviet proportions. In these instances the agents would visit the relatives of the accused themselves, often posing as prisoners who had been released or as interrogators. They would tell the relatives where they could go to get help for the prisoner. In fact, what they would do is give the address of a more important Soviet agent, a taker of bribes. Sometimes they would lure the money out of them on the spot, promising to take care of the matter themselves. In this manner, it was not only permissible to cheat the relatives of prisoners, but it was even sanctioned by the Soviet Security and organized by them.

It was understandable that after such a "good Samaritan's" visit the relatives of the prisoner did everything they could to raise money, sometimes even selling off the last of their possessions, hoping to help get their prisoner released.

The prisoner would be released and that would strengthen the family's belief in the "Samaritan." Then the prisoners would explain to their family that they had been released not because of the family's efforts, but because they had been found not guilty. There was no way of getting the lost money back because most of the time no one knew who the other agents were and did not know where they lived.

My Brother is Released: His Friends are Deported to Siberia

Jurgis's situation was not among the worst. He was facing a year and a half of forced labor in Siberia. The entire indictment was hinging on Vilius admitting that Jurgis could not have known what was written on the leaflet from the underground, even though Jurgis himself would not admit that. Together Antanas and I tried everything we could to prevent him from being exiled to Siberia. Often even strong, healthy, young men died after a few weeks in the Soviet Union's concentration camps for political prisoners.

One evening I remembered the letter left behind for Jurgis by the Red Army soldier Vosily. I decided to try and use it now. The next day I rushed to my father's farm to retrieve it.

I found Vosily's semi-literate handwritten letter and collected the signatures of all the people who had taken in Vosily on Jurgis's account. I delivered it to the appropriate Soviet agencies who confirmed the veracity of the information with the appropriate stamps and appendixes. Besides these documents, I managed to acquire a few more certificates from several Soviet officials who confirmed that during the German occupation Jurgis was of an anti-Nazi and anti-German orientation and had been loyal to the Soviet regime. I presented all of it to the city of Kaunas State Security Chairman General Voronckis. This attempt was my last hope to help my brother. My efforts seemed to be working; therefore, I did not mind giving bribes to a new round of officials.

At the beginning of May they released my brother, after they had gotten him to agree to inform for them. For a long time he deliberated whether he should take the trip to Vorkuta[48] or agree to becoming their stool pigeon. Only the knowledge that the partisans were organized all over the country convinced him to sign. He made the firm decision that once released he would join the partisans rather than inform for the Soviets.

---

48 A city in the Komi Republic. One of the areas where Lithuanians were deported.

I got the good news for the first time from my brother Stasys. I was standing in the food parcel line at the prison. I was shuffling for a better position in line, when Stasys tugged me by the collar from behind and said, “Did you hand over your parcel yet?”

He waited for me to say no. Then he continued, “Let’s go home then, you don’t need to do this anymore.”

Cold chills ran up and down my back. The first thought that went through my mind was that Jurgis had died. But when I saw the smile on Stasys’s face I relaxed.

“He came home last night,” Stasys said.

Hastily, I stumbled out of line. I divided up my food among the others waiting in line. The older women standing around me, kept muttering to themselves:

“Dear God, how lucky he is.”

My brother Jurgis, who was very physically strong, was not in that bad shape. However, his face was white as a sheet. They released him as usual from Freedom Avenue Number Six in the middle of the night. He happily told us that their group of five had it easier than the other prisoners. Our efforts had helped them quite a lot.

Jurgis’s friends were tried within two weeks. Some of them were sentenced to a few years. The others were sentenced to a few decades. Most of them were tried in absentia and only afterwards did the head of investigations read them their verdict.

After the “trial” they herded everyone into one cell, a cell that had previously served as the prison chapel and storage room. Here the prisoners waited to be deported. In this cell the Russian prisoners would rob the Lithuanians and take away their better clothing and food reserves. It was very difficult for the Lithuanian prisoners who caught the attention of the Russian thieves because of their goods. Not only were they defenseless against their aggressors, they were severely beaten. The prison administration would not react.

The first wagon train went in the direction of Moscow. The number of prisoners deported from Vilnius reached 2,000. From Moscow the train turned in the direction of the Komi Republic. Here the prisoners were divided into two groups. One group was assigned railroad work and the other was assigned to the coal mines. In both places the work was hard and the conditions dire.

The group that was assigned railroad work would be released into the wilderness. They had to chop down trees during raging blizzards, build their own barracks, and begin work on the railroad. Groups of up to a thousand men would finish their work in one place and then be moved further on, a few dozen kilometers away, leaving behind their barracks, only to build themselves new ones. Every prisoner was assigned a work quota for the day and if he did not fulfill the quota he would not receive his food ration. The climate was too cold for us Lithuanians. The blizzards were so severe that the exiles would set up wire runs to and from their work area, so that they could hold onto the wire in a blizzard and not be knocked down to the ground. The weaker ones began to die. In half a year more than half of them died. Their places were filled with new exiles, who were constantly being brought in from the West. The corpses were not buried. They were left strewn alongside the railroad line. In the springtime the guards would order prisoners to hook a metal hook into the dead men's chins and drag them a little further away from the railroad line.

Conditions were not much better for the coalminers. After half a year most of them died of starvation or contagious diseases. They did not receive packages from home because they were only allowed to begin writing letters home after a long time had passed. It took a few months for a letter to reach Lithuania. Often they disappeared altogether. Engineers and doctors found themselves in a better position. They were often given jobs in positions of leadership that enabled them to procure food, albeit illegally.

[Translator's Note: In the following section the author documents the activities of the resistance during 1944–1946. The events described are not necessarily in chronological order. Also, in this section Lukša purposefully gave misleading dates. The correct dates of each battle are in the footnotes. He describes battles where he was not necessarily present as a fighter or as an eyewitness. Lukša's descriptions in this section are reconstructed from oral testimonies, written memoirs, and written eyewitness testimonies. These accounts are woven into the fabric of the narrative of Lukša's account of his life as a partisan.]

The Armed Resistance

Organizational Concerns

In the early spring of 1945, the Lithuanian Freedom Council distributed proclamations to the public. It was the first time a wide-spread organized political resistance had appeared during this occupation. The Lithuanian Freedom Council attempted to educate the nation about the situation in the international arena while at the same time directing the nation on how they should conduct themselves during the occupation. The Council foresaw organizing units of technical workers whose job it would be to operate on the fringes of the Soviet system in order to legalize the number of individuals living in hiding all over the country. I was given responsibilities in this department. I was asked to maintain contact with Simutis.[49]

Unfortunately, the Lithuanian Freedom Council survived only until the middle of May when the NKVD succeeded in infiltrating their organization and arresting the majority of their members. The remaining members made an attempt to move to Vilnius, where they believed they could join forces with members of the same organization operating in Vilnius. They hoped to continue the type of work they had started in Kaunas. That turned out to be a mistake. Somehow the NKVD managed to trace them to Vilnius. In Kaunas, Simutis was arrested. After this calamity Būtautas[50] began pressuring me to go underground. Remembering the promise Simutis and I had given each other, not to betray each other under any circumstances, I was in no hurry to heed Būtautas's warning. It turned out that Simutis had been arrested when he had performed a specific task that was not tied in any way to the other members of the Lithuanian Freedom Council. Knowing this, my trust in him grew even stronger. As it turned out, he did not disappoint me despite the fact that during long sessions

---

49 Stasys Šimkūnas, 1918–1984, participated in the June 1941 uprising against the Soviets. While a student at Kaunas University, he joined the underground and became its leader. On June 27, 1945, he was arrested and in November was tried. He was incarcerated in concentration camps in Kniaz Pogost, the Komi Republic, and in Oziorny.

50 Bronius Barzdžiukas, 1918–year of death unknown. Barzdžiukas was a student of engineering at Kaunas University. He participated in the resistance against the Nazis. He was arrested in March, 1951, and was imprisoned in concentration camps in Siberia.

of torture the Soviet Security interrogators crushed all the joints in his hands. Meanwhile, I continued to walk around free and unmolested. During Simutis's interrogations it came out that he had been followed ever since the arrests of Vytautas,[51] Juozas,[52] Andrius,[53] and the others.

I was unable to get in touch with the remaining members of the Lithuanian Freedom Council, so I established contact with a new group, The Lithuanian Partisan Movement. The purpose of this organization was to establish ties with the partisan units operating all over Lithuania and to coordinate them into one organization with a common goal and organized tactics. I worked with Jurgis,[54] Jonas,[55] and Algirdas.[56] We worked together to build a few radio transmitters. We successfully established contact with Partisan units in Panevėžys, Kėdainiai, Kaišiadorys, Trakai, Kaunas, Marijampolė, and a few other regions. At first our work went well. We even managed to successfully transfer some commanding officers to different units lacking leaders. Only through communication could the independent activities of the units be coordinated by regulated orders and commands. We made contact with the underground press, which reached large numbers of people. Dzūkas[57] and Sausis[58] were especially active in this area.

---

51 Stasys Rainys, 1919–. Rainys was a student at Kaunas University. He resisted the Nazis during the German occupation. He was active in the underground. He was arrested in Vilnius on November 14, 1945. On March 26, 1946, he was sentenced to 10 years in a concentration camp and three years in exile in Siberia. He returned to Lithuanian in 1957.

52 Mindaugas Bloznelis, 1923–. Bloznelis participated in the June 1941 uprising against the Soviets. He was active in the underground. On April 6, 1945, he was arrested and sentenced to 10 years in a concentration camp and five years exile in Siberia. He returned to Lithuania in 1958.

53 Andrius Rondomanskis, 1922–. Rondomanskis participated in the June 1941 uprising against the Soviets. He participated in the resistance against the Nazis and in the underground during the second Soviet occupation. He was arrested January 9, 1945 and was sentenced to 20 years in a concentration camp and five years in exile. He was imprisoned in the Vorkuta concentration camp number 18. He was released from the concentration camp in August of 1956 and returned to Lithuania in 1958. In Lithuania he was constantly monitored and harassed by the KGB. In 2004 he was honored for rescuing Jews during the Nazi occupation.

54 Jonas Algirdas Antanaitis, 1921–year of death unknown. Antanaitis was active in the underground in 1940–1941. He resisted the Nazis and was active in organizing underground student organizations during the second Soviet occupation. He was arrested on May 30, 1945, and on September 24 was sentenced to 10 years in a concentration camp and five years in exile in Siberia. He returned to Lithuania in 1957.

55 Juozas Draudvila, 1922–1949. Draudvila was arrested on January 15, 1946 for his involvement in the underground. On March 14, 1946, he was sentenced to ten years in a concentration camp. He died in 1949, in exile.

56 Algimantas Ruzgys, 1924–year of death unknown. Ruzgys was active in the underground. In early September, 1945, he was arrested. He agreed to collaborate. When he was released he told the underground that he had agreed to collaborate and then went into hiding. On August 23, 1947, he was arrested and sentenced to 10 years in a concentration camp and five years in exile without any rights. He returned to Lithuania in 1955.

57 Feliksas Dziedulionis, 1907–1982.

58 No name given in the author's code.

We lost Jurgis in June. Soon afterwards we lost Jonas, Dzūkas, and Sausis. Through Anatoly[59] I was able to get in contact with Jankus.[60] Through him we were able to get in touch with Colonel Kazimieraitis [61] from Dzūkija. We tried to organize a central partisan headquarters around him. We invited Major M.[62] to work with us along with a few people working in the underground in various parts of Lithuania. I worked with Jankus in the organizational sector. After only three months' work we were forced to give up on this idea. Colonel Kazimieraitis was recognized by a few citizens in Kaunas and he was forced to go back into hiding. This time we managed to avoid any casualties, but all of us finally understood that it was impossible to carry out underground work and function as an underground organization while living semi-legally in a city. We decided to join up with active partisan units and by using only their established links and ties to work towards centralizing and coordinating the work of the underground. I established ties with the Partisans operating in the Suvalkija region.

In Vilnius, as in Kaunas, both strong and ineffective underground organizations tried to establish themselves. In addition to the already mentioned Lithuanian Freedom Council another strong resistance organization was the Unity Committee. The summer struck a lethal blow to this committee. The Soviets arrested sixteen of the organization's key members together with their chairman Captain Mataitis[63] and Professor Mir. S.[64]

The Partisan Movement

In the beginning of 1945, stronger and weaker partisan units were operating in the peripheries. This ever-growing movement had spread like wild fire across Lithu-

---

59 Arnoldas Steikūnas, 1924–. A medical student who was arrested and sentenced to 10 years in a concentration camp and five years in exile in Siberia. He returned to Lithuania in 1956.

60 Antanas Jauniškis, 1915–1979. He was arrested in 1945 for his involvement with the underground. He was sentenced to 10 years in a concentration camp. He returned to Lithuania in 1956.

61 Juozas Vitkus-Kazimieraitis, 1901–1946. He was heavily wounded in a battle against Soviet Interior Forces. He was arrested, but died on the way to prison.

62 Identity unknown. This man had a farm between Kaunas and Garliava.

63 Jonas Noreika, 1910–1947. Noreika was a captain in the Lithuanian Army. He worked as a lawyer and a journalist. He was arrested by the Nazis for anti-Nazi activities and sent to a concentration camp in Stuthof, Germany. He was liberated by the Russian army and returned to Lithuania, where he worked in Vilnius and became deeply active in the underground. In April 1946, he was arrested and sentenced to death. He was executed by a firing squad on February 16, 1947.

64 Tadas Petkevičius, 1893–1964 was a diplomat, a member of the Hague International tribunal, and a professor at Kaunas University. He was active in the anti-Nazi underground. He was deeply involved as a leader during the resistance to the second Soviet occupation. In April 1946, he was arrested and sentenced to execution. He was executed by a firing squad on February 16, 1947.

At the end of the war the Germans made a deal with the Lithuanian Freedom Army (Lietuvos Laisves Armija-LLA) to train about 200 of them and parachute them behind Red Army lines in order to perform reconnaissance and sabotage. Many of these, however, immediately joined the resistance.

ania, except in those regions where larger Russian units had their base-camps, like Paprūsiai or the northwestern regions of Lithuania.

Larger fighting units of men, ranging from a few dozen to several hundred, operated under the cover of the heavily forested regions of Lithuania. Areas like Rūdininkai, Prienšilis, Kazlų Rūda, Žaliosios girios, Labanoriai, and the forests of Tauragė had a number of partisan units. There was no common partisan leadership at the time. The territories under partisan command were small. Before executing larger scale operations, units would invite the help of other units. After the operation had been executed, everyone would leave and go back to their normal areas of operation, maintaining contact between the units. The organizational structure differed from unit to unit, as did methods and analysis of operations. However, everyone had the same common goal: to paralyze the activities of the Bolsheviks by interrupting the execution of their plans and to destroy the Soviet Interior Forces wreaking havoc in the provinces. Their other task was to maintain law and order and to protect civilians from the constant looting by Red Army soldiers and Russian civilians alike. They avoided open clashes with the Red Army units.

In the middle of January and in February and March the Germans parachuted their own spies into various regions of Lithuania—agents, radiomen, and Lithuanian paratroopers trained for sabotage. They also dropped a large supply of guns, ammunition, and explosives.

Most of the paratroopers were of a purely Lithuanian patriotic orientation and chose to help the Germans not out of any love or sentiment for the German nation, but because they had realistic calculations. They were trained by the Germans and given supplies necessary for the partisan units, and with the German help were able to infiltrate the country and join up with the partisans. They reached Lithuanian soil with the help of the Germans, but once they arrived they refused to cooperate with them.

These paratroopers, who had made their way back into Lithuania through a pro-German orientation or some form of it, were not immediately admitted into the partisan units. They were either isolated by the partisans or they isolated themselves. These missions were relatively rare and the activities of these paratroopers did not last very long because they could not survive for long without knowing the local situation.

In the middle of March nine paratroopers of somewhat pro-German loyalties led by lieutenant Astra[65] were dropped in the region of Prienšilis. Soon they were in contact with the leader of the local partisan unit, lieutenant Briedis[66] (Moose). They began negotiations that developed into an argument because lieutenant Astra did not only want to join the existing partisan units, he wanted to take over their leadership. Without compromise Briedis requested that Astra submit to his command and give an oath of loyalty to the fighting units. If Astra could not do this, Briedis told him he should leave and go back to where he came from. Without reaching any constructive agreement, the majority of the paratroopers took the oath and joined the partisan units, following Briedis's command. Astra was left with three men. They went their own way. After a few skirmishes with Russian units, all of the paratroopers who had joined Briedis's Unit were killed in action.

That group was an anomaly because it could not come to an agreement with some of the older partisan units. The other groups were much more patriotic. They quickly joined with the partisan units; they obeyed their orders; and they worked with the Germans only as much as it was materially beneficial to assist the

---

65 Julius Astra, 1918–1945, was a lieutenant in the Lithuanian army. He completed espionage school in Prussia and returned to Lithuania with a group of paratroopers. He fought as a partisan in the Dzūkija region. He died in battle in 1945.

66 Martynas Kuzmickas, 1910–1945 was lieutenant in the Lithuanian army. In 1944 he escaped to the West when the Soviets invaded. In January 1945, he returned to Lithuania with a group of Lithuanian paratroopers. He was elected leader of the Iron Wolf Partisan Regiment. He was killed on the night of April 13–14 retreating after the battle in Būdininkai.

ever-spreading partisan war. As a result of this cooperation with the Germans, the partisans were able to obtain a large amount of weaponry, ammunition, and communications equipment. However, this support was just a drop in the ocean for the growing partisan movement. The partisans had obtained most of their weapons and ammunition when the Germans were retreating.

It was not possible to hide the air drops from all of the local populace. Rumors spread across the region about a potential attack on the Bolsheviks. That encouraged the local populace to support the partisans even more. There was talk that the Germans, convinced that they were losing the war, might overthrow Hitler, draft a separate peace with the West, and join forces to crush the Bolsheviks.

At the time it was impossible to keep false information from spreading among the populace because there was no centralized leadership in the underground that could pass on accurate information. On the other hand, the cruelty of the Bolsheviks, and the massacres, that were becoming more and more frequent, incited the people against the occupiers. Day after day, the ranks of the partisans grew and their activities strengthened. By April there was a 30,000 [67] strong partisan army operating across Lithuania. These numbers grew on their own, fueled by the instinct of self-preservation, by the desire to defend one's nation, and one's religious freedom. The various rumors only fueled the fires.

Collaborators

In order to fight the partisans, in the autumn of 1944, Soviet local militia units were mobilized. They were called *Istrebitely*, which means "destroyers" in Russian. This Russian word was barbarized into *Stribai* in Lithuanian. About 30 men from each county in Lithuania were recruited into these Soviet local militia units. Their function was to fight the partisans. Anyone who joined was excused from military duty in the Red Army. These conditions at first tempted a number of Lithuanian men into joining, only because they did not know what their duties would consist of. The partisans did everything they could to disrupt the recruitment process because they did not want to have a situation where Lithuanians would be fighting Lithuanians. This move was done through personal contacts, proclamations, and sometimes through force. Often relatives and friends of the partisans joined the Soviet local militia. As a result of the partisans' efforts the Soviet local militia began to come apart: some of the Soviet local militia went into

---

[67] As mentioned in the Introduction, it is difficult to make an exact count. Lukša's number was a rough estimate.

Agents and informers over time became one of the most effective means for the Soviet Security to round up the partisans. This is a picture taken after the killing of the partisan leader Sergejus Staniškis–codename Litas–February 3, 1953. The photo together with posing Soviet Security officers was used as a kind of insurance to confirm the loyalty of the agent towards the Soviets.

hiding, others joined the partisans. The only people who remained in the ranks of the Soviet local militia were the criminal elements who had already committed crimes during the period of independence. In a word, the *Stribai* were society's trash. The *Stribai* were poorly armed. They usually only had rifles and every so often a machine gun. You could not call the partisan clashes with the *Stribai* serious battles because they usually resulted in the *Stribai* running away. In the spring of 1945, the *Stribai* began to run in droves. The reason their ranks fell apart was not only because of their losses in these clashes, but also because of the power of the myths surrounding the partisan activity. The remaining members of the *Stribai* lost the trust of the Russians.

The Lithuanian nation bitterly hated the *Stribai*. The Lithuanians regarded them as the blind tools of the occupier, as individuals who were helping to annihilate their own nation. That anger and hatred was only fueled by the fact that the *Stribai* answered to the Russians.

As one of the means to fight the resistance the Soviets set up paramilitary units recruited among locals who for one reason or another agreed to cooperate with the authorities. These were used to guard administrative facilities, to protect local party officials, to assist with the deportations and to patrol the villages in order to look for partisans. The name for these paramilitary units in Russian was Istrebitely–Annihilators. The locals called them, in a derogatory manner, Stribai or Skrebai, as a shorter form of this word. The Stribai were extremely disliked among the population, partly for cooperating with the Soviets, partly for their habit to loot, steal and harass the people in the villages, when looking for partisans. A large part of the Soviet casualties in the war against the resistance were Stribai and their relatives.

Partisans of Foreign Extraction

Through one means or another, individuals of German, Russian, or Latvian nationality ended up in the partisan units. Some of them were deserters from the Red Army, while others were prisoners of war who had escaped. The partisans accepted them into their ranks very reluctantly. They usually tried to convince them to go back to their home countries and start similar movements. Foreigners, notwithstanding their previous military rank, were only trusted as common soldiers, with the exception of partisans of Latvian descent. The activities of foreign partisans in Lithuania were very limited because each partisan was required to know the lay of the land, the local traditions, rituals, and the local people's psychology. None of them were completely trusted. They could help the enemy infiltrate our ranks. It did not go unnoticed that these foreign partisans sometimes used their position to loot from the local people. Because of the looting, in the spring of 1945, there was an organized analysis of who these foreign partisans were and a ban was placed on letting any more foreigners into the ranks in the future. In the 1945 statute that was put together in the Tauras district there was a clause that stated only persons of Lithuanian nationality could be partisans.

Among the partisans there were a number of foreigners. Some of them were German ex-soldiers who had been left behind at the end of the war and joined the resistance. The man to the right with the MG-42 machinegun was a German named Willy Richter. He was an airman who escaped from a prison camp and joined the Lithuanian partisans.

At the beginning of the conflict, in 1944–45, the partisans formed large units. Estimations give that at its peak about 30,000 men were under arms in Lithuania. The picture is taken in 1945 of a platoon-size unit in the Tauras military district in the south of the country.

The Iron Wolf Regiment

From the early autumn of 1944, there was already active partisan activity in the regions of Garliava, Prienai, Gudeliai, Sasnava, and Balbieriškis. These regions came under Briedis's command in the spring of 1945. Before that separate units had operated in the area. A little later neighboring units joined, forming the military "Forest Brothers" regiment. This regiment chose for itself the mythological name of Iron Wolf. My friend Uosis had been a member of the Iron Wolf Regiment from their very first day.

In the middle of January, 1945, the Iron Wolf regiment, having already rid its own territory of Bolshevik activity, organized an attack on Šilavotas. A unit of about 50 men was successful in overtaking 18 Soviet Security soldiers and *Stribai*, who had been organizing a raid. They attacked with lighting speed and forced the enemy to retreat. Only two Russians reached Šilavotas alive, where they connected with some reserves and evacuated to Marijampolė without resisting. The partisans collected the weapons abandoned by the Soviet Security soldiers and the *Stribai* during their flight. Facing no resistance, they occupied Šilavotas. They also took away the Russians' booty. They cleaned out all the government offices and cooperatives, collected all the documents, and confiscated the seals and supplies of the post office and the local Soviet government. After the operation was complete, the unit moved off in an undocumented direction.

Soon afterwards seven fighters from that unit—Uosis, Pjūklas (Saw),[68] Tetervinas (Grouse),[69] Durtuvas (Bayonet),[70] Lapė (Fox),[71] Žaibas (Lightening),[72] Bijūnas (Peony)[73] attacked the "Red wagon-train" transporting Prienai's NKVD officers. The Bolsheviks were liquidated and the partisans suffered no losses. A large quantity of requisitioned grain was taken.

In the beginning of February, eight fighters unexpectedly ran into six Soviet Security in the village of Dūmiškis. They fought for several hours until finally the partisans were able to surround them. They killed five and the sixth surrendered. The prisoner turned out to be a Lithuanian Jew. The partisans interrogated him. The man cursed his dead comrades and insisted that he was innocent.

"What do you think, gentlemen, that I, a Jewish intellectual, would throw in my lot with those vagabond Russians and the *Stribai*? That would be the day! Only, gentlemen, please don't kill me. I'll tell you everything," the man said, trembling.

"You say you're our friend, so why were you shooting at us?" Pjūklas asked.

"You shouldn't have been afraid. I was only shooting up into the sky. I was afraid to lift my head out of the puddle. Look at my shoes, they're wet and dirty," the man explained.

This back and forth would probably have gone on quite a while longer if Tertervinas had not brought over a Gymnasium teacher from a neighbor's house. The teacher had escaped from Prienai a few days ago. The teacher, Lieutenant Stravinskas,[74] recognized the man immediately. It turned out that he was in charge of the local network of Soviet agents. Stravinskas, now a partisan under the code name Kardas (Sword), had been forced to leave Prienai because of this man. The Director had tried to conscript Stravinskas to inform on his colleagues.

---

68 Zigmas Juška, 1923–1948 fought on the eastern front with the German army. Retreating with the Germans, he was taken prisoner by the Russians. He escaped from captivity, returned to Lithuania, and joined a band of partisans in Alytus. In 1945 he joined the Iron Wolf Regiment. In May 1946 he became leader of the Šiaurys company, and later the second company. He was betrayed and died March 17, 1948.

69 Petras Burinskas, 1924–1949. He was killed while hiding at the Kedžių farm.

70 Leonardas Bluzevičius, 1926–. He was wounded in battle and taken captive by the Soviets. He was tried and sentenced to 10 years in a concentration camp and five years in exile. He returned from exile in 1953.

71 Vladas Sabastijauskas, 1922–1947. Brother of the Iron Wolf Regiment liaison-woman Ramunė. He was taken alive January 30, 1946. He was sentenced to death, and on January 30, 1947, he was executed by a firing squad.

72 Antanas Markauskas, 1923–1946 died in a bunker on October 30, 1946.

73 Albinas Buzas, 1926–1947. He was betrayed and died December 25, 1947.

74 Juozas Stravinskas, code name Kardas (The Sword), 1914–1946 taught Mathematics, Physics, and Chemistry at the Prienai Žiburys Gymnasium. In the spring of 1945, Soviet Interior Forces tried to get him to agree to work for them as an informant. He joined the partisans instead. He was active in unifying the separate bands of partisans into a unified whole. He was betrayed and killed June 7, 1946.

The moment the Director of the Soviet Security Ministry laid his eyes on Stravinskas he lost his tonuge. He began shaking with fear and begging for mercy.

"So, Comrade Director, we've met almost at our agreed upon time, but not in Prienai as we had agreed, but in Dūmiškis," Stravinskas said angrily. "It was you who forced me to abandon my beloved students, threatening me with a jail sentence if I didn't volunteer to inform for you. As you can see, I didn't become a traitor. I was forced to leave my wife and children and a job I loved, and look where I am now."

Turning towards Uosis he added:

"Don't believe him. He wanted to fool you by making you think he was just a regular Officer. It's not true. He's the head of the entire network of Soviet Security Agents and all the agents answer to him personally, all of the ones who spy against the intelligentsia."

The remainder of the interrogations continued with Stravinskas present. The prisoner was forced to speak the truth because Stravinskas knew many of the details and was able to correct him any time he tried to evade the truth. It turned out that they had come to Dūmiškis to force citizen N. to collaborate. The interrogation revealed that many of the local teachers had already agreed to inform for the Russians, but that the Soviet Security did not expect much from them because they only conveyed news that everyone already knew or that had no significance.

After he had told the partisans everything he knew, the Director cursed the Communist Party and sincerely offered to join up with the partisans. However, his offer was declined.

Accounts of a Few Partisan Battles

Žemaitkiemis[75]

In February 1945 about thirty men from the Iron Wolf regiment attacked a strong Soviet Security unit in Žemaitkiemis. After the first few short battles, the partisans retreated from the local farmsteads to trenches that had been prepared during the war. Their position was strong. The Bolsheviks, who were unfamiliar with the terrain, did not expect the trenches. Twenty-seven Soviet Security soldiers were killed in battle. The partisans lost three men. Five were injured. Among the

75 This battle actually took place April 4, 1945. Three partisans died in battle: Jonas "Ališauskas", the school teacher Vasiliauskas, Jonas Kiselius.

dead was Audra[76] (Storm). He blew himself up. An explosive bullet had blown off his left leg. Audra handed his submachine gun to Uosis and asked him to prepare two grenades. He waited until the Red Army soldiers got close and then he detonated them.

Adventures while Preparing for the Attack of Šilavotas

During this time the Perkūnas (Thunder) Unit was inivited to join forces with the neighboring Briedis (Elk) Unit. During their first meeting together the Briedis Unit asked the Perkūnas Unit to help them prepare for an attack on Šilavotas. Also, at the same time contact had been established with the Dzūkija regional units. Plans had been made to join forces to attack the town of Prienai.

In preparation for these operations, the partisans had to acquire more weapons, ammunition, and bandages. To that end the partisans spread out across the local area to collect what they needed. During this "fund-raising" expedition they had a few adventures.

Anglas (The Englishman)[77] along with three other men stopped by his family farm near Pakuonis. Careful as a cat, he crawled up to his family home. Through the window he saw some Russian weapons set beside the door. The Russian weapons meant that there were visitors. Even more carefully, Anglas crawled towards the other end of the parlor. Glancing through the window, he recognized the Pakuonis region's most active Bolsheviks: a party agent and a regular agent. They were seated at the table enjoying dinner and making passes at Anglas's sisters.

Anglas went back to the kitchen window. He rapped lightly on the window and got his mother's attention. He and his mother discussed in whispers the best means of disposing of these uninvited "guests." Anglas's mother returned to the parlor. She kept one of the guests busy. Meanwhile, she sent one of the sisters back to the kitchen on an errand. The mother managed to convey to the daughter that she should announce to the guests that she needed to go out to fetch some water from the well, and that she should ask one of the guests to accompany her. Anglas would be able to finish that guest off without any problems.

And that's what happened. The Russian had just barely managed to get out the door when Anglas felled him with one blow. Then the other partisans rushed into the parlor. They grabbed the weapons left beside the door, and informed

76 Jonas Kisielius, 1924–1945. He exploded himself with a hand grenade after he was wounded in battle.

77 Kazys Ziutelis, unknown–1945.

the remaining guest, the regular agent, that he had overstayed his welcome. After this evening, two of the most cruel officers in the region were never seen or heard from again.[78] In Partisan terms, they went off to the Nemunas River to go "fishing."

The partisan Merkys[79] was out collecting weapons in another area when he and his friends stopped by a village just as the villagers were assembled together, chanting the rosary. Almost all of the village's population, from whom Merkys had planned on acquiring weapons or ammunition, were praying. So, the partisans went off to talk with the people at prayer.

When they arrived at the prayer meeting, they found that the villagers were only halfway through the rosary. Merkys crept over to the window and saw regional chief Kasevičius[80] sitting at the kitchen table, working his way through a bottle of vodka.

The partisans had been looking for this Communist for quite some time. He was known to have completely sold out to the Bolsheviks.

"Well," Merkys thought to himself, "while everyone else is praying, you're sitting here in the same house drinking all by yourself. This presents a perfect opportunity to do you in. By the time you die, the pious villagers will have had just enough time to toss in a few Hail Marys for your soul at the end of the rosary."

Merkys got the attention of the hostess. He asked her to do whatever it took to keep Kasevičius at the table until he could get himself into the right position to corner him.

And that's exactly how it happened. The woman went back inside just as the Communist chairman was reaching out with his shaking drunken hands to pour himself another drink while at the same time groping the woman seated next to him. At that moment Merkys broke in and knocked the shot glass out of the chairman's hands.

"Put your hands up, dear comrade. It must be boring drinking alone. Now we can sing together, but something a little more cheerful than what they're singing in there," Merkys said, emptying Kasevičius's pockets.

The chairman shook like an ash tree in the wind. He looked at Samas[81] fearfully, while Merkys pulled a Russian Nagan revolver and two grenades out of his jacket pocket.

---

78 Naprūža and Naujūnas.

79 Algirdas Juodis, 1924–1947.

80 Chairman of the Pakuonis Regional Land Commission Kunevičius.

81 No name provided in the author's key to his secret code.

In the beginning of the resistance, 1944–1945, the guerrillas could move around quite freely in large groups. For some time they practically controlled the countryside and it was very hard to find people who would agree to work for the Soviet authorities in the rural areas.
Note that one partisan in the middle is carrying a German Panzerfaust, an anti-tank weapon used by the partisans mainly to blow holes in brick buildings when attacking Soviet outposts, a common tactic used in the beginning of the conflict.

"He's ready to hunt rabbits," Samas joked.

But the comrade just stood there trembling with his mouth open, as though he had swallowed a bone. Only when they led him out the door did he manage to regain his voice and sputter:

"Men, you don't mean…"

But he never finished his sentence because Samas covered his mouth. The penitent worshippers never even heard a thing when the partisans shoved the functionary into their sledge and took him off in the direction of the Nemunas River.

An Unsuccessful Attack on Šilavotas[82]

In the second half of February the regiment leader Briedis invited the neighboring partisan unit led by Perkūnas (Thunder)[83] to prepare a second attack on Šilavotas. The Soviet casualties from the previous raid had been replaced with new men brought in from Marijampolė.

---

82 This attack took place on the night of February 22, 1945. Two partisans died in battle: Juozas Liniauskas, Vytautas Urbonavičius.

83 Jonas Gelčys, 1920–1945, was a partisan from 1944. He was killed October 16, 1945. The Russian threw his dead body in a shallow grave along the fence to the Bajoraitis farm. His remains were exhumed in 1991 and properly laid to rest.

A drawing by an unknown partisan, depicting an ambush on Soviet troops. The drawing is named "The Battle at Varčia."

Perkūnas arrived at night with 40 fighters and surrounded Pakiauliškis. Meanwhile, Briedis's men had taken Čepeliškes. When both units joined forces, Šiaurys (Northerner),[84] Perkūnas, and Tigras agreed on a plan of attack. The following night both units moved towards Klebiškis. Viesulas's[85] (Whirlwind) and Karys's (Soldier) squads were supposed to quietly occupy the Šilavotas cemetery and chapel, which was a few meters away from the Bolshevik "bastion." The main attack would begin early in the morning.

It had been agreed upon ahead of time with the head of the local *Stribai* that he and all the other *Stribai* and local functionaries would give themselves up alive. There were less than 20 Russians. Meanwhile, the partisans had 80 men and 17 machine guns. The strategic goal of the operation was to occupy the Šilavotas school, a brick building beside the Church, where the Soviet Security had its local headquarters. It would take heavier weapons than machine guns and submachine

---

84 Vincas Senavaitis, 1923–1945. He began fighting the Soviets in 1940 while he was still a high school student. In 1944 he organized a band of partisans in his native village and served as their leader. He was heavily wounded in battle June 17, 1945. The partisans hid him in the forest, but when they returned for him he'd disappeared. His whereabouts are still unknown. Four of his brothers and one sister died fighting in the resistance.

85 Vytautas Marčiulionis, 1921–1946. He was an art student. He joined the partisans September 8, 1944. He was killed in battle July 27, 1946.

guns to take this stronghold. Dešinys, Briedis's unit's squad leader, had acquired two German Panzerfausts[86]. They also had several tanks of gasoline, enough to burn a few houses.

Viesulas's and Karys's squads executed their orders smoothly and without incident. By midnight they had already occupied the cemetery. From choice positions they closely followed the bastille's guards, who were busy stamping their feet from the cold. At dawn the main forces began their attack. When the fighting began in the town, the Militia, the *Stribai*, and those Soviet Security soldiers who were housed separately, ran for cover into the brick school house. The entire town fell into the hands of the partisans with the exception of the school house.

Machine gun fire shattered the tile roofs, burned the roof joists, rafters, and the lathing and started a fire in the attic. The Bolsheviks defended themselves with machine gun fire, submachine gun fire, and by tossing grenades out the windows. They managed to quickly put out the fire in the attic. The partisans chased the Bolsheviks away from the windows with heavy gun-fire and got close enough to the building to use Dešinys's panzerfausts. However, luckily for the Bolsheviks, neither of the panzerfausts fired. The partisans tried carrying the tanks of gasoline closer, but the Bolsheviks shot holes in the tanks. They were soon empty. Both means of delivering the main blow to the fort had failed. The attackers' mood worsened because the machine gun fire only succeeded in making holes in the façade and did not penetrate the brick walls. The Bolsheviks had lost an insignificant number of men. Because of that neither the Militia nor the *Stribai* surrendered. After four hours of fighting, the partisans had no choice but to withdraw because there was no longer any hope of penetrating the Bolshevik stronghold. In addition, there was the danger that the noise would attract neighboring Soviet Security garrisons. After this failure, both partisan units separated and went their own ways.[87]

Margininkai[88]

After the failed operation at Šilavotas, the unit reorganized itself again. The fighters voted anonymously and elected Viesulas their new leader. Recently the size of the original unit had doubled. For tactical reasons, the unit was divided into four squads.

---

86 Rocket-propelled anti-tank weapons.

87 Two partisans died in the Šilavotas battle on February 22, 1945. They were Juozas Liniauskas and Vytautas Urbonavičius.

88 This battle took place March 11, 1945. Afterwards, on March 13 when they crossed the Nemunas River they were attacked by the town of Kruonis NKVD unit. Three *Stribai* were killed in the fighting.

The reorganized unit had its next serious battle in March in Margininkai (Pakuonis region) where the local Pakuonis and Kruonis Soviet Interior Forces were attacked. Tigras's squad began the battle. The other squads assisted him, firing from the wings. Their initial attack was successful. They regrouped and attacked again. The Bolsheviks retreated, leaving behind their horse and wagon, ammunition, and a few dozen dead.

After this battle, the unit crossed over to the other bank of the Nemunas River. For some time after they had recovered from the battle in Margininkai, the Kruonis Soviet Interior Forces harassed them. After they were defeated a second time, the Soviets left them alone for a while. Viesulas and his squad went deep into enemy territory along the Vilnija River, reaching as far as Užguostis. Here they struck against the local Communists, the NKVD and other similar types. Beyond Trakai they turned in the direction of the Nemunas River, closer to the Suvalkija region. They traveled only at night. Their direction was dictated by reports of where various Bolshevik agents were located, where they could find strong reinforcements, or where armed groups of looters were traveling. They would threaten some of these groups of looters; others received a beating, but still others, those who had committed serious crimes, crimes too serious to be forgiven or to expect reform, were sent "up into the trees."

Būdininkai[89]

The Bolsheviks suffered huge losses from the partisans in Būdininkai. The partisans who had been staying in the village were warned that large numbers of the enemy were approaching. These partisans moved to the edges of the forest and took up positions in the trenches. Briedis was leading a unit of 80 men. They were armed with over 20 machine guns. They lined up across an area of a kilometer and a half and waited for the approaching enemy. The Bolsheviks, not knowing where the partisan stronghold was, drove towards them in cars on the main road. When the cars arrived in the area where the ambush was set up, the partisans opened up. Several dozen Bolsheviks did not even have enough time to jump out of their cars. The ones who remained alive organized themselves into waves of attack, storming the partisan stronghold, shouting, "Hurrah." Notwithstanding the fact that there were several times more Bolsheviks than partisans, the partisans did not stop shooting and were able to destroy wave after wave of Bolsheviks. The Bolsheviks kept bringing in more reinforcements. With only short breaks,

89 This battle took place April 13, 1945.

the fighting continued for several hours. The Bolsheviks were not successful in breaking through to the partisans in the trenches.

Towards evening the Bolsheviks were convinced that their attack was not going to be successful, so they sent part of their forces to the other side of the forest. This part of the forest was not covered by the partisans. When it was already quite dark, the Bolsheviks approached the partisans from behind. When the partisans noticed their presence, they withdrew under the cover of darkness through holes in the positions created by the Bolsheviks when they had reorganized. During this battle the partisans lost only one of their own. The nurse Marytė[90] was shot while tending to the wounded. The Bolshevik losses consisted of over a hundred men.

Just a few days after the Būdininkai battle, the unit's leader, Briedis, was killed unexpectedly in a Soviet Security ambush. Dešinys was selected to lead in his place. At this time changing conditions dictated new directives for the partisans. Among other responsibilities, in addition to battles with the Soviet Interior Forces, a number of administrative duties appeared. An Administrative Unit was organized in the unit's headquarters under the direction of Šiaurys.

Degimai

After the reorganization, on June 11, 1945, the main forces of the Iron Wolf regiment engaged in a large-scale battle in the Klebiškės forest.

On the left bank of the Jiesa River, in the meadow near the Kukoriškės Bridge, five battle units were being taught fighting squad positions. At about four o'clock in the afternoon the guard posts in the Skerdupis fields sent a message that a large number of enemy troops were approaching from the direction of Pajiesis. Soon afterwards a similar message was received from the posts in Naujasis Klebiškis. The Soviet troops were advancing from Šilavotas towards the Klebiškis forest.

The partisans quickly crossed the Kukoriškės Bridge, occupying the right bank of the Jiesa River. They spread out their forces and prepared for battle. The first squad, led by Commander Dešinys, and the second squad, led by Uosis, established themselves in trenches on both sides of the Kukoriškės Bridge, so that they were perfectly positioned to fire out into the fields spread out before them. The two squads were separated by a country road that led to Pajiesis and Skerdupis.

---

90 Marytė Senavaitytė, 1921–1945 came from a large farming family. She was a nurse and worked in a hospital in Vilnius. When her brother Vincas organized the partisan movement in Prienai, she joined. She died April 13, 1945 in the Būdininkai battle while attending to the wounds of a fallen partisan.

For obvious reasons there are very few pictures available of combat scenes. In this picture members of the Vytautas regiment in Tauras military district fire at retreating Soviet forces in 1946, all of them equipped with German Sturmgewehr.
The Sturmgewehr assault rifle was one of the favorite weapons of the partisans, it was reliable and useful at both long and short range. The main problem was access to ammunition, a reason why it later had to be replaced. At the beginning of the resistance about half of the guns were German and half of them of Soviet origin. In later years almost all guns used by the partisans were Soviet made.

The partisans expected that the enemy would use this road to send reinforcements to join the advancing troops.

The third squad, led by Kareivis, took up position on the left wing, maintaining contact with the first squad. They had the mission of guarding the road that led from Naujasis Klebiškis to Čepiškės. The fourth squad positioned itself in the right wing, maintaining contact with the second squad. They had the mission of guarding against a possible attack from Pajiesis on the right bank of the Jiesa River. The fifth squad, led by Dautartas[91] was in position at the Vilkas[92] farmstead and had the Medic Unit with it. They guarded the road from Čepiškis.

---

91 Leonardas Bluzevičius, 1926–. Bluzevičius was wounded in battle July 4, 1946. He was arrested and sentenced to 10 years in a concentration camp and five years in exile. He returned to Lithuania in 1953.

92 Jurgis Vilkas, uncle of Juozas Lukša. He and his entire family was imprisoned and tortured. Jurgis Vilkas was exiled to Siberia for two years. His family lived for several years in the woodshed after their farm was burned down by the Bolsheviks.

They had just managed to secure their positions when a small group of Soviet Security scouts arrived from Skerdupis. They were heading, as the partisans had surmised, in the direction of the Kukoriškės Bridge. The Soviet troops were prepared for battle; their main reserves had gathered in the village of Skerdupis. The Soviet Recon party noticed the partisans' footprints in the Kukoriškės meadow. With extreme caution they approached the bridge doubled up. The partisans refrained from firing at them and allowed the recon party through their positions. Dautartas received orders to destroy the scouts in the fields surrounding the Vilkas farmstead. Dautartas reached his new position in time and engaged the scouts after they had left the forest and were sneaking towards the Vilkas farmstead. After a few minutes of heavy gunfire all the soldiers in the recon party had been killed, with the exception of two wounded, before they even realized where the gunfire was coming from. The partisans had opened up only when the enemy was out in the open fields and could not find cover quickly. The partisans quickly tended to the two wounded and instructed them to return to their units and advise them to go back to where they had came from. The prisoners were given a lecture by a fighter from this unit who went by the code name Mykolas[93] (Michael).

"Why did you idiots spill your blood?" he asked. "Isn't it enough that they made fools out of you in Russia! Starvation and the mistreatment of the working classes is not a problem in our corner of the world, but in the other fifth of the world, the part that's being destroyed by the Communists, it is! You've already seen all that for yourselves. Go back and tell your comrades that they shouldn't dare take on a fight with the partisans. We'll slaughter them all to the last man," Mykolas said, finishing his speech.

An agreement was made with Commander Dešinys. The wounded prisoners were allowed to return along the same road they had come. They were told to tell their comrades everything they had seen and heard. Neither of the wounded prisoners noticed that armed partisans lay in hiding along both sides of the bridge. They had no idea what the partisans' positions were nor did they have any idea of their numbers.

The partisans did not need to wait very long. Soon after the wounded prisoners returned with their report, the main Soviet forces moved out of the direction of Skerdupis and Pajiesis towards the Kukoriškės Bridge. The first Bolsheviks spilled into the Kukoriškės fields. The first two units of partisans opened fire, scattering the ranks of the advancing troops. Man after man fell. Not one of them

---

93 No name provided in the author's key to his secret code.

managed to reach the bridge. The rest retreated. Deceived by their own scouts, and having encountered the first partisan attack, the Soviets realized it would be impossible to reach the bridge, guarded as it was by machine guns and a few snipers. They ceased their attack and retreated to their first line of escape.

The partisans replenished their ammunition, strengthened their outlooks, and waited for a second attack. The main Russian forces headed south. The partisans needed to strengthen their left flank and prepare for unexpected attack from the other fronts. They were not caught off guard. After a good hour, the Bolsheviks waded through the fords about a kilometer and a half away from the bridge and began a large-scale infiltration of Commander Kareivis's region. This time the Bolshevik attack was much more fierce and more sustained. The Russians were successful in bringing in three heavy machine guns. Most of the rounds from this gun was explosive. This often caused confusion because it made it difficult to determine where the actual front was since the exploding bullets often exploded far off in the forest. The partisans withstood even this attack.

The strongest attack was the third Bolshevik assault. Commander Kareivis's squad had fought so well during the second attack that they had not expected a third attack from the same quarter. But the main Russian forces struck a strong blow. This time the Bolsheviks managed to break through the left partisan wing. Commander Kareivis died along with three of his best fighters while trying to bridge the gap the Russians had made. Left without a leader, Commander Kareivis's squad began to retreat from its position. They moved closer to the main partisan forces. Only with the help of the first and second squads did they manage to hold back the Bolsheviks.

Because of this retreat the partisan positions changed. Commander Kareivis's squad moved to the rear and their place was filled by the squad commanded by Commander Dešinys. The partisans reduced their front, slowly retreating in the northeastern direction of the Degimas fields, keeping the enemy at bay with ever-weakening fire. This third attack lasted until twilight. The battle was fought up close, in the dark, in the depths of the forest, along the edge of the Degimas fields. When darkness fell the partisans retreated and were not followed.

After five hours of fighting the Soviets had lost 67 men, among them their unit commander's major. The partisans had lost six men, among them the organizational squad leader Commander Šiaurys. Several partisans were heavily wounded, among them Unit Commander Dešinys.[94]

---

[94] The names of the partisans lost in this battle are: Liudvikas Dabrišius, Jonas Slavickas, Antanas Banislauskas, Kazimieras Gudaitis, Juozas Balčiūnas, Vincas Senavaitis, Juozas Šiugždinis (was heavily wounded, and died later).

Overnight the Bolsheviks reinforced their forces, hoping to take revenge on the partisans in the morning. However, by dawn the partisans were already 20 kilometers away. The only option left for the Bolsheviks was to collect their corpses and return to the "fortresses" they had set up in the local towns.

To satisfy their need for revenge, the NKVD arrested the farmer Vilkas, his wife, and his grown children. They confiscated all their livestock and any other goods they needed. Then they burned the Vilkas farm to the ground.

Paliai[95]

One partisan regiment chose the boggy swamps of Paliai as their base.[96] It was an area that was very difficult to navigate if you were not a local. The Russians ignored this area for a long time. At night "reconnaissance missions" around the local environs were organized. This partisan "swamp kingdom" was hard to find. Only a very few local inhabitants knew the confusing and dangerous system of trails through the swamps. Even fewer people dared attempt crossing the dangerous sections of quicksand. Besides, no one ever had any reason to.

Eventually, the success of partisan actions in the neighborhood of the swamps drew the Bolsheviks' attention. After several months of intense espionage Soviet agents were successful in ascertaining that the partisans must be hiding in the swamps.

In the beginning of August, on a Sunday, Soviet Interior Forces drew together large numbers of troops and deployed a small caliber cannon. They surrounded the Paliai swamps and began shooting at the partisans. After a few hours of cannon fire, the Russians got up their nerve to get into boats and row out into the swamps, searching for the partisans.

Up until this point, the forest brothers had not shot back. Now they let their guns articulate their response. They shot out the bottoms of the Bolsheviks' boats as they moved laboriously through the thick swamp. Very quickly the swamp was overrun with live, mostly wounded, Soviet Security soldiers thrashing around in the swampy waters going under along with the splintered remains of their boats. Some of the Bolsheviks struggled to grab hold of roots, but in vain, none of them

---

95 This operation took place August 3–10, 1945. The 133rd Soviet regiment attacked with tanks, light artillery, and even used reconnaissance aircraft in the operation. On August 6th the swamp was surrounded and the operation began. Tanks fired constantly at the small islands where the partisans were camped. They sunk all their boats. They established ambushes every 100–200 meters surrounding the swamps.

96 Six partisan units made their headquarters in this swamp: the Daukšas Unit, the Dzūkų Unit, the Muškietininkas Unit, and three others made up a total of 200 partisans. After this battle, the remaining partisans from these swamp units joined the Tauras District partisans.

survived. Most of them were swallowed up by the bottomless swamp, by the sink holes, and by the quicksand.

The battle lasted until evening. At twilight the partisans were able to cross the swamp using submerged pathways they had constructed ahead of time. They got past the Soviet Security Force's strongholds and escaped to the areas they had prepared in advance. The following morning, full of smiles, they were able to watch the Bolsheviks "swimming" in the swamps. They bid them "good luck" and left. The partisans lost 17 in this battle.[97] The Bolsheviks lost around 200 soldiers.

Daugšiagirė

A former Lithuanian army officer took the initiative to organize scattered partisan units in the regions between Kaunas, Pakuonis, Prienai, Punia, Butrimonai, Aukštadvaris, and Rumšiškės into one larger unit. He led this unit until the autumn of 1944. Operating under the code name Beržas[98] (Birch Tree), this former army officer destroyed a few informants, Soviet Security agents, a few of the more active local people who had sold themselves to the regional Bolshevik leaders, and a few bands of thieves who operated by day and by night. In December, while liquidating a band of armed Russian thieves, the unit leader Beržas was killed. The leadership of the unit was taken over by Aras.[99] His second was Audronis.[100]

By early January of 1945, this unit consisted of over 40 heavily armed men. The unit was divided into two squads, one led by Dobilas[101] (Clover) and the other led by Balandis[102] (Pigeon).

Dobilas's squad, to which the unit leader Aras belonged, made camp that January near Daukšiagire, on the right bank of the Nemunas River. From the opposite bank of the Nemunas they received news that a few NKVD were arresting people in the neighboring village. Dobilas and his men quickly crossed the Nemunas. Just then the NKVD were making themselves at home on the property of farmer Vaitkevičius. The partisans crept along the furrows right up to the farmhouse. They surrounded the farm and began shooting. All the NKVD men were

---

97 The names of the partisans lost in this battle are: Antanas Durneika, Juozas Karalius, Vytautas Lietuvninkas, Vytautas Linonis, Juozas Marčiukaitis, Antanas Meškelevičius, Juozas and Jurgis Stanynai, Jurgis Žukauskas.

98 No name provided in the author's key to his secret code.

99 Vincas Rukas, 1925–1945. Died in battle in January 30, 1945.

100 Jonas Marčiulionis, 1917–1945. Died in battle January 25, 1945.

101 No name provided in the author's key to his secret code.

102 Antanas Milenka, 1915–1945. Died in battle January 30, 1945.

killed. The nine arrested people were released, and a Russian machine gun was confiscated along with two submachine guns, and about 20 kilograms of meat and bacon that the NKVD officers had stolen from the local populace. The partisans suffered no losses.

Alšininkai[103]

Aras's unit suffered badly in February. A strong Soviet Interior unit was searching for partisans in the area when they met up with four men, who had just returned home after having driven Aras's men by sledge to Alšininkai. After a prolonged and torturous interrogation, the Bolsheviks managed to extract information from the men. Before dawn Soviet Interior Troops used the river's valleys to surround the farms that the sledge drivers had indicated. As the sun came up, they opened fire with heavy machine guns into the farmhouse and barns. Only two farms where the partisans were hiding had been revealed correctly. These units fought back. The heaviest and bloodiest fighting was sustained by Balandis's squad where the unit leader Aras was stationed.

The attack was sudden and unexpected. Most of the fighters had already taken off their clothing, had set aside their weapons, and were resting. By the time they were able to get some clothes on and get ready for battle, they had already suffered losses. The heaviest fire came from the Bolsheviks' heavy machine guns stationed on the river bank. Dobilas's squad was further away and had enough time to prepare for the attack.

Balandis's men fought stubbornly for a few hours. The Bolsheviks saw that they were not going to take any partisans alive and that the defense from the farmhouse and barns was not getting any weaker. They decided to burn the farm buildings.[104] Five partisans holding out in the farmhouse died in the fire: Aras, Balandis, Našlaitis[105] (Orphan), Kregždė[106] (Swallow), and Strazdas[107] (Thrush). Only three wounded partisans managed to break their way out of the flames: Tigras[108] (Tiger), Jovaras[109] (Sycamore), and Vanagas[110] (Hawk). Four men from

---

103 This battle took place January 30, 1945.

104 The entire Danilevičius family, Juozas, Marija and their sons Juozas and Jonas and daughters Anelė and Ona burned to death in the farmhouse during the battle.

105 No name provided in the author's key to his secret code.

106 No name provided in the author's key to his secret code.

107 No name provided in the author's key to his secret code.

108 Kazimieras Pyplys, also went by the code names "Mažytis" (Small), Audronis. 1923–1949.

109 No name provided in the author's key to his secret code.

110 No name provided in the author's key to his secret code.

the other group died: Žaibas[111] (Lightening), Perkūnas[112] (Thunder), Laimutis[113] (Good Fortune), and Gandras[114] (Stork).

Dobilas's squad opened fire from the flank and helped free up Tigras's fighters. They retreated to the north. Dobilas's squad survived the battle without losing any men. The Bolsheviks lost 23 men. During the battle the partisans had managed to take over one of the Bolshevik's heavy machine guns, but after renewed attacks they were forced to retreat quickly and leave it behind. Six civilians died during the battle. The entire Danilevičius family, Juozas, Marija and their sons, Juozas and Jonas, and daughters Anelė and Ona burned to death in the farmhouse during the battle.

Having suffered these losses, the partisans retreated towards Pakruonis where they elected a new leadership. Another partisan, who also went by the code name Perkūnas[115] (Thunder), was elected squad leader. Tigras was elected battle leader and Dobilas and Viesulas were elected squad leaders.

After this fundamental reorganization, the unit returned again to Alšininkai. The first order of business was to punish the man with the horse and sledge for not holding his tongue. The punishment was relatively light. His horses were confiscated. Then the unit had to take measures to fill in the gaps in the unit. They restocked ammunition used during battle.

Paverkniai

Just before Easter the unit came to the Nemunas River again, to the village of Paverkniai. At the time the unit consisted of 79 men. Besides other weapons, they always had 15 machine guns with them.

One day, while resting, the unit received news that Soviet Interior Forces the size of a division were approaching Paverkniai from Vosyliškai. It was clear from the direction in which they were headed that the Soviet Interior Forces were searching for this partisan unit. There was not enough time to withdraw without being noticed. So, the unit decided to test its courage against the troops. They hurried out of the local farms to the edge of the forest and positioned themselves to greet the "guests." Not even a half hour went by before the exhausted Russians showed up, spilling across the local environs, searching for the "bandits."

---

111 Juozas Bajoras, 1918–1945. Died in battle September 8, 1945.

112 No name provided in the author's key to his secret code.

113 No name provided in the author's key to his secret code.

114 No name provided in the author's key to his secret code.

115 Jonas Gelčys, 1920–1945.

The partisans opened fire only when the Russians were practically tripping on the muzzles of their guns. Understandably, the "bandits'" rudeness cost the Russians.

The partisans' machine gun and submachine gun fire did not stop for an hour and a half. The first line of Bolsheviks was scattered. Some died on the spot while others were wounded and taken away. However, this first partisan victory did not impede the division's task. New Soviet units were brought in from all over the region to replace the casualties. They surrounded the territory and reinforced the units leading the battle. When the partisans realized they were in danger of being surrounded, they quickly began to retreat. Their only line of retreat was across the swollen Verknė River. On the other side there was the Nemunas River.

By the time the partisans reached the Verknė and found the ford, they had to once again fight off the Soviet Interior Forces' first line of attack, which had rushed to follow them. A few partisans were killed in the fighting. They met no Russian troops on the opposite bank of the river. They had to hurry away, hiding their tracks. However, passing through the Vėbra Manor they ran into reinforcements. The partisans won this clash. The retreating Russians left behind a few dead and two wagon-loads of ammunition. Without changing direction, the partisans continued. With their newly acquired booty, having replenished their ammunition stores, the partisans followed the road to Birštonas. On the road they ran into more reinforcements, standing on the road with wagon trains of ammunition. The Soviet Security soldiers standing beside the wagon trains did not realize the men were partisans. They waved at them and shouted:

"Boys, over here, take the ammunition!"

The partisans understood immediately that the Russians did not understand whose "boys" they were. Six partisans dressed in Russian uniforms separated from the unit. They went over to the wagons and disposed of the Russians, using only their knives.

All of this happened without one shot being fired. That was pertinent at the moment, because gunfire would have exposed the partisans' position. The partisans crossed the road and separated into four squads and went off in four different directions. The Bolsheviks lost 94 men in this battle and the partisans lost 11.[116]

---

116 The remains of the partisan dead were taken away by the Russians and since many of the fighters weren't local, and since the local people weren't brought in to identify the bodies, the identities of many of the dead from this battle aren't known. The partisan dead who are known are: Vladas Siugždinis, 1924–1945, Kazys Ziutelis, unknown–1945, Petras Kurilavičius, 1924–1945, Konstantas Vaikšnys, 1920–1945. Two Germans were found among the dead. Soviet Interior Forces murdered 74-year-old Aleksandras Bačinskas.

The Expedition to Prienai

The forest brothers were not happy with just engaging in battles forced on them. They often took the incentive to organize "quick expeditions" to the enemy's dangerous prison camps, engaging in recklessly brave operations. These frequent operations terrified the occupier and became legendary for the local populace.

After the battle in Margininkai, six men from the unit, led by Merkys, left for Prienai. They changed into Russian uniforms and on market day went to the town and found five of the most notorious Communists who were known for their bloody crimes. They shot them on the spot. Then they went to the market. Impersonating the local *Stribai*, they began checking the market prices. When they found the prices to be too high, they threatened to confiscate the goods. One of the sellers, who showed no sympathy for the Russians, explained to them that the market dictated the prices. Other sellers, when confronted, began explaining their family ties to the *Stribai* and their ties with Soviet authorities. That was all the partisans needed to hear. They quickly organized their horses and wagons, unbuttoned their overcoats, showed their partisan badges, and in the name of the partisans confiscated the goods of the sellers who claimed to be working for the Soviet system. After dealing with Prienai in this manner, the men left the town, covering their tracks.

The Battle of Kalniškės[117]

In southern Lithuania the local inhabitants fondly remember the Battle of Kalniškės and like to tell stories about it. They have even composed folk songs about the battle. The battle took place in the spring of 1945 in the forest of Kalniškės. Eighty partisans, led by Lakūnas (The Pilot)[118] slaughtered over 400 Soviet Security soldiers over the course of a few hours.

Women fought bravely alongside the men in the battle. Lakūnas's wife, Pušelė[119] (Little Fir Tree), a former school teacher, fought throughout the battle just as bravely as the men. She replaced a fallen machine gunner. Even after both her legs had been shot through, she held on and kept on fighting.

The partisans had a stronghold in the highland forests. They were attacked by Soviet Interior Forces many times larger than them. These forces had been from the town of Simnas. The battle lasted for several hours as the Bolsheviks tried to

---

117 This battle took place May 16, 1945.

118 Jonas Neifalta, 1915–1945. He joined the partisans in 1944. After this battle, he became commander of the Mindaugas Unit in the Šarūnas District. He was killed November 20, 1945.

119 Albina Griškonytė-Neifaltienė, 1921–1945.

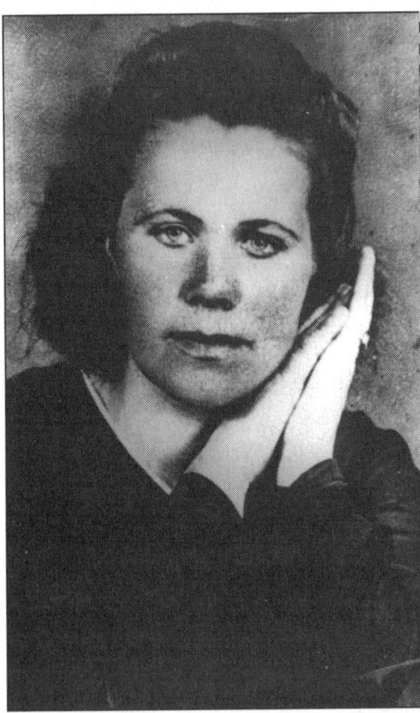

Albina Neifaltienė-codename Pušelė (Little Pine)-participated in the fight at Kalniškė forest in the south of Lithuania, May 16th 1945. She was married to the leader of the group, Jonas Neifaltas-code name Lakūnas (Pilot). During the battle she allegedly functioned as a machine gunner. The fight is legendary in the tales about the resistance. More than 400 Soviet soldiers from the so-called border security troops are said to have been killed by the partisans during the fight. According to available archives and reports the real Soviet casualties, however, were a fraction of these numbers. This gives an idea of the difficulties of retrieving proper information about the events, especially at that time. The event has a symbolic value though. It took place exactly one week after the end of the World War in Europe, thereby confirming that the war in Lithuania and Eastern Europe was not over yet.

break through the partisan positions. All the Bolshevik attacks were met with fierce resistance. The sierra was filled with bodies of dead soldiers several times over.

Only when they began to run out of ammunition, did the partisans move from a defensive position to an offensive one. With their last rounds, the partisans broke through the Bolshevik ring surrounding them and escaped into freedom.

The unit's leader, Lakūnas, was laid to rest on the sierra alongside his wife, Little Pušelė, and a number of other fighters.[120] Their final prayer was immortalized in the words of a folk song that has become a prayer for the tragic fate of our nation.

Sister, braid me a green wreath,
Bring it in secret,
Brother, plant a black wooden cross
Secretly in the deep of night

Sese, pink vainiką žalia,
Atnešk paslapčia,
Broli, juodą medžio kryžių
Pastatyk nakčia...

---

120 Unit leader Jonas Neifalta did not actually die in the battle of Kalniškės. Forty-four partisans died in the battle. Some of the dead were: Buzulis, Bražinskas, Leškevičius, Jurgis and Albinas Markelis (a father and son), Jonas Kaknevičius, Kazakevičius, Kostas Šulgauskas, Antas Voska, Edvardas Žukauskas. The dead partisans' bodies were tossed alongside the Krosna-Lazdijiai road. Later they were brought to Simnas and buried on the banks of the lake. In 1988, the remains were exhumed and buried in the Simnas Cemetery.

Žiemkelis

In January 1945, along the border of Veiverys county, just before Girininkais Antraisiais, on the edge of the Kazlų Rūda forest, after a completed operation, the Bolsheviks came upon Arlauskas's[121] unit. These partisans had spent the winter in bunkers.

There were 47 fighters among the partisans. The attacking Bolsheviks had over 300 men. The battle was fought long and hard. The unit commander Arlauskas was killed in the battle along with 16 fighters.[122] It was only the bravery of the commander, who sacrificed his life by covering the partisans, that allowed them to break through the ring of fire and escape into the depths of the forests, thus saving many lives in this unexpected ambush. Nonetheless, the Bolshevik losses were larger than the partisan losses.

Gerčiai

That same February on the other edge of the Kazlų Rūda forest near Gerčiai strong Soviet Interior Forces consisting of 2,000 men attacked the camp of Captain Meilius.[123] There were about 150 partisans present. The unit had prepared special trenches in the sierra with special bunkers where they had hidden weapon and ammunition stores. The battle lasted eight hours. The Bolsheviks suffered heavy losses. The Russians lost 290 men. The partisans lost 33.

Only at dusk did the partisans withdraw from their positions of defense and head for freedom in the forests.

The Northeastern Partisan Units

The northeastern forests of Lithuania, from Vilnius to Lake Narutis, housed the largest partisan units. For that reason the battles that took place in this region were on a scale far larger than in the rest of Lithuania.

---

[121] Alfonsas Arlauskas, unknown–1945, was a lieutenant in the Lithuanian army. He was one of the first organizers of the partisans in the Žiemkelis forest. On December 24, 1944 a group of Soviet Interior Forces arrived at Arlauskas's family farm in Pargiriai. He was not home, but they arrested his father and his neighbor Mickus. When they were being seated in the car, a group of partisans hiding in the forest shot and killed General Smirnov and wounded one soldier. The Soviets burned down the Arlauskas home in revenge. Arlauskas died February 26, 1945 in battle while covering his comrades.

[122] Of the partisans who died, only the identities of two who died from their wounds are known: Kostas Skatikas and Kazys Lapinskas.

[123] Jurgis Valtys, 1910–1945, was a captain in the Lithuanian army. He was a partisan from the spring of 1945 and helped organize the movement. He was betrayed and killed October 17, 1945.

In March 1945, Captain G.[124] led 800 partisans into a battle with strong Russian forces. Two Soviet Interior detachments participated in the battle. These divisions lost 800 men during the battle. The partisans lost 150 men. The unit captain was severely wounded during the battle. His leadership was taken over by Žalgiris.[125]

After this battle the unit had some relief from fighting. They retreated beyond the Lake Narutis to the Belorussian regions. Here the unit was able to establish contact with Belorussian partisan units operating on the Lithuanian/Belorussian border. The Belorussian units lacked good leadership and organization. They were more like unorganized bands, fleeing starvation and lacking any formal political orientation. They fought because they were unhappy with their living conditions under the Soviet occupation.

Žalgiris had lived on the Belorussian border since childhood and could speak the Belorussian language well. He understood their lifestyle and their thinking. He used his time in Belorussia to reorganize and cement this movement of loosely organized bandits into a military structure. He tried to give the movement a political orientation. He explained to the Belorussians the organizational system the Lithuanian partisans used, their operational methods, and their nationalist and political goals. At first the Belorussians liked the Lithuanian organization. Žalgiris even succeeded in organizing the disparate bands under one leader. However, his progress lasted only as long as Žalgiris and his men stayed in the region. When they returned to Lithuania, order fell apart among the Belorussians, because the leadership lacked experience and organizational skills and because of arguments between leaders. The bands lost sight of their higher goals.[126]

The Samogitian Partisans

During the first period of the partisan movement, roughly from the summer of 1944 to the summer of 1945, the best organized partisan units were in Samogitia. They first became organized during the German occupation when they needed to protect themselves from German looting. Almost the entire Samogitian partisan movement, from its earliest days, was organized under the *Lietuvos Laisvės*

---

124 It is not clear from the author's code who this person actually was.

125 Jonas Kimštas, 1911–1974, was a lieutenant in the Lithuanian army. He led the one of the platoons and later took over company leadership. On August 16, 1952, he was betrayed by a double-agent and was arrested. During interrogations he agreed to collaborate with the Soviet Interior Forces and became a double-agent.

126 In autumn 1944 the Polish army "Krajova" took the anti-Soviet Belorussian resistance under their wing and pulled them into their battalion. In the spring of 1945 the fighting Polish battalions began evacuating to Poland and their ties with the Belorussian partisans were severed. The Belorussians at that time became interested in being incorporated into the Lithuanian partisan union.

Vanagai [127] (Lithuanian Freedom Hawks). The largest number of former Lithuanian Army officers were organized in these units. The officers immediately began organizing the partisan movement and making necessary adjustments. In the first year alone droves of Lithuanian officers and partisans were laid to rest in the Samogitian earth. Among them the honorable General Pečiulionis[128] was laid to rest.

The Bolsheviks were unable to defeat these highly organized partisans in open battle. Therefore, they used subterfuge. This type of subterfuge only came to the other regions of Lithuania much later.

In February of 1945,[129] between Tauragė and Raudondvaris, several hundred Soviet paratroopers showed up dressed as partisans. They murdered every single "Soviet" official they came upon, not taking their loyalties into account. Somehow, they managed only to find and kill those functionaries who were working with the Soviet system for the good of the people, rather than for the good of the occupier. After a few weeks, this unit that had taken upon itself to slaughter innocent people, disappeared. A few days later it appeared again, but this time wearing Soviet Interior Forces uniforms. A second round of civilian murders began. All the people who had assisted them in any way, whether out of fear or loyalty, when they had arrived dressed as partisans, were now murdered. After just a few days many farms had been burned and several hundred citizens had been arrested. A large number of the people who remained alive joined the partisans.

The Partisans of Central Lithuania

Between Panevėžys, Ukmergė, Kėdainiai, and Kaunas Officer Vaitelis[130] and Jonas Blieka[131] terrorized the Bolsheviks. These rather large units based themselves in

---

127 This organization was formed in 1944, right at the beginning of the partisan wars.

128 General Motiejus Pečiulionis, 1888–1960, was the only general from the former Lithuanian army in the Partisan movement. He vehemently opposed any form of collaboration with the occupying Nazi forces. The Lithuanian Independence Movement left Pečiulionis with the mission of leading within the resistance movement. His expertise and experience was greatly valued within the resistance. He was arrested May 3, 1945 and, on April 25, 1946, he was sentenced to ten years in a concentration camp and five years in exile. He returned from exile in 1956 and died in 1960.

129 Actually, these units first showed up during the summer of 1945 and operated from Salamiestis to Panevėžys. At first they pretended to be German soldiers left behind. About 200 provocateurs terrorized partisan liaisons and support people during this period.

130 Danielius Vaitelis, 1913–1948, was a lieutenant in the Lithuanian army. When the Soviets occupied Lithuania in 1940 he was released from the army into the reserves. That autumn he secretly crossed the border into Germany, where he received training as a paratrooper. A few weeks before the war began he was parachuted back into Lithuania to guard strategic sites. He participated in the June 1941 revolt in Kaunas. From 1944 he fought as a partisan. He died in battle May 13, 1948.

131 Jonas Blieka, 1910–1947, was a lieutenant in the Lithuanian army. He was a partisan from 1944. He died in battle in December 1947.

the Žalieji forests. Over and over again some of their units infiltrated larger cities like Panevėžys or Kaunas. Often the Soviet Interior Forces in Panevėžys were overcome with fear by rumors that Blieka and his men had infiltrated the city.

Vaitelis also did his share. His men would secretly enter the center of Kaunas and attack Soviet Security offices. One of those attacks was directed against the Soviet Security buildings on Italija Street. They attacked in an attempt to rescue their imprisoned friends. The attack lasted only a few minutes, afterwards they sped out of the city in cars.

Jonas Misiūnas, known as Žaliasis Velnias (the Green Devil).

Žaliasis Velnias (the Green Devil)[132] operated around Trakai, Vilnius, Kaišiadorys, and northeast of Kaunas. He became a legendary figure for the populace. Stories of his clever operations and courage passed by word of mouth throughout the region, becoming myth.

The Partisans Act Against Bolshevik Plans

This was the face of the partisan movement during the first year of the Soviet occupation. People sympathized with the partisans; therefore, tales of their heroic deeds were often exaggerated to the extent that only a skeleton of the truth remained. The invisible hand of the partisans worked constantly. Bolshevik NKVD officers, virulent Communists, traitors, and bands of thieves and looters, disappeared constantly. Partisan activity became more and more secretive. The result was that the people mythologized the partisans. The people were impressed

---

[132] Jonas Misiūnas, 1911–1947, had served as an officer in the Lithuanian army. He joined the partisans in 1944 and was one of the movement's early organizers. In November 1945 he was lured into a meeting by the double-agent Jonas Markulis and was arrested. He was tortured to death on March 11, 1947, in Moscow's Butryk prison.

by the partisans' ability to acquire weapons, their organization, their discipline, their high morals, their secretiveness, and their sense of justice.

The result of their work was that in many places the Soviet administrative machinery was crippled. After a few months, there were no remaining local chairmen, no secretaries, not to mention collaborators—because once one collaborator was punished, others did not volunteer. No one dared take on any Soviet responsibilities without the partisans' knowledge or approval. This deliberate partisan plan to create havoc constantly undermined any Bolshevik plans to put together a five-year economic plan or institute any of their other orders. In this manner they accomplished their goal of slowing down the Sovietization process. Even the most important Bolshevik collaborators did not dare take on any duties that would be detrimental to the good of the Lithuanian nation. As a result the enforced Soviet structure was not as successful in quickly acquiring the people's wealth, property, and work force in Lithuania. Any new officials constantly had before their eyes the risk of partisan retribution.

The partisans were successful in blocking the occupiers from instituting the nationalization and redistribution of land. In August of 1944, a law was passed to institute the results of land reform and to further detail that reform. Under this law the Bolsheviks confiscated about a million hectares of land from the farmers. In this manner the Bolsheviks were able to create a much larger land fund than they had in 1940. If the land commission, which was made up of Communists, could be convinced (which was not difficult) that a citizen during the time of the German occupation had been forced to hand over food or goods, even though his land did not amount to the necessary limit of 30 workable hectares, then all of his land would be confiscated with the exception of five hectares. The fate of all citizens labeled "middle class" according to the Bolshevik mentality was the same. The label "middle class" was given to anyone who resisted the Soviet regime, even if that individual did not own much land—not even ten hectares.

Together with the land, farm equipment was confiscated. According to the Bolsheviks' statistics, 16,000 horses, 20,000 cows, and 11,400,000 various tractors and tools were confiscated from Lithuanian farmers. The farmers were not compensated for their land, their buildings, their animals, or their equipment or tractors.

The farmers who had land taken away from them were taxed so heavily on their remaining five hectares that they would end up having to give up this plot as well. These farmers were severely punished if they tried to hide part of their wealth. Punishments consisted of three years in jail or confiscation of all their wealth.

The Bolsheviks decided to donate a portion of the confiscated land to the "proletariat," which meant donating a portion of the land to the *Kolkhozs.*[133] The size of these farms reached up to 400 hectares. The landless were given 575,000 hectares of land; however, only 78,000 landless were given the land. Farms for various institutions were created out of 244,500 hectares.

The partisans came mostly from the working class or from small farms. In principle, they agreed with the need for social reform, but were against this manner of land redistribution. In the published partisan statutes all landless farmers were forbidden from taking land and other goods that the Bolsheviks had confiscated from farmers who owned less than 40 hectares of land. This partisan reorganization did not touch the relationships of the larger landowners and landless farmers. A situation arose in which there were far fewer individuals requesting land than there was land available for the taking. The newly marked plots stood unworked and without owners because the former and true owners of the land were forbidden to work it by the Bolsheviks, while the new owners did not dare step forward. Often land was forced on the landless. If they refused to take the land, they would be fined heavily as saboteurs and collaborators with the partisans. However, no amount of fear and no amount of promises could convince the majority of the landless to accept the land.

Even in 1946, the Bolsheviks were complaining that they had not yet distributed 180,000 hectares of land from the established fund. However, this number was far from accurate. The amount of land that had not been distributed was actually several times larger. To get a real picture of the "actualized" land "reform" (or more accurately, land confiscation) one must keep in mind that often even the land that had been distributed to the landless stood unworked and that the new owners had never even set foot on it.

For this reason it is not surprising that today only sixty percent of the land that had been worked before the war is under cultivation.

Bolshevik politics towards farmland were aimed at destroying individual farms, so they could institute collective farms.

Provocation Units in Suvalkija

In the summer of 1945, the Bolsheviks set out to paralyze partisan activity. They used methods similar to those used in Samogitia in the Suvalkija region.

---

[133] Soviet collective farms.

In July, Soviet Interior Forces dropped a large number of provocateurs from airplanes into the forest around Kazlų Rūda. These units consisted of Germans and Jews loyal to the Communists, some Russians who spoke a little German, and a few Lithuanian Soviet Security officers. They all wore German uniforms and were armed with German weapons. Pretending to be "paratroopers" they set up a partisan-like camp in the forest and started visiting the local populace, asking about ways to join up with the partisans.

They were successful in convincing some of the local populace that they were actually partisan paratroopers. The locals themselves set up communication with the Dabušis-Švyturys partisan units, operating on the eastern edge of the Kazlų Rūda forest. At an appointed time a few of the provocateurs came to visit the partisan camp. They invited the entire leadership to visit their camp and to engage in important discussions. The number of invited was fixed at 12 partisan leaders. Only nine of the 12 agreed to visit their camp. Three refrained because the "paratroopers" appeared suspicious to them.

When the nine departed, the remaining partisans grew uneasy.

Shortly afterwards, coming from the direction of the "paratrooper" camp, they heard an automatic weapon being fired. The gunfire did not last long and then the forest was silent. That only increased the remaining partisans' suspicions. No one discharged weapons in the forest without reason. The gunfire did not sound like it was coming from a battle, because it had come in a short burst. They quickly evacuated their camp, leaving only a few scouts to keep an eye on the situation. The rest of the partisans swiftly and vigilantly moved on.

The intuition of the cautious three partisans had not betrayed them. Not even an hour had passed before the partisan camp was surrounded by a large provocation unit. They had expected to annihilate the entire partisan group. But, instead they were left with nothing but an empty camp.

The provocateurs knew that they had been disclosed. With the help of about 2,000 troops, they combed the forests, killing and arresting the locals who had trusted and assisted them. The farmer Bilskis[134] was tortured in an exceptionally cruel manner. His body was found hanging by the legs from a tree. His head was crammed into a giant ant hill.[135] Bilskis was their first victim because he had collaborated with the "paratrooper-partisans" by giving them food. A number of other local people survived their torture sessions.

---

[134] Juozas Bilskis, a farmer from Girininkiai village. Tortured to death July 11–12, 1945.

[135] Juozas Lukša participated in removing Bilskis's remains after his death by torture. Bilskis's son recalls that all the flesh had been devoured off of his face and shoulders, revealing his bare skull and skeleton.

Eight of the nine partisans who had agreed to go to the "paratrooper" camp as "guests" were tortured to death even more cruelly than the farmer Bilskis.[136] Their bodies were discovered only a week later by local liaison women. The corpses were naked and were tied with barbed wire to tree trunks. Their skin had been peeled off. Their arms and legs had been either chopped off or burned off. Their eyes were gouged out. Each one had either the sign of Gediminas or the Vytis Cross[137] carved into their chest. Their mouths were stuffed with rags. Hunks of flesh or blackened skin lay scattered around the trees. Under their feet the moss was red with their blood. The unit leader, a former lieutenant in the Lithuanian army, was hanging from a pine tree in the center of the torture grounds. He was raised a few feet off the ground and hung by his own bayonet that had been used to pierce him through the throat into the trunk of the tree.

Only one of the nine had eluded torture. Group leader Stumbras's[138] body was found a little ways off riddled with bullets. It seemed as though he alone had managed to fight off the Soviet Security officers as they had tried to disarm him. He had fired off a few rounds. The rounds fired at him in return had saved the lives of the other partisans who had managed to escape in time.

The partisans were only able to retrieve the bodies after two weeks had gone by because the Bolsheviks kept a close watch on this area of the forest. The tortured men's bodies were buried by the local people. Their graves were covered with huge mounds of wreaths that demonstrated the people's love for their warriors for Lithuania's freedom.

---

136 The names of the murdered leaders do not appear in the author's code, but scholars have established that they are: Jurgis Paškevičius, Vitas Paltanavičius, Kazys Liaukus, Jonas Kalašinskas, Juozas Bacevičius, Julius Matulevičius. Arrested and tried were: Kęstutis Brundza, Juozas Juodžbalis, Kajetonas Naudžius. The three men who did not go to the meeting were: Jonas Sendzikas, Jonas Kazla, and Peony.

137 Lithuanian national symbols.

138 Stumbras: Kazys Liaukus, 1918–1945, was a craftsman from Skriaudžiai. He was arrested November 20, 1944 and imprisoned in Kaunas. He escaped but was later killed on the night of July 11–12, 1945.

II

Choosing the Fate of a Partisan

July 1945–January 1946

There Was No Other Choice

Our First Days Spent With the Partisans

Legal life was becoming more and more dangerous for me. I began working on establishing ties with the partisans operating in my native region, so that in a critical situation I would have somewhere to run. Up until this point my ties were indirect and only useful for receiving information. I needed a more direct link.

To this end that summer I received verbal permission to meet with the local partisans, who had promised to bring me to meet Kardas within a few hours time. He had replaced Dešinys and was the commander of the Iron Wolf Regiment. During the day I went to see Kazys Kėvalas[1] who lived in the village of Pajiesis. The partisans were supposed to meet me there.

At twilight three men dressed partially in Lithuanian army uniforms emerged from the banks of the Jiesa River. They had rolled up their uniform pant legs. These fighters were: Skirgaila,[2] Meškutis[3] (Little Bear), Vėjas[4] (The Wind). Skirgaila was carrying a light Czech machine gun over his shoulder. The other two were armed with submachine guns. Vėjas had a pair of bread sacks hanging from his shoulders, filled with ammunition for the machine gun. All three of them wore belts crisscrossing their chests, hanging with hand grenades. I knew Skirgaila the best of the three. We shook hands and he clapped me across the face.

---

1 Kazys Kėvalas, a farmer in Pajiesis village in the Prienai region. He was married to the author's aunt.

2 Klemenas Baltrušaitis, 1924–1947. In 1944 he was conscripted into the Soviet army, but managed to escape and join the partisans. When the Iron Wolf Regiment was formed he was elected to lead the Algirdas unit. He was an especially brave partisan and was responsible for killing the Soviet Security Agent F. Kukaitis-Žalgiris. On December 26, 1947, he was wounded in battle, was arrested, brought to Šilavotas, and tortured to death.

3 Meškauskas, ?–1945, was a student from Kaunas. He was a partisan in the Iron Wolf regiment from the spring of 1945. He would translate radio news from English into Lithuanian. He died from wounds in August, 1945.

4 Jurgis Grigonis, 1926–1982, was a partisan from 1945. He left the partisan ranks to begin his studies at Kaunas University. There he was arrested and sentenced to 10 years in a concentration camp and five years in exile. He returned to Lithuania from exile in 1959 and died in 1982.

Tauras District partisans. Juozas Lukša is in the front, to the left.

"So there's not enough room left in Kaunas even for someone like you," he joked. "I was expecting to find someone I knew here, only it was hard to guess who from the code name you've chosen."[5]

We exchanged a few more words and then left together. Skirgaila handed me his revolver, so that I could take myself out in case we were ambushed. Meškutis and Vėjas walked several dozen meters in front of us. When we reached a footpath we stepped in each others' footprints, Skirgaila walking last, so that his large footprint covered our smaller ones. Skirgaila explained that it was imperative to cover our tracks when walking on the footpaths, so that during the day the Bolsheviks' wouldn't notice the number of footprints. We walked backwards on some of the footpaths, so that the Bolsheviks would be unable to discern which direction we had been heading. We reached our destination and a local man standing in the bushes alongside the fence asked for a password. Vėjas replied correctly.

Kardas and I were both immensely surprised when we saw each other. It turned out that not only did we know each other, we were blood relatives. It was only natural that before this meeting I had imagined Kardas to be a very different person. In reality, I actually knew him quite well. It was often the case that you

[5] The first code name Lukša used as a partisan was "Juodis." In the pre-Christian Lithuanian faith a "Juodis" was the spirit of a dead soldier.

Partisans marching in formation.

only knew a partisan by his code name and by his actions. You did not know anything about his past or about his personal life, even after he was buried.

Besides Kardas, I was introduced to 11 more partisans, two women among them. One of them was the unit's lead liaison-woman, Audronė,[6] a Šilavotas High School teacher, who a few months ago had been forced to close the door on legal life. The second was the unit nurse Laimutė.[7] Six months ago she had left her job as a nurse in the hospital in the town of M. Five other nurses had left with her. The six of them had divided themselves up into small groups and had volunteered to serve as nurses in the various partisan units in the Suvalkija region. Each of them joined units far away from their native villages, so that if they were captured and interrogated it would be harder for the NKVD to locate their families or relatives.

There was activity all night long. Constantly, partisans would appear in the doorway with information or with matters that needed to be attended to. Kardas rarely made appearances in this region, so when he did he was called upon to

6 Petronėlė Pušinkaitė, 1923–1992, was a mathematics teacher at the Mikališkis elementary school. In 1945 she was transferred to the Šilavotas Gymnasium, where she taught Mathematics. From the beginning of 1945 she served as a liaison-woman to the partisans. In early May she was in danger of arrest, and so she joined the partisans full-time. She was responsible for communications between several partisan units and also provided the units with medicine and other supplies. She arranged the sewing of the regiment's flag. She was arrested November 9, 1945. She was sentenced to 10 years in a concentration camp and five years in exile. She returned to Lithuania in 1961. Petronėlė Pušinkaitė died March 23, 1992.

7 Domicelė Dičpinigaitytė, ?–1946, joined the partisans in May 1945. She died June 7, 1946 in battle.

Partisans sharing a meal.

attend to a variety of matters at once. Papartis[8] (The Fern) arrived and told us that in a village a few kilometers away the partisans had located, arrested, and interrogated a band of thieves they had been hunting for several weeks. Uosis had conducted the interrogations. It turned out that these armed criminals had committed 16 robberies. They had also committed murders. The ones who had only committed robberies were thrashed and warned that if they tried it again they would be hunted down. They were told that for a year they were not to touch alcohol and that they had to compensate the people they had robbed.

The two who had committed the murders during a robbery, killing a man named Veiverys, were shot.[9]

As the sun came up the posted guards were given instructions by the leader of the guards to change location. They moved from the bushes alongside the fence to the house's attic. From there they could better keep watch over the area. They

8 Vytautas Gudynas, 1922–1947, was a partisan from May 20, 1945. He was killed February 5, 1947 at the Jundilus farm in Gražučių village.

9 The brothers J. and K. Rinkevičius from Skerdupis Villaage in the Veiverys Region.

changed guard every hour. In case of danger we could retreat to the safety of the forest only a few hundred meters away.

At about ten o'clock Kardas sent Laimutė and Audronė to Kaunas to bring back lubricant for the rotary, stencils, and medicine.

At midday the partisan Liūtas[10] (The Lion) brought back the Veiverys district assistant to the head of the *Stribai*, Jankauskas.[11] He had been captured alive. This citizen was one of the cruelest members of the local Bolsheviks. He was a thief who had robbed not only the district's citizenry, but also his friends, the district leadership. Jankauskas was promised his life if on the following night he were to assist eight partisans (Uosis, Šatas,[12] Liūtas, Papartis, Vėjas, Špokas,[13] Speigas,[14] and Rainas[15]) to finish off the Veiverys district Soviet Interior stronghold. The traitor was quite frank during interrogation and promised his assistance. It was impossible for him to lie because Speigas, who participated in the interrogations, just two weeks before had fled his position among the ranks of the Veiverys local militia and had joined the ranks of the partisans. Speigas was familiar with the network, and knew where individual militias lived, what their work was, and the results. The partisans were interested in the officers, the interrogators, and the Soviet Security headquarters. These first three were to be dealt with without firing a shot. Jankauskas was supposed to invite each of them outside. The Soviet Security headquarters was meant to be taken with Jankauskas's help as well. He was to approach the guard and give the password. After the guard was killed, they would take the headquarters. They planned to use only knives and bayonets, so as to avoid attracting the attention of the Red Army, which was moving through the town from the west.

Kardas and I discussed a number of topics important to the underground. We agreed to move the radio transmitter from Kaunas, which had been under the

---

10 Juozas Stanaitis, 1912–1947, was an officer in the Lithuanian army. From 1945 onwards he was a partisan in the Iron Wolf regiment. He was betrayed and killed July 30, 1947.

11 No further information about the man's identity is available.

12 Kazimieras Jočys, 1923–1946, was a high school student from Marijampolė. From 1945 onwards he was a partisan in the Iron Wolf Regiment. He died from wounds incurred in battle on March 9, 1946. He was secretly buried in his family's barn. His remains were exhumed and reburied in 1991.

13 Bronius Vilkas, 1926–2002, a cousin of Juozas Lukša, was a partisan from 1945. In 1945 he left the partisans and studied at Kaunas University, using falsified documents. He was betrayed and was arrested on November 18, 1946. He was sentenced to 10 years in a concentration camp and five years in exile.

14 Antanas Gudynas, 1921–1953, at the beginning of the occupation in 1945 joined both the Soviet local militia and the partisans and acted as a double agent. From 1946 onwards he was a unit leader in the Iron Wolf Regiment. He was shot by a Soviet Security Force's agent in 1953.

15 Jonas Senavaitis, 1925–1947, came from a large farming family. All his brothers and sisters were partisans. He edited *The Freedom Scout*, an underground partisan newspaper that ran from 1945–1951 with a circulation of 1000–1200. He was killed in 1947.

jurisdiction of Algirdas, to his unit's supervision. We decided to communicate through Audronė in the future. From Kardas I learned that in the Suvalkija region the partisans were interested in the idea of a unified organization with a common command. There would be an agreed-upon unified structure in the individual units. They would adapt the configuration of resistance and set exact boundaries of operation between the units.

It was already late afternoon when I took a few copies of the Suvalkija region partisans' underground newspaper *The Freedom Scout*[16] and headed on my way, bidding my brothers-in-arms good luck.

The Atomic Bomb

On August 20th, according to our communications agreement, the liaison-woman Audronė found me and passed on Kardas's invitation to meet with me in the Mikalinė wood (Šilavotas district). She advised me that in addition to Kardas, I would be meeting with Major Mykolas Jonas,[17] whom I had not yet met.

At the agreed upon time we arrived at the meeting place in the forest where the partisan Vėtra[18] (The Storm) was waiting for us. He led us deep into the forest where among the thickets, in an amazing clearing, a group of partisans were gathered around a radio transmitter. They were: Mykolas Jonas, Kardas, Žalgiris,[19] Miškinis[20] (Woodsman), Ąžuolas[21] (Oak Tree), Vilius,[22] Plunksna[23] (The Feather) and a few more fighters.

---

16 A partisan underground newspaper in the Tauras district. It was published consistently 1945–1951 with a circulation of 1000–1200. It was mimeographed and distributed in Kaunas, Marijampolė, Prienai, Šakiai, and Vilkaviškis. The editors and writers for the newspaper were: V. Radzevičius-Vaidila, K. Matulevičius-Radvila, A. Baltūsis-Žvejys, J. Lukša-Vytis, A. Vabalas-Gediminas, A. Miškinis-Kaukas, V. Bazilevičius-Taučius, V. Vitkauskas-Saidokas.

17 Zigmas Drunga-Šernas, 1904–1946, was a pilot and a captain in the Lithuanian Air Force. Later he became a major. He was active in the underground and in uniting the partisan forces. He died on June 12, 1946.

18 Juozas Gylys, 1922–1946, was killed in battle June 7, 1946.

19 Feliksas Kutkaitis, 1900–1947, helped organize and lead partisans units in 1944–1945. He was a partisan general. He was an instructor in the Iron Wolf Regiment propaganda division. On June 1, 1946, he was surrounded and attacked in a bunker where he was hiding. He surrendered and agreed to collaborate with Soviet Interior Forces. In total he betrayed about 20 partisans, who died as a result of his betrayal. In the summer of 1947 he was killed by the partisans.

20 Antanas Stravinskas, 1910–1946, joined the partisans in 1945. He was one of the organizers of the partisan underground press. On March 19, 1946, he and three other partisans stayed over night on the farm of Kazys Ragucka. They were betrayed and Soviet Interior Forces surrounded the farm house and set it on fire. Stravinskas was wounded as he was trying to escape and burned to death.

21 Klemensas Garbaravičius, 1918–1946, joined the partisans in 1944. He was the head of the Iron Wolf Regiment's press and administration. He organized and launched three underground partisan newspapers. He died of wounds on June 1, 1946.

22 Unknown, possibly of German origin.

23 Antanas Pūkas, 1899–1946, was a partisan since 1944. He was killed in battle in the beginning of June 1946.

The partisan underground press.

This was an unusually happy day for the partisans. All of them were gathered around the radio listening raptly to a BBC newscast about the atomic bomb that had been dropped on Japan a few days ago. They believed that these new inventions would change the course of world politics. Everyone was thrilled to hear America's president talking about one world government united under one world leader.

After the newscast was over, everyone rubbed their hands together with joy and with heightened morale exchanged ideas. We believed that soon our suffering and hardship living as partisans in the forests would be over, now that the West was taking the fate of the world into its hands.

Ąžuolas set down the typewriter on a tree stump and right away began writing an article. Vėtra prepared the rotary press. Half an hour later Audronė eagerly pulled a special edition of *The Freedom Scout* from the rotary press. The extra edition announced to the nation how the split atom was being used as a weapon against aggressors. The Bolshevik press was silent about the atom bomb. They wrote in their press that Japan had been conquered by the victorious Red Army.

A few hours later the print run of that edition of *The Freedom Scout* was complete. Vėtra distributed the newspapers to the units, holding onto the necessary number allocated for the cities and for other faraway neighbors. The job was finished just as the evening nightingales came out to sing. Žalgiris tuned the radio to music from Warsaw. Three pairs of partisans linked arms and danced a waltz.

It soon became apparent why I had been invited to the meeting. Through Naktinis[24] (Man of the Night) the Iron Wolf Regiment's leadership had been invited on August 25th to attend a meeting of the Suvalkija region partisans to be held in Skardupis.[25] The invitation was signed by the leader of the Kazlų Rūda partisans Spyglys[26] (Thorn) and Vygandas[27] and Vampyras[28] (Vampire), the leaders of the Marijampolė region partisans. Mykolas Jonas and Kardas asked me to go and to represent the Iron Wolf Regiment at the meeting since neither of them had the necessary travel documents.

I also got to know Mykolas Jonas better. A few months back the Bolsheviks had found out that during the German occupation he had worked for the Lithuanian Front in the Kaunas district. The Bolsheviks had come to the conclusion that the same individuals who had resisted the Nazis in the underground were the ones who were now resisting the Soviets. They decided to arrest them all. Mykolas Jonas was lucky; when the Bolsheviks came to his home to arrest him, he was not there. His neighbors managed to warn him before he got home. Without even waiting or taking the time to say good-bye to his family, he headed for the forests of Suvalkija. On the way he was arrested by the Šilavotas Soviet Security, even though he was unarmed. They put him in prison, accusing him of traveling too far away from Kaunas—20 kilometers beyond the city limits—without permission from his place of employment. His seventh night in jail turned out to be his lucky night. After several days of silent hard work, he had managed to cut loose the bricks surrounding the bars in the windows. He pushed out the window and escaped before the Šilavotas Soviet Interior Forces received information from Kaunas as to who he was. Only a few days later did the Soviet Interior Forces realize that they had caught such a big fish and had

---

24 Andrius Popiera, 1927–1946, was a liaison man and a partisan. He died September 20, 1946, in battle.

25 A village 11 kilometers to the southwest of the city of Marijampolė.

26 Bronius Abramavičius-Abramatis, 1914–1945, was from a wealthy farming family. He was a lieutenant in the Lithuanian army. In 1944 he escaped to the West with his wife and three young children, but soon afterwards in 1945 returned to Lithuania to help lead the partisan resistance. He was betrayed and killed November 20, 1945.

27 Vytautas Bacevičius, 1915–1946, was a lieutenant in the Lithuanian army. He was active in unifying partisan units and worked with the underground press. He was arrested October 22, 1945, and sentenced to death by execution. He was executed November 26, 1946. His body was buried in a mass grave in Tuskulėnai in Vilnius.

28 Vytautas Gavėnas, 1922–1950, joined the anti-Soviet underground in late 1940. In May 1941, he was arrested crossing the border between Lithuania and Germany. When the war began between Germany and the Soviet Union, he was released from prison. He then joined the anti-Nazi underground. He lived underground from 1942 and since he was armed, carried out missions. In the summer of 1944 he began organizing partisan units. He founded the Vytautas division and participated in creating the Tauras District. He was betrayed and killed by a Soviet Security Officer March 9, 1950.

PRIESAIKA.

Aš prisiekiu Visagalio Dievo akivaizdoje, kad ištikimai ir sąžiningai vygdysiu Lietuvos Laisvės Kovos Sąjūdžio nario pareigas, kovosiu dėl Lietuvos laisvės ir nepriklausomybės atstatymo, negailėdamas nei savo turto, nei sveikatos, nei savo gyvybės, tiksliai vygdysiu Sąjūdžio įstatus, statutus ir savo viršininkų įsakymus, šventai laikysiu visas man patikėtas paslaptis, niekada su Lietuvos priešais nesusidėsiu, jokių žinių jiems neteikiu ir visą, ką tik apie juos sužinosiu, tuojau savo viršininkams pranešiu, saugosiu šalies gerovę ir visur elgsiuos, kaip doram, klusniam ir narsiam laisvės kovotojui elgtis pridera.

Gerai žinau, kad už sąmoningą uždavinių nevygdymą ir paslapties išdavimą man grėstų mirties bausmė.

Tepadeda man Viešpats Dievas mano darbuose Tėvynei Lietuvai.

oooo0oooo

Parašas ....

Tvirtina : KV

The Partisan Oath

I swear in the name of the Lord God, that with loyalty and conscientiousness, I undertake the duties of a Freedom Fighter for Lithuania and that I will fight for Lithuania's freedom and for the reinstatement of Lithuania's independence. I will not regret losing my wealth, my health, or even my own life. I will accurately and carefully carry out the Partisan leadership's orders, statutes, and my commanders' orders. I will keep all secrets entrusted to me sacred. I will never join together with Lithuania's enemies. I will not share any information with Lithuania's enemies. Anything that I learn about the enemy I will report immediately to my commanders. I will protect the well-being of my nation. Always and everywhere I will behave as is befitting of a humble, loyal, honest, freedom fighter.

I understand that the punishment for consciously disobeying my commanders' orders or betrayal of Partisan secrets is death.

May the Lord God assist me in my work in the name of the Lithuanian nation.

Signature

lost him. They posted warnings everywhere that a "dangerous bandit" was on the loose. They said he had a submachine gun strapped around his neck and was a threat.

Setting Up the Tauras Military District

Almost everyone who had been invited to the August 25th partisan organizational meeting for unit leaders had responded that they planned to attend. Everyone seemed to be thinking along the same lines—that it was time to unify the resistance. The results of the meeting were to unify the Suvalkija region political and armed underground resistance groups into one. All of Suvalkija was united into one district, named the Tauras Military District.[29] The Tauras District was further divided into the Vytautas, Iron Wolf, Žalgiris, and Šarnas units. The zones of activity for each unit were established, taking into consideration the zones where these units had already been operating. The Tauras District headquarters were organized with Kovas[30] at the helm. His assistant, the head of the political department, was Luobas,[31] an adjunct to Šarūnas.[32] Vygandas became the headquarter's leader. Raginas[33] became the Departmental Head of Public Order.

Šernas[34] (Boar) became the Head of Recruitment. Vaidila[35] (Shaman) became the Administrative Department Head, Vilkas[36] (The Wolf) became Medical Unit Head. Leaders of Communications and Liaison were decided upon. There was a chaplain assigned to the district headquarters, Father Ylius.[37] A Political Committee was established along with the Tauras Military District with its own Department Head.

The Head of the Political Committee was given the responsibility of preparing the Tauras District Partisan Statute, which was scheduled to be ratified at the next congress.

---

29 The Tauras District encompassed partisan units from Marijampolė, Vilkaviškis, Šakiai, Lazdijai, and the Kaunas and Alytus regions up to the Nemunas River. The Marijampolė region partisans initiated creating the Tauras District as a unified front. Their headquarters were established July 19, 1945, in the Skardupis Rectory. During the years 1944–1952, six thousand partisans died within the territory of the Tauras District.

30 Leonas Taunys, 1894–1946, was a pilot and a captain in the Lithuanian Air Force. From 1940–1941 he was the director of the Darius and Girėnas Glider School. He was a master stunt pilot. In July 1945, he joined the partisans and was active in organizing the Tauras Division. He was arrested October 22, 1945. He was sentenced to death by execution. On November 26, 1946, he was killed by a firing squad. His remains were buried in a mass grave at Tuskulėnai in Vilnius.

31 Liuvikas Butkevicius, 1881–1963. In June 1945, on his own initiative, he began publishing the underground newspaper *Girios Balsas*. He wrote all the articles himself. On August 15, 1945, when the Tauras District was formed, he was appointed head of the Political Unit. He was arrested on the night of 21–22 October and was sentenced to 10 years hard labor. He returned to Lithuania in 1955.

32 Jonas Pileckis, 1905–1946 was active in organizing the Tauras District. He was appointed head of the weapons department. He was betrayed and killed October 22, 1946.

33 Stasys Sackus, 1907–1992. He was arrested in 1946 and was sentenced to 10 years hard labor. He returned to Lithuania after serving his sentence and died in 1992.

34 Zigmas Drunga, 1904–1946, was a captain and a pilot in the Lithuanian army. He was active in the underground. He was wounded in battle June 12, 1946, and blew himself up to avoid capture.

35 Vincas Radzevicius, ?–1945. He was appointed editor of the underground newspaper *The Freedom Scout*. His activities were discovered by a MGB agent. He was arrested October 20, 1945 and died during interrogations.

36 Antanas Ylius, 1909–1994. He was a priest who, during the Nazi occupation, rescued and hid four Jews, who now live in Israel. He joined the underground and was active in organizing the Tauras District headquarters. He was arrested on the night of 21–22 October and was sentenced to 10 years hard labor and five years in exile. He returned to Lithuania in 1956. Because of his patriotic sermons and his positive affect on young people, Antanas Ylius was constantly harassed by the KGB. He was slandered in the Soviet press and a propaganda film was made to defame him. Only after he threatened immolation in 1974 if the slander campaign did not cease, did Soviet authorities leave him in relative peace.

37 Antanas Ylius, 1909–1994. The author purposely made it seem as though two priests were involved.

From the beginning the guerilla movement tried to centralize its activities in order to be able to act as effectively as possible. This is a picture from the inauguration of the Tauras Military district, July 19, 1945. To the left the first district commander Leonas Taunys–codename Marsas (Mars). A German Sturmgewehr is placed on the altar for the ceremony, performed by the chaplain Antanas Ylius–codename Vilkas (Wolf).

In the near future it was the task of the Communications Division to enter into contact with neighboring district units and to establish ties with the West.

Every participant in the congress was called upon to be competent in several areas at once. The plan was that this first underground organization to establish itself as a unified whole would serve as an example to the rest of Lithuania's underground forces. The plan was to invite General Maciokas[38] to serve as the commander of all of Lithuania's partisan forces.

The Freedom Scout was made the official newspaper of the underground. An editor was assigned to the newspaper. New staff was added.

Plans were made to encourage other underground organizations and partisan units to combine into units organized under a single regional division. At this time ties had already been established with partisans in Vilnius, Kaunas, Panėvežys, Raseiniai, Telšiai, and with some of the Dzūkija region units.

---

38 Mykolas Maciokas, 1899–1947.

The Political Committee of the organization established its headquarters at the place where the meeting had taken place in Skardupis. The other units divided themselves up around the Suvalkija territory.

There was some opposition to the new unit boundaries as they were established at the meeting. The root of the problem lay in the loyalty of partisans to certain areas of operation, although at the same time the spontaneity of the establishment of the organization had to be acknowledged. All the units were assigned leaders, or more precisely, the leaders they already had were acknowledged. Every sub-unit had its own territory and its own fighters.

The Tauras Military District initiatory group decided that a partisan unit needed to be established in the city of Kaunas. Organizers of that district were selected. They were to answer to the Tauras Military District leadership.

One of the last points on the agenda, a point that was considered of great importance, was the partisan leaderships' opinion on the Soviet Interior Forces General Major Bartašiūnas's[39] offer of amnesty to the partisans.

Bartašiūnas's Amnesty

During the summer, in order to commemorate the end of the war, the Soviet Security General Major Bartašiūnas announced an amnesty for the partisans. The amnesty encouraged the partisans to stop fighting, to return home from the forests, and promised that the partisans would not be punished and no revenge would be taken against their families. The partisans needed to issue a response, and quickly, because before the meeting many partisans had decided to take advantage of the amnesty and return home. The partisan leadership knew perfectly well that the Bolsheviks would show no mercy to their political and ideological enemies, especially not to those wearing arms. Nonetheless, they decided against stopping any partisans who wanted to turn in their weapons and to register as civilians. There were several reasons to justify this decision: first, the number of partisans at that moment was too large for the types of operations they were interested in accomplishing; second, it was harder to feed and maintain a larger number of partisans: it put a burden on local farmers who supported them and made it too easy for the Soviet Interior Forces to find and punish their supporters. These conditions forced the partisan leadership into a corner; they agreed to allow each partisan to make up his own mind, however, the leadership made it clear that those partisans who registered as civilians would be eliminated from

39 Josef Bartašiūnas, 1895–1972.

the partisan ranks, so that when they were tortured and interrogated they could not betray their brothers in arms. In addition, the partisans who were leaving were asked to exchange their weapons for weapons of poorer quality, since one of the conditions of the amnesty was that the partisan had to surrender a weapon. They were also given a proclamation in which it was made clear to the fighters that the Bolsheviks would not accept them without punishing them. Partisans who, up until this point, had never been registered by the Soviets were encouraged not to give themselves in, because by revealing their identity they could compromise the safety of their relatives.

With the discussion of this point the meeting ended.

Soviet Security General Major Josef Bartašiūnas. During the summer of 1945, to commemorate the end of the war, Bartašiūnas announced an amnesty, encouraging the partisans to stop fighting and to return home from the forests.

The Church Choir

The second meeting of the Tauras Military District leadership was planned for the end of September on the feast day of Saint Michael (September 29). Partisans from the Suvalkija region who could not attend the first meeting for various reasons were expected to attend this meeting. In addition, the meeting was attended by the District Commander, the Head of the Political Committee, the heads of each headquarters, the unit leaders, two members of the Political Committee, the Vytautas Unit leader, and representatives from the Žalgiris, Iron Wolf, and Šarūnas leadership or liaison-women from those units. The meeting took place in Skardupis. All the participants gathered at night. They had been warned ahead of time in the event of danger to listen to the directions of the farmer who would be hosting them. He would lead them to safety. The farmer's family was very surprised when they returned home and found all their beds occupied. When they asked the people in the beds who they were, the answers were even stranger: Deer, Wolf, Boar, and so on. It was as though their home had been possessed by evil spirits or wild animals.

The guests were awoken by a bell in the morning. They quickly got dressed and ready. They prayed and then sat down to breakfast. During breakfast the last of the expected guests arrived, Mykolas Jonas, accompanied by Audronė.

There were a number of organizational questions that were to be attended to during the meeting, among them ratifying the Tauras Military District Partisan Statute. With small breaks, the meeting went on until noon. At the end of the meeting the Head of Liaison spoke about the Samogitian partisans' activity and their organizational situation. Only half an hour previous he had returned from Telšiai. As it turned out, our brothers, the Samogitians, had not fallen asleep on the job. They were real competition for the Suvalkija region. They had already organized themselves into a district under one command, as in Suvalkija. A decision was made to meet with them in six weeks.

In the evening all the participants went to confession. Mykolas Jonas gathered anyone who could sing and hastily prepared them for the feast day mass.

The following morning we were awoken earlier than on the previous morning. We all went to church. We accepted the Holy Communion. We all prayed to the Lord for his blessing in our battle, asking Saint Michael to watch over the partisans. During mass the women in the church kept turning around to see who these "angels" were who were singing so well throughout mass. They took us for clerics.

Afterwards we mixed in with people departing the village after mass and all left in separate directions.

The Tragedy on October Eighteenth

The Tauras Military District required more activity from certain underground organizers. The Bolsheviks took notice. The NKVD managed to get its hands on newspapers from the underground press because so many papers were printed and distributed around the Suvalkija region. From the confiscated underground newspapers the Bolsheviks learned that the underground had organized itself into a unified whole. They also found in *The Freedom Scout* an appeal to the Lithuanian nation written by the Supreme Committee for the Liberation of Lithuania.[40] The NKVD began to carefully follow the activities of *The Freedom Scout*. They managed to uncover the locations of several liaisons who were delivering the newspapers. They did not apprehend them right away. Instead, they observed them, hoping they would lead them to a larger concentration of partisans.

---

[40] A Lithuanian émigré organization that operated in the West.

October 18th was an unfortunate day. That night 17 individuals were arrested. Among them were General Butkevicius,[41] Major N.,[42] Captain Taunys,[43] Lieutenant Bacevicius,[44] Father Ylius and two more priests,[45] the engineer Dulinskas,[46] the athlete Šačkus,[47] the agronomist Radzevicius,[48] Kulbokas,[49] and others. The next day the arrests continued, but with less impact. The fledgling Tauras Military District had suffered a huge blow. Although the Bolsheviks did not manage to find the headquarters, which had been built securely underground, they did know that it had to be somewhere in the vicinity. Therefore, they poked around. The press had to temporarily cease its activities, as did headquarters. Only after the Bolsheviks lost interest in the area was it possible to transport the printing apparatus to a new location. The members of the headquarters leadership, who had not been arrested, quickly changed their location of operation.

These arrests in the Tauras Military District had a direct effect on me a month later. On November 18th my colleague Regina Budreikaitė burst into my room and told me that the room I had just moved out of three days ago had been ransacked by the NKVD. Luckily for me, I had given my former landlady an incorrect forwarding address for my mail. I had done that purposefully because I had a feeling that trouble was in the air for me too. I learned a few details from my friend. That same night our friend Bronius,[50] who had lived in the same apartment with us, had been arrested. It turned out that in the evening eight NKVD had taken positions in the house across the street and were waiting to make arrests during the day. They had not seen me and my brothers moving around in the apartment, so they sent a girl over. The girl asked the landlady where I was, saying that she was a friend of mine from the University here on university business. When the landlady told her I had already moved, she did not believe her because she had seen Bronius coming home that night. As soon as it grew dark the NKVD busted into my apartment. They waited in the apartment until dawn and then they left. They arrested Bronius later at the university, not at home,

---

41 Liudvikas Butkevicius.
42 Unknown.
43 Leonas Taunys.
44 Vytautas Bacevicius.
45 The names of the priests are not provided in the author's code, however it is likely that one of them was Pranas Adomaitis 1911–?
46 Juozas Dulinskas, 1919–?
47 Stasys Šačkus.
48 Vytautas Radzevicius.
49 Vincas Albinas Kulbokas, 1906–1955.
50 Bronius Vilkas-Kekstas.

so no one could warn us in time to stay away from the apartment. Fortunately, things turned out differently.

We had to move quickly, before my luck ran out. I did some checking and found out that all the places I usually frequented, even places that had no connection with my work with the underground, were swarming with NKVD and that arrests were being made. Jurgis and I destroyed the underground documents that we kept hidden in a variety of locations. After contacting the necessary people, we headed towards the border of the Iron Wolf Regiment.

Our youngest brother, Stasys, who had no ties whatsoever with the underground, took the risk and stayed in Kaunas to continue his studies. He believed that our going into hiding would not affect his status. He was wrong. Already the following morning the Soviet Security had found our new apartment. In the early morning hours they drove into our street. They shut off their headlights and rolled their car up to our house. A few of them surrounded the house, while the others ordered the landlord to unlock the door because they had an urgent matter to attend to. When the landlord opened the door, he was greeted with the muzzles of several guns and flashlights burning into his eyes.

The Bolsheviks had no luck here either. They did not find the men they were looking for. They interrogated Stasys and wanted to bring him in, but then thought better of it. They thought he would not be of much use to them. They satisfied themselves with confiscating his papers and ordering him not to leave Kaunas. All of them had a good cursing session, but left without waiting for dawn.

Left without his papers, Stasys felt convinced that the time had come for him to give up on his studies and take a "vacation." He left close on the heels of the Soviet Security, and under the cover of darkness, succeeded in getting himself past the difficult check points.

Before leaving Kaunas I managed to meet up with Jankus, who told me that Deksnys[51] had come back from abroad with his friend.[52] Jankus and I set up a method for communication for the future. I took it upon myself to transmit the news of Deksnys' arrival to the Tauras Military Leadership.

---

51 Jonas Deksnys, 1914–1982. He returned to Lithuania from the West in 1945. Later he was recruited by the Soviets and worked for them.

52 Klemensas Brunius-Patroklas, 1906–1976. He returned from the West to Lithuania in 1945 determined to work in the underground. On December 27, 1946, he was arrested by Soviet Interior Forces and sentenced to 25 years in a concentration camp in the Komi Republic. He was released in 1956 and returned to Lithuania. In 1976 he died in an automobile accident believed to have been set up by the KGB.

I left Kaunas by taking a route I had never used before, knowing that at any moment. I could run into a Soviet Interior Forces checkpoint. Even though during his interrogation Stasys had told the NKVD that I had not run away, that I had only gone to Vilnius for the day, I knew that I was not safe anywhere in Kaunas. I also knew they would be hunting for me on the road to Vilnius.

It was absolutely clear to me now that I would no longer be able to show myself again in legal life. I had to quickly and safely reach the Iron Wolf Headquarters and continue working with the partisans. My only insurance of safety was to arm myself.

In the Iron Wolf Regiment

The lives of the armed partisans followed a strict routine. The wave of arrests that had affected the district's Headquarters did not frighten the armed resistance. Only, now they had to continually check the legal status of individuals involved in the underground's leadership.

On All Saint's Day (October 31) the Iron Wolf Regiment organized ceremonies to bless the newly acquired regiment flag.[53]

The newly blessed blood red flag fluttered in the wind against a backdrop of autumn leaves. The entire Iron Wolf family swore their loyalty to the flag. All the partisans confessed their sins and accepted Holy Communion during mass.[54]

Almost all the partisans had given their oath of loyalty when they joined the Iron Wolf Regiment. However, during this holiday all of the partisans repeated their oath of loyalty according to a new text that had been included in the new Tauras Military District Statute.

Afterwards, the feast day was observed with a dinner. Meanwhile, as the Bolshevik press was rejoicing with artificial pomp over its wave of arrests and the impending liquidation of a group of "bandits" here in the forests of Suvalkija, large numbers of partisans gathered, vowing before the cross not to lay down their weapons until the war with the Red fascists had been won.

A few days later I went to stay with my friend Vilkas.[55] I was completely prepared to become a partisan. My brother Stasys, who had safely reached the village

---

53 The flag was sewn in Kaunas. V. Kryževičius organized having the flag sewn and P. Pušinskaitė-Vilija brought the flag to the Iron Wolf Regiment by wrapping it around her body and wearing it under her clothing.

54 The flag was blessed by the Father Antanas Mieldažys (1907–1990), who was later arrested, tried, and exiled to Siberia.

55 Antanas Vilkas, also referred to as "Lupaitis."

without his documents, was also determined to join the partisans. He was temporarily staying with farmer Jančoras.[56]

I sent a message to Kardas, explaining my situation and my brother's predicament, requesting that we be accepted into the partisan ranks. I received a reply shortly after sending my message. I was also given a mission and told to prepare myself for battle. The elections to the Supreme Soviet[57] were coming up. The Bolshevik pre-election propaganda machine was already in full swing. The partisans were planning on playing a major roll in the elections themselves.

The Thieves of Vainatrakis

In the middle of 1945, the Russians were still looting en masse from Lithuanians. There were so many looters that the residents had to come up with creative means of defending themselves. The Russian looters were especially active near the larger towns and cities, near larger roads, and close to Soviet Red Army camps—places that were difficult for the partisans to protect. All the citizens in the suburbs around Kaunas had set up a system of gongs. When the looting started, someone would sound the alarm and households prepared to defend themselves. Neighboring towns and villages would hear the gongs and would sound their own alarm. By this means, in the dead of night, people were able to warn each other of the approaching looters. Often the looters would hear the gongs and run away.

Unfortunately, that was not always the case. After a few incidents, the Russians no longer paid any attention to the gongs. This was the case in the village of Vainatrakis.[58]

At midnight the people were awoken by villager Gegužis's gong. All the neighbors' gongs rang in answer to his. But this time the looters were bold. They paid no attention to the gongs ringing throughout the village. Soon the villagers heard calls for help from the home that had sounded the alarm. The screams were coming from one of the farm houses.

Eight of the braver men, armed with clubs, axes, and other blunt objects, rushed off to help the neighbor who was being robbed. Along the way they ran into Bielevičiūtė, a young woman dressed only in her nightshirt. She told them

---

56 It is believed that Stasys stayed with Ignas Jančoras from Pajiesio village.

57 Mock elections were held in the Soviet occupied countries and in Soviet Russia in which puppet Communist candidates were "voted" by the people into governance. These elections were staged to prove to the West that the people of the Soviet Union enjoyed the same rights and privileges as people living in democratic nations.

58 Actually, the incident took place in Girininkų village in the Pakuonis county.

that the looters were three Russians and that one of them was armed with a submachine gun. As she was running away, they had broken down the door and were already emptying out the parlor.

Thus informed, the men decided to attack the looters as they left with their loot because it would be too dangerous to try to fight them indoors in the dark since one of them had a submachine gun. They crept up to the house. Four of them hid in the currant bushes near the door, while the others hid along the four corners of the house, guarding the windows.

The robbery took several hours. Standing outside, the men could hear glass being smashed inside and the closets being hacked apart. Of course, as was typical with the Russians, a stream of vulgarities followed each crash. Finally, one of the Russians had enough loot and began telling the other two that it was time to leave. The other two lingered, searching every corner for whatever they could still find.

The one who had enough loot eventually grew tired of waiting for his companions and left on his own. The villager Gegužis grabbed the Russian as he was leaving the house. He slammed him to the ground and rifled through his clothing, searching for weapons. He found a grenade and relieved the Russian of it. However, Gegužis lost his grip on the Russian's mouth and he began to scream for help. The other two leapt out the door, but when they saw their friend was down on the ground, they ran back inside the house and threw a grenade out the window. After the grenade went off, one of the Russians pushed his sack through the open window and jumped out after it. But he landed on his own sack and fell over. Village J.[59] took advantage of the situation by hitting him over the back of the head and was prepared to hit him again if he tried to get up.

The third Russian, seeing that the situation was grave, began shooting out the window, wounding K.[60] However, the village men held their ground. They crept behind the house, out of range of the windows, and waited for the "brave" Russian to run out of ammunition. Then they marched into the house and subdued him too.

After thrashing them, the men chucked the Russians into B.'s cellar. They decided to quickly inform the Panemunė Communist leadership[61] about the incident.

The regional secretary was given the responsibility of conveying the news. He got on a bicycle and within a few minutes was in Panemunė. The "leadership"

---

59 Unknown.

60 Unknown

61 The town was actually Pakuonis.

was pleased that for once the citizenry had been "conscientious" about capturing the "bandits" and holding them captive, so that they could be handed over to the appropriate authorities. Only there was some confusion as to how to interpret the word "bandit" and who a "bandit" actually was. The Communists referred to the partisans as "bandits," not the looters. This time, they misinterpreted the report to mean that the villagers had captured three partisans.

They jumped into their cars and drove off at top speed. The head of the local Communist government, Savickis, the head of the local Soviet Security, and eight soldiers raced to the scene, rubbing their hands together with glee that at last they would get their hands on those "bandits."

When they reached B.'s yard, they all leaped out of the car. The head of the Soviet Security spoke expansively, praising the men who had apprehended the bandits, and recommending that the other villagers follow their example. He promised to give the villagers weapons and special permissions to carry weapons. After this speech all the Russians, including the local government official, armed themselves with some large clubs and prepared to greet the bandits as they were released from the cellar. B. opened the cellar door and the head of Security stuck his head inside the dark hole and in a sarcastic tone called out:

"Out you come, you criminals, come and get what's yours…"

Reluctantly, the first looter climbed up the stairs hanging his head. Savickis was standing closest to the cellar opening. Fully believing this man to be a partisan, he brutally thumped the looter over the back. The looter howled in pain and ran back down into the cellar.

"Stop, damn it, that's Lieutenant Scipin," the Soviet Security chief called out, recognizing the man from his voice.

Everyone grew quiet. The Soviet Security chief glared angrily at the people gathered around him. Then he grew confused and muttered:

"Come out, come on out, nobody's going to hit you. Comrade Lieutenant, get up and climb out of the cellar."

One after another, the dirty, blood-covered thieves climbed up out of the cellar. Among them there really was the Red Army artillery Lieutenant Scipin. The other two were infantry. They all belonged to the Panemunė artillery division. Neither Savickis nor the Soviet Security were prepared for this surprise. They gazed at their bloodied friends, confused, not sure what to do next. The looters just spat and muttered curses through clenched teeth at everyone present.

Savickis felt very uncomfortable. He was the head of the local Soviet government and yet he himself had struck the wounded Red Army lieutenant. He stood there now with lowered eyes, trying to avoid the stares of the local villagers. All the villagers stood there with serious expressions on their faces, yet their eyes danced with laughter.

The expressions on the villagers' faces said something entirely different about this tragicomic situation: *For once you were given the punishment you deserve. We taught you a lesson. You have called every complaint an act of slander against the Red Army, and now look. We've held our own court without your help or blessing. Take those bloody lice away with you.*

Lieutenant Scipin was furious both with shame and anger. He began asking about the villager who had beat him the most, explaining that the man had shamed the honor of the Red Army. The situation was saved by the chief of the Soviet Security who ordered everyone into the cars. He decided to kill the issue by quietly retreating. He could not voice any complaint against the villagers, and so, he could do nothing but give in.

The man whose house had been robbed wanted to request compensation for his broken door and shattered furniture. He sought council among his neighbors, but they told him:

"Be happy to be alive and leave well enough alone. You're not going to get any justice here. A crow never pecks out the eye of another crow."

That was the rule of life and the man who had been robbed had no choice but to accept it. As the cars drove out of the yard, the village men only regretted that they had not beaten the looters harder. Now they had to live with the fear that one night Scipin would come back with "reinforcements" and take his revenge against the entire village.

The Interrogator Varnas

Another interesting event that took place was liquidating the Bolshevik Varnas. He was the Pakuonis county Soviet Security Interrogator. He was despised as a collaborator. He was personally responsible for the deportation of almost every single Lithuanian from the Pakuonis region to the concentration camps of Siberia.

However, his reign of power was not to last indefinitely. Varnas and Semenev, a Russian NKVD officer, stopped by a Lithuanian farm to take care of some business. They were unlucky. A few partisans were visiting the farm too. When they learned that the "honorable guest" was the one and the same Varnas they had been hunting, they decided to assassinate him. It was a good opportunity, since he only had one Russian guard with him.

The partisans Gluosnis[62] (Willow Tree) and Vėgėlė[63] (Burbot) changed into peasant clothing, armed themselves with pistols, threw scythes over their backs, and went out on the hunt. Without much trouble they tracked the two men to the Banionis fields[64] and killed them. They buried the bodies in the turf. Varnas had been carrying a briefcase with him containing lists of names of families destined for deportation to Siberia, as well as other important NKVD documents and lists of names of collaborators with the Soviets.

The Battle at the Laukas Family Farm

A few weeks previous the partisans had killed Misiūnas, also a NKVD officer. After this killing, the partisans Tiger, Naktis[65] (Night), Automatas[66] (Submachine Gun), and Radastas[67] visited Misiūnas's liquidation spot, the empty Laukas family farm. They wanted to pick up some things they had left behind. They had left their things in the granary, but the Soviets had locked the door and sealed it. They had no choice but to break the door down.

The noise attracted the attention of some Russians in the area. The partisans had barely managed to load the last of their things into the cart and ride out of the yard. Radastas, who was on guard, warned them that some Bolsheviks were hurrying their way through the orchard. Naktis grabbed a second horse and cart. Tigras and Radastas prepared the machine gun to greet the enemy. As the Russians rounded the corner of the house they were met with machine gun fire. Six fell on the spot.

As Naktis was running for the horses and carts, he bumped into a second group of Russians who had gotten ensnared in the barbed wire fence. He opened fire at them and killed three. On the other side of the farm, holding the "front," Automatas was occasionally able to get a shot from his position.

After those initial losses and after taking fire from three directions at once, the Soviet Interior Forces were confused. They dropped to the ground and shot blindly in all directions. The partisans jumped into their horse-drawn carts and took off.

---

62 Bronius Banionis, 1922–disappeared after his arrest in 1946.

63 Unknown.

64 Supporter of the partisans. 1879–1945. He was arrested August 30, 1945 and deported to Siberia where he died.

65 Justinas Jasaitis, 1917–1948, was a lieutenant in the Lithuanian army. He joined the partisans in 1944. He was killed while on a mission January 5, 1948.

66 Unknown, however it is known that this partisan was of German origin.

67 Albinas Švedas, 1919–1950. He was betrayed and killed February 9, 1950.

Dealing with Thieves in Paprienis

A few weeks before the battle on the Laukas farm, the partisan Kariūnas[68] (Crown) was killed in the Pašventis village during an operation. The platoon commander, Viesulas, was wounded.

A few Russians often rode over to this village to loot. After every robbery they would stop by at farmer Gelčys's farm house to spend time with his daughter. At the farm they would get drunk, flirt with the girl, and pay for their visit with possessions they had stolen from the farmer's neighbors.

Their last visit ended badly. As they were making themselves at home in the village, Viesulas's platoon was made aware of their presence. The platoon was determined to end these visits once and for all. They decided to kill the Russians at the girl's house because they would already be drunk and fewer people would get hurt.

They sent Gaidys[69] (Rooster) out as a scout. Viesulas and four other men prepared themselves for the task.

The scout, dressed as a civilian, reached the Gelčys farm. There was a full moon that night. Three saddled horses were tethered inside the barn. Inside the house the drunken Russians were singing and the girl was laughing along with them. It was hard to tell exactly what was going on inside because the windows were covered.

Gaidys passed on the information about what he had seen and heard. Viesulas, Kariūnas, Šarūnas,[70] Naktis, and Žvaigždė[71] (Star) hurried off in the direction of the noise.

The situation had not changed. The horses were still munching hay in the barn. The same noises were coming from within the house. The partisans crept alongside the barn towards the cottage. The dogs began to bark. One of the Russians pulled back the curtain. Caught unawares, the partisans were exposed. The Russian saw their silhouettes. The noise inside ceased. Three of the partisans ran to the door. The other three surrounded the house. Viesulas knocked on the door, pretending to be a neighbor, asking to be let inside. The Russians suspected that they were partisans and so, instead of opening the door, they fired a few rounds through the wooden door. The first shots hit Kariūnas, who was standing close by and wounded Viesulas.

---

68 Unknown.

69 Justinas Kvainauskas, 1925–. Arrested July 9, 1948 and exiled to Siberia.

70 Vytautas Juodis.

71 Kazys Bartulis, 1924–1945. He was killed December 25, 1945 at the Liukaitis farm.

Naktis ordered all the civilians to leave the house. The girl obeyed immediately. She had been alone inside with the Russians. The partisans tossed grenades through the windows, killing two of the thieves. The third was wounded. He jumped through the window and ran. Gaidys was stationed closest to him. He took aim and fired. The shot missed and the Russian ran away. The partisans were heavily equipped and could not catch up to the last Russian. He managed to escape. Gaidys and the others followed his bloody footsteps to N.'s[72] farm where they lost his tracks. The farmer was sure that the Russian had kept on running beyond his farm. Although they could not find the tracks, the partisans trusted the farmer's word.

A few days later it turned out that the farmer had been forced to lie to the partisans. The wounded Russian had been hiding behind the stove, holding a gun to the farmer's wife, threatening to shoot her if the farmer told the partisans where he was. In the end, however, the Russian was not able to outrun death. He died from his wounds there beside the stove.

The Grain Collectors

On December 24th, I stopped by to see my acquaintance Povilas.[73] As I was talking to his wife, the dogs began barking outside.

"What's this now," Povilas said, leaping to the window, "the dogs only bark like that when it's the Russians coming."

I rushed to the window myself. Outside a number of Ivans were milling around. The dogs were straining at their chains, barking at them.

"Your dogs weren't lying," I said, looking around for a place to hide.

Povilas saw that I was concerned. "Wait, there's nothing to worry about yet," he said. "Maybe they'll leave soon. I'll go outside and talk to them and you keep watch. If there's any trouble jump into that pile of wood shavings in the corner. It'll never occur to them to look there."

There really was nothing to worry about. When the Russians saw Povilas, they ordered him to hitch up his horses and to drive where they directed him. One of the twelve Bolsheviks was covered in blood. His friends were holding him up. At first we thought he was wounded. But when they lifted him up into the wagon and he began to vomit we realized we were wrong. The drunken Russian had fallen on the cobblestones and had cut himself. We would have been surprised if this group had not been drunk.

---

72 Unknown.

73 Antanas Vilkas and his wife Petronė, relatives and friends of the Lukša family.

Povilas ran inside. While changing his clothes, he said:

"That's the Prienai county grain collector and 11 NKVD troops. They're terrorizing citizens who haven't yet paid the government their grain allotment. They're all drunk as pigs—and they stink!"

Rushing through the door, he added, "Good-bye, wait until I get back."

Cursing and staggering, the Russians piled into the wagon with their weapons and drove away. The dogs in the yard strained against their chains, barking at them.

It grew dark. The distant forests were covered in frost. Still, Povilas had not returned. Suddenly, the evening stillness was shattered by the sound of gunshots coming from the direction of the town of Prienai. Afterwards, there was a short silence. Then, the sound of automatic weapons followed, echoing for several minutes without stopping. Soon the gunfire gave way to the sound of grenades going off and volleys of gunfire followed by interludes of quiet.

The partisans are picking off the Ivans, I thought to myself.

Povilas's wife was also listening to the gunfire. She began to fret over Povilas. "God only knows where Povilas has got to," she said. "It's already dark and he's still not home. I hope he's alright."

"Don't worry," I said, "Povilas is clever. He'll find a way out."

I did not believe my own words. I had a bad feeling about the situation. It really was strange that Povilas had not returned yet. Anything could happen with a band of drunken NKVD officers. I felt uneasy. I went outside to see if I could hear his wagon wheels returning.

Povilas returned an hour later. He left the horses outside, not even unharnessing them from the wagon. He staggered inside and fell into a chair at the end of the table.

His wife was overjoyed to see him. Much relieved, she asked, "What happened, Povilas dear, what took you so long?"

"You wouldn't believe it," Povilas said, lifting his hand heavily. "Just be glad I made it home alive." Then Povilas told us what had happened.

It turned out that when the Russians had left the yard they had not gone directly to Prienai, but had stopped over at farmer Petrauskas's[74] where they drank until it grew dark. The grain agent had ordered him to bring in the surrounding neighbors who hadn't deposited their grain. He threatened to arrest them. The NKVD beat the farmers. This lasted until nightfall.

74 Petrauskas from Mogiškių village.

Finally, they were ready to leave Petrauskas's farm. All of the soldiers were very drunk. They sat in the wagon and shouted out Russian songs.

When they reached the Nuotaka hill the partisans opened fire on them. The ones who were less drunk rolled out of the wagon and ran. Povilas managed to roll out of the wagon and into a ditch, but he was still exposed there. Luckily, it was not quite dark yet and the partisans could distinguish between those in civilian clothing and those in uniform. The partisans managed to round up the soldiers on foot at N.'s brick factory. One of Povilas's horses had been killed in the crossfire.

After some time the partisans returned. They unharnessed the dead horse and gathered up the weapons from the ground. There were many more weapons than corpses. Another treasure turned out to be the agent's briefcase with documents inside in which the grain collector had registered the names of citizens who had not turned in their grain.

Povilas was pleased that the NKVD soldier who had given him and his neighbors the hardest time had been shot in the scuffle. That soldier had been furious with Povilas because he thought he was driving the horses too slowly. Afraid of traveling in the darkness, the officer had beaten Povilas with his weapon and grabbed the reigns away from him.

After he was finished telling his story, Povilas took a deep breath and gazed at the bloody harness in his hand.

"I feel bad about my horse," he said. "He was such a good horse."

"Just thank God that you are alive," his wife said, heading for the kitchen. "We can get another horse."

I said good night to Povilas's wife. I went outside with Povilas to have a look at the damaged wagon. Then I headed on my way.

All of the local citizenry was pleased that the grain documents had ended up in the hands of the partisans. Now the county offices could no longer check which farmers owed the government grain. The Bolsheviks were dependent on the goodwill of the farmers to come forward and admit their grain debits, but of course that never happened.

A few days later the partisans hung posters around the county informing the Soviet authorities that under certain conditions they were willing to return the lost documents and briefcase. The Iron Wolf Regiment Kęstutis Unit commander Dešinys signed each poster himself.

Celebrating Christmas Eve with the Partisans

On Christmas Eve Kardas, Uosis, and Miškinis came to my father's farm to celebrate Christmas with our family. They arrived just as we were finishing up preparations for the evening's celebration. Their eyebrows were covered in frost and their cheeks were red from the cold. Their clothing was only partially military. They were dressed in boots, army pants, and army overcoats. They wore hand-knit warm sweaters and special partisan hats made from rabbit or fox. Their civilian suit jackets did not match their partial military outfits. On their lapels they wore small medallions with the image of the Virgin Mary on one side and Jesus on the other. On both sides the holy pictures were covered with lacquer. The corners were painted with Lithuania's national colors: yellow, green, and red.

They all wore wide belts crisscrossed over their shoulders. Ammunition and their gear, pistols and grenades, hung from their shoulder belts. They all wore binoculars. All of them had the same basic weapons—Russian submachine guns.

At our humble Christmas Eve table the mood reflected the present situation in our country. For seven years already changing occupying forces had invaded our land and had annihilated our nation. With pain in our hearts, we prayed to the Lord that our lost freedom and independence would be returned to us.

This holiday of peace and serenity was all the more painful for us because we were celebrating it outside the boundaries of legal life, cut off from normal life. We needed God's help more than ever before because we were being hunted like wild animals. We suffered all of it only because we would not kneel before the occupier, because we would not deceive our own conscience, and because we still honored our most sacred ideals: we wanted to be free and we wanted our nation to be free.

After we said good night to Kardas, he and I agreed that on New Years Day Stasys and I would join his partisan unit. We agreed on a meeting place at N.'s farm. Kardas told us that the new military district commander, Mykolas Jonas, would be present at our meeting. Mykolas Jonas had taken over after Kovas had been arrested.

A Partisan Christmas

Just as on every other day in Lithuania, blood was spilled on Christmas day. The Bolsheviks were especially active during the holidays. They were aware that on Christmas Eve every partisan would try to return to his family to spend time with them according to the Lithuanian tradition. For that reason the Soviet Interior Forces kept a careful watch on the farms suspected of belonging to partisan families.

Because of this danger the partisan leadership put out an order forbidding the partisans to visit their families during the high holidays. However, it sometimes happened that individual partisans missed their families so much that they ignored the order and risked their lives to see them.

Viesulas spent Christmas Eve together with most of his unit. A few days before the holidays, in a predetermined place, they gathered food confiscated from Communist officials or collected as donations from the people. Guests from neighboring units, as well as members of the partisans' families, sat down together with them at the Christmas Eve table.

On Christmas night Viesulas, Tigras, and Gaidys went out to visit with the neighboring unit. They reached the village of Pašventis. Not knowing their way beyond the village, they stopped over at a farmer's house to ask for directions. The farmer, according to Lithuanian custom, sat the partisans down at his table and served them food.

A neighbor in a house close by had seen the partisans enter the farm house. The farmer had not drawn his curtains, so the neighbor was able to watch them from his window. Tigras thought the man was a Russian in uniform, but Viesulas and Gaidys argued with him that this was not possible. That night they almost paid for their inattentiveness with their lives.

Luckily for them, they did not stay long at this farmer's house. After twenty minutes they finished eating. The partisans were getting ready to leave. Someone knocked on the door. The farmer asked who was there. The person behind the door did not identify himself, but demanded in an authoritarian tone that the farmer open the door at once. The man spoke Lithuanian, but the voice was not familiar.

The partisans prepared their weapons. Gaidys and Viesulas only had pistols with them. Tigras alone had been vigilant and had brought a German MG 36 machine gun with him. He was their only hope.

Tigras asked the farmer to move away from the porch door and into the other room. He positioned himself with the machine gun close to the front door. He spotted a few armed Bolsheviks in the yard. Tiger needed no more encouragement. He opened fire.

A few rounds of submachine gunfire were fired from outside. They were fired by the Prienai county Soviet Security Interrogator Captain Arkady Kruglov. Fortunately, Tigras's skin was thick. The bullets that came through the door embedded in Tigras's overcoat, but not one of them penetrated his skin. Tigras responded with a new round of machine gun fire. The machine gun made a hole in the front door large enough for a dog to jump through. The Interrogator Kruglov lay sprawled outside the hole. Tigras replenished his ammunition. Now Gaidys began to fire. They opened the front door. Tigras sprayed bullets into the yard. Not one shot answered them back. They could hear the wounded in the bushes cursing in Russian.

The partisans tumbled out into the yard. They faced no resistance. Gaidys listened for shots. Nothing. Then he ran to their sled and brought back more ammunition. Gaidys armed himself with a sub-machine gun that he took from the corpse of Kruglov. Only then did several rounds of automatic gunfire come from out of the hay stacks. The gunfire grazed Tigras's pant legs. He got angry and headed for the hay stacks. The Russians grew quiet. This time Gaidys was able to help Tigras.

After this firefight the partisans left their horses behind and retreated on foot.

They later found out the reason why the Russians had been quiet. With his first burst of gunfire, Tigras had killed three Security Officers: Captain Kruglov, Lietutenant Marcinkevičius, and one more Russian officer. With their entire leadership killed, the remaining Soviet Interior Forces were not sure what to do next. They allowed the partisans to retreat without shooting at them.

My Brother and I Finally Set Out

After Christmas, my brother Stasys and I prepared ourselves for our new lives as partisans. From various sources we gathered the necessary clothing and weaponry. We dismantled some Russian submachine guns we had been hiding for a few years and began polishing them. Even though these weapons had been lying in their hiding place since Christmas 1943, they were not that rusty. After a few hours of careful polishing, the guns looked like new. Even their wooden parts looked newly painted. Stasys turned out to be cleverer than I was. Somehow he had managed to get hold of some ammunition and a few grenades. The grenades were rather rusty, but we did not bother polishing them. Stasys did not mind that they were rusty. We only checked to make sure the stems were good. Most of the ammunition was not in good shape. We had to polish most of it and check it. Almost all of the ammunition powder was wet, so we dried it out like we would dry out nuts, by pouring out the powder from the capsules and setting it out to dry in a sunny place. Once the powder was dry, we poured it back into the capsules, checking to make sure the capsules were not damaged. Even after this procedure, we could not trust our ammunition that much. Our home-made shells could be deformed and could jam in the barrel of the gun. Therefore, we filled the first cartridge clip with the better looking bullets and set aside the ones in worse shape.

Afterwards we pulled straws to see who would get the better gun. Stasys got the better-looking gun. I got the one with the better barrel and better chamber clip. We argued over whose weapon would prove to be more dependable in the end.

Like real greenhorns, we considered ourselves armed well enough. And if our future comrades-in-arms thought differently, we were sure they would provide us with better weapons because they knew from practice what a partisan needed or did not need.

Over time the forest brothers developed unconventional methods in order to solve the complicated supply problems. One of the most sophisticated matters was how to store ammunition. One of the solutions was to store the bullets in air tight bottles, in order to prevent corrosion.

New Years, 1946

On New Years Day we went to the agreed upon farm where we were to meet with Kardas. We waited impatiently for him to arrive. When it grew dark, I asked the farmer to take his dogs inside while I stood watch myself.

Not even a half hour passed after darkness had fallen when I heard them in the darkness, one of their weapons clanged accidentally against the metal orchard fence. The partisans were here. Without hesitation, I headed towards the gate.

"Who's there?"

A familiar voice answered: It was Skirgaila.

"It's me, the new recruit," I answered and laughed, standing where I was.

Skirgaila recognized my voice and approached me first. He held out his hand.

"Happy New Year to you as you begin your new life. You already are bragging about your new life. From now on we will travel together," he said, smiling broadly.

After that Skirmantas,[75] Kairys,[76] and Laimutė came forward. We all greeted each other and wished each other a happy New Year. Then we went inside, leaving Skirgaila outside as the guard.

Soon the military district commander, Mykolas Jonas, appeared in the doorway. He was accompanied by the unit leader, Kardas, and a few other partisans. Skirgaila gave the command, "ten-hut," and began his report. After his first few words, he was stopped by the commander's "at ease." The greetings and conversations continued. The hostess invited everyone inside where a New Year's dinner was laid out on the table. After grace everyone began to eat, tell jokes and stories, and share their thoughts.

Dinner was interrupted by the Military District Commander, who explained the current political situation and our nation's tragic state. He emphasized how important it was for the Lithuanian nation to keep on fighting and thanked the partisans for their sacrifices that year. He thanked them for living up to their sacred oaths. He expressed his wish that they continue carrying out their duties this year.

"Our nation's suffering and the amount of our brothers' spilled blood, and the blood that continues to be spilled every day in this horrific tragic moment, should not deter us from carrying our flag forwards and continuing the fight," he said, finishing his speech.

After he was finished, everyone around the table grew silent. The meditative silence was broken by one of the partisans' favorite songs:

Far beyond the forests the sun was setting
The brothers sang as they plowed the fields
The farmers of the land sang
Plowing the dark fertile land

Toli už girių leidosi saulė,
Dainavo broliai ardami,
Dainavo tėviškės artojai,
Arimą juodą versdami...

The men's voices rang loud and strong:

Mama, you stood beside the gates,
You said the evening was lovely...
Nights you never slept
Rocking your babies...

Stovėjai, mama, tu prie vartų,
Kalbėjai—vakaras gražus...
Ir per naktis tu nemiegojai,
Prie lopšio supdama vaikus...

---

75 Juozas Baltrušaitis, 1926–1949.

76 Petras Mockapetris, 1925–1951.

The men sang on. Their voices were filled with sadness, making the words of the song even sadder.

Now you long for your green orchard
For your children scattered far away
And the evenings are so long
Without any joy, without song

But wait for me mother, I'll come back,
I'll come back to kiss you...

Dabar ilgu žaliajam sodžiui
Toli išklydusių vaikų.
Ir vakarai čia taip nuobodūs,
Be jokio džiaugsmo, be dainų.

Bet lauk, motule, aš sugrįšiu,
Sugrįšiu tavęs išbučiuot...

The stanzas of the songs flowed one after another, making everyone sad, filling everyone's soul with longing and forcing everyone present to lose themselves in thought. I watched Laimutė, a young partisan woman. Her eyes were brimming with tears that threatened to overflow with every word. This evening was much sadder than usual. Perhaps it was because of the holidays. Many of the partisans were wandering far from home, far from their families.

After that another partisan song rang out. Skirmantas led the song with his tenor. His friends joined in:

The first blue violets bloomed.
The bird song rang out merrily.
The brothers went out to defend
their nation,
Silent, but brave as falcons.

The old mother bent her head
in the window,
And the girl cried alone...
She knew as storms were brewing,
How hard the fate of a partisan was...

Pražydo pirmos melsvos žibuoklės.
Paukštelių daina skriejo linksmai.

Tėvynės ginti išėjo broliai,
Tylūs, bet narsūs, kaip sakalai.

Lange parimo sena motulė,
Ir mergužėlė verkė viena...
Jinai žinojo, kad vėjai siuto,
Kad partizano sunki dalia...

This song brought visions of the partisan life before everyone's eyes. As they sang, they remembered their brothers who had died.

Sleep quietly, partisan,
Your native land will mourn you.

Miegok tyliai tu, partizane,
Tavęs gimtoji šalis liūdės.

Laying down your head in the bloom of youth,	*Pačioj jaunystėj padėjęs galvą,*
You see always before you a free Lithuania.	*Lietuvą laisvą visad regi.*

The final words of the song rang out. There was a short silence. The entire time we had been singing, the Military District Commander sat, leaning on the muzzle of his weapon, lost in thought, as though he were contemplating every word of the songs in the depths of his soul.

After the singing the guests spoke together in small groups. Mykolas Jonas took the opportunity to pull me aside and go into another room to talk together with Kardas. From this day onwards I was a partisan and already they had a mission for me—I was to head the military district's press.

They familiarized me with the military district's press situation, which was not enviable. The recent arrests had left gaps in the operations and in certain other of the districts headquarters' operations. The press was temporarily paralyzed. It was imperative to begin publishing *The Freedom Scout* again and to organize the necessary means to do so as well as the necessary personnel. The idea was that if *The Freedom Scout* were to appear again it would ease the burden of arrested staff members in jail. The Soviet officials would have a harder time proving that they had run the press. I was given this task.

At this same meeting, with only Uosis present, we discussed the partisans' methods for boycotting the approaching elections to the Supreme Soviet. The underground press had to at least partially off-set the massive Soviet propaganda machine. We already knew ahead of time that according to Soviet methods the official statistic for the one and only Communist Party was that 90% of the voters would vote in its support. But this did not concern us. Our goal was to fight the Soviets' application of force against the voters, so that we could show the real will of the Lithuanian people to the outside world. We would act, so that later history could judge our actions. Besides, it was imperative that the Lithuanian nation stand up to the occupier by voicing a clear "No" to their lies, to their violence, to their use of force.

We finished our meeting and returned to the table. We did not stay much longer at the table because the partisans had to continue onwards to take care of other business. A few minutes after midnight their footsteps faded into the night's darkness.

Stasys and I did not sleep. According to our agreement with Kardas, the two of us would set out behind them and meet them at an agreed-upon place 15 kilometers away. We quickly thanked our hosts and rushed to get ready for our journey. All of our partisan gear had been stored at a neighboring farm. Here we dressed in our partisan clothing, hung the ammunition belts across our chests, fastened on the grenades and ammunition, and then, clutching our weapons, went to say good-bye to our family.

Tears rolled down our mother's cheeks. We both went to her and kneeled before her, waiting for her blessing. She stretched out her work-worn, though gentle and motherly, hands and pressed our heads to her. Quietly, she whispered her blessing. She blessed the road we had chosen. We had chosen it because we deeply loved our native land; because we wanted to oppose the decimation of basic human rights; because we opposed this type of slavery, unheard of in the twentieth century.

"May the Lord God protect both your footsteps," our mother said. Those were her only words, her last words to us.[77]

In our hearts we asked God to bless us and then we took our first steps as partisans out across our native land. Our native land—for that land we had vowed to sacrifice everything, all or our earthly joys, hopes, and our lives. This road had already drawn thousands into this holy battle. Today my brother Stasys and I took our place in the long line of brothers of the night, a line of men who were ready to sacrifice their lives so that their land might be free again.

77 Members of the Lukša family recall that Ona Lukšienė also said to her sons, "Do not let them take you alive."

III

On the Partisan Road

January 1946–May 1947

Taking My First Steps as a Partisan

Recon

It was now January 1946. Outdoors the midnight cold hit us. Through the thick darkness we moved in a direction we were only vaguely aware of. We made every effort to place our footsteps carefully. We anticipated danger with every sound. Because we were new at it, we were not doing a very good job. The frozen earth crackled under our every footstep, breaking the tense silence in the air. Every now and then someone would step on the thin ice forming between the furrows. To our tense ears the breaking ice sounded like glass shattering. In the faraway nighttime darkness dogs barked lazily.

When we reached the forest, we traveled parallel to the main road. It was too dangerous to travel on the road itself: there was always the danger of running into the Russians. It was also too dangerous to travel on the smaller trails through the forests—it was too dark and we did not know the trails well enough. We could have easily gotten lost. We would orient ourselves by following the road's reflection on the horizon.

We successfully traveled several kilometers through the forest and ended up in an open field. A light snow began to fall, accumulating slowly. Because of the snow, we were leaving footprints behind, but they were not dangerous—the fresh snow would cover them shortly. The thin layer of snow cut back on the crackling noises our footsteps were creating.

The rest of our trip would have been pleasant if we had not come across a river that we needed to cross. The river was quite swollen. The cold had come late this year and the river, which typically flooded in autumn, had not yet returned to its natural course. Because we did not know where the river's shallows were, we were forced to cross at the point where we had arrived. Sloshing through the icy water, we arrived at the opposite bank. We made use of partially submerged shrubbery to cross and only our legs got wet. After a few more kilometers, we reached our goal. Here we met up with seven partisans who had arrived ahead of us: Mykolas Jonas, Kardas, Uosis, Miškinis, Rainis, Šatas, and Kairys.

My brother and I were nervous. We did not feel comfortable. We were not sure how to talk or how to conduct ourselves among the partisans. Our relationship with the partisans lacked the naturalness our friends shared with them. We handled our weapons clumsily. We didn't know if we should stand, holding onto them or set them down somewhere. But what we lacked most was the partisan spirit. We lacked the partisans' characteristic survival humor, that unique wit they applied to every situation. It was a sense of humor that allowed them to accept even the most tragic situations with amusement.

The partisans decided we would spend the coming day at Skučas's farm. A few of the partisans' dozed stretched out on the wooden benches. Others stayed up and talked quietly. From time to time they changed guard.

Before dawn our guard burst into the house and told us that a long line of vehicles was traveling on the road from Prienas heading towards the Dambrava manor. This news got everyone up on their feet. Kardas ran outside to observe the line of cars with binoculars. The remaining partisans hurried to get dressed.

Once everyone was ready we received orders. We took cover by traveling between farms, heading towards the forest. To cover our fresh tracks, our host chased his herd out of the barn and after us across the field. We quickly reached the river we had crossed the night before. We crossed again, and in groups of threes headed for the forest, all the time keeping an eye on the headlights of the unending stream of cars heading towards Dambrava. We reached the forest when it was already quite light. We decided not to stay because the forest was not deep enough to provide us good cover. We crossed the overgrown banks of the Jiesia River and ended up in the forests around the town of Garliava. The Russians never noticed us.

We crept into the depths of the forests and started a fire from dry underbrush, so it wouldn't smoke too much. While the others crowded around the fire to dry their wet clothing, Uosis and I went out as scouts. Uosis familiarized me with the lay of the land and explained the basic concept of scouting. I pressed myself close to a rather large fir tree. Under cover of the fir's branches, I scoured the area with binoculars. Along the edge of the forest, thirty meters away from our camp, I saw the road. Beyond the road, in the flat plains, a few farms lay scattered among thickets. A few kilometers away stood the Dambrava manor. To the left was the river. I did not see anything suspicious, so I set down the binoculars and was just about to warm my frozen hands by clapping them, when two Russians appeared on the road to our left. They nearly walked right past us. I squatted down, letting go of the binoculars. I pulled Uosis under the fir tree with one hand and grabbed hold of my gun with the other. The Russians did not notice us. They sauntered along lazily. One of them held his gun ready. The other had his weapon tossed over his shoulder. Just to be careful, Uosis had already taken aim on one of them. The muzzle of Uosis's gun slowly followed the Ivan as he passed; he was ready to fire at any given moment. But there was no need to worry. The Russians never even realized they were in danger. They passed us without ever even noticing us, and so we had no reason to shoot them.

"Those Ivans are slick," Uosis joked, "they passed right under our noses and nothing. They got lucky, otherwise there would have been a funeral."

Attentive to the lesson of our carelessness, we moved further back into the forest to an area better suited for reconnaissance. We stayed there a few hours unnoticed by the massive movement of Russians. Then we returned to our friends, who were still drying out. The second set of guards took our places.

That afternoon the guards returned with a local civilian who told us in detail about the Russian movement and its purpose.

Nine hundred Interior troops had arrived at the Dambrava manor to organize a pre-election rally. Several hundred local residents had been brought to the manor by force. Every one of them was brought into a separate room and indoctrinated with issues relating to the elections and forced to "promise" they would vote. The individuals who refused to agree to vote were beaten and locked in the cellars. This was done, so that they could have the opportunity to "change their politics." Because of this activity many of the local people went into hiding in their hay barns or ran for the forests. This man too had fled for the forest. The empty farms were being looted of food and valuables by the Soviet Interior Forces.

Around three o'clock we crept to the edge of the forest to watch the Bolshevik rally. Groups of Russians dressed in furs organized into long lines were going from farm to farm, surrounding each one and chasing out the inhabitants. With our own eyes we watched the Soviet Union's "most democratic" election preparations.

"Study their methods and think about what methods you will need to use to alleviate these people's fear and to convince them not to be afraid to voice their own will when election day comes," my commander said to me.

"I believe in my people's conscience and in their persistence," I said to my commander, "and that is worth a lot more than the enemy's methods of terror. Those masses of people being chased through the cold and beaten, they won't vote. Commander, allow me to organize one of the Bolshevik's most favorite tactics—a socialist rally—only this time the result will be a boycott of the election."

The commander smiled slightly, without saying anything, he continued watching the activity in the direction of the Dambrava manor.

When it began to grow dark, we left our position and headed through Lapupis towards Išlauža. Most of the farms were filled with Russians, so we had to be very careful as we passed through the area. Vehicles were still traveling in on the main road. Every so often we would have to lie flat in the frozen fields or hide in the bushes as their headlights streamed past.

Just before Dambrava we heard the hum of many engines and saw their headlights. The blackness of the night sky was cut by flares going up to signal groups that were still working on the "operation" to return to camp quickly.

The goal of our march, Uosis explained to me half way through our hike, was to visit Viesulas's unit. Our commander, Mykolas Jonas, was determined to visit every partisan group in the Tauras Military District. This time the visit was to take place in our region.

We were met by Viesulas's second in command, Naktis[1] (Night) with several men from his company: Tigras, Radastas, Gaidys, Dalia[2] (Fate) and others. They had all adjusted to the snowy conditions and were wearing white camouflage. These men had all been blessed with height. All of them were nearly two meters tall. Their polished machine guns were impressive beside their height.

Discussions and instructions took about three hours. Then we took three hitched sledges and moved to the Kozeris woods. We expected that we would be able to spend the day quietly in this area because only yesterday the "rallies" had taken place here. We choose two farms side by side, split our group into two, and parted to rest.

About two o'clock in the afternoon our guards announced that a group of about 30 Russians were approaching from the opposite bank of the river. Mykolas Jonas ordered us to leave the farms immediately and to hide in the Kozeris wood. That way we would avoid confrontation. Using the farm buildings for cover, our group reached the forest unnoticed. We set ourselves up in the trenches along the edge of the forest, ready to fire in case our second group did not reach cover safely. The second group made its escape late and was spotted by the enemy. Led by Naktis, they moved in a line towards the forest.

The first Bolsheviks were closer to us than our retreating friends. When they noticed the partisans, they stopped moving forwards and did not attack, despite

---

1 Justinas Jasaitis, 1917–1946.

2 Elena Nausėdaitė, 1921, was arrested February 22, 1947 and sentenced to seven years and three months hard labor in Siberia.

the fact that the partisans were outnumbered by far. They were probably frightened by the partisans' unusual height and the three machine guns they were carrying. The Bolsheviks had no machine guns with them. Our friends reached the forest quickly. The Bolsheviks did not even dare open fire.

We couldn't feel safe. We had been seen and we could only expect that they would reinforce their numbers. The wood was surrounded. We quickly traveled to the other end of the Kozeris wood. From there we traveled unnoticed to the Klebiškis forest.

We took cover about half a kilometer inside the forest. It was growing dark. We collected dry underbrush and twigs and started a small fire. As the fire sputtered, the district commander led us in prayer. We said the partisan prayer and then very quietly, singing with only half our mouths open, sang a hymn to the Virgin Mary and then the Lithuanian national anthem. The last of the fire died just as we ended the anthem. We scattered the ashes around in the snow and traveled closer to the edge of the fields.

When it grew quite dark, we split into three groups: Viesulas's men left for their area of action, the district commander, Kardis, and Uosis left to solve some communications issues, and the remaining five us of were left to spend the night in the forest.

The district commander and the men accompanying him intended to return by morning. However, things did not go according to plan. We waited until day break in the agreed-upon place, but they did not return. Large numbers of Interior troops swarmed the area.

We later learned that the Klebiškės forest was being used as cover by more partisans than just us. The night before Dešnys's unit had arrived and had spent the night in an empty farmhouse. They were attacked by the Bolsheviks in the morning. The partisans repulsed the attack and retreated for the forest. As they were retreating, Dešnys's soldier Ramybnas[3] was killed. Because they could not hide their footprints in the snow, the partisans were followed and constantly under fire as they retreated.

The five of us crossed paths with the pursued partisans. We were worried. From all sides we were under fire, from both the enemy and our friends. It was impossible to make out who was who. We lay close to the ground and waited until one of the groups got close enough so that we could communicate with them either by words or gunshots. We waited in this position for a good long

[3] Juozas Morkūnas, 1910–1946.

while. Once the other partisans reached advantageous positions, they were able to fight back against the Bolsheviks. Both sides entrenched themselves and exchanged fire for several hours. When the Bolsheviks tried to surround them, the partisans retreated. We took advantage of the opportunity. Under fire from both sides, we retreated towards Anatiniškis until we were able to get out of the firing range. Just then it began to snow heavily. In a few minutes our tracks were covered completely.

We reached an area in the forest where trees had been chopped down and a pile of branches had been left behind. We crawled inside this pile of branches, determined to wait out the storm. The raging blizzard covered our hide-out. We were relieved. The storm would completely cover our footprints and our present hiding place. It turned out that our hide-out was quite safe. The exhausted Soviet Interior Forces, with their eyes practically shut against the driving snow, stumbled past our hide-out and saw nothing but a pile of branches. We thanked God that we had managed to avoid a confrontation because it would have been an uneven fight—several hundred enemies against the five of us. Besides, out of the five of us only two could have fought, Rainis and Miškinis. Šatas was almost out of ammunition and my brother Stasys, who now went by the code name Tautvydas, didn't have much either.

That night when we left the forest we found out through a liaison-woman that Mykolas Jonas, Kardas, and Uosis were leaving us for a while to work on a separate mission. We were given a two week leave because of the storm.

Tautvydas and I said good-bye to our friends and left for our native regions, hoping to use our leave to get our hands on more ammunition and badly needed guns.

Working for the Press

Two weeks later Kardas and Uosis showed up at headquarters. We left for Plunksnas's[4] (The Feather) region where they had the necessary equipment to get the press running. Our first assignment was to publish *The Freedom Scout* and anti-election proclamations.

Our work was difficult. Uosis and I had to prepare the manuscripts. After that, it was my responsibility to compose the vignettes. Besides the proclamations I was assigned the task of coming up with two cartoons that would represent the

[4] Lukša did not identify this individual in his secret code; however, scholars believe this man to be Antanas Pūkas (1899–1946). He was a former policeman who joined the partisans in 1944. He was killed in battle in June 1946.

"most democratic" Soviet elections. It was a painstaking job preparing the plates for printing because we lacked the proper equipment. We ended up tapering the point of a bullet and using it as an etching tool.

We printed using a rotary press. All this work was done in a tiny bunker out in the woods. We had to do the typing, the engraving, and the printing. It took us three days to complete the work. When we were done 900 copies of *The Freedom Scout* and 1,400 anti-election proclamations and cartoons lay before us.

We distributed the press according to instructions we received from our leaders. The first method of distribution was straightforward. In the dead of night partisans would glue the proclamations in crowded public areas. The second method was to use the Bolsheviks' administrative machinery. In the provinces we accomplished this by using methods of coercion against the local Communist leadership. Often they were forced by the partisans to make sure that every citizen in their district receive a copy of *The Freedom Scout*. Some of them accomplished this task by covering the front page of *The Freedom Scout* with an officially sanctioned Communist newspaper and circulating it around the village. Others, the ones who were known to cater more to the Bolsheviks, were required by the partisans to go to the homes of the villagers themselves and personally read *The Freedom Scout* out loud.

A portion of the proclamations and the cartoons were displayed in the larger intersections and mines were planted around them. Quite a few Bolsheviks lost their lives trying to tear them down.

Ten days before the elections a truck full of agitators was heading down the road to Pakiauliškis. They were accompanied by Soviet Interior Forces. At the last intersection before the town they saw a tree covered in proclamations and cartoons. One of the larger cartoons was pasted onto cardboard that was wired to a mine. Three Ivans jumped out of the truck to tear down the cartoon. All three were killed when the mine went off. Two others were wounded when the tree came down on them.

After this incident the Bolsheviks no longer dared touch the partisans' proclamations, cartoons, and newspaper. They were on display in the open for weeks until larger detachments passed through.

The Trip to Dainava

After our assignment with the press was complete, Kardas, Uosis and I were ordered to travel to the Dzūkija region partisan units. Plunksnas's men accompanied us to our first destination, the border of the territory of operation of

Tabokius's[5] company. Here we found that communications had not been properly set up and we were unable to make contact with the liaison. We had to discharge Plunksnas's men so they could return to their unit. The three of us waited until we could get in touch with their liaison-woman Pinavija.[6] She informed us that we needed to head to another village to meet with a certain farmer. We decided to spend the day with the farmer until Pinavija could get us in touch with Tabokius.

At the farmer's house we stood outside in the bitter cold for a long time until the farmer finally decided to let us inside. We asked for something to eat. The farmer would not even talk to us. We asked him politely and then we threatened him, but he still would not give in. He muttered at us angrily and refused to assist us in any way. We asked if he would give us a corner to sleep in for a few hours. We received the same type of reply. All the beds, pillows, sheets were being used by his large family, he told us. In an effort to get rid of us, he told us to go stay with his neighbors—they had a smaller family and more money.

We realized that the farmer thought we were either the local *Stribai* or provocateurs. There was nothing left for us to do but to gather up some rags, sweep the dirt floor, and lie down. We forced the farmer to go out to the barn and bring us some hay. We patted down the hay, spread rags on top, and lay down, propping up our heads with our fists. There were four hours left until dawn.

I woke just as it was growing light outside. I looked around the room and saw someone gazing at us through the window. I woke Kardas. He jumped, recognizing the face.

"It's Lapinas[7] (The Fox)" Kardas said, sitting up.

Lapinas smiled at us through the window and then momentarily disappeared. He reappeared at the front door.

Now it was clear to us why the farmer had treated us the way he did. Lapinas had been using the farm house as his hide-out. Because the Bolsheviks often wandered the area at night, threatening the locals, the farmer had been warned to be wary of any unknown armed men that visited his farm. He had been told not to get friendly with these types of visitors no matter how hard they tried to convince him that they were partisans. The partisans had put out a directive that unknown partisans in the region be introduced by known partisans to local sup-

5 Pranas Senavaitis, 1917–1945. He was killed in fighting in the Prienai forest. His body was publicly defiled and left on display the cobblestone streets of Prienai.

6 Identity unknown.

7 Stasys Marčiulynas, 1924–1949.

porters. These instructions were well known to our farmer. That was the reason why he had not given us anything to eat and not even one single pillow. Now he approached us in an entirely different demeanor and apologized profusely for his rudeness. He promised us that he would make it up to us. We praised him for being so careful and conscientious and told him to not worry about making anything up to us. We shook hands and started the day on a new foot.

Lapinas took up watch and we crawled into two warm beds and slept a few hours longer.

The farmer woke us at eleven as promised and served us breakfast.

Lapinas had received orders to find the company commander as quickly as possible. He left us in the care of the farmer. We felt safe here because the area was quiet. The Russians rarely showed up here. In these parts the partisans usually carried out their orders during the daytime dressed as civilians.

The day passed quickly. Our farmer, having found out from Lapinas that we were officials from Headquarters, fed us accordingly. He even sat down with us and told us all about his life—about his past problems and his present problems.

Visiting With a Former American

When our host was barely twenty, he had left to try his luck in America. He had earned some dollars, but was tormented with homesickness. He returned to Lithuania and purchased 16 hectares of land. He married and had many children. During the years of Lithuania's independence he did well. He and his wife had to work very hard, but they never went hungry. They sold grain and livestock. They earned enough money to maintain their buildings and to repair their tools and to feed their ever-growing family.

The Bolshevik occupation had brought his farm to its knees. The Bolshevik requirement that farmers "voluntarily" donate grain above the required norm meant that he was required to hand over more than 1,700 kilograms of grain. In addition to the grain, he was required to donate 1,900 kilograms of potatoes and 320 kilograms of meat. He was also expected to bring in hay, wool, linen, eggs and milk. Sixty percent of the grain had to be of bread quality. During the first year of the Bolshevik occupation he received no compensation for the crops he was required to donate. None of the Lithuanian farmers received any compensation for their donations. This year the Bolsheviks had begun "compensating" the farmers; however, the compensation was not worth much. It was merely symbolic. For every 100 pounds of rye Lithuanian farmers received five rubles. For those five rubles our farmer was able to buy a comb.

For all the donated standard duty combined he received around 400 rubles. For that sum he was able to buy one pair of shoes (naturally, on the black market since at the time no other market existed in Lithuania). His property tax along with his insurance payment, war time debts, and other tributes reached around 5,000 rubles. In other words, his debt to the Soviets was eleven times more than the compensation he received. In order to pay his debts, with the "state" controlling prices, our farmer, like all his neighbors, had no choice but to sell his livestock on the black market. During the years of independence he had owned six cows. Now he only had two. Several of his neighbors were unable to make their payments and had ended up in jail. Even the present duties would not have been that difficult to pay if his harvest was the same as before the Bolshevik occupation. However, his harvest had decreased by half because he lacked workers, farm equipment, and fertilizer. The state had taken away his hired men by piling all sorts of additional work onto their shoulders without taking into account the amount of work that needed to be done on each individual farm. Three months out of the year he was required to work with his horses in the forest. The state had assigned him work in the forest 20 kilometers away from his farm in Prienšilys. They did not pay him anything for the forced labor.

He could not even think about any type of improvements on his farm. There was no money to renovate his farm buildings. There was no money to purchase new equipment. Working under these conditions, over time he would have no choice but to join his land with a collective farm or donate his land to a *Kolkhoz* or *Solkhoz* and go and work there like a starving serf.

These Bolshevik policies had a clear goal—to impoverish the small farmers as quickly as possible, so that they would sell off their livestock on the black market and sign their land over to the collective farms. Farmers who were unable to fulfill their grain and other quotas to the state were punished with large monetary fines or were arrested or had all their land and wealth confiscated.

Our farmers could not understand why the grain that was collected by the state was not guarded. In the autumn the grain was poured out onto the fields into hastily assembled bins. When it rained the grain would open and sprout and would soon be ruined. The bins of potatoes rotted. Also, the grain collectors would force the farmers to hand over their crops before they were ripe. In the provinces, almost without exception, all the grain agents were Russians. In the name of the local farmers they would announce competitions between counties just to get the farmers to hand over their grain more quickly. The entire district would be pulled into a grain-competition in which the winner would be given the opportunity to have his name

The farmers were extremely harshly treated by the Soviet authorities who demanded large quantities of grain and other products for a symbolic compensation. In the picture a line of farmers deliver grain to the state storages. Since this is a propaganda picture there is a banner in Russian reading "Our first grain delivery to the state!"

displayed on a plaque of honor. These competitions were arranged between the grain agents who would hurry the farmers into surrendering their grain so that it could be sent to Mother Russia, which, of course, was bursting with its own grain.

The funniest part was when the Soviet newspapers reported that the Lithuanian Soviet Socialist Republic had won the grain and rye competition against some Asian Soviet Republic. Our farmers, who had never even heard of any such Republic, would walk around their barns cursing Stalin for inventing some idiotic Republic that he had to "race" against.

The Bolshevik and the Partisan Press

We sat and talked until late in the afternoon until the company leader Tabokius arrived. He was two meters tall and broad shouldered. Instead of a handgun, under his overcoat he carried a Russian submachine gun, the PPS-43. The partisans named this gun "Amerikanka" (the American).

After he gave a thorough report of his company's activities, Kardas reprimanded him for his poor liaison network. Because of his poor communications we had not been able to get in touch with him for a long time and the local residents never received the underground press. The Bolsheviks had created reading rooms around the county and had forced the directors of the reading rooms to make sure the local residents subscribe to a predetermined number of Communist newspapers. If the director could not get the right number of people to subscribe to the newspaper, then he was stuck having to make up the difference himself by subscribing to that number of newspapers in his own name in order to avoid facing unpleasantries.

These apostles of the Soviet press, or, better said, these self-sacrificing individuals, usually were the village school teachers. By subscribing to a Communist newspaper an individual displayed his loyalty to the Soviets.

We put off our journey for a few days because we needed at least a few more escorts to lead us to the first company of District A., under the command of Raganis.[8] Because communications with our neighbors were to be orchestrated by the company commander, Tabokius, he now had to be in our escorted group. Because he had important business to attend to that could not be put off, we agreed to put off our trip for one day. We spent the night getting to know the company's men, listening to their stories, and hearing about their living conditions. We still had not agreed upon the district's precise borders because up until that point they still had some differences with Skirmantas's[9] territory.

Once it was dark we transferred to another place where all the fighters began to assemble at the orders of the company commander. This company was the smallest in our district and was made up of only 12 men. However, all of them were well-equipped with carefully concealed living quarters, food, clothing, and footwear for the entire year. All of it was in line with the district's administrative instructions.

The local citizens and the partisans alike complained that they lacked access to the underground press. This time we handed over 300 newspapers to them, shortchanging our future hosts, the Dzūkai. We promised in the future to send them 200 copies of each issue of the newspaper with the condition that they assist us in acquiring paper and other supplies. We asked that they not forget to donate something to the newspaper, since our production costs were high.

---

8 Kazimieras Degutis, 1907–1946.

9 Juozas Baltrušaitis.

We spent the entire day with Tabokius's men, sleeping only for a few hours. In the evening we set out on our journey to Raganis's territory.

Under Astra's Supervision

Tabokius and Pjūklas escorted us. The company commander carried a German machine gun. The rest of us were armed with Tokarev SVT-40s semi-automatic rifles.

The night was unusually dark. We marched listening to each other's footsteps.

We traveled through Vartus and Kunigiškius, until we reached the Balbieriškis forest. We did not want to travel on the main roads, so we turned right, hoping to travel on side roads and footpaths. Things did not go as planned. In the darkness we wandered away not just from the side roads, but from the footpaths as well. We walked blindly through thick underbrush, that tangled up in our clothing and weapons and scratched our faces. We were constantly stepping on branches and creating noise. Our map was of no use to us because we had no point of orientation. We trusted Tabokius's conviction that if we walked straight we would soon find the necessary road leading where we needed to go. We patiently broke our way through the undergrowth.

Some women actively fought together with the men. These two girls, Jadvyga Žardinskaitė–codename Daktaras Dolitlis (Doctor Dolittle)–and Marijona Štarolytė–codename Audros Kudikis (Storm Baby)–fought in the Vytis military district. They were captured in 1952 and 1953 respectively.

Half an hour later we reached a footpath. We followed the foot path from then on. We intended to correct our mistake from here. Somehow, crossing some sort of a creek, we had reached the edge of the forest and saw the silhouettes of farmhouses against the sky. As it turned out, we were exactly where we needed to be. Tabokius had had his bearings right. Within a few minutes we were talking with Astra,[10] the clear-eyed liaison-woman for Raganis's group in District A.

Astra was lovely. She was tall and strong with blond hair and sky-blue eyes and a slightly masculine face. Her masculinity showed itself in how she carried out her mission. The partisans called her the commandante of Raganis's group. When Tabokius explained his business to her, she promised to deliver us to Raganis's camp in the morning. She quickly prepared rye pancakes with honey for us and offered to take on guard duty, so that we could lie down on the benches and rest.

In the Forest Camp

Just as the sun was rising we slipped into the forest. Astra slipped a 9 millimeter pistol into the sleeve of her fur coat and led our group, together with Pjūklas. The rest of us followed behind, trying our best to step inside their footprints.

It had snowed a little before dawn, so when we traveled along larger footpaths we had to hide our footprints. As we marched the sun rose. Soon day broke.

We slipped through a thick forest of firs and one behind the other entered a road. We tried to disguise our footsteps by walking inside the tracks left behind by sledges. We walked like that for quite some time until Astra put up her hand. That was the signal for attention. We had to move quickly to the side and not leave any tracks. Astra broke off a few fir branches and spread them out beside the road. She stepped onto them and then took a great leap into a thicket of bushes alongside the forest. We all followed her example. The last one of us scattered the branches across the road, so that it would look as though they had fallen off the back of a sledge. We hid our footsteps another hundred meters deep into the forest. We jumped from bush to bush that had not yet been covered in snow.

As we got closer to the camp, we began to see traces of the partisans. Soon we met up with the first set of guards. We exchanged passwords and were led further in. We traveled a few hundred meters further and came upon a few of their lean-tos. They were covered in fresh snow, camouflaged by nature to blend in with the landscape.

The lean-tos were built simply, very much in the way that shepherd children build shelters against the rain and wind out of branches and sticks. Four strong posts were driven into the ground in the shape of a square and were secured on

---

10 Aldona Marčiulynaitė, 1925–1947.

the top and the bottom with twine. The front posts were half a meter longer than the posts in the back, so the roof sloped down towards the back. The lower sides of the lean-to, both ends, and the roof were covered in fir branches. Inside the ground was covered with a thick layer of dried pine needles that served to insulate from the cold and served as a "comfortable" bed to sleep on. In front of the higher section of the lean-to near the opening were stacks of chopped oak logs. They provided protection in the front of the lean-to and were also used as firewood.

The camp guard had thrown a few logs together and was calmly warming himself before a crackling fire. The oak logs burned nicely and did not create much smoke. The other men had just returned from their night missions and were sleeping on pine-needle beds in the lean-tos. They had no blankets to cover themselves with. They lay with their clothing on, wearing their shoes and with their weapons close by, prepared to jump up and defend themselves if attacked. It was strange to watch these partisans covered in white frost, with snowflakes gently falling down onto them and rising back upwards from their breathing. Weapons hung above their sleeping bodies or were leaning up against the lean-to walls. One partisan was a little more comfortable and was lying at the eastern end of his lean-to. There were no weapons at his end of the lean-to. The camp guard explained that a few days ago his spine had been wounded in a battle with the Bolsheviks, and that he had to take a few days to recover.

After he showed us around the camp, the camp guard Aušra[11] woke the unit leader Raganis. He lifted his head, saw Tabokius, gave him a sleepy smile, stretched, and climbed out of his lean-to.

"I never dreamed I'd wake up to find such honorable guests," he said, greeting each of us in turn. "Who'd ever believe that a respectable person would come visit us in this wolf's den… Unless, that person was being hunted by the Bolsheviks," he joked.

"Perhaps it's the other way around," Kardas replied, "we're planning on driving those Bolsheviks up into the trees during their election."

After the night's march we were rather tired and preferred to rest rather than socialize. Our host noticed this immediately. He went and woke up a few of the fighters sleeping in the lean-tos and offered us their places to lie down in.

"All I can offer you is this bear's den," Raganis said, "I'm afraid I don't have better accommodations for my guests."

---

11 Identity unknown.

"The den is princely, don't complain," said Uosis sitting up in his bed of pine needles and joining our banter, "only we doubt the nature of their fleas—they might go to war with ours."

Raganis and the men laughed.

"Our purebred forest fleas won't kill your field fleas. Ours are quite peaceful," I said.

We accepted the invitation, loosened our belts, and following the example of our hosts, set up our weapons. We asked them to give us the day's passwords in the event of danger. Then we went to sleep.

I awoke around two o'clock. Without lifting my head, I listened to the sound of bacon crackling as it was being fried over the camp fire. I realized that I had gotten up just in time for lunch. The scent of the cooking food aroused my appetite. I had not realized how hungry I was. I heard the sound of men's footsteps in the snow around my lean-to.

Kardas had gotten up earlier and sat talking with Raganis. Raganis noticed that I was awake and invited everyone over to eat. Astra was the cook, circling around the fire hard at work. She handed out plates and utensils to all of us and began ladling out large portions of food to the fighters. She did not have to invite us to eat—after our journey, we were hungry as wolves. We quickly devoured our meal, ignoring our usual table manners.

After lunch we had a meeting with the forest brothers. Among them I met my old school friend Rimvydas.[12] For tactical reasons the partisans here had two camps. The second camp was three hundred meters away from this one.

Most of the partisans looked exhausted. The area was not wealthy. There were many partisans here and most of them had to live in the forests. Because of the danger of leaving tracks, during the winter they rarely left the camp. That made their life even more difficult. They not only froze, but often went hungry. Their weaponry and uniforms were also of much inferior quality to ours.

After staying with the partisans for a few hours, we prepared to continue our journey. Our travel companions, Tabokius and Pjūklas, were replaced with Raganis and Patrimpas.[13] We said goodbye to the men and camp and a good hour before dusk set out with Raganis leading.

---

12 Jurgis Krikščiūnas, 1919–1949. He had earned the degree of lieutenant in the Lithuanian army. He studied at Kaunas University. He accompanied Lukša on his first trip to the west.

13 Juozas Antanas Petraška, 1916–2001. He served with the independent Lithuanian military. After the Soviet occupation in 1944, he went into hiding. In 1945, he joined the partisans. He quickly rose in the ranks. He was taken alive during a battle with the Soviet Interior Forces on August 11, 1947. He was interrogated, tortured, and sentenced to 25 years hard labor in Siberia. He returned to Lithuania from Siberia in 1958. He died in 2001.

The Journey by Sledge

Before dark we reached the edge of the field. The white expanses of Dzūkija spread out before our eyes. Standing on the edge of the forest we carefully assessed the surrounding area to make sure nothing suspicious was going on. Then we snuck along the edge of the forest and into a farmer's house. We found out from the farmer that the area was peaceful. We took the opportunity to dry out our wet socks and shoes on the stove. We all shaved our beards and cleaned ourselves up, so that we would make a better impression on the people of Dzūkija. Only when it grew completely dark did we move onwards.

Our goal this night was to make contact with the Ūdrija's[14] group leader Linksmutis[15] who was also the district's adjunct. We marched for about 15 kilometers and then stopped in at a local farm to check on the area. We learned that this area was peaceful as well. The Russians were around only during the daytime when they rounded up the local civilians and brought them off to pre-election demonstrations. In the evenings they returned to their usual posts. The situation allowed us to relax and be at ease, even in foreign territory.

A few kilometers down the road we reached a liaison, who was to deliver news to us about the rest of our journey. The elderly farmer, dressed in long furs, led us for the rest of our journey. After a good half hour we were conversing with Linksmutis and his friends.

They were also in the throes of the pre-election campaign. The men had thick bundles of the newspaper *For the Homeland*[16] and piles of proclamations ready to be transported. The technical editor of the newspaper was Labutis.[17]

We were forced to change our poor impression of the Dzūkija partisans. We'd formed that opinion from observation of Raganis's group. Labutis's men were exceptional. Most of them were in full uniform and were decorated according to rank. We exchanged a few words with the local unit's leader, Žižmaras,[18] and then crept into our hiding places to rest.

---

14 A unit belonging to the Dainava division that operated in the towns of Alytus, Krokialaukis, Simnas, and Miroslavas.

15 Identity unknown, however, believed to be Adomas Baciuka, 1910–1947.

16 This underground newspaper was published between 1945–1946 by the Dzūkija division of partisans. Twelve issues were published with a circulation of 5,000. The first issue was published June 1, 1945. The newspaper was edited by A. Markeliūnas, code name Labutis.

17 Antanas Markeliūnas, –1947. He was the leader of the Kęstutis group headquarters from July 23, 1945. He was killed January 11, 1947.

18 Vacys Petraška, 1926–1947. He was killed in battle.

Later, we left to meet the district leader, accompanied by Laimutis,[19] Labutis, Patrimpas and eight other fighters. This time we almost did not have to cover any ground on foot. We traveled in two sledges. There were several dozen heavily armed men in our unit. We felt rather brazen and enjoyed racing through the town of Ūta with our two machine guns poised. In this manner, we traveled to Panemunikiai. Here the sledge drivers let us out and we continued the remainder of our journey on foot.

The Approaching Elections

We met up with Ąžuolas[20] (Oak Tree) a few hours later at a farmer's homestead.

At midnight a man of around 50 years strode into the room. He was very tall and had an olive complexion. His beard was frozen over with ice. He was led inside by Labutis. He was the District Commander. Our discussions began immediately.

It turned out that our directives and the directives for the District A., as delivered by Ąžuolas were similar. The main aim was to boycott the elections and by so doing to demonstrate to the world and to the Bolshevik Russians the true face and intentions of the Lithuanian nation. To that end we resolved to strengthen the underground press and to use the press to reveal the Bolsheviks' future plans. In order to protect the voters from the Bolsheviks' aggression, we decided to take these measures:

1. To collect passports from all citizens several days before the election. Since nobody could be admitted into the polls without a passport, this would give the people a valid excuse not to cast their votes. Moreover, since their passports would be missing, it would be impossible for Soviet officials to tell whether or not the passports contained the mark indicating whether the individual had "voted" when that person applied for a new passport later on.

2. On the eve of the election (February 9th) to damage or blow up important local bridges, cut telephone lines, and shoot up the poling stations. Such measures would make it impossible for local Communists to contact central installations. These actions would also prevent any additional guards from reaching the

---

19 Vytautas Duliūnas, 1924–1945. He died in battle.

20 Dominykas Jėčys, 1896–1947, joined the independent Lithuanian army in 1919. He fought for Lithuania's independence and was taken prisoner by the Poles, but later escaped. During the Soviet occupation he lived in hiding. He helped organize the partisans in 1944. He rose through the partisan leadership ranks. He was betrayed and killed in his bunker August 11, 1947.

polling stations and at the same time would discourage the local NKVD from venturing out and dragging people to the polls.

3. On election day (February 10th) the partisans would patrol all surrounding areas to prevent the Russians from rounding up voters by force. The patrols would kill any Communists caught bringing citizens to the polls at gunpoint.

These were the tactics we agreed upon to protect the local populace from Bolshevik terror. Having settled all pertinent questions, Ąžuolas and Kardas began discussing more detailed operations between the Vaidotas Unit of the District A. and the Šiauris Unit of the Tauras District.

I discussed the underground press with Labutis. We agreed to exchange newspapers on a regular basis. I also promised to pass on matrices to them since they were far away from any city and could not easily get any.

Having resolved all our pertinent matters, we shook hands and wished each other good luck and went our separate ways. Ąžuolas and his adjunct left for their headquarters. We headed towards home, accompanied by seven fighters. We marched a few kilometers. As we approached the town of Alytus, day broke. We spent the day in an interesting manner. We slept a while in the morning and then we talked until evening. We had the opportunity to hear quite a few local partisan songs. Almost all of the men leading us had good voices. This region was known for its love of music. Their favorite song, and I think the most expressive in military terms, was this song:

Through the old house, through the cherry orchard	*Pro seną pirkią, pro vyšnių sodą*
We'll greet the enemy with red bloody fruit.	*Prieša sutiksim kruvinom vaišėm.*
Don't cry Mother, we are going away,	*Neverk, motule, mes iškeliaujam,*
We are traveling beyond the wayside cross.	*Mes iškeliaujam pro seną kryžių.*
To battle, to battle, to battle, my friends,	*Kovon, kovon, kovon, draugai,*
The homeland is calling us,	*Tėvynė šaukia mus,*
Soon the fields will smell of gun powder	*Greit paraku pakvips laukai*
And blood will darken the skies...	*Ir krauju raus dangus...*

It is too bad that I can only remember these two verses.

On the following night we reached Žižmaras's squad. These men had recently stepped up their struggle against the Russians' systematic destruction of the Lithuanian forests. I have already mentioned how farmers were being forcibly recruited to strip the timber of all forested regions of Lithuania. When such activity was begun in Žižmaras's district he and his men surrounded the forest and herded all the woodcutters together. Then he ordered the supervisors and the other Soviet functionaries to be flogged before the woodcutters' eyes. Then he ordered the woodcutters to leave the forest at once and to never show their faces there again. The farmers, most of whom had been dragged against their will from great distances, were more than happy to comply. They silently rejoiced that this intolerable burden had been lifted off their shoulders. They returned to their home districts where they complained that partisan activity had made fulfilling their obligations impossible.

As a result swarms of NKVD and Soviet Interior Forces were scouring the forests searching for Žižmaras, as he was entertaining us, less than a mile away. After giving the Communists work in the forest, he thought he would feel safer on the outskirts. We had our doubts, but it turned out he was right. The Russians tramped the woods all day long while we sat and laughed at their efforts.

On the way back to headquarters we had to advance much more cautiously. Twenty to thirty Russians had been posted in every electoral district. At night they attempted to ambush the partisans. But in Raganis's region it was the Russians who suffered—two were killed during a clash with our men. When the Kungiskis electoral district Soviet Interior Forces police, who were in Tabokius's region, heard about this, they set to work strengthening their position and piled a layer of sand bags nearly six feet deep outside their ground-floor room.

The partisans' white handbills petitioning the people to boycott the elections were posted everywhere along the roadside.

The Pre-Election Campaign

When we returned Kardas informed the district leader about our journey and the results. We then put together detailed instructions on how to interrupt the pre-election and elections. Those instructions were swiftly delivered to individual unit leaders.

The people within the boundaries of our unit's area of activity were informed not only through the partisan press, but by word of mouth that the elections should be boycotted. The partisans were ordered to circulate among the local people and to tell them about the fraud being practiced by the occupying forces against them. The partisan's task was to convince the people not to go to the polls.

Several days before the elections the drive to collect passports began. It went smoothly. I saw this for myself when I visited Viesulas's unit headquarters. Around midnight the men who were out collecting passports began to return. They came back in twos and threes lugging baskets overflowing with documents. In order to mock and deride the Communist penchant of carrying out every task with pomp and ceremony, the men had adorned the baskets with red-colored paper flowers and Communist slogans. There was a lot of talk about competing as to who would collect the most documents. "Fraternal" republics were encouraged to break all collection records. Thousands of passports made their way into the Partisan's archives.

At first district officials tried to issue temporary papers to those deprived of their passports, but the masses of people swarming the district offices were so large that soon the Communists lost patience and ordered everyone to go home.

The attacks on the polling stations were scheduled to begin on the evening of February 9th. Our first goal was to tie the Russian garrisons to the spot, so they would not be able to prepare traps for the armed resistance movement or interfere with the destruction of telephone lines and important local bridges. Our second goal was for our constant shooting to keep the Russians awake and on watch all night long, so that on election day they would be sleep-deprived and exhausted and it would be that much more difficult for them to recruit prospective voters by terrorizing the local people.

Finally, these incidents were to be staged to provide the nonvoting local inhabitants with a valid excuse for not showing up at the polls. It was simply too dangerous.

Each company in our partisan unit was responsible for covering one polling station. Kardas, Uosis, and I were assigned the Šilavotas "fortress." There was a garrison of roughly 200 troops stationed there awaiting assignment to the polling stations in our district. We were to begin operations in 24 hours. On hearing our shots, the other companies were to follow suit.

After having examined and cleaned our weapons and after replenishing our supplies of ammunition, we set out. A death-like silence reigned outside. Although it was February, a drizzling rain was falling. The weather was unusual for the this time of year. Deep mud caused by the rain impeded our progress. Soon all of us were soaking wet.

When we finally reached Šilavotas, we entrenched ourselves in a ditch several hundred meters away from the Soviet quarters and awaited their commander's order to shoot. We had decided to discharge fifty rounds. The moment we heard their command "Fire!" our semi-automatics opened up. The Russian "Maxim" machine guns responded immediately afterwards. The machine gun bursts and tracer bullets flew above our heads and buried themselves somewhere in the pine grove behind us. After discharging the agreed number of shots, we heard Kardas squeaking like a mouse. This was our signal to withdraw. Uosis let fly a few grenades for good measure. The Russians intensified their fire. But we just laughed at them and took off across the mucky fields. We were not about to abandon Šilavotas so soon, however. We were planning on giving the Soviet Interior Forces more fire from the other side of their stronghold.

Plowing our way through the sticky mud, we began back-tracking. The going was tough. The terrain had become a quagmire. The warmth of the air combined with the heavy gear we were carrying caused us to drip with sweat. Somehow we managed to reach a hillock where we could rest. At last, we had a chance to see what was happening. The whole district looked as though it had been transformed into a battleground. Signal flares streaked skywards from the polling stations. Automatic weapons clattered away. Grenades exploded at regular intervals. We celebrated the fact that our comrades were doing so well and resumed our trek back to Šilavotas.

Once again we found ourselves adjacent to the Soviet Interior Forces stronghold, but this time the darkness prevented us from finding any good vantage points. We finally settled for the slopes of a slippery buff and opened fire again. The Russians fired back more promptly and more accurately than before. Their bullets whizzed past our ears, forcing us to stick close to the boggy ground. Moreover, this time a searchlight in the church tower swept back and forth across the area, to ferret us out.

After midnight the scene grew even more animated. After the telephone lines were destroyed, the Bolsheviks panicked and began sending up flares of every description. They lit up the sky for kilometers in all directions that helped us find our bearings during the march.

Election Day

Around five in the morning we reached Dūmiškis Village. We went to the house of a friend and, resting our heads on the muzzles of our guns, caught a few hours sleep.

In the middle of the morning, after a good breakfast, we left for Prienšilis. Our mission now was to capture the Šilavotas–Prienas road. We expected that in the morning the Russians would try to transfer part of their forces from Prienai to Šilavotas. We were prepared to ambush them along their way—we had found a good spot in Prienšilis.

Outside it had gotten much colder. Everything was frozen. Instead of muck, we now had fresh snow under our feet. We emerged into a path along the edge of the woods.

When we reached the Prienas Road, we planted several anti-tank mines that we had brought with us from the bunker at predesignated spots on the Prienai road. We had already mined the route over which the Russians would try to send reinforcements to Šilavotas. As soon as this operation was finished, we took cover in nearby trenches and waited there to pick off whatever enemy troops might try to escape the mines. The vigil proved unpleasant. We were still soaked from the previous night's rain and sweat. Our limbs began to grow numb and our teeth chattered. We waited an hour, two hours, three hours, but the Russians did not show up. We could not endure waiting any longer than noon. We unmined the road and began walking. We pulled out our field glasses and carefully scanned the surrounding area. Nothing was moving. Everywhere the wonderful stillness of a winter Sunday afternoon reigned.

We decided to abandon the forest and look in on a nearby farmstead. We wanted to find out what was going on in the village.

Shaking the snow from our feet, we entered the farm house. A family of five sat dining at the table—the parents and three children under the age of ten. They glanced up at us timidly.

Pretending to be a Communist official, Kardas said in Russian, "Enjoy your lunch! How did the voting go comrades? Did you vote already?"

The husband and wife glanced nervously back and forth at each other. Finally, the farmer opened his mouth:

"We didn't know anything about the elections.... The village elder didn't tell us anything." The man was around 45. He did not raise his eyes from the table when he spoke.

"How is it you didn't know? We had so many meetings. Stalin's constitution was explained to everyone and he says he didn't know!" Kardas raised his voice.

"I had no time to go to those meetings," the farmer said, "I was sent to the forest to chop wood for the state. The women were forced to go to the meeting, but as soon as they got home they forgot the date of the elections. The entire time the meeting was taking place all they could think about was the piglets at home and whether they'd get stolen while they were gone."

"So much for that," Kardas said, "but now you'll have to vote."

The farmer bore his eyes into his bowl, as though searching for words in his soup that would get him out of this situation.

"Are our votes really that important to you?" he muttered. "They'll elect whoever they want without us. And we don't know the people we're voting for. We don't know who they are."

As the farmer was talking, I had been poking around the house. Suddenly I spotted an old woman—the farmer's mother—crouched inside a huge barrel in the other room. When she had seen the armed men enter the yard, she had been convinced they were coming to drag her to the polls, so she had concealed herself in this absurd and uncomfortable hiding place. It was all I could do to keep from laughing out loud.

Until now we had been speaking among ourselves in Russian. I now switched into Lithuanian and said:

"It's a tight squeeze in there, Auntie, let me help you out."

"You can speak Lithuanian?" the little old lady said, trembling, doing her best to climb out of the barrel. I led her into the main room. Her face was lined with tears. I proudly told my friends that she was avoiding the vote by hiding.

Seeing the tears in the poor old woman's eyes and sensing her fear, we resolved not to torment these people any longer. Smiling, Uosis and I unbuttoned our fur overcoats and revealed our Partisan badges.

"So tell me men, why did you have to scare us like that?" the old woman said, jumping towards Uosis and planting a joyful kiss on his cheek. "I was in such a rush to hide, I scraped my knee," she said. Then she called out, "Hey, old man, come on out!" She opened up the small metal door to the masonry stove and an old man came crawling out.

We all burst out laughing. The old man crawled out with his gray hair toussled and covered with soot. He was the farmer's father. He pointed at his son, still seated behind the table, and said:

"It's fine for him. If they try to force him to vote, he has an excuse. He can say, what's the rush, I've got until nightfall. Not so for us old folks. There's nothing left for us to do but hide in the hen house or the stove. You see, they told us that they were going to deliver the vote right to our doorstep. They said we don't need to make the trip to the polling station."

"I'm not going to vote in their election, the devil take them!" the old man continued, growing agitated. "I might die tomorrow and they're going to force me to sell my soul to the devil in my final hours! They'll never catch me! They can all take a trip to hell!" The old man was brushing the soot and ash off of his clothing as he talked.

"They've taken my life away from me as it is," the old man started up again. "There isn't even a scrap of rye bread left to eat. They found those devils themselves, let them vote for them themselves. What do they need us for?"

The room seemed more cheerful now that everyone was smiling.

"Come and join us as our guests," the farmer's wife said, "although we don't have much to give you. Well, we do have some warm beet soup. Jonas, do you have any ham left at all?"

The farmer's wife had remained quiet the entire time, but now she got up and motioned for us to sit down and eat. The farmer stood up and disappeared through the door. He returned with half a liter of vodka.

"Men, you've got to warm up. You look as though you've been outdoors all night. My wife and I didn't fall asleep until three. How could anyone possibly get any sleep with all that racket. Oh, but did you ever scare off those bums," the farmer said, rubbing his hands together, "you couldn't get them to come out today even if you tempted them with a piece of cake."

We took a few drinks with the farmer and then asked about today's elections. It turned out that not a single person from their village had voted yet. Although it was Sunday, no one had gone to church either. They were all afraid that along the way to church the Bolsheviks might grab them, drag them off to the polling stations, and force them to stick their hands into the voting boxes. Even the most devout Catholics had not gone to church today.

We thanked our host for his hospitality and his determination not to vote. Then we left for the edge of the forest to keep watch over the area. For a while, everything was quiet. The villagers remained at home, waiting. At about three o'clock some movement began. Tired of waiting for voters, the Communists began descending on the villages closest to their garrisons. Because the telephone lines had been cut, they could not receive instructions from headquarters and were acting on their own. Some of them had even brought the ballot boxes with them. However, they did not get many votes or voters. Most of the villagers fled for the forest when they saw them coming. Only the elderly and infirm remained indoors.

Towards evening we spotted three Bolsheviks driving down the road. They brought a bright red ballot box in their vehicle. We decided to observe the voting procedure. We saw that they were heading towards a local farm. We hurried for the farm. Kardas took cover behind a stack of firewood. Uosis and I hid inside the house. We were resolved to get rid of the Russians and their box if they tried to force the family to vote.

We had hardly settled into our hiding places when the election vehicle clattered into the yard with its three passengers. We asked the farmer to go outside into the yard and discuss the voting with them. An NKVD lieutenant leaped from the car and barked at the farmer in Russian:

"Well, farmer, how about voting?"

The farmer replied in Lithuanian that he was just on his way to the polling station to cast his vote. The Russian at first did not understand what he was saying. The farmer repeated what he had said and added hand gestures. Once the Russian understood his meaning, he surprised us by acting polite and satisfied with the farmer's reply. He turned, jumped into his car, and drove off to call on others. Kardas rushed to the window and shouted:

"Men, the ballot box is empty! It wouldn't pay to touch it. If we destroyed it now, the Russians could claim it was full and that the votes had been tallied."

We decided Kardas was right and considered our mission accomplished. We sat down to a friendly chat with our host as we waited for evening. As it grew dark, people began returning to their homes, figuring there was less of a chance that they would be dragged to the polls at night. We learned from the farmer that the Russians usually saved their most effective methods of coercion for the people who lived further away from the safe haven of the forests. Here, on the outskirts of the forest, they were not insistent. They were afraid of partisan retaliation. They satisfied themselves with making perfunctory inquiries and leaving it at that. As a result, the only Lithuanians who found themselves voting in such areas were the men hired to drive the Russians around the villages and then back to the polls. For them there was no escape. The only ones eager to vote were the Russian soldiers in the garrisons stationed in the vicinity of the polls.

Some of the electoral regions were attacked by the partisans during the day because the Bolsheviks in those areas entered the villages and tried to force the villagers to vote at gunpoint. Only along the edge of the forests or in other protected places were the partisans able to take advantageous positions, forcing the Russians to retreat back to the polling stations.

Commissions had been formed to manage the voting districts. The Communists made up these commissions from people who were loyal to them and from local residents. Notwithstanding their loyalty, out of fear or conviction some of the members of the commission hid on election day while others feigned illnesses, while others found excuses to leave the area.

The Election Results

Polling ceased at midnight when the votes had been counted. The troops at the polling stations had forced all the members of the electoral commission to vote and all the horse-cart drivers. The lucky ones managed to get themselves too drunk to vote or had disappeared. Only the garrison soldiers voted loyally.

Soon we had the election figures. We obtained them from members of the electoral commissions themselves. The figures were favorable to us. Our resistance operators had done their job. Within the confines of our detachment's activity, only two and a half percent of the eligible voters had turned out to vote. The number of people voting in all the localities where the Tauras District had been active represented only 17 percent of those eligible to vote. But the Tauras District was beaten by the Dzūkija District where only 12 percent of those eligible had cast their votes. In other parts of Lithuania the percentages were higher. This was particularly the case in those rural areas where Russian garrisons were stationed and in large cities like Vilnius or Kaunas where the political machinery was highly organized. On election day the city wards were canvassed by a brigade of "persuaders" who went around in groups of twos or threes to the homes of the people named on their lists. They began calling on people early in the morning. A little later in the day, they would show up again. Then, sometime during the afternoon, they would come around with ballot boxes, just to be absolutely certain that no one forgot his obligation to vote. Needless to say, many city dwellers were coerced into voting. In fact, the cities accounted for the majority of the votes cast. However, those votes had been obtained under duress.

Even so, according to the partisans' calculations, less than 40 percent of eligible voters in Lithuania had cast their votes.

The votes of the Russian garrisons were the only votes that had been cast voluntarily. If, from that total of 40 percent, one were to subtract the Russian garrisons' vote and their families' votes, which made up 12 to 13 percent of all eligible voters, all of whom voted at the expense of the Lithuanians, then only 27–28 percent of the Lithuanian population voted. This percent of voters did not equal the urban population of our cities. That meant that even in the cities, where the people had no partisans to defend them, people risked their freedom and well-being by not voting in this farce of an election.

The Bolsheviks published an announcement stating that over 96 percent of Lithuanians had voted.

As it turned out, the Bolsheviks collected about 27–28 percent of their vote by terrorizing the Lithuanians. They took this percentage and multiplied it a few times and announced to the world that the Lithuanian nation gave more than 96 percent of their vote to the Communist puppet candidates.

Searching the Forests and Villages

When the elections were over several partisans and I went to visit Ainis's[21] company. However, when we reached Ainis's region we found a real battle in progress. Soviet Interior Forces, which were here guarding the polling stations and forcing people to vote, had now merged into larger units up to 200 men and were hunting the partisans who had given them so much trouble during the elections. We had to wait until the enemy withdrew. Moreover, Ainis's company, numbering about 150 men, had split into smaller groups in order to keep safe.

One such small detachment of five resistance fighters was surrounded on a farm by 30 Russians. The partisans had only two machine guns. While defending themselves, they took down about 20 Russians. Then they ran out of ammunition and fresh forces arrived to help the Russians. Our men began to force their way out of the farm. Only one of them, Apinys,[22] made it out alive. Four died. Badly wounded, he managed to reach the forest, where he remained hidden in a bunker until dogs led the Russians to the spot. There were cartridges in the shelter, but Apinys could not defend himself. He was too weak. The Russians dragged him from the shelter alive and stabbed him to death with bayonets.

The other units managed to avoid battle with the Russians. After two days the Russians withdrew.

The Fate of the Proletariat

After the Russians retreated, we often left the edge of the forest to go see the liaison Girinis. It was rather easy to reach him. His dilapidated cottage was barely twenty steps from the edge of the forest. Near the pigsty stood a large pile of firewood that hid the approach from the forest completely. Besides, this "safe" house seemed rather safe. In general, the Bolsheviks believed and tried to convince their troops, that the partisans came from the upper classes. Because of this prejudice they often misjudged which local people were aiding the partisans. That's how it was with our Girinis. The Bolsheviks would pass by his decrepit cottage, which was practically sinking into the ground, and never guessed that this proletariat's home could be the liaison headquarters of the local partisan movement.

---

21 Pranas Kučinskas, 1913–1947. He joined the partisans in 1945. He quickly rose in the partisan ranks. He was betrayed and killed December 26, 1947.

22 Identity unknown.

Inside that cottage you would see a family that really deserved pity. Five small children circled around the crumbling stove. They were all pale as sheets, very thin, and dressed in patched clothing. They were always crying that they were hungry. There were two simple beds in the room nailed together from boards and a simple wooden table along the wall flanked by two long wooden benches. There was a dilapidated cupboard in the corner and a few shelves for food. There was no other furniture. Girinis stored his tools in one of the corners—his hammers, saws, carpenter's squares, and something wrapped in paper. Beyond the bed, on the wall, hung two axes and a few other tools. The cottage's windows were made out of various shards of glass glued or welded together. The clay walls were decorated with a few pictures of saints.

Once we talked and it turned out that this family had been newly formed just as Lithuania lost its independence. The husband and wife both had worked for local farmers as hired hands. Together they saved 1,500 lits and were able to purchase two and a quarter hectares of land. After they bought the land, they married, and planned to save more money to buy themselves a better house. When the Bolsheviks occupied Lithuania, they had 300 lits in the bank. When that money was converted into rubles, it lost its value almost completely. Daily life during the war became harder and harder. Their family grew and they needed more and more. It became nearly impossible to earn enough money even to buy bread, not to mention anything else. This current occupation had brought with it unbearable poverty. The farmers tried to work their land without hiring help. This was because for each hired worker they would have to pay the government about 3,000 rubles a year. It was dangerous for a worker to work secretly for a farmer because if they were caught not only would the farmer be punished, but the worker as well. Because of this it was very difficult for Girinis to find any work. Before, during his free time when he was not hiring himself out as a worker, he would build sledges, carts, feeding bins, clogs and other items out of wood. Now no one needed his handiwork. Everyone lived for that day only, using whatever they had, no matter what condition the equipment was in. They were afraid to buy anything new, lest the Bolsheviks take it away. Besides all that, a lot of his time was taken up by the forced labor—the orders to cut down lumber to work on road repairs and so on. The government paid him nothing for this sort of work. And so, a hunk of bread was hard to come by in this little cottage. During independence he could earn enough rye to feed his family for a month in two or three days, now it took ten days, and those ten days rarely came.

This is why often when we stopped in at Girinis's cottage we found his children clinging to his wife's dress, whining with hunger. Often we shared our own food with the children. The children grew so fond of us during our four day visit that afterwards their mother had a hard time dragging them away from the frozen windows, where they sat, gazing outside, waiting for the "bandits" to come.

From the Gymnasium to the Forest

We waited out the four days, and, once the Russians had withdrawn, we went to meet with the men of the company. It appeared that their numbers had grown too large. This complicated their ability to hold out throughout the winter. It was not easy for them to reduce their numbers because more and more victims of Communist terror were applying for admission into the partisan ranks. The influx of university students and students from the local gymnasiums and high schools into Ainis's company had increased dramatically. Among them was an entire class from a local high school. We reproached the company commander and demanded to know how he could admit so many inexperienced underage young people into his ranks. He confided in us that he no longer knew the exact number of young people who had joined. He explained that the class had arranged everything with a private in his company. They had killed the only *Komosol* (member of the Communist Youth League) in their class, got hold of a few weapons, and took off for the region of Ainis's company. When the company commander berated the private for inciting the students to join, the private explained that he had only been joking with them and had never dreamed that they would take his invitation to join the partisans seriously.

The private and the company commander spoke to the students and tried to convince them to go back to school and continue their education. But they were not about to budge. They argued that every day the NKVD took a friend or two from their midst and put them on mock trial and then added them to the deportation list to Siberia. "We can't just sit around waiting with our arms folded for our turn to come," one of them said.

I became better acquainted with the students and found them to be disciplined, orderly, conscientious, and as daring as seasoned partisans. We still tried to persuade them to return home, but in the end only three left.

The Ford and Studebaker Bonfire

After taking care of other matters, we returned to our headquarters. Along the way, we stopped at a number of liaison points. Everyone we met was talking about the success of the various operations against "the most democratic elections in the world." It appeared that the various company commanders had not wasted any time in submitting reports of their activities. Some of them were quite interesting. One good story was about how Dešinys had gone about "clearing" the road in the Prienai-Šilavotas sector. Several days before elections he took four machine guns and a number of men and chose a convenient spot in the Prienai pine forest. He monitored and inspected all passing vehicles, looking for those being used for "electioneering." Two partisans dressed in Russian uniforms were stationed on the road with field glasses. They scanned the terrain for any red cars with election placards. Whenever a "Red" car approached, the partisans would dash out of the bushes, stop the car, disarm the passengers, then push the car from the road and hide it in the forest. Within four hours seven cars on election business were stopped and all the men inside of them were disarmed without a shot being fired.

Only one car transporting a Red Army Major caused a problem. The Major refused to surrender easily. When his car was stopped, he leapt out and attempted to roll underneath it, clutching his pistol. The partisan Griausmas (Thunder)[23] yanked him back and slammed him up against the car's wheel with the barrel of his machine gun. The Major managed to let out only half a curse:

"Atchady, bla..."[24]

Audra (Storm)[25] jumped forwards and removed the Major's belt and pistol. Comrade Major begged for his belt, but Audra answered him with his own words:

"Atchady, bla..."

Two disarmed Red Army soldiers and a few NKVD regulars were standing near by. They began to laugh. One of them said:

"Because of that, Comrade Major has ten years in Siberia to look forward to."

The inferior confiscated weapons were tossed onto the partisans' campfire and burned. The superior weapons were appropriated by the partisans. After that, the partisans separated the Communist Party members from the regular Russians. They lined up the Communist Party members. After they were lined up, Dešinys gave the order to shoot. The first Communist Party member in the line was handed a weapon and told to shoot his comrades. As the executions took place, the regular Russians stood by, rubbing their hands with glee.

---

23 Klemensas Maceina (1923–1947). Maceina joined the Iron Wolf Regiment on April 28, 1945. He was decorated for valor. He was killed March 5, 1947.

24 Get away, bit...

25 Vincas Morkūnas (1925–1946) joined the partisan Viesulas's Unit in December 1944. He was killed September 6, 1946.

"For once, the bastards got what they deserved," one of them said.

The regular Russians were given three of the confiscated vehicles and sent on their way. The election placards were destroyed. The remaining four American automobiles—three Studebakers and one Ford—were drenched in gasoline and burned. It would have been impossible to hide them from the enemy.

The rest of the reports contained the particulars about methods of distributing the resistance press, about information for the citizenry, and interruption of Bolshevik communications.

The Deportations

After our mission of boycotting the elections, we spent some time at our main headquarters, affectionately called *Sėklyčia* (the Parlor).[26] We worked on various projects, one of these involving the publication of a new newspaper. We had turned *The Freedom Scout* over to the staff of a neighboring area unit shortly before we left, but had yet to see the appearance of a new issue. To fill the gap, we put out another newspaper, which we named *On the Road to Battle*[27] (Kovos Keliu). In order to confuse the enemy, we indicated the organization LAF[28] as the publisher of the newspaper. To honor our own regiment, we decorated the top of the first page of newspaper with an emblem of the Iron Wolf howling with the city of Vilnius and the hill of three crosses in the background.

We distributed *On the Road to Battle* not only in our own district, but also sent 100 copies to Dzūkija and the Žalgiris territory. We added a gift for the Dzūkija partisans—100 matrices for their press.

After delivering our newspaper to the distribution points, on the morning of February 17, 1946 we were engaged in collating the data of the electoral precincts

---

26 The Parlor was the main bunker of the Iron Wolf Regiment. Located on Kazys Varkala's farm (Varkala was the partisan Uosis's father and himself a former volunteer in independent Lithuania's army), headquarters consisted of four bunkers, one located under the cottage's floor boards, one in the shed, one under the woodpile, and one under a hill of gravel. Varkala had a code name and himself carried out dangerous secret missions for the partisans. His daughters, Janė and Kazimiera, also performed missions that required courage and integrity and acted as liaisons.

27 The Iron Wolf Regiment's newspaper. In October 1945, after the Soviet Interior Forces liquidated the district headquarters and the editorial offices of *The Freedom Scout*, the Iron Wolf Regiment leadership under the initiative of Juozas Lukša in the beginning of 1946 began publishing several more newspapers, such as *Kovos Keliu*, a new edition of *The Freedom Scout*. After the June 2–3 district leaderships congress it was decided to discontinue publishing *Kovos Keliu*. The circulation was 800. It was printed by rotary press.

28 LAF: Lietuvių aktyvistų frontas (The Lithuanian Activist Front). An anti-Soviet resistance organization that was founded in the summer of 1940 and which organized and enacted the June 23, 1941 revolt against the Soviet occupation. On June 28, the German occupying forces managed to disarm LAF and shut down their activities on September 22. The former members of LAF went on to organize several anti-Nazi resistance organizations.

for publication. As we were working, Rūta[29] ran into the room and informed us that there were Russians in the yard. We hastily gathered up our papers from the table, grabbed our weapons and made for the root cellar. As we were climbing down the stairs, we heard our host, the farmer, talking loudly in the doorway, in an attempt to stall the enemy from coming inside. Hardly had we managed to adjust the trapdoor, when we heard the footsteps of the Russians and the farmer in the kitchen above our heads. We were considering whether we should sneak through the emergency opening, in case the uninvited guests should decide to take it into their heads to conduct a search. But then we heard the Russians inquiring as to the name of the locality. From their polite tone we understood that they were not here to conduct a search but rather to gather information. For safety's sake, the farmer led them to the other end of the house. Rūta took advantage of the opportunity to report to us:

"Don't worry. It's only a few of the bosses. Most likely they consider Father one of their own. They're probably looking for someone in the neighborhood. They've brought a radio transmitter with them. They've opened up a map. It looks as though all the staff officers have descended upon us. There's one major, two captains, five lieutenants, and one shaggy non-commissioned radio operator. You ought not to get in each other's way. At night you can slip out and get away."

"Just our luck! Damn it! The bosses of the bosses," Uosis said and added a choice curse. Then he laughed, "Oh well, maybe it's better that way. The bosses are less argumentative."

Although we were not afraid of a search, we kept as quiet as possible under the floorboards until evening. You could never tell. The bosses might take it into their heads to steal something and ransack the cellar, hoping to find loot. If that were to happen, we'd have no choice but to kill one of them and maybe even one of us would be forced to take a trip to visit Abraham. As it turned out, that day we coexisted like perfect gentlemen. They didn't take any interest in us and we ignored them. After they got their bearings straight, they demanded the farmer bring them some home brew. As they were drinking and shuffling through their papers, our host noticed some sort of lists authorized by the head of the Prienas Soviet Security Services. The lists were backdated January 30th.

It was already late afternoon when this group of Soviet Security Officers decided that the farm's geographic location was not favorable enough to them and left.

---

29 Kazimiera Varkalaitė.

***

February 18th was a historic day for this region. It was a day of horror. All day long on the 17th large units of Soviet Security troops raged across southern Lithuania. There were so many troops present, that the partisan units were forced into hiding. On the 18th the mass deportations of civilians began. Only then did we understand the nature of the lists of names that the farmer had seen that day when the Soviet Security Officers entered his home. As it turned out, already at the end of January the Bolsheviks had put together the lists of names of people destined to be exiled to the concentration camps of Siberia. These lists of people were prepared by the Russians without interrogating any of the people or providing a trial. The lists had been drafted at the end of January. But because of tactical considerations—in order not to scare the people away from participating in the elections and reducing the physical numbers of voters—they decided to postpone the deportations until after the elections. Such a postponement had yet another advantage. The people would regard the deportation as punishment for the boycotted elections and pledge themselves in the future to put up with any kind of fraud. The lists of deportees were mainly made up of families who during the one and a half years of the Russian occupation had not yet been completely impoverished. These mass deportations would have begun in 1945 had the transport been available at the time. But at the time the transport was being used by the armed forces for carting away goods looted throughout various areas of Russian-occupied Germany. In 1946 the means of transport were more available and it was therefore possible to carry out the mass deportations.

The deportations were carried out much in the same way as in 1941. Trucks filled with NKVD and regular soldiers would drive up to a house or a farm. They would surround the house, burst in, conduct a search, and order the residents to prepare to leave. Very little time was given for preparations—a few minutes or a half hour at the very most.

The people would hardly know what to grab to take with them. They were terrified. All members of the family would be taken away, including the elderly and the infirm, pregnant women and infants. No regard was paid to the fact that it was winter and that these people were being exiled to an even colder climate. Many of the older women and more sensitive younger ones were so overwhelmed that they lacked the strength to climb into the trucks and would collapse in the snow. The elderly would beg the soldiers to finish them off on the spot, on the land where they had worked and suffered, rather than send them to a lingering death in the Russian hinterlands. Their requests were ignored. The people would be shoved unceremoniously into the trucks, which were already overcrowded. Terrified children would scream. Their mothers, unable to reach them, would cry out and wail. Infants would cry incessantly. The deportees were given less than fifteen minutes to pack their belongings. Then, these unfortunate people would be transported to the nearest railroad station. There the soldiers would yank their food and warm clothing away from them. The local Bolsheviks participated in this thievery. They'd toss the deportees a pile of useless rags in exchange for their coats and clothing.

During the deportations of 1941 the men had been separated from their families and could do nothing for them. The men had been sent to separate concentration camps where they quickly died of starvation or froze to death. Bitter experience had demonstrated that family units remained intact only as far as the train. Only infants were allowed to remain in the arms of their mothers. For this reason, if they could, the young and the strong tried to flee.

In 1941 the deportations had lasted three days. In 1946 they lasted much longer. People suffered terribly. Even those who were not deported suffered. Many who had gone into hiding soon proved unable to endure the hardships of the fugitive life. Exhausted by cold, hunger, and lack of sleep, they began drifting back to their homes. Of these people, only the ones whose names had not been on the proscribed list in the first place escaped deportation. The rest were rounded up and deported almost at once.

The mass deportations were among the cruelest episodes in the annals of the Soviet Union's undeclared war against Lithuania. At the same time, they constituted some of the vilest crimes against humanity. In a little less than ten days over 20,000[30] Lithuanian men and women and children were packed into cattle cars and shipped to unknown destinations in Siberia.

As these atrocities were being perpetrated, representatives of the Soviet Union were present at the Nüremberg Trials and were demanding the death penalty for Nazis who had been accused of exactly the same crimes. At that moment, somewhere far away in the West, conferences were held, toasts were raised for victory, for the Soviet allies, for the cynical murderers of our nation.

The free world made no protest on the deported people's account. Except for the partisan press, not a single newspaper in the West so much as mentioned the plight of the Lithuanian people.

---

30 The deportations described took place February 18–21, 1946. The exiled were collected from the towns of Alytus, Lazdijai, Marijampolė, and Tauragė. The deportation was directed against people who had participated in the partisan underground and against other "illegal" families. The order for the deportations was signed by the Soviet Security Officer J. Bartašiūnas on February 15, 1946. The list was began to be prepared in October 1945. According to available Soviet Security records 501 families were deported, a total of 2,082 people.

The partisans could do very little to stop the deportations. Their hearts were with the deportees, but their minds counseled prudence. For one, the number of Soviet troops carrying out the deportations was massive. The partisans were greatly outnumbered. Any partisan attack would have cost the lives of many innocent people. The Russians would have retaliated by shooting all the deportees on the spot and would have killed off the partisans.

Guarding Deserted Farmsteads

As a result of the deportations and continued arrests, many farms in Lithuania were left abandoned, derelict, without any supervision. The Communists set about destroying the farms. Buildings were demolished and their timber was used for firewood. Other building materials were transported to the towns to be used for the construction of jails, storehouses and other buildings. At the same time, the Russians appropriated whatever property remained on the farms. Sometimes the neighbors of the deported people did the appropriating. There were also people who took advantage of the situation to loot.

The partisan command took steps to protect the abandoned farms in their districts. Livestock and other property that required tending were turned over to the owners' relatives and the farms were frequently mined to ward off vandals. There were also notices posted in the vicinity stating that trespassing, vandalism, and looting were strictly prohibited. Anyone who ignored such notices would be punished.

A partisan who belonged to the Dešinys unit of the Iron Wolf Regiment noticed that his father's farm was being vandalized. To prevent further plundering, he mined the stables, the barns, the house, and the harness room. A few days later several Russians pulled up in a cart with the intention of knocking down the house and using it as fuel. Just as they moved through the gates, two anti-tank mines exploded. The explosion killed the horses and one of the Russians, wounding two others. The shocked survivors did not venture to enter the farm from another point. Instead, they collected their firewood from the Prienai Pine forest. Only a few weeks later, another group of Russians showed up. They must have forgotten what had happened to their comrades. They headed straight to the harness room to loot. They had barely entered the building before a concealed mine exploded, costing them their lives.

In this manner, the farms whose owners had been deported to Siberia were protected.

The Fighter Nastė

At the end of February the news reached us through the nurse, Dalia, in Viesulas's unit, that a few days previous our district fighter from Ainis's Unit, Erelis,[31] had returned to our district from Kaunas. In January, while fighting the Soviet Interior Forces in Živavodė, he had been wounded. The bones in the upper portion of his leg had been shot through. The partisans were not equipped to tend to a wound this serious. Therefore, they put together falsified documents and had him brought to the former Red Cross Hospital in Kaunas. Because the NKVD would routinely check the hospitals for partisans receiving secret medical assistance (they figured that hospital personnel would hide partisans and treat them in the hospitals) we had prepared a statement that Erelis had been kicked by a horse. After a few weeks of treatment, before his leg had mended in its cast, the NKVD managed to figure out, or at least suspect, that Erelis was in fact a partisan. The nurse, Nastė,[32] realized the danger he was in. She alone had been trusted with Erelis's secret. Not knowing which unit he actually belonged to, she resolved to secretly remove him from the hospital under the cover of darkness, bring him to her native region and hand him over to the unit in charge there.

Nastė's mission was completed successfully. During the day she found a farmer from her region and made an agreement with him to take Erelis away at night. It would have been impossible to remove him during the day because the NKVD remained on guard. She availed herself of the necessary documents, medical supplies, tools, and medications. She hurriedly stacked it all into the farmer's sledge and successfully made it to our district. At that time she also made the decision to leave her job at the hospital and to join our unit herself. Leaving the hospital with the wounded partisan meant that she could look forward to an NKVD trial, since the Soviet Security Officers knew that Erelis had disappeared with Nastė's help. The punishment for these kinds of acts was at least ten years hard labor in Siberia.

We helped replace the cast on Erelis's leg and sent a message to his unit that he was with us and would return to them once his leg had mended. The journey had weakened him considerably. In the end, Nastė brought a doctor[33] to replace the cast on his leg.

---

31 Juozas Prajara, 1921–1947. He joined the partisans in the spring of 1945. On January 6, 1947 he ran out of ammunition while surrounded in battle by Russians. Rather than giving himself up alive, he blew himself up with a grenade.

32 Anastasija Rinkevičiūtė, 1918–1946. She worked as a nurse at the Red Cross Hospital in Kaunas. From February, 1946, she fought as a partisan with the Iron Wolf Regiment's partisans. She was killed February 24, 1946.

33 Doctor Gedminaitė.

After two weeks under Nastė's care, Erelis was in much better condition. He was able to return to his unit. Nastė reached Ainis's unit and, accompanied by a few men, returned to retrieve Erelis. Near Plutiškės they were attacked at night by a group of Soviet Interior Forces. Nastė was killed in the fighting along with one other partisan.[34] In this battle Nastė proved that she could deftly handle a weapon. She fought bravely. She was adept not only in medicine and in her ability to plan and strategize, but also to fight. She was still seated in the sledge when she was wounded by machine gun fire in her legs. Unable to retreat, she fought from the sledge, wounding a Russian artillery man, who had climbed out of a ditch alongside the road and was attempting to cut off the partisans' escape route. By the time the partisans were able to organize their defense, it was too late to save Nastė's life. She was killed by a new round of machine gun fire.

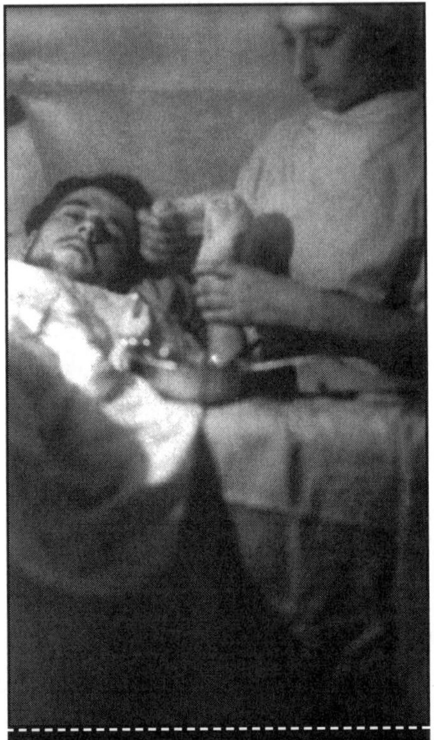

The support from the civilians, when it came to medical care, was crucial for the endurance of the armed resistance. On the picture the partisan Juozas Trakauskas-codename Jureivis (Sailor)-is treated for bullet wounds by Angelė Senkutė-codename Aušra (Dawn).

Blood for the Press

The Freedom Scout did not reach us for quite some time. We realized that we would have to satisfy ourselves with a newspaper that circulated only in our district. We had not received any orders from our regiment's leadership to publish *The Freedom Scout*, so we decided to prepare another issue of *On the Road to Battle*. At the same time, the district leader, Kardas, ordered me to take on the position of head of the district's Propaganda Committee. In reality, I had been handling the duties of that position since January.

34 Jonas Demikis.

I wanted to raise the quality of *On the Road to Battle.* I decided to increase the number of people working for the newspaper. I wanted to set up liaisons to handle news from abroad and to prepare a few people to report the current news and to write lead articles as well as secondary articles. Only the coordinator, the technical editor, the press liaison (who also took care of logistics) remained in the headquarters' propaganda office. This method of collecting, preparing, and distributing the news proved to be effective and functional. No one, besides Kardas, Uosis, Tautvydas, Miškinis, and I, knew where *On the Road to Battle* was printed and who was on its editorial team. We published up to 1,000 copies of the newspaper and in a single night delivered it to five liaison points. From there armed members of the resistance took the newspaper and distributed it according to their instructions. There was no danger that, in the event of the Bolsheviks intercepting the newspaper, they could trace it back to the place where it was actually printed.

At those same liaison points we would find materials provided by the district's units: paper, ink, rotary presses, and so on. We ordered every unit leader to have ready and in reserve radio equipment, a rotary press, and even underground bunkers prepared for the work of printing the newspaper. The unit that was the best prepared in this regard, received the largest number of newspapers from us. The need for the news grew and grew. We ran out of frames for our later issues. We would have to use two.

On March 19, while undergoing the duties of the Propaganda Committee, a fighter from out our regiment's headquarters, Kardas's brother, Miškinis, was killed. He had been given the mission of recovering two good radio transmitters and receivers and a rotary press that had been left behind by the retreating Germans and hidden among the local populace. He was undertaking the mission with two other partisans—Ąžuolas and Vėtra. The area where the objects were believed to be hidden was not far from Šilavotas, where there was a very strong Russian presence terrorizing the environs. As they were checking in on local people, they went to see Juozas Raguckas. They walked in on him and his neighbors celebrating his name day. These people invited the partisans to join the party. Just as they sat down at the holiday table the Bolsheviks surrounded the house because the civilians who were on guard duty did not notice them in time. They burst through the door and fired a round of machine gun fire. Miškinis was shot in the chest and collapsed on the front porch. Vėtra and Ąžuolas managed to escape through the back door. Miškinis's corpse burned inside the burning house. None of the people at the table or even his friends noticed the moment he had been killed because he alone had tried to escape through the front door.

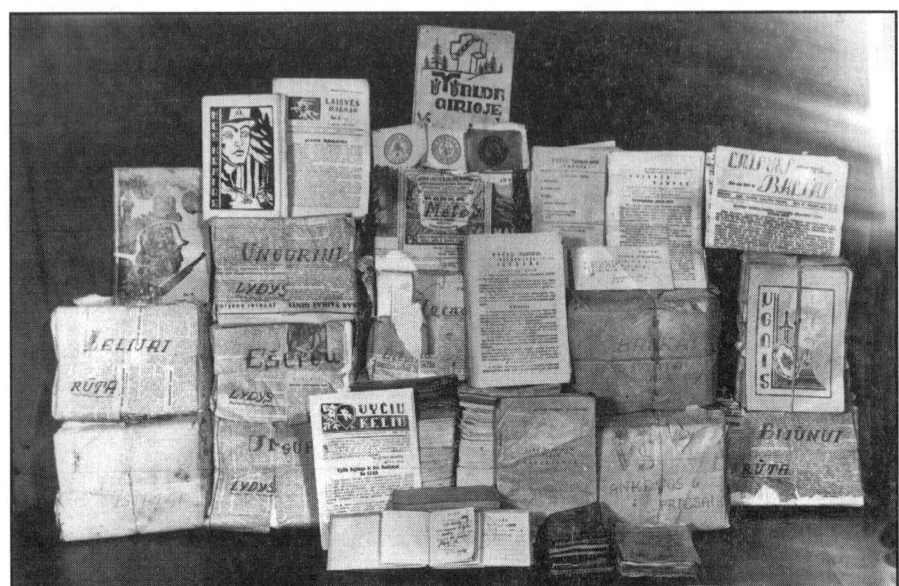

Over time the importance of propaganda and written materials increased. About 50 different newspapers were published during the period, together with flyers and other kinds of material.
The first picture on the opposite page shows the front page of the Freedom Scout, a newspaper edited by Juozas Lukša for a period of time. This issue is from the 2nd of February 1947.
Not only newspapers were published; the second picture shows the cover of a poetry book, with the ironic name "The Red Paradise."
Huge efforts were made to reveal the whereabouts of the places where the newspapers were produced. The Soviet Security would at times patiently wait for months to strike out against people involved in the underground press in order to pinpoint the source. The great number of confiscated issues from all over Lithuania on this picture gives an idea of the scale of the reaction. This was one of the most important means for the resistance to continue also after the end of the armed conflict, all the way to the end of the Soviet Union.

For a long time we did not actually believe that we would never see him again. A week later his sister went to clean up the ashes from the badly burned house and came across his bones. She recognized her brother's remains from the metal parts of his weapon and from the rosary she had given him as a gift. We had been hoping that perhaps he had been wounded and was recovering somewhere in secret. Losing him was tragic. He had been well-liked. We called him the Head Matchmaker as an ironic compliment.

In that issue of *On the Road to Battle* I wrote: "Dear Lithuanian, treasure the underground press, for it is paid for in blood."

LIETUVIAMS

LAISVĖS ŽVALGAS

1947 II 20 | TAURO APYGARDOS L L KOV. ORGANAS | Nr 5(50)

Bolševikinių "rinkimų" tiesa.

S.m. Vasario mėn. 13 d. bolševikinė spauda ir radijo paskelbė "rinkimų" į LTSR aukščiausiąją tarybą rezultatus. Pasak tuos pranešimus rinkimuose į tarybą dalyvavo 97,31 procentų rinkėjų. Iš šių sufabrikuotų "laisvų ir demokratinių" rinkimų bolševikai pasidarė "didelę pergalę". Tačiau kiekvienas, kas sekė rinkimų eigą, matė ir žino, kad Lietuvos kaimas, kuris sudaro virš 80 procentų gyventojų, visiškai boikotavo šiuos rinkimus. Numatydami tokį rinkimų boikotavimą, rusai sutraukė į kaimus apie 100000 kariuomenės, kurią panaudojo rinkimams. Kadangi kiekvienoje smulkesnėje rinkiminėje apylinkėje buvo apie 20-30 ginkluotų kareivių, tai jie, nesulaukę balsuotojų rinkiminėse apylinkėse, vaikščiojo po ūkius versdami gyventojus balsuoti. Esant dideliems šalčiams ir norėdami rinkimus "paspartinti", kareiviai patys įmesdavo biuletenius į urnas. Atsisakantiems balsuoti buvo grasinama išvežti, buvo atiminėjami pasai bei kiti dokumentai. Tačiau ir tie priversti balsuotojai metė biuletenius, išbraukdami atstovų pavardes. Nežiūrint didelio skaičiaus kaimo ir miesto gyventojų, kurie boikotavo rinkimus, bolševikai paskelbė, kad visi įstatyti kandidatai į deputatus buvo išrinkti.

Dabar kyla pats svarbiausias klausimas, ką bolševikai išstatė ir "išrinko" į LTSR aukščiausiąją tarybą. Iš paskelbtų sąrašų aiškėja, kad iš bendro 180 atstovų skaičiaus 1/4 yra rusai. Bet ar jie yra bent Lietuvos rusai? Ne. Tai atsiųsti iš Maskvos lietuvių tautos smaugikai; įvairūs įgulų generolai, NKVD, NKGB viršininkai ir Maskvos bolševikai. Imant atskirose apskrityse ir miestuose rusų skaičius yra dar didesnis. Štai Vilniaus mieste iš 13-kos išrinktų atstovų keturi /4/ yra rusai, Kauno mieste iš 12-kos atstovų – 4 rusai, Vilniaus apskrityje iš 8 išrinktų atstovų – 7 rusai, Švenčionių apskrityje iš 6 atstovų – 4 rusai, Trakų apskrityje iš 5 atstovų – 4 rusai ir t.t. Pagal Lietuvos gyventojų statistiką rusai Lietuvoje niekad nesudarė trijų pilnų procentų; tuo tarpu dabartinės okupacijos metu rusai pravedė daugiau kaip 25 procentus atstovų. Turint galvoje, kad išrinkti lietuviai atstovai yra skirti tik reklamai ir propagandai, nes jie neturės jokios sprendžiamos reikšmės, rusai, Maskvos įsakomi, tvarkys ir atstovaus Lietuvos reikalus. Ar reikia iškalbingesnių argumentų už vadavą Lietuvoje lietuvių išskyrimą nuo valstybinių reikalų! Visiems lietuviams yra aiškūs rusų užsimojimai. Tačiau ir visas pasaulis gerai žino, kad joks lietuvių valios klastojimas nebus užskaitytas rusų naudai. Ateis valanda, kada Lietuva galės pareikšti, nežudoma rusų ginklų, savo tikrąją valią – būti N e p r i k l a u s o m a.

A Prohibition on Home Brew

Alcohol was the Bolshevik's best friend and the executor of all its plans. It was impossible to imagine a Soviet official without a bottle of vodka in hand. Drunkenness knew no bounds. People drank at work, at home, and in the streets. Vodka was regarded as the most suitable and valuable bribe for taking care of business in official Soviet offices. Almost every Russian subsisted from nothing more than a bit of dry bread, but he had to have his vodka.

Often the Bolsheviks were crueler to the citizenry when they were drunk. When they were drunk, they lost all sense of morals or conscience or even fear. They robbed and they killed while drunk. And there were many opportunities to get drunk.

The local people also drank a lot. For one, they drank because they were disappointed with life. Secondly, they drank because they had grown accustomed to drinking with Soviet officials. There was no way to say no when a Bolshevik demanded that you drink with him. Besides, many people had begun drinking during the German occupation. And when people drink, they talk. They often completely forgot the instructions the partisans had given them and they complained far too much about how unhappy they were under the Soviet system, no longer paying attention to the fact that among the drinkers there were informers. And sometimes, even knowing the NKVD system, they would talk, just to vent their anger. Because of that many of them ended up in Siberia.

The partisans suffered because of alcohol also. Often the civilians would be too kind to the partisans and would give them too much to drink. Sometimes the result was that the partisans became less careful, or too bold.

Because farmers produced home brew on such a large scale, it resulted in hunger for the people. Home brew was produced mostly from rye, which was badly needed for bread.

For all these reasons, the partisans decided to take action against the production of alcohol and its use. In our region we began by writing about all the disastrous effects of alcohol in *On the Road to Battle*. However, these methods proved futile. There was real reason to begin looking for better methods.

Therefore, the commander of the Iron Wolf Regiment was forced to issue two orders, effective as of April 15th, 1946. One of them made it a crime for farmers to either manufacture vodka or to drink it to excess. The other prohibited partisans from accepting alcohol from any farmer. The penalty for violating these prohibitions was a fine of 1,000 rubles or its equivalent. The order went into effect on April 15th.

The example of the battle with alcohol in the Iron Wolf Regiment was endorsed by the entire Tauras district and neighboring partisan districts.

As it happened, on the evening of April 15, Kardas, Uosis, Tautvydas, and I prepared for another trip, this time to visit the Šiaurys Unit. We were to be led by Tabokius. Passing through the village of Šidiškis, a few hundred meters away from a farmstead, we heard some noise coming from the house. We heard a woman crying out and a man shouting in a threatening tone, then we heard glass breaking. We thought that the Russians must be robbing the place because we could not make out which language the shouts were in. We broke up into pairs and surrounded the house from both sides.

We were surprised to find, instead of looting Russians, two drunk civilians fighting each other with bricks. They had managed to smash out all the windows in the farm house. They fought near the fence as the women looked on, screaming.

We herded the drunk men into the room and ordered them to sober up immediately and to pay the fine for drinking. In a fearful tone, they explained that of course they had intended to honor the order, but in their rush to finish off the remainder of their home brew, they had drank their way past midnight and now hardly realized what time it was. Tautvydas entered the kitchen and found their stash. In the corner they had set up their equipment and were mixing up a new batch of home brew. Barrels of home brew stood in the corners of the room.

Tautvydas and Uosis turned over all the barrels and emptied their contents onto the floor. They took apart the equipment and brought the hoses and pipes into the front room. They broke everything in front of the drunks' eyes and asked the toughest of the men to destroy the distiller by himself. He proved that he could not only smash heads in, but beat up a distiller as well.

Both the men had to apologize to each other, pay for the damage they had done to their host's home, and kiss each other good-bye.

"We passed that law ourselves, and now we were the first to test it," Kardas mused as we walked along the road.

Desecrating Fallen Partisans

During the spring the Bolsheviks began terrorizing the people and intensifying their control. The reason was the NKVD General Bartašiūnas's order, announced on February 15, 1946. The long winter and the fact that snow remained on the ground did not allow the partisans to change their old bunkers for new ones. Almost every day we would hear about the increasing number of partisan skirmishes with the Soviet Interior Forces. Almost always they ended in bloodshed. The Bolsheviks

Rarely were the partisans and the families of partisans able to properly lay their dead to rest. This photo depicts a partisan funeral.

Women mourn a dead partisan

were furious with the partisans' persistence and stubbornness. Because they had not yet defeated the partisans, they came up with more and more cruel methods. Up until this time the Soviet Interior Forces had not removed the partisan remains from the battle sites. They were satisfied with collecting their own dead. This year it was as though they had come upon a new gruesome method of fighting the partisans. When the partisans had to quickly retreat, leaving their dead behind, the Soviet Interior Forces would gather the bodies and desecrate them in the local town market squares. They believed that the brutalization of partisan remains would discourage new people from joining the partisan ranks.

At the end of the winter several dozen Soviet Interior Forces in the Garliava region (near Juodgiria) attacked a group of 14 men from Viesulas's Unit led by Žvangutis.[35] The partisans managed to kill 23 Bolsheviks. Then they broke through the circle surrounding them and retreated, leaving their leader Žvangutis behind and six dead fighters.[36] The Bolsheviks gathered up all the bodies and brought them to the town of Garliava. In the town square they propped up Žvangutis's

35 Antanas Juodsnukis, ?–1946. He was a partisan in the Iron Wolf Regiment from March 15, 1945. He was killed on the night of March 10–11, 1946.

36 Among the dead were: Aloyzas Maceika, Kazys Maceika, Antanas Juodsnukis, Antanas Rakauskas, Alfonsas Dobkevičius.

corpse against a wall, using boards to hold him up, and shoved a water pipe into his open mouth. They set up the rest of the corpses in a semi-circle around him, as though a meeting were being held. The Bolsheviks required every active member of the Communist party to go to the town square and to release their anger on the corpses by kicking them and beating them with clubs.

Some of them shouted, "And now go ahead and take advantage of the proletariat!"

The corpses were set up in such a place that they could be easily monitored from the NKVD's windows. If they saw people passing by the corpses who revealed sadness or pity, they would go out and arrest them and torture them, demanding that they reveal the names and surnames of the dead men. The citizens could not reveal the dead men's names because they were not from that area. But they could mourn them as unknown fighters.

At the same time the Bolsheviks began a campaign of destroying the graves of partisans, scattered across the country near forests, in the forests, and even out in the meadows. These graves were tended and decorated by civilians and partisans both. Every spring flowers were planted on the graves and watered by the tears of young Lithuanian women or by the falling rain. Every region was proud of the care it took of the partisans' graves.

If possible, the partisans were buried properly and the graves looked after. Two girls attend to a grave in the Tauras military district, summer 1949. A large part of the remains of the fallen partisans have, however, never been retrieved.

Undoubtedly, the nationalism expressed by the care taken for the graves, decorated with national flags, symbols, and flowers, infuriated the occupiers. They began breaking down the fences surrounding the graves, tearing down the crosses, and hacking apart the headstones.

On the edge of the Klebiškis forest on the way to Šidiškės were seven partisan graves. The good people of the local area had built handsome fences around the graves, had crafted lovely gravestones, and had set up identical crosses for all seven. They planted moss and flowers in the shape of the Lithuanian coat of arms and in other Lithuanian symbols on the graves.

The Soviet Interior Forces found these graves and destroyed them. The local unit leader Papartis (Fern) swore to get even. Papartis and his men restored the fence, the graves, the crosses, and the national symbols created out of flowers and moss. To prevent the graves from being desecrated again, the area was mined and a warning written in both Lithuanian and Russian was posted on the newly constructed fence. It should have kept all but the blindest fanatics away, but it didn't. A few weeks later a gang of Russians showed up and went to work. As they were tearing down the fence, a mine went off, wounding three of them and sending the others running for cover. But this did not discourage them. They entrenched themselves in a ditch not far from the graves and attempted to finish their job by tossing grenades at the graves.

This manner of desecration of graves took place all over the country. In some places the Soviet Interior Forces themselves destroyed the graves, while in others they ordered foresters to do their dirty work or intimidated the people on whose land the graves stood.

The Right to Choose Work

In 1944 many Lithuanian farm workers had taken work in various wartime industries, hoping by this means to avoid recruitment into the Red Army. Because of the system, the pay for the work was very poor. They were required to work ten hour days, while their monthly pay, after subtracting fees and taxes, was only 170 rubles—or the price of a kilogram and a half of butter. They managed to survive only with the help of food parcels from their families and the hope that things would get better after the war. But, by 1946, the war had been over for more than a year and the situation showed no sign of improvement. Tired of starvation, many of them returned to their villages where they hoped to subsist by cultivating their own plots. But they had forgotten that they were no longer living in a free Lithuania. If the Soviet Union protected the rights of the working man, it did so only in theory. In practice things were quite different.

The NKVD decided that these working men were saboteurs and began rounding them up. Scores of them were arrested and sentenced to ten years of imprisonment in concentration camps. The rest headed for the forest and joined the partisan ranks. At the same time the agricultural industry in Lithuania began to suffer from a shortage of manpower, even during this "springtime of peace."

Uniting the Partisans

The first organizational steps taken by the Tauras District from its founding on August 25, 1945, were undermined by the number of arrests that autumn. Only the enthusiasm of the new district leader, Mykolas Jonas, managed to keep the district's morale high, winning more and more organizational gains. The Samogitian region partisans first contacted the Tauras District, founding the Kęstutis District. Then the Dzūkai founded the Dainava District. The other regions organized themselves in Lithuania more slowly.

Through the liaison-girl Rasa[37] we received documents from the Samogitian leadership in which they described the advantages of organizing into a district and in which they updated us on their future plans. In their letter they invited the various districts to form one large organization under one command and thus centralize partisan activity throughout Lithuania.

During the meeting the statute of the Southern Lithuanian partisans was published and the basic structure of a future Lithuanian government was put together by the Supreme Committee for the Liberation of Lithuania. This meeting and its resolutions were published in partisan newspapers all over southern Lithuania.

At the same time Kazimieraitis took on the responsibility of establishing ties with the partisans of the Aukštaitija region. Mykolas Jonas took on the task of working with the Samogitian partisans.

The documents delivered by Rasa from the Samogitian partisans made Mykolas Jonas's mission so much simpler. They had already shown the initiative to unite. He immediately answered their letter, not as the leader of the Tauras District, but as the assistant to the leader of the entire region of southern Lithuania, offering to meet in the near future on the shores of the Nemunas River.

While engrossed in this work spring arrived and nature burst into full bloom. Our district leader released a statement in which he encouraged all the partisan fighters to become more prayerful and to ask for God's blessing in our bloody battle for our homeland and for eternal peace for our dead brothers-in-arms. At the same time he encouraged the unit leaders to restore the graves that had been desecrated by the Bolsheviks and to look after their upkeep.

However, no one could tend to the fresh graves that had appeared in the town dumps, the ditches, or in the swamps. All we could do to honor those graves was

---

37 Nina Naudėsaitė, 1924–2004. She was a technical student at Kaunas University. In 1945 she joined the resistance. She became the head liaison woman between the Tauras, Kęstutis, and Vytis Districts. On February 25, 1947 she was arrested by the NKVD. She was tortured in the NKVD prison in Vilnius. On December 6 she was sentenced to 10 years hard labor in Siberia. She returned to Lithuania in 1956.

to register the areas, note the code names of the partisans buried there, and convey the news to their relatives.

At that time, in the first May issue of *On the Road to Battle* Mykolas Jonas was given space on the front page for an article he wrote honoring Mother's Day. The mothers of Lithuania deserved the most honor and respect in this fight for freedom because in their hearts they bore the most pain.

Evaluating Our Activities

When the district leader visited our unit, he ordered all the officers and unit leaders to prepare reports on that year's activities. We were told that the reports would be presented at a meeting in which the district leader would participate. He would evaluate their work. The meeting was scheduled for May 1, 1946, in the Prienai forest.

A summary of the year's [1946] activities were as follows:

Seventy-two partisan fighters died in the Tauras District that year. The number of enemy dead, including the local Communists and criminals, was five times that.[38] That the year the district had lost 90 weapons, among them several dozen light machine guns. Much attention was paid to the numbers of civilians dead as a result of the fighting.

The Committee for Social Assistance had not been developed as much as it should have been. The number of people needing assistance was growing. This was an area that needed development. The people working in this committee were encouraged to take personal initiatives to collect more funds.

The Medical Committee received praise. During the year 59 fighters, with both serious and minor wounds, had been treated. The nurses had enough medicine and bandages. The only thing they lacked was sufficient hidden bunkers in which to nurse the wounded back to health.

The Reconnaissance Committee was found to be satisfactory.

I could account for the Propaganda and Press Committee only from January 1st when I had begun my duties there. Five thousand five hundred newspapers had been printed (*The Freedom Scout* and *On the Road to Battle*). About 4,000 proclamations had been printed and about 2,000 political cartoons. We were criticized for lacking analysis on developing political ideals. The Propaganda Committee

---

[38] Because the occupying administration carefully hid its losses, even after large battles the reported dead numbered no more than one or two wounded. Therefore, in terms of historical analysis, the partisan count may actually be more historically accurate.

had two reserve methods of publishing the newspaper and was well stocked with paper and other materials.

The Administrative Committee was found to be lacking. They had not made up lists naming all the fallen fighters; lists of the individuals exiled to Siberia, nor had they listed the farmsteads that had been destroyed by the Bolsheviks.

The district leader evaluated our committee's work as positive. We had done better than some of the neighboring units. The number of people who had voted in the elections in our area of operation was not only the lowest in the Tauras District, but in all of Lithuania. That was achieved by initiating a boycott and by the intense pre-election press encouraging the citizenry to resist the Bolsheviks and by raising the citizenry's political awareness.

It was almost evening by the time we finished delivering our reports. The unit commander, Dešinys, noted that his own report was not yet complete because at the very last minute his liaison had given him the news that at five o'clock seven men had killed eight Communists from Prienai who had been collecting money from the local citizenry.

At first, rank-and-file civilians were recruited by the Communist party to act as collection agents among the farmers. It was not difficult for the partisans to deal with them. In the evening they would simply take away any money the collection agents had collected during the day and return it to the farmers. They would also destroy all records of the farmers' obligations. Once the Russians became aware of these partisan tactics, they turned the job over to the NKVD. They would descend on the farmsteads and villages in carloads, often making it impossible for the partisans to protect the people without engaging in battle.

Dešinys's unit took on the NKVD when they became too brazen about fleecing the local populace. Partisan Jungas and six others were selected to set an example. Armed with three machine guns and various other automatic weapons, the partisans opened fire when the collectors were within approximately fifty yards of the Maciūnai Hill. After a few minutes, only one NKVD remained alive. On that occasion the partisans not only carried out their mission successfully, but also acquired eight automatic weapons and a long list of obligation records and a considerable sum of money.

After the battle the partisans had to retreat quickly because they heard machine gun fire in the distance. Two Soviet Security Force Units, a total of 60 men, were hurrying over from Prienai. Only they were too late. The partisans retreated to the Kozeris forest. They could not hide in the Prienai forest because they knew that we were having our meeting there. In the village of Mogiškis 30 Russian units

Over time the resistance–literally–went underground. All over the country the partisans dug a huge number of bunkers, in all kinds of locations. These bunkers were often extremely difficult to find without some information of their whereabouts.

blocked their path, but after an engagement with the partisans, they retreated and lost their will to approach further.

When our meeting ended, men from Tabokius's unit brought in guests from the Dainava District. The men from the Dzūkija region, Labutis, Aras, and Tauras, were given the task of establishing better ties with us. We spoke for a half hour with our guests and then we ended our meeting with a prayer. Most of the people present at the meeting hurried off before it grew dark, so that they could begin the long march home to their districts. Other guests spent the entire night with us.

Building the Bunker

The following day Mykolas Jonas, Kardas, Uosis, Tigras, Tautvydas, Skirgaila, Gegužis,[39] Vabalas[40] and I began building a bunker in Prienšilis for us to work in. We chose a spot, collected tools, enough food to last us a few days, and got to work. The weaker men were assigned the easier work—guard duty and cooking.

39 Juozas Gelčys, 1922–1946. He was killed in a bunker on September 4, 1946.

40 Antanas Aglinskas, 1924–1946. He was a former school teacher who joined the partisans in 1945. He died on September 4, 1946, in a bunker.

The drawings show Soviet Security drawings of revealed bunkers, in a ridge in the forest and in a well at a farm.

On the third day the bunker was completed. It was three meters long, two meters across, and two meters high. There were two long openings to be used as exits. The top was so well concealed that we could barely see it ourselves. Inside we built bunks, racks for our guns, shelves for the radio equipment, files, printing equipment and other supplies.

The picture shows partisans and supporters digging a bunker inside a house.

Civilians provided support to the partisans, assisting them with food and shelter and providing liaisons. This photo shows a system used to quickly remove dirt and dig a bunker under the floorboards of a cottage. Partisans Vėtra, Neptūnas, and commander of the Tauras District Aleksandras Grybinas-Faustas are shown working to dig this bunker. Photo taken June 2, 1946 in Užnemunis.

Once we had completed our work, we closed off the openings and experimented with our weapons. It turned out that in terms of noise we could not have done better. Vabalas's machine gun fire could barely be heard a hundred meters away.

As we were leaving Prienšilis we ran into Anbo.[41] He delivered some sad news. The previous night in a battle with the Soviet Interior Forces from Šilavotas, Tabokius had been killed. He was the fifth member of the Senavaitis family to die in battle. His sister Marytė has been killed and his brothers Šiaurys, Zuikis,[42] and Rainis.

Again on Unification

On May 18th the representative Juozas Albinas Markulis, code name Erelis (Eagle)[43] came to our district to meet with Mykolas Jonas. We chose a meeting place in a forest in an area that was difficult to reach because it was surrounded on all sides by swamps. By the time we reached the meeting place we were all soaked to our knees because there was no dry path to get there.

---

41 Jonas Bulota, 1917–1947. He was a pilot in the Lithuanian army. He joined the partisans in 1944. He was betrayed and killed September 24, 1947.

42 Kazimieras Senavaitis, 1928–1946.

43 It later turned out that Markulis was acting as a double agent for the NKVD. Juozas Lukša, who worked closely with Markulis from Vilnius to set up a meeting of Lithuania's partisan leaders, realized that Markulis was a traitor in time to stop the meeting from taking place, saving the lives of all the partisan leaders who would have been present.

During the meeting Markulis explained to us that he represented what remained of the Unification Committee and some of the partisan units in the Aukštaityja region. He told us that the purpose of his visit was to make contact with the partisans of southern Lithuania to unify all the partisans under one leadership. He also informed us of the international situation and his organization's concern that we ought to look for new methods of continuing the resistance as it would be difficult for the partisans to hold their own during the summer. He talked about new opportunities to establish ties with the West and about the possibility of receiving material aid from the West. He informed us of the partisan situation in Aukštaityja and told us that they wanted to join forces with us and to exchange fighters, weapons, and ammunition with us. He also informed us of the situation in neighboring Poland and Belarus.

Mykolas Jonas informed Markulis in the name of the partisans of southern Lithuania of what activities had taken place and what on-going organizational work we were engaged in. He also told him about the obstacles we faced. He explained our position on our southern and eastern neighbors. Kardas gave a report on partisan military activities.

On both sides the need for absolute unification under one leadership was obvious. We agreed to maintain strong ties and to work towards this goal. We decided to move towards this goal quickly so that the armed resistance would not suffer too many losses throughout the summer before we received the necessary assistance we expected from the West.

Markulis, Mykolas Jonas, Skirgaila, Skirmantas, Tautvydas, Kairys, Laimutė, Gegužis, Tigras, Vabalas and I participated in the meeting. We put together minutes of the meeting and then accompanied our guest on his journey home, passing on greetings to our fellow brothers-in-arms.

A few days later we meet with Kirvis (Axe) a liaison leader from the central Lithuanian partisans. He asked that we help them put together their own district or that we accept them into the Tauras District. We instructed him on which units he should confer with. For the time being, we suggested that we satisfy his request by providing him with underground newspapers.

Two Visitors from the West

On May 25th Mykolas Jonas received a message through Skirmantas's unit that two Lithuanian men from the expatriate underground had arrived and were in contact with Vampyras. They were Jonas Deksnys and Vytautas Stanevičius-Staneika. Mykolas Jonas gave the order to bring them to our camp.[44] From the message we knew that one of the two men, Deksnys, had been in Lithuania six months ago. He went by the code name Daunoras.

We took care of liaison matters and expected our guests' arrival on the night of May 26. It was the feast day of Šeštinės. After a mid-day prayer, we had lunch, and were resting in the sun in small groups. At camp there was: Mykolas Jonas, Uosis, Tigras, Vabalas, Gegužis, Arminas,[45] Durtuvas, Dėdė[46] and myself.

At about two o'clock one of our liaison men[47] arrived at camp and informed us that Soviet Interior Forces units had shown up at several farms neighboring the forest where we were meeting. We had no idea why they had shown up, but Mykolas Jonas gave the order to immediately evacuate the camp and prepare for battle. We thought about it some more and came to the conclusion that perhaps our camp had been discovered since we had been camping here already for several weeks. We quickly began hiding the valuables, which we would not be able to carry with us in the event of a battle. We hid our typewriters, our paper, printing plates, and oil for the rotary press. We covered the paths that led to the camp as best we could and retreated a few hundred meters away. When we reached the deep forest we stopped. Some of us slept, others played cards. Mykolas Jonas and I discussed our concerns.

About fifteen minutes walk from our camp we saw a rabbit bounding through the forest. Dėdė, who knew animal behavior well, grew suspicious. He said that a rabbit never moves out of its den in the forest during the day unless someone frightens him out of it. The rabbit had been frightened out of his den somewhere in the area around our camp. Dėdė took his gun and walked towards the camp. As we watched, he quickly turned around and ran back. When he reached us, he whispered that our camp was already swarming with soldiers.

He had barely finished telling us what he had seen when I spotted a tall Central Asian man about thirty meters away, pointing his submachine gun in our direction. That was the right wing of the Soviet Interior Forces that had surrounded our camp. The Russians had not noticed us yet. I put the Central Asian in my sights and asked Mykolas Jonas if I should fire or wait for a command. He gave no answer. He took aim with his submachine gun and fired. I also took off my safety and fired. The Central Asian fell backwards like a post, dropping his

44 The camp was located in the Mozūriškis forest, not far from the village of Juodbūdis.

45 Antanas Lukša, the one surviving brother of Juozas Lukša.

46 Juozas Išganaitis, 1921–1949. He joined the partisans in 1945. He was betrayed and killed February 13, 1949.

47 Vincas Lukša.

weapon. Tigras followed suit, cutting down another soldier. Our fighters, who had fallen asleep, woke up to the sound of our weapons. There was no need for commands. The Russians fired back immediately. Their fire was concentrated from two machine guns, one *sturmovik* and three submachine guns. We shot at the Russian front and slowly began to retreat, keeping up our gunfire. The Bolsheviks had had enough of a fight and rather than pursue us, they collected their dead and retreated back to the edge of the forest.

We had no losses with the exception of one backpack in which there were several hundred sheets of paper for the press and 3,500 rubles in donations for the newspaper. The Russians did not find any of our hidden things in the camp except for one soup pot with some left-over soup in it. They finished off the soup and afterwards shot up the pot. They tore up all the tree stumps around the camp, poked through the moss, and turned over some trees. They had no luck.

We found a new place to meet with our guests in Skirmantas's region.

On the morning of the 27th, after we had checked the trustworthiness of our guests, we began our meeting. With the arrival of Daunoras[48] and Lokys[49] (Bear) the question of how we would maintain links with the West was solved. This spring's efforts to unify all of Lithuania's partisan forces under one leadership coincided nicely with the new ties we established to the West through our guests. All it would take now was work to coordinate everything.

From Daunoras's and Lokys's lips our district heard for the first time direct news from the West. Their reports were pessimistic. It appeared that the conscience of the West was taking its sweet time waking up to our problems. We had come to the conclusion that the genocide taking place in the Baltic States did not concern the West and that it would take a long time before we were free again. In the meantime, there would continue to be bloodshed—something we really did not want.

We talked until evening. Daunoras, Lokys, Mykolas Jonas, Kardas, Uosis, Žalgiris, Tigras and I participated in the discussions.

---

48 Jonas Deksnys.

49 Vytautas Stanevičius-Staneika, 1913–1977. He was a lieutenant in the Lithuanian army. In 1943 he was arrested by the Nazis for his work in the anti-Nazi underground and brought to the Stuthof concentration camp. In 1945, the Russians liberated the camp and he was conscripted into the Red Army. As the train was bringing troops through Poland he escaped out the train window and went into hiding. In January, 1946, he crossed the border into the English-occupied zone. In May, 1947, with Jonas Deksnys he secretly crossed the border into Soviet-occupied Lithuania. He participated in meetings with the partisan leadership. On the night of June 26, 1947, along with his wife, Jūratė, he was brought over the border to Poland by the partisans. He found refuge in Sweden and there worked for Lithuanian underground organizations. He emigrated to the United States in 1953 where he edited various Lithuanian émigré newspapers. He died in 1977. He was fiercely loyal and trustworthy, and politically active until the end of his life.

In the evening Mykolas Jonas and Kardas rushed out to a meeting of the leadership at headquarters, leaving the guests under my and Uosis's protection.

The Trip Through the Cleansing Operation

In the second half of May, 1946, our scouts told us that very large formations of Soviet Interior Forces were assembling within our district's territory. It was clear to us that these were the first units to begin the massive manhunts—a Bolshevik tactic that we were now well familiar with. Only, we did not expect them this early this year. It turned out that the group we had engaged after we had evacuated our camp were scouts for these formations. They used tactics similar to those of the partisans. They moved along the edges of the forest in units of several dozen men, carrying large supplies of ammunition with them, searching for the partisans, trying to find their hiding place. These wandering units were not attached to the local Soviet Interior troops. They ate at people's farms and often slept in the forest at night.

Over thirty men from our camp were prepared for action because, according to the information we had received from our liaisons, the edges of the forests were crawling with mobile Interior units. At one time we had even been engaged in battle and had held our positions for a full hour. Our guests Daunoras and Lokys joined us in battle, armed only with pistols. During the day there was no line of retreat out of the forest, so we decided to risk staying in the forest, hoping to go unnoticed. Our forest butted up against Šilavotas where there was a detachment of several hundred Soviet Interior Forces, but that did not worry us. The partisans were accustomed to keeping their camps right under the very noses of the NKVD. In these instances there was less fighting. The partisans were more cautious and the Bolsheviks never even imagined that their hunted enemy would brazenly set up camp so close to their bases of operation.

The previous night a dozen or so men had gone out to the villages to find out, among other things, how many Russians were in the area.

In the morning the returning partisans were ambushed. During the night the Russians had surrounded the forest. Luckily, the partisans slipped away without any losses. They reached camp and told us the situation was dire. One out of every three partisans who had gone out at night would not reach camp until morning. During the ambush the NKVD stated the direction the partisans took into the forest. It was clear that there would be a confrontation that day. Skirmantas and his men decided to retreat from the camp towards the Žaliasis Forest. Both our guests, Uosis, and I stayed in place because our guests refused to move in that direction. Unfortunately for us, Uosis did not have a good gun because he had switched it with a partisan who had gone out on scouting duty. That partisan had not yet returned to camp. This company in general lacked good quality arms. This was because a few months ago the company had taken in several dozen university and high school students who had still not yet been properly armed.

At daybreak, Skirmantas took 30 of his men and several Iron Wolf staff officers and headed for the outskirts of the forest to see if he could break through to a safer area. Uosis and I accompanied them to a very dense thicket where all of us took cover. Because of our inferior arms, we had to resort to evasive tactics. Because we would not be spotted by enemy troops unless they came very close, we decided to hold our fire until they were just a few meters away from us. Then our plan was to take down the ones closest to us and to make a run for it.

The thicket was filled with tree stumps. Using these stumps as supports, we sat facing in four different directions and kept a look-out for the enemy. But my mates could not keep up this inactivity for very long. Soon, they were fast asleep. The men from abroad were still exhausted from their journey and Uosis had not slept for a day and a half. I also felt sleepy, but I felt responsible for our lives, and so I fought off my drowsiness. Everything around me was unusually still. I could hear each bird awakening and preening its wings for the day. I shared my loneliness with a field mouse that emerged from a hole beside Lokys's feet. It leapt in tiny leaps from one tuft of grass to the next. Every time one of my comrades snored, the mouse twitched with fright.

Suddenly the sound of loud machine gun fire broke the silence. It was Skirmantas. The firing had come from the direction he had gone in. The battle had begun. Not only did my friend the mouse disappear, my comrades sat up, startled.

"What was that?" both our guests asked at once.

"That was Skirmantas fighting his way out of the forest," I said.

"Yes, I can tell from the sound that we took the first shots," Uosis said, listening intently, "that was hellfire from Vilius's[50] and Durtuvas's Dreiser. Tigras is not far behind."

"Or maybe that was Špokas's[51] gunfire?" Uosis wondered out loud. Then he added, "Or maybe the Russians got him?" Uosis could differentiate between the sound of the Russians' machine guns and ours.

---

50 Vilhelm, a German soldier who had fought on the front and was an expert at handling the machine gun. He died together with the Tauras District leader J. Stravinskas in battle on June 7, 1946.

51 A. Pažėra. He also died in battle June 7, 1946, with the partisan leader J. Stravinskas.

We could hear spats of machine gun bursts punctuated by grenades detonating and then submachine gun fire.

"This is really war here, men," Lokys said, listening closely. "I'd like to be there too, with a good machine gun in my hands. Let the Russians know that Lokys doesn't just shoot for nothing. We shouldn't have stayed with you. We should have gone with Skirmantas."

After a while the shooting ceased altogether. We heard a few more shots here and there, but they came from a different direction. We hoped that Skirmantas and his partisans had managed to break through.

Around 11 o'clock we were hungry and so we ate some of the canned food brought by our guests. They wanted to return to the abandoned camp because a few days previous they had made arrangements to meet some local residents there. Although Uosis and I knew that after today's fighting no civilian would dare set foot in the forests, we decided to humor our guests. We set out, walking Indian file. The closer we came to camp, the more cautious we became. We were afraid to so much as stir the leaves on the bushes.

About half a kilometer from camp we encountered four partisans who had been away on assignments at the time Skirmantas left. They were Plechavičius,[52] Vilkas,[53] Jūrelė,[54] and Šerkšnas.[55] One of them was still carrying the automatic weapon he had borrowed from Uosis the previous evening. The eight of us formed a fairly respectable group. We rested a while in a nearby glade and from there picked up the path that led to camp.

Around three o'clock in the afternoon bursts from Russian submachine guns and grenades shattered the quiet. There were enemy troops some two hundred yards ahead of us. We fell back about a hundred and fifty yards and discussed what to do next. Uosis thought that the Russians were firing to see if the gunshots would bring any hidden partisans out into the open.

Plechavičius speculated that they were firing at a small underground shelter occupied by two of our men. In any event, we all agreed it would not be wise to remain in the area for very long.

We walked along without incident until we came to a clearing. We scrutinized the clearing through our field glasses, but did not notice anything unusual. We

---

52 Juozas Raguckas, 1919–. He was arrested March 3, 1947, and was sentenced to 10 years hard labor in Siberia and five years in exile. He returned to Lithuania in 1956.

53 Antanas Vosylius, 1924–1949.

54 Vacys Bumblys was a student who fought in the Iron Wolf Regiment from March, 1946, onwards.

55 Domas Bumblys, brother of Vacys Bumblys. He was a student in the Pedagogical Institute. He joined the partisans with his brother in March 1946.

decided it was safe to cross. We sprinted to the other side of the clearing. Uosis followed directly behind me. However, just as Lokys was stepping into the clearing, we heard shots coming from somewhere to our left. It was a Russian lookout signaling to his comrades the direction in which we were traveling. It was necessary for us to hide our tracks, but as though to spite us, the grass was knee-high and brittle. By the time we found a place that seemed hidden enough and sat down to rest, we were bathed in sweat.

Scarcely twenty minutes went by when we noticed some Russians trailing us. Since we no longer had any place to retreat to, we decided to take a chance and sneak past them, right under their noses. Luckily for us, these NKVD soldiers were exhausted, and therefore not very observant. As soon as they were out of sight, we took off running. We headed in another direction, but we saw too many footprints to feel safe. Concealing our tracks, we tried our luck in another direction, crawling on our stomachs, so the Russians would not spot us. Here again we found too many footprints. The Russians apparently were scouring the entire forest. At last we reached what looked like a safe spot and decided to stay there until after sunset. In the meantime, we carefully scanned the surrounding area and waited.

It was just beginning to get dark when we arrived at the edge of the forest. Here we succeeded in making contact with a liaison officer who told us what Plechavičius had already guessed—that the Russian volleys we had heard and wondered about had indeed been directed at an underground partisan shelter. We also learned that a partisan named Ąžuolas, who had been wounded during this attack, had blown himself up with a grenade rather than allowing himself to be taken alive. He used the grenade to make sure that no one could identify his body and find his family and friends and arrest them.

We asked the liaison officer if he had any news of Skirmantas, which he did. Skirmantas had not succeeded in breaking out of the forest. Like us, he had spent the whole day dodging the Russians. Only now did we realize the danger we had been in. It turned out that an entire Russian battalion had left the town and had searched the forest—about 100 Russians for every single partisan. There was talk that even a Russian general was seen in Šilavotas.

There was little time to waste. We had to get moving as quickly as possible. Without waiting for the cover of darkness, we crawled out of the woods and into the fields, anticipating attack at any moment. We could expect it all the more because 13 Soviet Interior troops had been killed during the clash with Skirmantas. Skirmantas had not lost a single man. The Russians were out for blood.

Three days later we found ourselves back in our permanent headquarters. We learned that our District Commander, Mykolas Jonas, had not yet returned from the forest. We held onto the slim hope that he had survived.

The Partisans Ambush the Bolsheviks

After the district leaders' meeting, all the units did not immediately disperse. We decided to say goodbye by putting together an ambush for the Bolsheviks. Not far from their meeting place they were organizing a demonstration. High level Bolshevik leaders from Marijampolė were supposed to come to the demonstration. This posed the perfect opportunity for the district's leadership to demonstrate to its fighters that they could also do a good job of taking on the enemy.

Kardas was assigned leadership of the operation. Several machine guns were taken from the Vytautas District and a few men were asked to help. The edge of the Šunskas forest was selected for the ambush.

Two fighters disguised as civilians went to the demonstration and took a few shots at the local Communist leader. They let him escape to Marijampolė to get some help.

They did not have to wait long before a vehicle carrying 30 Interior soldiers rushed to the local Communist leader's aid. They were met with machine gun fire several kilometers away from the demonstration. The burning vehicle crashed into a ditch on the side of the road. The driver had been shot too soon, which made it harder to pick off the surviving Russians. Still, the Tauras District leadership was able to display their skill. Out of 30 NKVD men, only two escaped with their lives. Not a single partisan was so much as injured. Everyone wiped away their sweat, shook hands, and bragged to each other over their day's work.

"That's how all the men in the Tauras District ought to fight. Eighteen men took down 30. And, we got enough weaponry to arm half our company."

In the Market Square

We and our guests had succeeded in getting rid of the Russians for a while. For some time things went well for Skirmantas and his men too. They joined forces with the group headed by Kardas and were making their way towards headquarters by slipping past the Soviet encirclement. However, living like that, constantly on the alert, had exhausted them. Not only were they unable to rest during the day, they had to stay awake for the better part of the night on alert.

As a means to subdue the resistance, the Soviets for some years dumped the bodies of killed partisans on the square in the nearest town. This was done in part to create fear among the population, but also to identify the bodies by perceiving how by-passers reacted when looking at the corpses. If somebody showed remorse, they were interrogated as to whether they knew the identity of the dead. The pictures are taken by the Soviet security, as a mean of identifying the dead. No written instructions, however, to use this mean are available from archives. On the picture there are three dead partisans from the Vytis militarydistrict, with their weapons dumped on top of the bodies. The three are: Vytautas Kadžys-codename Šešiapūdis (Six pounder); Antanas Valikonis-codename Grietinėlė (Cream); and Jonas Kalvanaitis-codename Pažistamas (Acquaintance).

* * *

On some rare occasions partisans actually survived. On this picture to the left we see Petras Gumauskas-codename Pipiras (Pepper)- photographed together with his dead comrades in 1952.

Women were dumped together with the men on the squares. In the middle is an unknown woman together with two partisans, one of them has most probably blown up his own face with a hand grenade in order to avoid identification.

On June 3rd Kardas, Laimutė, Skirmantas, Strazdas[56] (Thrush), Dėdė, Saugūnas,[57] Vėtra, Jazminas, Špokas, Studentas[58] (Student) and Gintaras[59] (Amber) reached the Pagraižis forest just before morning. It had rained that night. The exhausted fighters did not properly cover their tracks. Unfortunately for them, as soon as the sun came up a truck full of Bolsheviks traveling on the road from Veiveriai to Šilavotas spotted their tracks leading towards Pagraižis. The Russians called for reinforcements from Šilavotas and arrived at the area where the tracks had been found and began hunting for the partisans using dogs. The partisans were found very quickly. They were all asleep. The Soviet Interior Forces surrounded them and began firing at them with machine guns from up close. Vilius and Špokas, the best in the unit at handling a machine gun, grabbed their guns and managed to get off a few rounds. Only Saugūnas and Skirmantas managed to escape with their lives. All the rest were either killed on the spot or were killed a short close by, except for Dėdė and Strazdas, who were spared because they were away at the time procuring breakfast.

The Russians collected the partisans' bodies and brought them to Šilavotas where they dumped them in the market square. Even though there were several hundred Soviet Interior troops on duty in Šilavotas at the time, the wives and

[56] Juozas Samuolis, killed in battle July 4, 1946.

[57] Antanas Šiurpienas, killed in battle July 13, 1946.

[58] Identity unknown, he was killed in battle June 7, 1946.

[59] Jonas Naujokas, 1926–1946, he was killed in battle June 7, 1946.

sisters of the partisans managed to honor the dead under the cover of night by bringing flowers and wreaths and covering their bodies with them. The following day Kardas's, Laimutė's, and Vėtras's corpses were brought to the larger town of Marijampolė to be identified. They brought Kardas's wife[60] out of jail and made her stand before the corpses. They beat her brutally, demanding that she reveal their names. She refused to give out the names, so they tossed the bodies back into a truck and brought them to Prienai where they demanded that the local high school teachers come and identify them. Most of the bodies were partially undressed while others were left completely naked. The Russians set up Laimutė's corpse in an indecent pose out in the open market square.

Mykolas Jonas is Killed

On June 6, 1946, the Tauras District suffered another painful loss. That day the Russians began combing the forest in the northern part of our district's area where the Žalgiris unit was operating. Two divisions of Soviet Interior Forces, supported by armored cars, infiltrated the Kazlų Rūda forest exactly at the time our district commander Mykolas Jonas happened to be there. They surrounded him along with the partisans from the Sakalas unit. Since the Russians could reinforce their troops at a moment's notice, the little band of partisans was threatened with complete annihilation. The district commander, therefore, ordered them to refrain from trying to take on the advancing troops and to concentrate instead on breaking through the Russian lines with a single coordinated maneuver.

The Sakalas partisans were fully experienced in this kind of warfare and the break-through succeeded. Thirty six Soviet Interior Forces troops were killed as opposed to five of our men. Among our dead were Sakalas[61] (Falcon) himself, who was the company head, and Brangutė[62] (Precious), an important company leader.

The following day the Russians seemed to have quieted down and District Commander Mykolas Jonas made preparations to return to headquarters. Towards evening, accompanied by six volunteers who had traveled with him as far as Samogitia, he left camp and headed for the edge of the forest. When he and his companions stopped to rest, they were ambushed by a detachment of Russians who had been hiding in the forest. A fierce and unequal battle ensued. Three men

---

60 Kastutė Mieldažytė-Stravinskienė, 1920– . She was arrested December 19, 1946, and imprisoned in Marijampolė. A military tribunal sentenced her on September 3 to seven years hard labor in Siberia and five years in exile. She returned to Lithuania in 1957.

61 Bronius Brazauskas, 1914–1946.

62 Juozas Sidabra, 1926–1946.

from the unit died and another four fought for a half hour more. Mykolas Jonas was eventually heavily wounded. The partisans were forced to retreat. Mykolas Jonas could no longer fight, so he pulled out a grenade and blew himself up. Only two freedom fighters survived. Thirteen Russians were killed in the fighting.

The dead partisans' bodies were brought to the small township of Kazlų Rūda. Here the corpses were desecrated. Some of the bodies were bridled with the rosary beads that had been found on their persons. Others had prayer books shoved into their mouths. The Lithuanian insignia, the symbol of Grand Duke Gediminas, was carved into their flesh.

We Lose Vabalas and Gegužis

After the meeting on May 10th, 1946 we planned on building more bunkers. Things turned out differently. We were swamped with a number of organizational duties and as we were taking care of them we found ourselves unprepared for a manhunt directed at us.

As the manhunt proceeded, Vabalas and Gegužis requested Tigras's permission to return to their previous homes because the fighting got in the way of any of the work they had been assigned to do. Tigras agreed to their request. They returned to their former areas of operation.

After a few days Vabalas received news that his sister,[63] who had been exiled to Siberia, had returned home. Both fighters, without waiting for the manhunt to end, decided to go and visit Vabalas's sister. It was a beautiful July afternoon. Vabalas and Gegužis emerged from their underground bunker lightly armed and set out on their journey. At just that moment a Soviet Interior Forces company emerged from a nearby rye field and spotted the two partisans. The partisans rushed back to the bunker to retrieve their heavier weapons. By the time they got there, Gegužis was already wounded. They realized there was no way they could survive. Gegužis blew himself up with a grenade, so that the Bolsheviks could not identify him. Vabalas did not hold out long on his own. After a few minutes he held a grenade to his head and detonated it.

The NKVD brought Gegužis's father and brother[64] to the scene and ordered them to remove the bodies from the bunker and to transport them to the town of

---

63 Marytė Aglinskaitė, 1928–. On August 30, 1945, she was arrested for assisting the partisans. Together with her parents, she was jailed in Vorkuta, Siberia. On July 18, 1946, her case was dismissed and she was granted permission to return to Lithuania.

64 Antanas Gelčys and Motiejus Gelčys. Motiejus Gelčys was also a partisan in the Iron Wolf Regiment. He was arrested December 27, 1947, and was sentenced to 10 years hard labor in Siberia. From 1956 onwards he lived in Siberia in exile. He was released in 1967.

Garliava where there was an area in the market grounds set aside to display the corpses of partisans. Gegužis's family managed to save themselves by arguing that they did not know of the bunker's existence and that they couldn't recognize the face of the body. Gegužis's father, carrying his dead son to the market ground, did not betray his son's identity to the Bolsheviks by shedding a single tear.

Vabalas's sister, after everything she had suffered in hard labor in Siberia, did not get to see the last member of her family still alive. They did finally meet, only not there where Vabalas had dreamed of meeting, but in the Garliava town square where, hiding her tears, she glimpsed him from a distance.

More Manhunts

While Uosis, Daunoras, and I were concerned with matters of organization and continued to publish the underground newspaper, the Russians staged a partisan manhunt in our vicinity. It began during the first week of August 1946 and continued for a couple of weeks. Every farm was searched several times over. Houses, stables, barns, cellars, and any other place where a partisan might hide were ransacked.

To protect themselves during these searches, the Russians always forced a member of the farmer's family to walk ahead at gunpoint and act as a human shield. There were times when we thought our own headquarters were in danger of being discovered, but they never were. Nor did the Soviet search parties find any other partisan detachments.

Around this time, we raided the state-owned Išlaužas dairy and carried away a supply of butter. We also managed to get a hold of the ledgers in which the dairy officials kept records of how much of the required quotas of milk farmers in the area had "contributed." We took those along with a batch of blank receipts. Each farmer who had failed to meet his quota received from us a forged receipt acknowledging delivery of the required quantity as stated in his ledger. Since we destroyed the ledgers afterwards, the dairy officials had no way of telling the quota-completion receipts issued by us from the ones that had been issued by their agents.

But this raid had been no more than a diversion. There was far more serious work to be done if we intended to achieve our goal of building a strong and unified armed resistance. For this purpose, I had been delegated to go to Vilnius where I was to participate in the formation of a partisan general staff. It was strange to think I would be soon walking around in the open in the light of day and mingling with people in "legal" life. No less strange was the sensation I felt when I boarded a train out of Kaunas.

Over half the passengers were Russian military personnel. There were NKVD officers, Soviet Interior Forces, and ordinary Red Army soldiers. Just a few days ago I had been shooting at these men, and now here we were, conversing pleasantly, seated together in one coupe.

For my own protection, I decided to strike up a conversation with a NKVD major. I thought to myself, if I have to talk to them, then why not start with the biggest fish. In this way, when the time came for a document check, the functionaries delegated to the task would assume I was a friend of the major and leave me alone. My plan worked. A few stations later soldiers boarded the train and began checking the passengers' documents. They also examined suspicious looking suitcases and parcels. But they did not give me so much as a second glance. They did not dare disturb the major's conversation. I had been chatting with him about various aspects of university life. I was surprised to find out that he knew quite a bit on the topic himself. He even knew that officials in Moscow had accorded the University of Kaunas top rank among universities in the Soviet Union and that it was placed on equal footing with the universities of Leningrad and Moscow. He agreed with me that the standards of Lithuanian universities were very high.

Taking on a Position of Leadership

For Bravery and Courage

In Vilnius[65] Tautvydas and I got in contact with Daunoras. The Samogitian, the Great Battle, and the Vytis Division leaders had already arrived ahead of us. My first task was to set up permanent communications between the Tauras and Kęstutis Military Districts.

In the beginning of September, 1946, we helped Deksnys break through the border to Poland where he would meet up with Lokys.

We were planning to compile a headquarters for the armed resistance by using cooperating members from various districts. Then, after we had settled a number of organizational matters, we would have to set up reliable communications.

Each district had to select representatives for the Political Committee. With the participation of the headquarter's military college leadership, statutes were put together.

In October 1946, among the members of the military college, there were representatives from several districts.

From the first of November, 1946, I was appointed adjunct to General Vytis, the head of partisan headquarters.[66]

My first mission out of Vilnius with an assignment from the armed resistance partisan leadership headquarters was to the Tauras District. That journey took place at the end of September, 1946.

I returned to the Iron Wolf Regiment together with Uosis, who had been appointed District Commander. On September 15, 1946, we reached the Vytautas Regiment where we had hoped to find the District Commander. The new Division Commander was Žvejys,[67] who had earlier been Chief of Staff. I did not get to meet with him, because at that time he was visiting the Žalgiris District.

---

65 In Vilnius, Markulis set up Juozas Lukša with falsified documents as a student.

66 A. Kamarauskas. He was a captain in the Lithuanian army. He agreed to work for the NKVD as a double agent with the code name "Vlasov." Under the leadership of double-agent Jonas Markulis, code name Erelis (Eagle) he worked within the structures of the partisan leadership under the code name Vytis.

67 Alfonsas Vabalas, 1909–1948.

I took care of matters with Gediminas,[68] who was the head of the Tauras District Political Committee.

After the meeting both Uosis and I were invited to the Vytautas Regiment's ceremony for both the passive and the armed resistance. Several of the fighters were honored for their bravery.

About 35 men were honored on the first of the ceremonies. The district commander, Vampyras, and other leaders participated in the ceremonies.

After the district's adjunct, Kunigaikštis,[69] read the District Commander's orders regarding the badges "for courage" and "for bravery," he led the leadership in thanking the men for their service to their country and asking them to continue in the fight.

After these words, medals were pinned on the men by the District Commander himself. He shook every man's right hand. The official part of the ceremony was concluded with a remembrance of the partisans who had died fighting. Everyone sang the first stanza of a song dedicated to the dead partisans:

You died for freedom in an honorable fight,	*Jūs žuvot už laisvę garbingoj kovoj,*
Hawks of your native land.	*Gimtosios šalies sakalai.*
For eternity Lithuanians will remember you in song,	*Per amžius lietuviai minės jus dainoj,*
And honor will follow you into eternity.	*Garbė jus lydės amžinai.*

Afterwards, everyone hummed as Kunigaikštis spoke the words to the second stanza out loud:

Already the light is dawning in Lithuania	*Jau Lietuvai teka skaisčioji aušra,*
And soon the Red Star will set	*Ir greit nusileis raudonoji žvaigždė.*
The first partisans are lying in their graves	*Pirmus partizanus jau slegia kapai,*
And the flowers whisper, "Farewell."	*O gėlės jiems šnabžda: "Sudiev".*
But no, you will live among us forever.	*Bet ne, jūs gyvensit tarp mūs ažinai.*
Lithuania will announce your names.	*Lietuviai jūs vardą minės.*

---

68 Vytautas Vabalas, 1919–1947.

69 Antanas Markauskas, 1922–1946. He blew himself up with a grenade in his bunker October 30, 1946.

Generation after generation, the old and young	*Ir kartos į kartą, seni ir vaikai*
Will keep you in their hearts in prayer.	*Maldoj ir širdy jus turės.*
You died for freedom in an honorable fight,	*Jūs žuvot už laisvę, garbingoj kovoj,*
Hawks of your native land.	*Gimtosios šalies sakalai.*
Lithuanians will remember you in song,	*Per amžius lietuviai minės jus dainoj*
And honor will follow you into eternity.	*Garbė jus lydės amžinai.*

After the singing, the official part was over. Then we sat down at the table to eat. Uosis and I were asked to give speeches: one of us representing the Iron Wolf Regiment and the other the Headquarters of the armed resistance. During dinner the fighters, led by the chaplain, sang a popular partisan song.

The following night members of the passive resistance were honored. These were the liaison people and the supporters of the resistance. They received small epaulettes "for support" and "for bravery." The ceremony was the same as on the previous day, only with less formality and with a shorter program.

The Vytautas Unit held an award ceremony for the first time in over two years. The most loyal, conscientious, and the oldest fighters were honored. The unit commander had been given the right to distribute the awards by the district leadership.

Requisitioning Food for the Partisans

The armed resistance managed to provide themselves with food from two principle sources. Some of it was forcibly extracted from Lithuanians who were known to be Communist sympathizers or who maintained friendly relations with the Communists. Most of the food, however, was willingly donated by local farmers. Farmers who had benefited from partisan assistance in the past were especially willing to donate food. Unfortunately, Lithuanian farmers had recently been so hard-pressed by the Soviet authorities, who were pressuring them to join the collective farms, that very few of them had anything left to contribute. The partisans understood their plight and did not wish to impose on their generosity any further. The time had come to look for another source for food supplies.

In the autumn of 1946, the new Tauras District commander, Žvejys, instructed the various units, detachments, and squads operating in his district to begin confiscating the food stores of the Soviet state operated farms, the *sovchoz*. The *sovchoz* system had been established on some of the larger estates and were being administered by members of the Russian Red Army. The estates also served as storage depots for the grain that had been confiscated from Lithuanian farmers.

The partisans were to requisition enough provisions to feed themselves for a year, including grain, livestock, and other necessities. A small portion of the produce thus requisitioned was to be sold in order to obtain funds for various military and organizational expenses.

To illustrate the efficiency with which these food-confiscation operations were conducted, I will describe how the partisans of the Šarūnas company raided the state operated storehouses on what used to be the Pagermanis estate.

The night before the raid was scheduled to take place, the men of the Šarūnas Unit set up camp about a kilometer away from their objective. On the following day, the storehouse and the area around it were thoroughly reconnoitered. Some thirty sturdy carts were rounded up and concealed until such time as they would be required. Towards evening, heavily armed bands of partisans were sent out to patrol the main road.

One group of partisans surrounded the storehouse while another moved the carts closer to its gates. The partisans had already learned that only the supervisor and the political affairs director of the storehouse were armed. Therefore, the first order of business was to put them out of commission. Tigras and two others set out to carry out this task. Climbing into one of the carts, they proceeded to the door of the administration building, singing loudly in Russian the entire time. Pretending to be Russian drunks, they demanded to be let inside. The real Russians, however, were wary about opening the doors. Luckily, just then more partisans appeared, dragging with them the orderly who guarded the horses at night. He was known to be the supervisor's confidant. Tigras grabbed him and ordered him to tell the supervisor that there were NKVD men outside the door, demanding a horse and wagon. When they heard the demand from the orderly, they opened up the door.

The partisans immediately knocked the supervisor to the ground and took away his pistol. Then he was taken to his private quarters and ordered to surrender whatever weapons he had there. His wife produced an ordinary rifle and some cartridges. But Tigras wasn't satisfied with that. He proceeded to search every room for concealed weapons and finally came up with a submachine gun that the supervisor's wife had apparently "forgotten" about. It supposedly belonged to the political activities director who was away that night.

After subduing the administration, the partisans drove the carts into the yard of the compound and fell to work. Grain was the first item on their list. Laborers from the storehouses were quickly mobilized to do the sacking and carting, while the partisans supervised them. The work went smoothly. One group of workers poured the grain into sacks and a second group loaded the sacks into the carts. All of them seemed to be enjoying themselves immensely. The grain-sackers even challenged the sack-loaders to engage in a Soviet-style "competition" to see who could work faster. Both groups scurried around like ants, urging the other to hurry. Each cart was filled in a matter of minutes. In less than three hours all the carts were loaded to full capacity, including four carts that belonged to the state. These had been confiscated for good measure along with the horses needed to pull them. In this manner, the partisans acquired 250 centners of grain, most of it choice quality wheat.

Having relieved the storehouses of most of the grain and all of the carts and horses, the partisans turned their attention to the livestock. Ten sleek black and white spotted cows were removed from their stalls—one cow for every five partisans in the company. Bacon lovers helped themselves to several fine porkers from the "private reserves" of the supervisor, the political affairs director and the aforementioned night orderly. This individual, an informer whose denunciations had cost several Lithuanians their lives, was denounced and shot in full view of the workers at the conclusion of the raid. None of the workers were harmed, nor was anything taken from them. They had performed their task willingly and efficiently. Most of them were as poor as the partisans themselves.

As soon as the carts were moved out of the storehouses, the bulk of the partisans withdrew. Only a few remained behind to maintain "discipline." They did this by locking the supervisor and his family in their rooms and telling the workers to help themselves to whatever grain was left over. What followed was a flurry of activity no less animated than before. Bags, aprons, even ordinary caps, were filled and refilled with grain as the workers vied with each other to build up reserves to augment their meager rations. By dawn all traces of the grain had disappeared. And so had the partisans. A detachment of Soviet Interior troops did their best to track them down, but their efforts were in vain.

During the months that followed similar raids were staged by partisans throughout Lithuania. When the Russians tried to thwart them by placing heavy guards around the *sovchozs* and food depots at night, the partisans began conducting their raids during the day. They would strike swiftly and efficiently and would vanish long before the Soviets had the time to bring in their troops. In this manner nearly all the partisan detachments were able to provide themselves with a year's supply of food.

Taking Measures Against the Stribai

Another problem facing the partisans in the autumn of 1946 was the recent restoration of the Soviet so called *Istrebitelyy*, or Soviet local militia. Just as the Nazis had employed the services of French militiamen to combat the French underground, the Russians were fighting the Lithuanian resistance movement with Lithuanian collaborators.

It was therefore necessary for the partisans to devise tactics whereby the *Stribai* would be demoralized and their organization disbanded once and for all. To that end, Commander Žvejys ordered every partisan unit in his district to select a point where the Soviet local militia garrisons were known to be concentrated and to obliterate it by means of an all-out attack. The measures used to effect this total destruction included panzerfausts, as well as anti-tank missiles and phosphorus grenades. In order to spread fear among the Soviet local militia operating outside the areas of attack, handbills circulated throughout the district, threatening terrible reprisals against all those who did not immediately lay down their guns and stop fighting their fellow countrymen.

Shortly afterwards the attacks commenced. Some of them were executed with no difficulty whatsoever. For instance, the entire Soviet local militia garrison at Gižai was wiped out in broad daylight by scarcely more than a handful of partisans. Keeping the *Stribai* at bay with machine gun fire, the partisans surrounded their headquarters and set it ablaze with phosphorous grenades. The Soviet local militia immediately took refuge in the basement, but there was no escaping the flames. After half an hour most of them suffocated and the remainder were shot the moment they set foot outside the basement door.

The attack on Kačergynė proved to be more difficult because the Soviet local militia headquarters were spread out over several buildings. In this instance, the partisans struck at night, employing a force of nearly one hundred men. Although some were killed in action, the rest achieved their objective and the Kačergynė Soviet local militia were totally annihilated.

Considering the deadly efficiency of these attacks, it is easy to understand why the Soviet local militia units were soon thrown into a state of sheer panic. For one thing, they had no idea what kinds of weapons the partisans had used to inflict such devastation. Therefore, the partisans deliberately circulated a rumor that they planned to attack with even more powerful weapons in the future. The *Stribai* then decided that it was time to part company with the "people's defenders" and quickly left their units. Many of them went into hiding. Others managed to officially resign. Others requested permission from the partisans to join their ranks or looked for work that was looked on more favorably by the partisans. Only those individuals who had carried the destruction and betrayal of their countrymen too far to be able to turn back remained in the Soviet local militia. But the number of these men was comparably small and amounted to no more than a handful in any given community. Their numbers were higher in areas with a denser concentration of Russians.

The victorious campaigns against the Soviet local militia and the successful food-confiscation operations gave a much-needed boost to partisan morale after a summer spent dodging the NKVD manhunts. However, no matter how optimistic we might have felt that autumn, our elation was tempered by the realization that every single day the lives of our fellow partisans were being snuffed out all over Lithuania.

Žvainys is Arrested and Interrogated

Five men from Dešinys's unit—Žaibas (Lightening),[70] Žvainys,[71] Kalnas (Mountain),[72] Linas (Linen),[73] and Šimtametis (Century)[74]—had managed to maintain a bunker for about six months in the forest of Mozūriškės. The Soviet Interior Forces were constantly searching the area, but couldn't find any partisans hiding in the villages. Then they started searching the forests. The unit was unlucky in that this particular forest was rather damp and it was impossible to completely hide one's tracks.

One night an NKVD patrol spotted two of the men as they were returning to the bunker after having visited a village close by. The ground along the outskirts of the forest happened to be very damp for that time of year. The NKVD who came around to check out the report early the next morning had no difficulty picking up the partisans' tracks. With the help of bloodhounds, they managed to find the bunker and immediately began their attack.

The five partisans were trapped. There was no way they could fire back at the Russians except through the bunker ceiling. But there didn't seem much sense in shooting at empty air. They could not escape out of the bunker because it was surrounded by Soviet Interior Forces troops two-circles deep. Their only remaining option was to blow themselves up with grenades. Four of the partisans in the

---

70 Povilas Buzas, 1919–. After torture in the Marijampolė prison, he was sentenced to ten years hard labor in Siberia and five years in exile. He returned to Lithuania in 1956.

71 Juozas Luiza, 1889–1946. He blew himself up with a grenade in his bunker October 30, 1946.

72 Kazys Stravinskas, 1925–1946. He blew himself up with a grenade in his bunker October 30, 1946.

73 Albinas Krušinskas

74 Antanas Kulikauskas.

bunker died that day by exploding themselves, but the fifth man, Žvainys, was wounded by his comrades' grenades and lost consciousness before he could detonate his own. Since he was drenched in blood when the Russians found him, they took him for dead and dumped him along with the bodies of the others outside the rectory in the town of Veiveriai.

After a few hours, Žvainys regained consciousness and sat up. Because he was so groggy, he did not realize that he ought to play dead or run away. He just sat there, gazing around him, until he attracted the attention of several NKVD officers nearby. Of course, the NKVD where surprised by this "miraculous resurrection" and rushed over to investigate. Žvainys finally came to when he saw the NKVD men rushing over towards him. By then, it was too late. Although he tried to run, he did not get very far because he was still too weak. Gasping with pain and exhaustion, he was picked up and dragged to the NKVD headquarters for interrogation.

There at the headquarters he was beaten so viciously that the blows reopened his wounds. In spite of the torture, he refused to divulge any information about himself or his comrades. The NKVD kept up the beating for hours. Finally, after the Soviets grew tired of the strain of beating the half-dead man, all but two of them left the room. Seeing this as his last chance, Žvainys summoned every remaining ounce of his strength and managed to wrestle a submachine gun away from one of the two men left to guard him. But when he pulled the trigger, the gun wouldn't fire. In desperation, Žvainys brought the gun down hard on the head of the NKVD guard who had been standing between him and the window. He hoisted himself up on the sill. Just as he was about to jump out the window, the second NKVD guard grabbed hold of his legs. Žvainys desperately fought to kick himself free, but he didn't stand a chance. Alerted by the noise, a horde of NKVD men charged into the interrogation room and beat Žvainys senseless with the butts of their guns.

Much later, when Žvainys came to again, the interrogation was resumed with a new vengeance. Žvainys remained steadfast to the end and no matter how much they tortured him, he refused to answer their questions. They beat him to within an inch of his life.

The Journey by Train

In early November, 1946, I was sent to the Vytis District as a representative of the Partisan Headquarters' leadership to meet with the district leader Vaitelis. The meetings were to take place near Panevėžys in the Green Forests. The partisans in these parts were far worse off than the partisans in the Tauras District. They lacked discipline, organizational skills, weapons and ammunition and did not have enough time to procure food and clothing. They seemed to take on too many offensive attacks. Because of this they had provoked large reprisals from the Soviet Interior Forces. Besides all that, they had too many partisans in their ranks. It was clear that their ranks needed to be thinned. In addition, their newspaper came out irregularly and was not distributed in any orderly manner.

In the second half of November, Markulis and I met the Partisan Headquarters' leadership in the Tauras District. During this meeting we ironed out a lot of difficulties. From this date the Tauras District was joined to the centralized organization. At the same time another representative of the Partisan Headquarters was in the Dainava District working on the same organizational concerns.

On December 5th Markulis, Girėnas,[75] and I took the train to the Kęstutis District. This journey made a huge impression on me. Through connections we were able to get three very good tickets—second class sleeping compartments. We took the Moscow–Kaliningrad train. In our compartment we had one Red Army aviation general, one journalist for the *Peasant Newspaper* and the director of some factory in Šiauliai. I felt rather uncomfortable in the company of these Bolshevik officials and was inclined to remain silent rather than to speak. I undressed and, ignoring them, nodded off. I thought that they must consider me some sort of Bolshevik official. Yet our compartment did not look Soviet at all. Our eyes had grown accustomed to Soviet filth and disorganization, but here the luxuries surprised me. I realized that this group was the cream of the Soviet elite. Along the way we paid 25 rubles for our bedding. That was less than 12 percent of the price of our tickets.

Our impressions were entirely different when we got off the train in Radviliškės. We had to wait four hours for the next train going our direction. We made the remainder of our journey in third class because no other types of tickets were available. The entire train was crammed with recruits. They had all been born in 1927 and were being brought to East Prussia for military training.

Up until this point Lithuania's recruits had been trained in their region's towns. Moscow had agreed with the Soviet Lithuanian government to allow recruits to

---

75 Algimantas Vincas Zaskevičius, 1917–. He was arrested March 11, 1947 and during interrogations agreed to cooperate with the NKVD. He became one of the most cruel double agents, betraying dozens of fellow partisans and even murdering them with his own hands.

be trained close to home. It was likely that if they had been put onto trains, they would have all deserted, thinking they were being deported to Russia.

Already as early as the autumn of 1946 the last batch of new recruits born in 1926 were called up and trained in their towns of origin. The training was completed within a few months according to the new "*Stachanovini Method*."[76] Of the already short training period three sevenths of that time was of no use because the Soviets allowed the recruits a three-day weekend, so that they could go home and bring back food for the rest of the week. During training the recruits wore their own clothing. Some of them were even then being trained in East Prussia. They were the men who came from areas close to East Prussia. These soldiers suffered from starvation because they were made to train constantly and could not take time off to procure food. Often, not being able to stand the conditions, they would steal their weapons and make a run for it.

Now the recruits born in 1927 were being exposed to precisely that kind of suffering. They were guarded by Red Army officers, so that they couldn't possibly escape.

From Radviliškės we reached the area we needed to visit. District Commander Visvydas[77] attended the meeting along with the leaders from the Political, Administrative, and Information Committees. The views of this district differed significantly from the others. We resolved to further discuss their concerns at the congress of the partisan leadership.

The journey back was not as comfortable. Once we reached Radviliškės we had to wait 18 hours for the next train. The train station was overfilled with soldiers from various Red Army units, civilian people, and many beggars and homeless people from Russia. At the entrance to the station they had laid out their bundles and had stood waiting several days already for the train. To get into the station you had to climb over people and their bundles. The Lithuanian travelers were usually enroute either to prison or to military bases. A number of them were young people from the universities. The Russian nation was represented by a variety of bums and opportunists who had traveled here from Belorussia looking to buy food on the black market. Others came here simply to beg. You could also see a lot of Soviet soldiers who had been demobilized from Prussia and Lithuania and were on their way home. Others had come here on military assignments.

---

76 Stachanovich was a coal miner who was capable of doing the work of three miners in one shift. He was held up as an example of efficiency by Stalin. The *Stachanovini Method* was a means of forcing workers or soldiers to be as productive as possible.

77 Juozas Kasperavičius, 1914–1947.

All the train tickets were sold out. Several hundred people, nonetheless, stood pushing and shoving in line at the ticket windows. Only Party Communists, important NKVD and Soviet Interior Forces personnel and the demobilized officers, by sticking out their elbows in front of them, were able to shove their way to the front of the line and curse the ticket sellers and get themselves tickets. People talked the demobilized soldiers into buying tickets for them, offering to pay them with vodka.

I had to finagle tickets for all of us. I could not get close enough to the Red Army soldiers to talk to them, so I decided to go look for the train station leadership. It was more than clear to me that the head of the train station took bribes. With the help of my friends, I figured out by the style of hat who was the train station head and positioned myself so that I would have the occasion to get close to him. When right the moment came, I greeted him and immediately got down to business. I told him that I was a Professor in the Kaunas University Technical Department and that my friends and I absolutely had to get on the train because I was scheduled to lecture at 11 o'clock the following morning. I saw in the head's face that he was not satisfied with this story.

I thought to myself, my story is not convincing enough. I thought hard about what I could say to catch his interest.

He scratched his head and then he surprised me.

"Fuck your lectures," he said.

I got the picture immediately and shoved 100 rubles into his palm. He squeezed the money in his palm and turned to face me. Everything changed.

"I'll do my best," he said, "wait in the corner over there," he said, nodding his head in the direction of the corner. Then he disappeared.

Twelve minutes later he brought me the tickets, asked me to pay for them, and warned me that I would need to prepare one more bribe for the steward on the train (every wagon had its own steward). After that we ignored each other like complete strangers. My friends were pleased with my success.

In half an hour the train we had been waiting for arrived from Klaipėda. It stood in Radviliškės for fifteen minutes. There was a huge push towards the train. The stewards guarded the doors and would not let anyone in, cursing at the passengers. They even got into fist fights with the soldiers. The civilian passengers, most of whom did not have tickets, did not bother to push their way towards the stewards to get inside. Instead they clung to the steps, the buffers, the roof ladders, or the platforms at the end of the wagons. The crowd surged crazily from wagon to wagon searching for places to grab onto. They were constantly beaten down and chased away by the militia and the stewards. In this mess the three of us were separated. Markulis managed to get inside a wagon with a bribe. Girėnas and I managed to get a foothold on a small platform at the end of the train and resolved to hold our own when the train began to move.

We learned from the passengers disembarking from the train that overnight in this train, between Klaipėda and Šiauliai, two murders had taken place. It was believed that the murders were committed by looting Red Army soldiers enroute to their "paradise." The corpses had been tossed out the train windows. It turned out that certain coupés had been designated for soldiers only. Some of the soldiers had let a few civilians in the coupés for bribes. Along the way they murdered them and robbed them and tossed the bodies out the windows.

On the platforms in Radviliškės several suspicious types dressed half as civilians and half as soldiers milled around. The area around the train station was dimly lit.

When the train began to move, Girėnas and I managed to get a foothold on the small platforms we had staked out. A student with a suitcase jumped onto the stairs in front of us. Once the train began to move the suspicious types we had seen on the platform leaped towards the student and ripped the suitcase out of his hands, almost dragging him down with them.

"Help! They stole my bread!" the student shouted.

But who was going to help? The ones who were supposed to protect people from criminals—the militia or the *Stribai* were themselves experts at performing these kinds of robberies.

"Just be glad they didn't rip you off of the stairs or knife you in the back," Girėnas said, calming down the student.

We began to talk. He told us that he had packed food from his family farm and was on his way to the Kaunas Finance Technical School. We had a hard time calming him down and getting him used to feeling like a "proletariat."

Around Kėdainiai I too had an incident. I was standing with my back to a door with the glass shattered out of the window. Suddenly a hand came through the hole and grabbed me by the back of my neck. But my combatant had not anticipated my reaction. I instinctively squatted down and with a knife I had kept ready in my sleeve I sliced the hand. The hand yanked back through the hole and disappeared. We realized that the thieves who had committed the murders the night before were still on the loose in the train. Girėnas and I moved to the standing space opposite and prepared to defend ourselves against an attack.

Soon the sun came up and that made the remainder of our journey somewhat safer.

Visiting the Vytautas District

The final district we visited was the Vytautas District. At headquarters we discussed the state of the armed resistance. We made adjustments to our plans. We established the territories of the larger companies, and formalized the duties of the leadership of those companies, organized the statutes so they were similar and edited the wording. We were encouraged to take the initiative to prepare more fighting units and to also put out an order to the units that more men keep diaries of the activities of the resistance.

Christmas Eve 1946

Dešinys decided to celebrate Christmas Eve of 1946 together with the men from his unit. That seemed a lot safer than allowing individual fighters to risk returning home to their families on Christmas Eve night. Since the partisans felt as though they were a family, this type of celebration was acceptable within the Lithuanian tradition. The second in command, Papartis, selected a site for the unit to celebrate. The unit adjunct, Tigras, was invited to join the unit.

Papartis found a place to celebrate in Skerdupis. The men gathered at dusk. Tigras and Dešinys and the other fighters arrived only around ten o'clock at night. They assigned two men to guard duty and everyone else sat down to the Christmas feast. After a short prayer, we passed the Christmas wafers around the table, kissing them and breaking them as they passed from hand to hand.

The second guard shift came in and reported that they had seen about twenty Interior troops passing through the village. The partisans hastily left the table, laden with food, and rushed to prepare for battle. It did not make sense to retreat since it would have been impossible to cover their tracks in the snow. Quickly they broke up into two groups. Dešinys took command of one group and Tigras the other. One group remained in the western edge of the village and the other rushed to the eastern end. They allowed the Bolsheviks to come close enough and then opened fire on them. The Bolsheviks were as confused as sheep and retreated. The partisans surrounded them in a semi-circle and continued to fire at them.

They chased the Russians a few kilometers and then returned to the house, gathered up the table cloth by its four corners, folded it together, and carried off what remained of Christmas dinner into the forest.

Retreating from Vilnius

Our affairs with the West again were not going well.[78] We did not receive the promised aid through Daukantas[79] and our ties had broken off.

Our liaison woman, Kregždė, who had maintained our district's communications with the Vytis District, was arrested. When the NKVD started breaking her limbs, she began to talk. The Bolsheviks learned that the center of the resistance was in Vilnius. We needed to quickly address this exposure so that the central leadership we had so painstakingly put together would not be liquidated and our work interrupted.

On December 28, 1946, we met in small groups. The situation became even more dire when a member of our leadership was arrested. We decided to leave Vilnius as soon as possible[80] and to move up the date of the meeting of the leadership and hold it within the Tauras District. Each one of us took it upon ourselves to make contact with the various districts and ensure that they did not send their liaison people into Vilnius. Everyone was assigned a part of communications and was instructed to change the location of central headquarters.

Tautvydas and I were given the task of warning the leadership of southern Lithuania's partisans. Several of the leaders of headquarters were planning on staying in those areas as well.

Those of us who had worked in the armed resistance did not know the entire structure of the passive resistance and therefore we entrusted Būtautas with the task of warning them all. We promised to provide a base.

Setting Up the Birutė Regiment

The Bolsheviks turned out to be quite flexible in their fight against the partisans. They constantly changed their tactics, always trying to adapt to the ever-changing conditions of the fighting. Just as soon as the partisans changed their tactics, the Bolsheviks accommodated themselves to them. In this manner, the two sides engaged in a deadly game of hide and seek.

For these reasons, on January 22, 1947, the leadership of the Tauras District decided to establish a new unit of operation, the Birutė Regiment, which would partially be located in the city of Kaunas. The founding of this regiment was

---

78 A. Daukantas was arrested before he even reached Poland.

79 In reality, the ties to the West were interrupted and the resistance was experiencing arrests because Jonas Markulis was acting as a double-agent, informing to the NKVD on partisan activities.

80 At this point Lukša had figured out that Markulis was acting as a double agent and that the partisan leadership was in danger.

meant to strengthen resistance activities in the city of Kaunas and its suburbs. It was especially intended for the conditions of operating within the city. This regiment was also vital to central command.

I was given new duties. I was assigned leader of the Birutė Regiment. All of the organizational work of the regiment lay on my shoulders.

The "Black Cat" of Kaunas

In January, 1947, in Kaunas, a band of thieves from Belorussia who called themselves the "Black Cats," and who operated during the night, made their appearance. Working in small bands they would rob people out on the street after dark. They would rob anyone they could catch, and would take away all their clothing, often murdering them. They also would break into apartments. It took a while until the people figured out their tactics. They would stand outside an apartment door and mew like a cat until the people inside opened the door. Then they would break into the apartment, steal the people's money, their valuables and clothing, and whatever else they could carry. Not a single night went by in Kaunas without someone being murdered. Red Army soldiers and other Soviets participated in these nightly robberies.

At dusk, people in Kaunas would lock their doors and not go out. If anyone was resolved to go out to the movies or the theater, then they would organize a large group of people to go out together, arming themselves with clubs.

As a result, whenever we had to go out at night to take care of business, we would have to spend a long time at each person's door convincing them that it was us and that it was safe to let us in.

After several months of operation in Kaunas, the "Black Cat" moved on to Vilnius, and then they left Lithuania for other countries.

Poverty in the City

The Birutė Regiment suffered much more material hardship than the other partisan regiments. The quality of life for the residents of the city and its suburbs was not something to be envied. Laborers and office workers earned around 450 rubles a month, the price of four kilograms of butter. Almost half of their wages were taken away as taxes. People working in intellectual fields were not much better off. My former colleagues, who now taught at the University, were earning so little that they were dependent on their families in the countryside to provide them with food.

I got to know one family, the Griausmas family. They lived in one of the city's suburbs. During the years of independence the father had worked at a food factory, now he worked for the Soviet railroad. His wife worked as a cleaning woman in a factory. Both of their salaries combined amounted to 240 rubles. This salary did not nearly satisfy their needs. Therefore, after some time the mother quit her job in the factory and began buying and selling on the black market. But even this type of work was not profitable under the Soviet system. They could barely make ends meet.

All of the city's workers lived in that kind of abject poverty. The luckier ones had factory jobs. They could steal goods from the factories behind their bosses backs and sell them on the black market. From two incomes they could cobble together a meager existence.

The Partisan Provocateurs

In 1947, in the regions further away from the cities, a new wave of Soviet provocation took place. Several dozen units of NKVD men who had trained in Major Sokolov's[81] *Osobyj Banditskij Otdiel* (OBO)[82] showed up in the southern regions of the Tauras District with the goal of infiltrating the partisan units. The provocateurs came from NKVD training schools and were of Russian, Lithuanian, and Jewish origin. They were thoroughly acquainted with Sokolov's methods of infiltrating the partisan ranks and destroying them from within. There were a few former partisans in the ranks. They had turned themselves in under the Bartašiūnas amnesty and had been forced to join the OBO. The provocateurs wore actual partisan uniforms. On their sleeves they wore badges similar to those of the partisans. They had all been provided with authentic partisan caps. They acquired these uniforms by taking them off the corpses of killed partisans. The partisans would be laid out naked in the town market squares. The provocateurs tried to simulate partisan cordiality when they met with the local people. They exercised self-restraint, and were polite, well-mannered, and pious.

Several dozen provocateurs arrived in the Tauras District and tried to fool the local people by posing as partisans from the Samogitia region. They invented a story that they had been separated from their unit during battle. Some of them

---

81 Aleksey Aleksyivich Sokolov, 1903–1973. He was born in Nizheny Novgorod, Russia. He worked in the Soviet Intelligence from 1927 onwards. He was a major and then later a general in the NKVD. He came to occupied Lithuania from occupied Ukraine where he had gained significant expertise in infiltrating and liquidating partisan units. From 1946 onwards he organized bands of *smogikai* or infiltrators. He instituted a new tactic. The *smogikai* units were to not be made up from Soviet local militia or NKVD, but from former partisans captured alive and tortured or coerced into cooperating with the NKVD. Sokolov is one of the most significant war criminals in Lithuanian history. He actively participated in organizing the genocide of the Lithuanian nation in 1949–1950. Under his leadership 150 partisans were killed.

82 A special unit within the NKVD structure to fight against the partisans.

One of the most sinister-and effective-tactics used by the Soviet security was the special units used to infiltrate the resistance, dressed as and acting as partisans. The concept was first used in Ukraine, where a certain major Aleksey Sokolov has been credited for developing the concept. Already in the 1920s Sokolov had successfully used this technique for capturing and killing riot leaders in Russia. The Soviet security used captured and recruited partisans to set up units of false resistance fighters, who, by using very cunning methods, gained information, captured and killed partisans.

remained in the Vaišvydava forest, and the others, the ones who spoke Lithuanian and a few of the Russians, around midnight approached the farm of a family known to support the partisans. They woke up the farmer and asked to be let in. When the farmer[83] opened the door, they left four men outside posted as guards while the rest stumbled inside. Out of 18 provocateurs only three of them talked. The others remained silent because they either did not speak Lithuanian or spoke it so poorly that it would soon give away their origins. The unit leader wore an overgrown beard, just like a real partisan. On his sleeve he wore not only a badge, but marks indicating that he had been wounded six times. Their weapons were all different and looked as though they had been collected in various battles. The bearded man demanded the farmer bring them food. The farmer told them he did not have enough food on hand to feed that many men. They apologized but proceeded to search for food themselves. They explained that they had not eaten for days. Before they ate they all tried to make the sign of the cross, but the farmer

83 K. Petrusevičius.

These units were further used to lure Lukša into an ambush and kill him. A spectacular part of this operation was a photo of Lukša, having returned from the West, but the heads of his comrades have been replaced by the heads of special agents.

immediately noticed that most of them did not know how. They either started from the wrong side or made it upside down.

After they ate, the partisans asked to be brought to the local partisan unit. They explained that they were out of ammunition. They also said they needed to receive instructions. The farmer noticed that these partisans were uncharacteristically nervous. Every single time they heard the slightest innocuous noise, one of the guards would run inside and tell their "leader" who would then alert his men to prepare for battle.

For two hours the partisan "leader" argued with the farmer to be brought to the local unit. The farmer stubbornly kept telling them, "I don't know anything and I don't know anybody. I have no ties with the partisans." After the two hours, the "partisans" gave up and tried their luck elsewhere. The farmer then rushed off to see the local NKVD leadership. He informed them that about 20 "bandits" had broken away from their unit during a battle and were wandering the area searching for their unit.

The following night the provocateurs showed up ten kilometers away. Here they killed two local Communist leaders, accusing them of collaborating with the Bolsheviks. It later turned out that the Soviets knew that those two Communist leaders were actually collaborating with the underground. The Communists used the provocateurs to get rid of them. After the killings, the "partisans" visited a number of local homes. At some of the homes they asked for support. At other homes they were cruel with the people and led some of them out into the forest to be executed. The people who were led into the forests were the ones who refused to feed or house them or give out information. They were tortured in the name of the "partisans" and accused of "collaborating" with the Soviets. There were a few instances in which people who wanted to avoid torture chose to give out the whereabouts of the actual partisans. They were released.

On the following day the provocateurs faked a battle with the Soviets in the forest. Around eleven at night two cars filled with Soviet Interior Forces arrived near the forest and took positions. They started firing. In the evening they deposited two corpses dressed in partisan uniforms in the local market square.

At night the provocateurs showed up at the homes of the people who they had already visited. The ones who had fed them or given them any kind of assistance were shown their NKVD badges. Then they were dealt with on the spot. Then they went to the people who had refused to assist them and showed them their partisan uniforms and punished them for "treason." Two people who were actually friendly to the Soviet cause died in this manner.

We later figured out that the two bodies that were tossed in the market square after the "battle" were actually the bodies of two German prisoners of war that were brought from a concentration camp for this specific purpose. They dressed them in partisan uniforms, executed them, and tossed their remains in the market square.

Smaller units of provocateurs operated in the Darius and Girėnas Unit region. They numbered around ten, although a larger number of reserves hid in the surrounding forests. They had no success in provoking the local people, since they had already been warned ahead of time.

It was very difficult for the partisans to enter into battle with the provocateurs. For several weeks in a row the units were on guard duty, scouting the villages. However, they could not manage to catch up with the provocateurs. In the village of Agurkiškės they encountered the provocateurs, but these retreated without firing a shot.

New Assignments

I had barely managed to set up the groundwork for the new regiment in Kaunas when I was pulled off the project and given a new assignment. The new assignment was of vital importance. I was ordered, together with Partisan Rimvydas, to break through the Iron Curtain and to go to the West in order to find out what progress was being made among the Lithuanians who had fled to West to bring about our independence. We had not heard from the two representatives we had sent earlier. Nor had we received a single message from the partisan Daukantas, who had accompanied them.

As it turned out, we had to postpone our trip for a while because the Soviets were preparing to hold "national" elections to select delegates for the newly-created Lithuanian "Supreme Soviet." Or, to be more precise, the Lithuanian puppet parliament. Elections were scheduled to take place February 9, 1947—a date that was innocent enough, except that by coincidence all the other so-called "independent" Soviet republics had scheduled their elections on the same day for their Supreme Soviets.

Just like a year ago, the Russians embarked on a massive propaganda campaign months before the elections were scheduled to be held. In the cities all civil servants and white collar workers were "recruited" for the task of electioneering, while the managers of businesses and officers were instructed in advance to make sure all their employees voted when election time came round.

Since the greatest opposition to this forthcoming election was expected to come from the rural population, the electioneering in these areas was conducted by various officials of the Soviet Military and the political forces stationed there. These included the NKVD, the secret police, and the Red Army. The Soviets must have been expecting strong opposition because 60,000 Red Army soldiers were brought in from Russia—a force twice the size of Lithuania's peacetime army.

Detachments of Red Army troops and Soviet Interior Forces were dispersed throughout the electoral districts in the ratio of 25 to 32 men for each precinct. These garrisons guarded the polling stations at night, made periodic tours of the villages, and herded citizens to political rallies on the appointed days. They conducted house searches whenever they pleased.

One of those house searches, conducted on February 3rd, interrupted the work of several partisans, including me. Four of us were visiting partisan Skirgaila, who had set up temporary headquarters in a sympathizing farmer's house. Skirgaila and I were forging passports and other documents for people in the resistance while the others were putting together lists of Lithuanians who had been tortured and deported by the Soviets or whose farms had been destroyed.

We were so intent on our work that we were not even aware that the Russians were approaching the farmstead until they were already inside the yard. At this point it was too late for us to reach our bunker outside. We had just enough time to conceal ourselves in the root cellar beneath the kitchen floor. Skirgaila and I grabbed the documents—about 1000 in all—while the others hastily collected the lists and anything else that might give us away. These we carried into the farmer's kitchen and through the trap door into the cellar. As soon as we were inside, the farmer's wife camouflaged the door by scattering wood shavings all around it. Then, to be on the safe side, she put a bench directly over it. She placed a basin of water on the bench, as though she were taking a sponge bath. She had already stripped off most of her clothing and was splashing herself with water when the Russians entered. The moment they did, she let out a terrible scream and began covering herself.

They were so surprised, they forgot about searching the kitchen. They mumbled their apologies and made a few perfunctory stabs with their bayonets at a sauerkraut barrel and then went off to search the room in which we had been working. Later, we realized that in our rush to hide we had left a few things out in the open that would have given us away if they had searched more thoroughly. For instance, we had overlooked two rubber stamps and several pages from our list that had fallen to the floor and lay under a bench. We also had left the cover of an American typewriter lying on top of the brick stove. Fortunately, the farmer's father had stayed in the room. Noticing these pieces of incriminating evidence, he gathered them up and slipped them into his pants pockets. When the Russians entered the room, he was seated beside the stove, placidly smoking his pipe. He stayed there all throughout the search, placidly smoking his pipe and carefully studying their movements as they went about their work.

When they grew tired of searching, the Russians summoned the farmer and ordered him to bring them something to eat. The latter hemmed and hawed. He complained that his family was so big, that he could not feed strangers. But in the end, he had to feed these unwelcome guests. Then he had to promise them he would attend the political rally scheduled for that day. He promised just to get them to leave.

After the Russians left, we emerged from the cellar prepared to continue our work. It was then that we noticed one of our rubber stamps lying on the floor in full view. The farmer's father hadn't noticed it either. The amazing thing was that none of the Russians had noticed. Most likely because they were not looking as hard for partisans as they were for things to steal. When the farmer took inventory, he found that 300 rubles and his daughter's gold bracelet were missing.

This time the partisan opposition to the forthcoming elections primarily took the form of various underground publications urging the people not to vote. We did not feel it was necessary to take more serious measures because we suspected that the people themselves were as reluctant to vote as they had been the previous year and would not be going to the polls unless dragged there. Moreover, these elections were limited to Lithuania, so that even if considerable numbers of voters were pressured into casting their ballots, they would not, by so doing, be acknowledging political ties with the Soviet Union.

Subsequent events proved that we had estimated the Lithuanian people's attitude correctly. More Lithuanians stayed away from the polls than ever before, especially in the rural districts. According to reliable sources, the ratio of those who voted of their own free will was roughly two or three individuals for every 50 families.

The Russians resorted to their usual forms of coercion and intimidation on election day. At twelve noon (Moscow time) troops were dispatched from each voting district with orders to canvass nearby villages and increase voter turn out. However, many of the villagers had been anticipating something of the sort and had either locked themselves in their houses or had gone elsewhere for the day. The ones who had not taken such precautions were hauled away to the local militia where they were tortured. But even among these unfortunates, a significant number remained adamant and refused to cast their votes, no matter what.

The farms and villages that lay farther away from the polling districts were canvassed by troopers with portable ballot boxes. But they too seldom found anybody "at home." The individuals who had been enlisted to drive these troopers around reported that after a while they did not even bother climbing out of their carts when they reached a farm. They were afraid of being ambushed by the partisans. As a result, the few people who did actually voluntarily go to the polls discovered that, according to the records, they had already voted. However, in such instances the Soviets were resourceful, and each of these voters cast his ballot in someone else's name.

Predictably, the election results turned out to be overwhelmingly in favor of the Soviets. According to their statistics, 97.91 percent of the enfranchised were supposed to have voted this time and nearly all of them cast their votes for the Communist Party. An article in the February 11, 1947 issue of the official Communist publication *Tiesa* (Truth) hailed the election as "a splendid triumph for the Communist Party." But the Lithuanian people knew very well what sort of triumph it was. They recalled only too vividly how relentlessly the followers of their "father and teacher" Comrade Stalin had pressured and persecuted them. Not even the dead had been allowed to rest in peace. To cite just one example, the bodies of five partisans (including that of a woman, Aurelė) had been left unburied for nearly two weeks. The reason was so that the bodies could be dragged through the village of Veiveriai on election day so that the people would think twice before boycotting the polls.

The Massive Interrogations

The Soviet authorities were furious about the resistance to the electioneering in the rural districts. These areas were hit with massive arrests afterwards. The action was undertaken partly as reprisal, but primarily as a means of unmasking the partisans who, the Soviets insisted, had to be the farmers and villagers themselves. Their opposition to the elections clearly showed that they were partisans or were strongly influenced by the partisans. They also reasoned that so few partisans were apprehended in the rural areas because the same people posed as peaceful farmers during the day, and did it so convincingly that the authorities had never before suspected them of their nefarious activities of the night. The Soviets were completely wrong, of course, but they did not realize it until after countless innocent Lithuanians had been subjected to persecution.

Heavily armed security officers supported by Interior troops descended on Lithuanian farms and villages, promptly arresting everyone in sight. The arrested were herded into open-air compounds and afterwards taken one by one into interrogation rooms where they were asked question after question about the partisan life. However, most villagers and townspeople did not speak or understand Russian; and the NKVD did not speak Lithuanian. Because the two languages share little common vocabulary, there were many misunderstandings. Because of these linguistic misunderstandings one simple-minded villager was almost shot.

The interrogator demanded to know:

"Do you know Saulė[84]?" (Lithuanian for the sun).

The interrogator meant the local unit leader who went by the code name Saulė [sun]. The villager misunderstood him, thinking he was referring to the sun up in the sky.

"Oh yes, yes, of course I know," the villager said in a mixture of Lithuanian and Russian and took the interrogator by the sleeve and led him outside.

The interrogator was excited, thinking that finally he would be able to make an arrest. He grabbed his submachine gun and allowed the villager to lead him through the throngs of people and outdoors. Here the man pointed up at the sun in the sky and said, "Comrade Captain, that up there is Saulė."

The interrogator rammed the butt of his submachine gun into the simple man's back and shoved him back inside.

"Which one of the partisans is Barsukas (Badger)?"[85] He demanded. Barsukas, a leader of one of the other partisan units, had recently killed a group of Bolsheviks in the Pakuonis region. But the man thought he was talking about badgers.

"Oh yes, here in our forests we used to have a lot of them, that was during the Smetona era," the villager said, rolling himself a cigarette.

"Wait a minute," barked the interrogator, "you had partisans here during the Smetona era?"

"What partisans, Comrade Interrogator? You were asking me about badges," the man said and his face lit up. He obviously was eager to have a conversation about badgers.

"Damn it! You fool! You claim you don't know any partisans, but you probably run out at night to meet with them," the interrogator shrieked.

---

84 Alfonsas Aliukevičius, 1915–1947. He had military experience from the Lithuanian military. He was married and had two daughters. From 1944 onwards he led the partisans units in Darsūniškės. He was the head of the Viesulys Unit in the Tauras District from February 20, 1945 onwards. He was killed in a bunker in 1947.

85 Antanas Išganaitis, 1924–.

He pulled out his belt and hit the villager across the face.

The interrogator was met with similar answers when he asked about the partisans Viesulas (Whirlwind), Papartis (Fern), Žentas (son-in-law), Naktis (Night), and a number of others whose code names were the names of animals or plants. The Russians, even this far into the conflict with the partisans, still had not figured out that the Lithuanians chose code names that had actual meanings in nature. They could not understand a word of the local language.

The interrogator grew more and more frustrated with his miscommunications with the villagers. He wanted to lead the simple villager outside and shoot him on the spot. The only thing that stopped him was that others intervened on the man's behalf, explaining that he was simple and did not grasp what was going on. Only in this way did the man escape getting shot.

Most of the people brought in for interrogation were then brought to prison because they had aroused the suspicions of the interrogators. Only, most likely, the reason they were suspicious was because they did not speak Russian.

Mažvydas and Pušelė's "Engagement" Party

Ever since 1944 the partisans had been following the activities of the Communist leadership in the city of Marijampolė with concern. Lulled into a sense of security by the vast concentration of troops in that area, the Russians and their collaborators were growing more insolent with every passing day. They seemed to forget that there was a resistance. By 1947, the Vytautas District decided to do something about it. They devised a simple plan. They would invite the most active members of the Marijampolė administration to a party and assassinate them all. After some discussion, the partisan leadership decided that the best time to hold such a party would be the Tuesday before Ash Wednesday—a traditional feast day in Lithuania, the Mardi Gras. They announced a wedding engagement between partisan Mažvydas[86] and liaison officer Pušelė.[87] The staff allocated 3,000 rubles for expenses and instructed Mažvydas and Pušelė to work out a plan.

Pušelė had been selected for obvious reasons. Her brother Giedrutis had been killed among the partisan ranks. At the same time, her job as an accountant at the Marijampolė Trade Union Commission put her in contact with many important officials and administrative department heads. Since she was on friendly terms

86 Kazimieras Pyplys, who also went under the code name Tigras.

87 Anelė Julija Senkutė, 1922–1947. She was a liaison officer since the spring of 1946. On October 15 of that year, after killing five Communist officials at the "engagement party" she joined the fighting ranks of the partisans. She was betrayed and killed in a bunker on April 27, 1947.

with most of these officials, it seemed natural that the fake engagement be celebrated in her house. She bought the provisions and made other arrangements while Mažvydas concentrated on devising a method of killing off the guests. The easiest method seemed to poison them. He would only need to get them thoroughly drunk and then introduce a small quantity of arsenic or cyanide or some other equally virulent poison into their glasses. Acquiring vodka was no problem. Anyone could buy as much as he wanted in the state-operated stores. The difficulty lay in obtaining the poison.

It was impossible to get any poison in Marijampolė. Therefore, Mažvydas traveled to Kaunas to search for poison. He acquired a Soviet passport, a work permit, a union card, a certificate that stated he had completed his military obligation, and an affidavit attesting to his proletariat origins. Then he boarded one of the perpetually late-running trains and rode to Kaunas in a cattle car that had been set aside for the local citizenry. He left the train just as it slowed down at the bridge outside the city limits and completed his journey on foot. Mažvydas had lived in Kaunas his entire life and he was worried that he might be recognized in the train station.

Conditions in Kaunas were bad. People were dispirited and continually harassed by the Russians. As a result, they were extremely cautious and fearful. After two days of searching, Mažvydas still had not found any poison. Unsuccessful, he decided to leave.

There seemed to be no other way of killing the guests other than shooting them. Mažvydas selected 12 men from the Vytautas Unit to do the job. They were to assemble at a pre-arranged destination on the evening of the party and to wait there for his signal. In the event that unforeseen circumstances interfered with these arrangements, Mažvydas and Pušelė would carry out the assassinations themselves. In general, the plan seemed simple. However, there were a few problems that arose because of Mažvydas himself. These problems had to do with his size. It was nearly impossible to get him the right clothing for the occasion. The first problem was with his dress pants. He was so tall, the pant cuffs had to be let out completely. Then it turned out that it was impossible to obtain dress shoes in his size. We finally settled on dressing him in his field boots, but polishing them to a high shine. We hoped that the trousers would cover up the fact that he was wearing field boots.

Finally, the groom was ready. His suit fit perfectly, not a single crease was evident. His boots shone like mirrors. His tie and the handkerchief that protruded from his breast pocket were both the same color—red. What the color represented was open to interpretation. Red could symbolize anything from burning love for his fiancé to a newly discovered political awareness of the Communist Party.

Now that he looked presentable, Mažvydas began checking his guns. He selected two Walthers and loaded them with ammunition. He spent so much time fussing over his weapons that the hostess of the event began to tease him that he ought to be thinking more about "love" for his bride than his guns. Mažvydas stuck one Walther in his belt and the other in his pocket. He checked himself in the mirror. Because of his long suit jacket, the weapons were well concealed.

Then, the hostess fed Mažvydas a liter and a half of fat to give him something to absorb the alcohol he would have to drink that night.

Pušelė's sister led the young fiancé through the neighborhood to the apartment where the party was to take place. Mažvydas took a good look at the surrounding areas and noted the best escape routes.

This is where the play began. Pušelė was with her friend, Albina, and two other young women who had come early to help prepare the food and set the table. One of the women was Saulutė, a member of the passive resistance who knew what was going to take place that evening. The other was a woman with the surname Karveliūtė who was a member of the Communist Youth.

Wanting to keep up a front for her girlfriends, Pušelė greeted Mažvydas with a passionate kiss. She introduced him to the women and the evening's performance begun successfully. In order to keep Albina and Karveliūtė from growing suspicious, Mažvydas had to play-act the role of the happy man in love. This was hard for him to do. Several years of fighting as a partisan in the forest had hardened him. The hundreds of battles he had engaged in had left a mark on him. It was difficult for him to act pleasant and relax and laugh and have a good time when inside he felt agitated. Then, it was hard for him to act out his love for Pušelė when he was preoccupied with the details of the assassinations that would have to take place that evening. It was difficult to make interesting and pleasant conversation, knowing that he, the fiancé, might get killed later that night. Nonetheless, the show had to go on.

After the preparations were completed, Albina rushed out to change into her good clothes. The guests were due to arrive soon. The minutes crept past slowly. A half hour went by and still no guests arrived. More time elapsed and not a single invited guest showed up. Mažvydas began to worry.

Another half hour passed and the door was flung open by the Russian chairman of the Executive Committee. He was already partially drunk. He saw all the food and liquor that had been prepared. The bride to be begged him to go out and find his friends and bring them back, so the party could begin.

"Fuck, they must be crazy to be late," he said, taking in the spread on the table.

Pušelė threw on her coat and went out with him to search for the others.

As soon as they had left, Karveliūtė took over the party and began shooting questions at Mažvydas. Where was he born? How did he meet Pušelė? When did he meet her? How soon would the wedding take place? Would they live in Vilnius? And on and on. Mažvydas was worried. He knew that Pušelė must have told her some sort of a story, but he did not know what the story was. He knew that because this woman was in the Communist Youth League, Pušelė had put a lot of effort into befriending her. Therefore, he tried to answer her ambiguously and turn the talk in another direction. Saulutė helped him. But Mažvydas was concerned. Why was this woman asking so many questions? Could the Communists be onto their plan? Could they be plotting a counter-attack?

Then Pušelė and the Russian returned, bringing with them two more of the invited guests. They had even managed to find an accordion player somewhere and had brought him back too. Of the new guests, one happened to be the secretary of the Marijampolė District Executive Committee (also a Russian) and the other was a Lithuanian collaborator by the name of Steponas Bakevičius. He was the Secretary of the Marijampolė Communist Party and had been recently elected as Marijampolė's delegate to the Lithuanian Supreme Soviet. Without waiting for the other guests, they all sat down at the table and the celebration began.

Soon a series of toasts began. The first toast was to the happy couple's future together. The second toast was to Stalin, the next to the glorious Lithuanian Soviet Socialist Republic, and then to the Red Army, and then to the Communist Party, and then the glorious Soviet youth and so on. Toast followed toast in rapid succession and the alcohol flowed. Soon everyone around the table was drunk and their cheeks were flushed. Saulutė began flirting with Bakevičius. She was so convincing, that through the prism of alcohol Bakevičius even began to believe that he was in love. He sat there in adoration, tossing down shot after shot of vodka.

The time came to tip off the waiting partisans as to the situation. Pušelė slipped out to meet them. She told them of Mažydas's concerns and that he might just be right because the larger number of invited Communist guests had not shown up. They began to doubt whether it was worth the risk to carry out the assassination when so few Bolsheviks had come to the "party." Vampyras left the deciding word up to Mažydas and retreated with his men to their hiding place.

Pušelė's abrupt departure had made Karveliūtė suspicious. From the moment Pušelė left, Karveliūtė kept her eyes glued to the door and continued to pry, firing question after question at Mažydas.

Pušelė rejoined the party and cuddled up to her fiancé in such a way that it suggested that even the brief separation from him was too much to bear. But her real intention was not romantic at all. It was the only way she could get close enough to Mažydas to tell him what she had discussed with the partisans outside.

At that point conversations were interrupted by the arrival of a certain Gurevičius, who headed the passport office. He came in the door, out of breath.

"I ran almost the entire way from Sasnava on foot," he panted, "just to keep my word and be here tonight."

"Maybe the bandits were on your tail," Albina laughed.

Everyone laughed. And that only made Mažydas more suspicious. He thought to himself, maybe running from the wolf you have jumped onto the bear?

Gurevičius asked for quiet. Then he explained that he had been running because he was delayed at the office. A thousand passports, the type that enable the bearer to travel in border zones, were missing. He and his staff had spent hours trying to track them down, but with no success. They could not even figure out how the passports had disappeared.

"Most likely the bandits stole them," Gurevičius concluded. "They probably got the *Stribai* drunk and then the committed the robbery."

Because he was late, Gurevičius had to catch up with his drinking. He tossed shot after shot in rapid succession.

Albina, whose cheeks were red and who was in a good mood from all the vodka, stood up and gave a speech dedicated to the happy couple.

Bakevičius also wished them luck and drained his glass in one swift movement. But he did not stand up to give a speech. By this time he could barely formulate a coherent sentence. Meanwhile, Gurevičius was doing his best to catch up to the others. Besides drinking toasts to the health and happiness of the couple, he drank a toast to the speedy recovery of the passports and then went on to toast whatever shot into his head. The only person to stop drinking was Karveliūtė. She refused all offers to fill her glass and seemed agitated by the situation. Perhaps she smelled death in the air.

Knowing what was about to happen made Mažvydas uneasy as well. Whenever the guests made a chance remark, he fell into analyzing it in his head, trying to figure out if they were on to him or not. He indulged himself in grim thoughts. Here, these people were talking about what they would do tomorrow, and yet not one of them would live an hour or two longer. He also debated with himself whether they should go through with it or not. He got to the point that even the most innocent remarks seemed filled with innuendo.

Pušelė seemed nervous and unsure also. When Bakevičius asked if they had enough vodka to last the night, she answered, "Don't worry, you'll never finish it all."

It was a polite answer, but it sounded wrong. It sounded like an accidental tip off.

The accordion player struck up a waltz and everyone stood up to dance, except for the happy couple. They remained seated, tapping their feet to the beat, concealing their nervousness.

Mažvydas became even more nervous when he saw Karveliūtė go out into the hall and whisper something into Gurevičius's ear. Because the music was so loud, he could not hear what they were saying, but Karveliūtė's expression was deadly serious and she kept shooting suspicious glances at him as she talked.

Then, Gurevičius came to the table and began asking questions. Again, Mažvydas answered the same questions.

The music stopped and people came to the table and ate and drank again. Mažvydas began to regret eating the fat because the alcohol had no effect on him and he had to play-act being drunk. He copied the table manners of drunk Russians, and groped for the food with his hands, forgetting to use his fork and knife.

When the time came for another dance, he and Pušelė backed out, saying they felt tired. She wrapped her arms around Mažvydas and began caressing him, hoping to hide his mounting anxiety from the other guests. Mažvydas, meanwhile, racked his brains over what to do. The small numbers of guests weighed towards postponing the assassinations. But what good would that do? The Soviets were now suspicious of him and they would arrest him the moment the party was over. Then Pušelė would be watched very carefully, she would be useless to the partisans and her own life would be disrupted. Even if they suspected nothing, it was still problematic. Under what pretext would the partisans be able to stage such a party in the future? And who could guarantee that more Soviet officials would show up? No, he decided, it was better to stick to the original plan and get it over with.

Just as Mažvydas reached this conclusion, he heard loud voices out in the hallway. Although the music drowned out the voices, he got the drift of the conversation. Karveliūtė had warned Albina to be careful because something about Mažvydas did not add up. Mažvydas's suspicions were confirmed when he distinctly heard the safe coming off of a pistol. It was Gurevičius. Now he only hoped he could prevent the Communists from striking the first blow.

The room was dark because it was illuminated only by two candles. The electricity was turned off at ten o'clock each night. Taking advantage of the dim light,

Mažvydas slipped his Walter out of his jacket pocket and cradled it in his hands. His position gave him the advantage to fire first if Gurevičius rushed at him with his own gun. However, this didn't happen. Gurevičius came forward slowly with Albina at his side. He broke away and sat down beside Mažvydas for a chat. Pušelė leapt up from the table and announced that there was something she had to do in the kitchen. The situation was too tense for her to take. She needed time in the kitchen alone to calm her nerves. Again, Mažvydas was asked the very same questions by Gurevičius. What he couldn't figure out, was what to do with the gun in plain view under the table. Fortunately, Gurevičius turned away from him to pour them both a drink and Mažvydas was able to slip the gun back into his jacket pocket.

"It's time some one took care of you," Gurevičius said. "Engaged men are so love-struck they forget all about drinking."

Mažvydas forced a smile. "I'm seeing double," he said, "I can't even stand up anymore." He took the glass and emptied it.

They were joined by the chairman of the Executive Committee, who wanted to know where Pušelė had disappeared to. That provided Mažvydas the perfect opportunity to get away from both of them. He assured them both that he would go and fetch his wayward fiancé and bring her back to the table. He stood up and staggered off in the direction of the kitchen.

By the time he stepped inside the kitchen, he was resolved to finish the job.

"The time has come, Pušelė," he said. "It's dangerous to wait any longer."

It was impossible to get a message out to the waiting partisans without being noticed. Except for the accordion player, every single guest seemed to know what was up.

Pušelė was frightened and suggested they wait.

"Absolutely not," said Mažvydas. "The Bolsheviks are not going to let me out of this party without checking me out. You and Saulutė go out there and invite them all to sit down at the table. I'll come out and take care of them. If anything goes wrong, you shoot. Only four of them are armed."

Pušelė agreed. She took a loading grip on her pistol and tucked it into her purse. She went out and invited the guests to sit down at the table. During that time Mažvydas prepared his Walters. Pušelė signaled Mažvydas and he came out into the room. He held both hands behind his back with the prepared guns. He approached the table and fired with both weapons. The first victim was Gurevičius, the second was the party Secretary of the Executive Committee, and then in rapid succession he shot the District Deputy Secretary Bakevičius and the Russian chairman of the Executive Committee. Karveliūtė was also shot and killed.

The musician made a run for it, dropping his accordion on the stairs outside the apartment door. Mažvydas removed the weapons of the dead Soviets. It was much darker now because one of the candles had been accidentally shattered by the first round of shots. Then Mažvydas noticed that one of the bodies was moving. It was the chairman of the Executive Committee trying to get up from beneath the table. Mažvydas shot him again and rechecked the other bodies. Then he noticed Albina. She lay in a corner, trembling. It was shock. Pušelė and Saulutė had been hit by ricocheting bullets. Pušelė's hand had been shot through and Saulutė was wounded in the shoulder. Mažvydas quickly saw to the girls' wounds and they ran from the apartment, taking with them two accordions and a few other things. Albina was left behind.

They had to hurry because a member of the *Stribai* lived next door and was sure to have alerted the Soviet garrison. They ran through the streets of Marijampolė, but although the women knew the city well, they got lost. Mažvydas had a compass with him. He checked the direction and led them out of the city into the safety of the forest.

When they reached the partisan bunker safely the district commander extended his hand, "Congratulations for making it out alive and leaving the others dead. Tonight marks 60 kills on your record."

For the first time that evening Mažvydas smiled and took a deep breath. That smile had been missing throughout his entire engagement party. Now he was able to kiss the two women and shake hands with his comrades. Without assistance, Mažvydas had taken down 60 Bolsheviks. He was considered one of the bravest of the partisans.

Before hearing the entire story, the partisans took care of the women's wounds, bringing them to their company nurse. After the wounds were attended to, Mažvydas smoked and told the others about the events of the evening.

The Aftermath

As could be expected, that very night the manhunt for a tall man and two blond women began. Soviet Interior Forces thoroughly checked all means of mass transit. The Soviets had learned about the assassination of their officials later that same evening. It turned out that during the shooting, the musician had been wounded in the throat. He escaped the scene of the shooting, and was spotted hurrying towards one of the bridges that led out of town. On the bridge the sentry ordered him to stop. The musician was terrified. He was convinced that the partisans wanted to kill him too. He also couldn't speak because of the wound to his throat. He tried to explain through hand gestures what had happened, but the sentry could not catch his meaning. The sentry brought him to the militia.

There, at the militia's headquarters, he wrote down his version of what had happened, although he himself was confused about the details and was not sure how the shooting had started.

The head NKVD interrogator Greisas[88] was brought in to take on the job. He too had been invited to Pušelė's engagement party, but he had not attended because he knew of her ties to the underground and was suspicious of the motives of the invitation.

Albina was arrested immediately and a wide-scale investigation and man-hunt was launched. By morning all roads leading out of Marijampolė were blocked. Every method of transportation was carefully monitored and the passengers scrutinized. Soviet troops patrolled the streets and searched house after house.

Elaborate funeral preparations were made for the dead. On the day of the funeral all theaters and movie houses were closed down. The day was declared a day of mourning. The funeral was attended by a number of Soviet dignitaries, including the puppet president of Soviet Lithuania, Justas Paleckis.[89] However, Paleckis was so angry at the gullibility of the victims that he refused to say a word of eulogy at the grave. He claimed that if the victims were stupid enough to fraternize with "bandits," then they deserved what they got.

After the funeral, the Marijampolė NKVD launched a massive wave of arrests. Anyone whose activities were in the least bit suspect were arrested and taken into custody.

Although Interrogator Greisas escaped being killed at the engagement party, ironically he was killed a few days later in the midst of the man hunt. Greisas, accompanied by an armed Russian trooper, arrived at the Marijampolė Gymnasium, marched into the lecture hall and arrested one of the students, a boy by the name of Šarūnas[90] who was a member of the passive resistance. Thinking on his feet, Šarūnas asked Greisas if he could stop by his house and pick up an overcoat since he had come to school that morning only with a light jacket and the weather

---

88 Aaron Greisas, 1908–1947. He was a secret member of the Communist Party since 1929. In 1935 and 1937 he was fined by the democratic government of Lithuania for his seditious activities. From 1940 onwards he worked for the NKVD in Lithuania. As an interrogator he was known for his cruelty and brutality. He would force people to admit even to petty crimes. He was also a known rapist.

89 Justas Paleckis, 1899–1980. One of Lithuania's most significant collaborators. He actively participated in all aspects of Lithuania's occupation and was the temporary prime minister and then puppet president of Lithuania.

90 Bronius Petrauskas, 1928–1949. After his escape from Marijampolė he joined the Vytautas District partisans. He was betrayed and killed in a bunker February 10, 1949.

Some Lithuanian communists acted as "Quislings," formally taking the responsibility for the country joining the Soviet Union and acting as the local government. In this picture of the Supreme Council, taken April 5th 1948, Justas Paleckis, the chairman of the Supreme Council is sitting to the right.

had suddenly turned cold. Šarūnas knew that he had a pistol hidden in his wardrobe and under the pretense of taking out his coat, he could retrieve the pistol and shoot Greisas. Greisas, on the other hand, welcomed the opportunity to conduct a search of the boy's house and find other family members.

When they reached Šarūnas's house, Greisas posted the Russian outside the door as a guard and accompanied the boy inside. Greisas began searching the premises. Meanwhile, Šarūnas retrieved the pistol and slipped it into his pocket. Šarūnas pulled the safety and was about to open fire but Greisas, hearing the click, rushed into the room and grabbed the boy's arm. Šarūnas held on to his gun and with his other hand punched Greisas in the head. A struggle ensued and Šarūnas managed to get Greisas on the ground and shoot him in the forehead. Šarūnas grabbed Greisas' pistol and made a run for it. The guard, seeing the arrested boy hurrying towards him without the interrogator, figured out what had happened and began to chase him. Šarūnas shot at him as he ran, but missed every time.

Šarūnas hurried out of the city on foot. Along the way he saw a farmer driving a horse-drawn cart. He jumped into the cart and at gun point demanded that the farmer drive him out of the city. In this way Šarūnas managed to escape.

Greisas had the most information about the resistance and knew details that would have implicated many people in the underground. All of this information died with him. The Bolsheviks never caught up with Šarūnas or the partisans who had staged the "engagement party" massacre. They pursued the investigation a while longer, but finally gave up, marking the case closed.

More Bolshevik Killings

After this success, the Vytautas Unit partisans planned a second attack on the Marijampolė Soviets. They decided to stage a massive assault on the Soviet Interior Forces troops stationed in the neighboring town of Liudvinanvas. An assault of this size could not be safely carried out in close proximity to civilians. Therefore, the partisans had to devise a pretext to lure the NKVD a safe distance away from the town and into the countryside. They decided on raiding a Soviet storehouse for vodka located several kilometers away from Liudvinavas on what was formerly known as the Butka estate. The NKVD were bound to be informed by telephone of the raid and would come rushing out to stop the raid. Then the partisans could ambush them on the road leading to the store house.

Early one morning a handful of partisans snuck into the compound before the sentries would realize what was happening. They seized the entire contents of the distillery along with most of its grain supply. Then they headed for the Butka Forest to conceal the stolen goods.

In the meantime, more partisans entrenched themselves along both sides of the road about a kilometers away from the distillery. This operation was led by Vampyras and Mažvydas. Entrenched alongside the road, they waited for the Soviet troops to show up. Two hours went by. They still had not shown up. The partisans could not figure out what was going on. Not until a reconnaissance scout returned with the news that the storehouse and distillery's telephone lines had been accidentally severed during the raid, did they realize that telephone communications were impossible. If the report was to reach the Soviets, it would have to be done by a messenger. Apparently, the officials from the store house were afraid to venture out of their stronghold to convey news of the raid.

Two of the partisans changed into civilian clothing and set out quickly in the direction of the distillery. When they came in view of the officials, they began play-acting that they were drunk, staggering around, slurring their words. They shouted that they had walked the entire way from Liudvinavas just to sober themselves up.

The officials knew that the partisans did not tolerate public drunkenness and punished whoever they caught drunk out in the open. They figured that the partisans must be gone and that it was now safe to come out. One of the sentries was sent to Liudvinavas with the report.

Very soon reconnaissance scouts reported sighting three, horse-drawn sledges filled with Soviet Interior Forces personnel heading down the road towards the distillery. As soon as the sledges came into their range the partisans opened fire. The bullets were released so quickly that most of the men in the sledges were killed instantly. The ones who escaped into the ditches alongside the road were then picked off. Within ten minutes the entire unit of 21 were killed and their weapons confiscated. Two partisans were killed.

Then the scouts reported that reinforcements were on their way to the aid their comrades. They must have heard the gunfire. The partisans realized that the gunfire had probably been heard all the way in Marijampolė and that reinforcements would soon be sent from there. They would soon be heavily out-numbered. The partisans decided to withdraw rather than engage in battle. They held the next two sledges full of Soviet Interior Forces at bay with machine gun fire and allowed their scouts to escape. Then they themselves withdrew into the Butka forests.

This operation turned out to be quite profitable for the partisans. The partisans had acquired a large quantity of wheat, a stockpile of Russian weapons, and around 400 liters of 200 proof alcohol, which they sold on the black market for a good price.

IV

Breaking Through the Iron Curtain to the West

June 1947–December 1947

The First Journey

Approaching the Border

In March we completed preparations for a journey to the West to restore communications. We provided ourselves with various supplies, including special drugs to treat against dog bites, since dogs were used to patrol the border. We then reported to various organizations to obtain final instructions. Unfortunately, we had to pass through an area where just a few days ago an important liaison man had fallen into the hands of the Soviet Interior Forces. The Russians had succeeded in learning from him the location of the Iron Wolf Regiment staff headquarters. They also succeeded in confiscating part of the archives. Now they were working to find the location of the resistance center and for this effort had amassed a sizable segment of their Security Forces in the surrounding countryside.

Some detachments had closed off the roads. Others occupied positions in high lying places, armed with machine guns. A third force carried out exhaustive searches among local inhabitants. Dozens of NKVD would surround a farmer's homestead and conduct a superficial search. Then an exhaustive search would follow in which the Russians would turn the houses upside down in their raid. Sometimes, they would even dismantle the stoves and turn over all the fodder and litter in the barns. In some buildings they dug up the earth to the depth of a meter. They were searching for partisan bunkers and for archives. They used special metal spits two to three meters long to prod the earth. With the spits, they would probe the entire farmyard; they would probe along the edges of fences, stables and barns. They broke down walls to discern whether they were double. They measured the houses from the inside and from the outside.

On the strength of reports from local Communist intelligence, the Russians suspected a certain farmer of having an armed resistance bunker on his premises. They conducted an exhaustive search and found nothing. So, they dragged in the farmer's wife and demanded she show them where the bunker was. She refused. They set trained dogs on her. Drenched in her own blood, with her flesh literally torn from her bones by the dogs, the woman still refused to tell the NKVD where the bunker was hidden.

The Bolsheviks went mad searching for the important archive of the resistance. At farmer K's in the village of N. the NKVD destroyed the floor to his storeroom and then, using buckets and sacks, removed more than a meter and a half of earth. They found nothing. During the raid a staff liaison woman called Palma[1] was arrested. But she outsmarted the Soviet Security Officers, and they got nothing out of her. After a brief interrogation, they released her.

* * *

According to the orders I had received from the Iron Wolf Regiment we were to be led further by fighters from the Birutė Unit. We met at M., said good-bye to the fighters who had accompanied us to this point, and continued onwards. Changing our liaison personnel frequently, we traveled through the Darius-Girėnas Unit region and reached the Kęstutis District and Varnas's[2] (Crow) Unit. Considerable searches were being conducted in this area as well, but we were lucky. Within two days we were able to establish contact with the unit leader. He passed on our leadership's instructions and gave us some final suggestions. We took two days to carefully discuss our mission. Then we moved on closer towards the border, to the Vytautas District. We were accompanied by several fighters from the Kęstutis District: Klajūnas[3] (Wanderer), Tūzas,[4] Perkūnas[5] (Thunder), Genys[6] (Woodpecker), and Gardenis.[7]

We reached the pre-arranged liaison points in the Vytautas District region where ten well-armed men from the unit met us. Among them was the District leader, Vampyras, and my good friend Mažvydas. We spent some time hiding with the unit because of the white nights. It was too light at night to safely pass through the border. Also, we were unfamiliar with the border zone. We used the time to acquire additional documents and to familiarize ourselves with the activities of the unit.

---

1 Birutė Ališauskaitė. 1924–.

2 Jonas Rimša, 1914–1947. He was a lieutenant in the Lithuanian army. He was arrested January 1, 1945 and exiled to a concentration camp in Vorkuta. In July 1945, he escaped from the concentration camp, returned to Lithuania, and joined the partisans. He blew himself up on August 19, 1947, together with his wife, Monika, in a bunker.

3 Jonas Brazys, 1921–1949. He was a partisan from 1946. He was betrayed and killed January 16, 1949.

4 A partisan from the Kestutis District.

5 Bronius Dženkauskas-Augustinavičius, 1925–1947. He was a partisan from 1945. He was killed July 27, 1947.

6 Vladas Kučiauskas, 1922–1947. Joined the partisans in 1945. He was killed in battle July 10, 1947.

7 Identity unknown.

* * *

When we reached the territory of the Vytautas District, we learned of a terrible misfortune that occurred on April 27, 1947. The unit staff had installed a dwelling in the Gulbiniškiai Village where the chief of staff, Kunigaikštis and two other functionaries hid. Among them was Pušelė. After the "engagement party" in Marijampolė and the incident in Butka, the Communists had strengthened their reconnaissance. Meanwhile, the duty officer, Kunigaikštis, had to go out every night on various assignments. During those white nights the Russians were able to see the activity on the farm.

After several hours of searching the suspected farm, Soviet Interior Forces began stripping the floor of the house. As they were probing the ground, they came upon the site of the shelter. The partisans heard them probing and began destroying documents and equipment. The Soviet Interior Forces began to dig with spades. The bunker had been designed for living purposes and not for defense; therefore, the partisans hiding inside had no alternative but to blow themselves up.

They put all their weapons on the table, the typewriter, and other printing supplies, so that they would not fall into the Bolsheviks' hands. Kunigaikštis and Baritonas each took an anti-tank grenade and detonated them at the same time. The explosion was so powerful that the shelter roof flew into the air and all four walls collapsed. The Soviet Interior Forces found only ruined weapons, destroyed supplies, the ashes of burned documents, and the corpses of unrecognizable partisans. Among the partisans who perished in the explosion, only Pušelė's face was not mutilated and recognizable. All three bodies were brought to Marijampolė.

A few days later we came to visit the scene of destruction. The cross that had hung on the wall inside the bunker and the Lithuanian national coat-of-arms had been left in the rubble among dismembered limbs.

It was a beautiful time of year—the first half of May. However, the beauty of nature bursting into bloom only worsened our mood. The contrast between the beautiful world the creator had made for us and the hopelessness of our present situation was almost too much to bear. We thought of the thousands of eyes who would not be seeing the beauty of this spring.

Everyone in the area mourned the death of Kunigaikštis. Women could not speak of him without tears coming to their eyes. Whenever Kunigaikštis had appeared in someone's home, people rejoiced. He could dry the tears of weeping women, cry over their dead sons with them. He could comfort sisters who had lost their brothers and children who had lost their fathers. He managed to give hope to people who could find no hope under the Communist nightmare. But the people who mourned his death the most were his wife and the children he left behind.

Saulutė also suffered. Pušelė had been her best friend. She had accompanied Pušelė on this path of hardship, battle, and death after the "engagement party" in Marijampolė. Now she was left alone without any close relatives or friends. All of her relatives had either been killed in the fight for freedom or had been deported to Siberia. She alone had managed to stay alive in Lithuania. It had been a little more than a year since she had left the Kaunas Conservatory where she had been a student. Since that time she had been active in the resistance. She was a gentle, sensitive, innately musical person who carried in her memory the texts and melodies of hundreds of partisan songs.

* * *

After ten days we moved closer towards the border. Vampyras and a few other partisans accompanied us. At night we covered fourteen kilometers. We traveled very carefully because the searches were not yet over. We would rest every few kilometers. Our first night of walking revealed to us that we were no longer accustomed to longer, more rigorous, hikes. Our travel was hindered by our heavy backpacks, our weapons, and other supplies. By dawn we were completely exhausted. The clothing we were wearing for the hike was too heavy because the weather had warmed unexpectedly. Rimvydas and I had the hardest time since we were carrying the ammunition and our backpacks were heavier than the others.

By dawn we reached Menkupis. The nature here was incredibly beautiful. As the sun came up hundred of birds sang in the bushes. Their songs refreshed us. We walked faster because daylight was upon us and we still had half a kilometer to go.

A few fighters met us in a pre-arranged spot. Under their leadership, we reached safety within a half hour. At the safe place we met ten more men. Among them, three, Stumbras[8] (Bison), Nykštukas[9] (Elf), and Rudaitis[10] were to accompany us across the border.

---

8 Aleksas Keleris, 1921–1981. During the 1940 Soviet occupation of Lithuania he was jailed for his patriotic activities. When the war began he joined a self-defense unit. In 1945 he was taken prisoner by the Americans. The Americans trained him for espionage work, but he was accidentally parachuted into Poland. He crossed the border into Lithuania and joined the partisans. He participated in leading emissaries from the West through the border from Poland into Lithuania and from Lithuania into Poland. He was arrested July 31, 1947, and deported to Siberia. He returned from Siberia in 1956.

9 Stasys Gurevičius, 1918–1951. He joined the partisans along the Polish border in 1945. Later he became a leader of the Polish partisans. He died fighting in Poland in 1951.

10 Bonifacas Rutkauskas, 1922–1947. He joined the partisans along the Polish border in 1945. He shot himself when surrounded by the enemy in his bunker.

The three of them, Vampyras, the unit leader Karvelis[11] (pigeon), Rimvydas and I deliberated on the further details of our journey. The area near Punskas where the border had been previously crossed, now seemed dangerous. We did not think it would be possible to get through without engaging in battle. The Bolsheviks had reinforced this area with a system of concrete bunkers, special fox holes to hide lookouts, and double barbed wire and other traps.[12] Therefore, we decided to make our crossing far to the right of Punskas. We decided that the following night we would get closer to the border and with increased security spend the night there. The following night we would break through the border. Our guides knew the area very well.

We Break Through the Iron Curtain

Once we had determined the exact details of our expedition, we said a short prayer, and then set out in the general direction of the Polish border. Although there were fifteen of us, Rimvydas and I were accompanied by just three experienced guides who would make the crossing with us. The remaining members of our party would return to their units just as soon as the five of us were safely on Polish soil. They had accompanied us in order to protect us along the way and were fully prepared to serve as live targets in the event of an enemy attack. They would engage the enemy, and we would pass through the border.

The night was very dark and the journey was extremely difficult, especially for me. I had developed a fever the day before when I had foolishly stretched out on a patch of wet grass. Now I felt dizzy and decidedly uncomfortable. I must have been running a high fever because every pore of my body was oozing with sweat. But I said nothing to my comrades. They took my unusual dispiritedness as worry rather than illness.

Our progress was slowed down by unexpected delays making contact with liaisons and obtaining food supplies. We did not reach the border until daybreak. Once we came close to the border we decided to stop and rest until evening. We took care to conceal ourselves among the underbrush, but not until after the sun had dried the dewy grass, concealing our footsteps, did we begin to feel a little more secure.

---

11 Feliksas Čereška, 1912–1952. He joined the partisans in 1944. He was betrayed and killed April 2, 1951.

12 The border between occupied Lithuania and Poland was treacherous and consisted of a 100 meter "death zone" where nobody set foot. About 20 meters in Lithuania's direction there was a double barbed wire fence. The barbed wire was interspersed with rockets and mines. Beyond that was a 500 meter "no-man's land" where all the local inhabitants were forced off their land. Beyond it was zone II, which was approximately two kilometers long, and then came zone III, which was 10 kilometers long. Civilians needed special permission to enter these heavily patrolled zones.

Immediately after lunch, Vampyras and two of his men set out to recon the area. For one, they had to determine the point where the crossing could most easily be made. For another, they had to discern the exact schedules of the border patrols and the locations of the concealed sentry posts. They returned an hour and a half later. They brought back some worrying news. It appeared that they had almost inadvertently given away our entire plan. That set Rimvydas and I cursing. They explained what happened. The three scouts had studied a strip of terrain some 730 meters from the border for quite a while. With not a single Russian in sight they fell into a false sense of security. As a result, they failed to notice the approach of a mounted border sentry until the man was practically on top of them. They dove into the bushes, but the Russian was so close he could hear their breathing. He leapt down from his horse and pulled out his automatic.

"Who's there?" he barked in Russian.

Vampyras and his men remained perfectly still, holding their breath. The sentry waited and listened for what seemed like an eternity. He did not hear another sound, so he climbed back onto his horse and rode away. His departure suggested that he had probably not noticed the scouts. He had most likely attributed the noise to a wild boar in the bushes and left it at that. But we had no way of knowing for sure. The five of us decided to break away from the others and to make the crossing at once before he could bring in reinforcements. We reasoned that there was no need to risk so many partisan lives unnecessarily. We were well-armed with anti-tank grenades and semi-automatic weapons. We would be able to defend ourselves in the event of an attack.

It was a good quarter of a mile to the crossing point and it was broad daylight. We crept forwards slowly and cautiously, keeping a vigilant and constant lookout for concealed outpost installations. After an hour or so we arrived at the spot where the Russian sentry had narrowly missed intercepting our advance scouts. We found a cap lying on the ground. In their haste to get away one of our scouts had lost his cap, but the Russian had not noticed it. The fact that we found the cap and not a troop of Soviet Interior Forces meant that the Russian had probably not attached much significance to the incident—at least not enough to warrant further investigation.

We were relieved. We concealed ourselves in the same bushes and remained there for the rest of the afternoon. We were much too close to the border to risk traveling during daylight.

As soon as it had grown dark enough, we emerged and prepared ourselves for the final segment of our journey. Stumbras, who had crossed into Poland many

Juozas Lukša, accompanied by a fellow partisan Jurgis Krikščiūnas-codename Rimvydas-on their way towards the Polish border, spring 1947.
Both are equipped with the Russian submachine gun PPD (Pistolet Pylemjot Degtyareva) with a magazine of 71 bullets. This was originally a Finnish constructed weapon, used in the winter war of 1939–1940 by the Finns against the Soviet troops. The weapon proved effective and easy to handle so the Soviets copied it.

times before, took the lead. The rest of us followed behind him at about fifty meters distance. For a while we trudged along a densely-wooded ravine. After three hundred meters the ravine ended and we found ourselves facing a wide stretch of open terrain. This was the most dangerous part of the crossing. We advanced stealthily, holding our weapons in constant readiness and keeping our eyes on Stumbras. Suddenly, he raised his hand in our pre-arranged signal to stop. We fell flat onto the ground and listened. We heard the sound of Russian voices not very far away. These voices were succeeded by silhouettes. Before long four border patrol guards came into view. We tracked their every move with our weapons, but they were so engrossed in conversation that they walked right past without noticing us.

Soon afterwards, Stumbras gave the signal to advance again. Since it was much darker now, we closed the distance between us and continued on our way. The closer we came to the border, the more tense we became. I looked around and saw that I was not the only one drenched in sweat. We all were. Finally, Stumbras signaled again. This time to indicate that the place where we would be making the crossing lay ahead of us. It consisted of a strip of land that had been ploughed and harrowed and then mined. Stumbras knew where each of the mines were located. We had to follow his instructions. We moved forward cautiously, stepping inside each others footsteps, so that in the morning the Russians would not be able to tell how many people had made the crossing. Finally, we found ourselves facing the two posts that marked the border. The post on the Lithuanian side was painted red while the post on the Polish side was painted in red and white stripes.

It is impossible to describe the feeling of elation we experienced the moment we found ourselves beyond the Iron Curtain. Such moments of pure ecstasy happen only very rarely in a man's lifetime. We wanted to jump and shout for joy, and we might have if Stumbras had not insisted on absolute silence. We still had to worry about the Polish border patrol.

We were able to finally rest about four hundred meters beyond the border zone. We thanked God for our successful crossing, shook each others hands, kissed each other, and then collapsed down onto our backs to rest.

On the Polish Side of the Border

We rested for only a very short time. We had all sorts of duties to attend to. Stumbras ordered all of us to lift up our shoes. He painted our soles with turpentine. The Russian border guards had been known to track people who had crossed the border with dogs up to 20 kilometers into Polish territory. We were soon on our way again.

The further we moved away from the border, the more light-hearted we felt. Everything about the countryside seemed new and wonderful. The scent of elderberry permeated the air. We decorated our buttonholes with clusters of elderberry blossoms.

The night sky twinkled with millions of stars. Here and there passing through villages we heard Lithuanians singing at the May Masses. We were surprised to hear that all the words to the masses and the hymns were in Lithuanian and were very similar to what we used to hear at home in Lithuania. Young people piled out of the churches, and walked home, singing together in Lithuanian. We almost ran into them a few times. We were resolved not to let anyone see us, and therefore we often had to dive into a ditch or into the bushes to let a giggling, singing group of young people pass.

For the first time I observed this region of Lithuania that had been torn away by the Poles twenty years ago. Entire counties had remained Lithuanian. Poles made up a small minority of the inhabitants. The local Lithuanians had a name for them, *Mozūrai.* Naturally, the years of Polish occupation and the intense polonification of the region did a lot of harm to the local Lithuanians. The Polish government had dragged the schools and the Church into their goal of altering the local

Lithuanian ethnicity into a Polish one. All of these politics could be felt in the Vilnius region where a Lithuanian surname was considered a pagan surname. The cooperation of the Polish church with these nationalist politics had done a lot of damage. Their demeanor shamed the Catholic nation of Poland. But here along the Polish borders Lithuanians were still praying in their mother tongue.

Entire occupied regions resisted this intensive polonification campaign. People who had escaped from Soviet-occupied Lithuania would come here to revel in the Lithuanian spirit. Nykštukas told us that many families in the region did not even know how to speak Polish.

The entire look of the region was decidedly Lithuanian. The crossroads were still adorned with folk art crosses. These crosses had been destroyed by the Bolsheviks all over Lithuania. Granted, many had been damaged by the Nazis as well.

Our guides had crossed this border many times, accompanying a variety of Lithuanian leaders with a variety of missions.

When we reached the farm where we were headed, we quietly slipped past the dogs and crept inside the farm house. The family was made up of four people: a grandmother, a mother and a father, and a son. When she saw us, the grandmother burst into tears.

"Dear God," she said in their particular local dialect, "what do I see? It's a miracle!" This woman, who had been broken by hardship, climbed out of her rough bed. "We thought the Russians had killed you all," she said, "It's been an entire year without any news."

"Don't cry Mother," Nykštukas soothed her, "you know what it takes to kill a Lithuanian. One is killed and several more come and take his place. Quite a few of us old-timers are still around."

The son reached for his accordion and began to sing: "Lithuania dear one, my homeland, the land where heroes sleep in their graves." After several days of intense stress during our journey, this was a very pleasant reprieve. We were in a foreign country, but at the same time we were standing on our ancestral land. All of our exhaustion evaporated instantly. The boy was a good musician and when we started singing our partisan songs, he quickly caught on to the melodies. Just to be safe, we asked the father to shut the windows, although on the whole we knew we were safe here. The Polish border guards do not patrol here and the neighbors had already returned from the May Holiday Mass. We enjoyed the company of this family for about an hour and then traveled on our way. So that we would not get lost, we asked the father to accompany us. Traveling in this region it was important for one to be familiar with the area since there were still many areas that were mined from the war. The local people knew their way around the mines.

The hike through the Polish countryside was very different from the hike through the Lithuanian countryside. There we were constantly on the look-out and had our weapons prepared, ready to shoot. Here we walked quietly, careful not to run into civilians, yet all of our weapons had the safety on and were tossed onto our backs. Only occasionally did we glance around at our surroundings.

Our friend led us about ten kilometers and then said good-bye. Stumbras led us for the remainder of the journey. A few kilometers before our meeting place, we sat down in a ditch to rest. The smokers among us enjoyed a cigarette, while the rest of us studied the map. The meeting place was quite far from the border and seemed safe enough. The area seemed suitable for self-defense. We were roughly a third of a kilometer away from our meeting place.

We walked the remainder of the journey carefully. The sun was rising and we might easily stumble upon people. We walked wide circles around the farmsteads, placing our boots in each others' footsteps.

When we reached our location, we surrounded the farmstead and monitored the activity inside. When we were sure that nothing suspicious was going on, we went to wake up the master of the house, careful not to set off the dogs barking. We were not successful. We had barely slipped through the gate when two dogs started barking—one in a deep baritone and the other in a high-pitched howl. To shut them up, Rudaitis and I ran over to their dog houses and lifted them up by the chains. My little dog shut up immediately. Rudaitis struggled with the German Shepherd for quite a while until he settled down. The master of the house came rushing outside in his night shirt to rescue us from his dogs.

We spent about an hour with the family. Our arrival had taken them completely by surprise. For a long while none of the Lithuanian partisans had passed through their house and so they thought that our activities had been completed extinguished.

Here we learned more about the situation in Poland. We were especially interested in the activities of the Polish partisans. As it turned out, that spring an amnesty had been granted and almost all of them had returned from the forests to civilian life. There had been a few incidents in which individuals who had chosen to continue fighting had been killed off by their comrades-in-arms who had chosen civilian life. They told us that just recently in the forests around Suvalki a partisan general had been hung. This general had been actively involved in the resistance from the beginning when Poland first lost its independence. This spring, when the amnesty was offered, most of the partisans from his unit were tempted into registering as civilians and leaving the unit. He decided to remain in the forest because in his opinion Poland still did not have independent rights and was a puppet of Moscow. Several of his former officers were given a mission by Polish Security Forces to take him alive and bring him to Suvalki. They performed their duties zealously. The general was betrayed and brought to the Polish authorities. Within a few days he was formally hung.

As day broke we went to lie down in the barn on the hay left over from last winter. Outside, the farmer's sons took up guard positions. Inside, we took turns keeping guard.

The day was absolutely perfect. The sun was shining. We were filled with new impressions and in a good mood. We had no desire to sleep at all. We climbed up into the loft and gazed around at our surroundings. The nature in the area was beautiful. The fields were filled with farm workers. The farmsteads were in worse condition than those in Lithuania. The buildings were not set up in a logical, geometric pattern, like in Lithuania. The farm buildings were usually built too close to each other, giving a crowded effect. The farm buildings themselves were in worse repair than in Lithuania. We got the impression that farmers in independent Poland had had a harder time than farmers in independent Lithuania. We had brought some Lithuanian sausage and lard with us and we now shared it out.

After lunch the farmer's family had more time to spend with us. They were very interested in hearing about our lives in Soviet-occupied Lithuania. They listened with horror as we told them about the tragic state of our nation.

Only when it got dark did we go out to the meeting place. The hike was very much like the previous night's hike, only now we had to hide more since many civilians were out and walking around.

Here we met with our partisans.[13] We learned from them that like us, they too had no news of Deksnys, Lokys, or Daukantas. However, they were of the opinion that the Polish Security, the UB,[14] had not arrested them because their liaisons remained in place.

---

[13] On the Polish side of the border in the Punsk and Seinai regions, the Perkūnas and later the Vytautas District Number Four Unit partisans were stationed. This unit consisted of about 10 individuals. These partisans occasionally crossed the border over into Lithuania to fight. Then they would return to Poland. They would return to Poland in uniform and armed and would then change into civilian clothing and work on the Polish farms as farmhands. They had fictive Polish documents. In total, around 62 partisans hid among Polish farmers and in the Polish forests. Most of them were eventually arrested by the Soviets and exiled to Siberia. Several dozen were killed. A few are still alive and live in Poland. The farmers who sheltered these partisans were arrested and punished, and either jailed or exiled to the formerly German regions of Poland.

[14] Urząd Bezpieczeństwa.

The West Recommends We Return and Wait

We safely arranged to make contact with Deksnys in the West. Everything went seamlessly. Ten days later, on May 19, we met with Deksnys.

It turned out that Deksnys and Algirdas Vokietatis (code name Lokys) had both successfully reached the West. Things had not gone so well for Daukantas though. He had been arrested along the way by the Soviets. A few packages containing supplies and information for the resistance in Lithuania were confiscated en route to Lithuania. Now we understood what had occurred with our ties to the West.

We delivered all the documents intended for the West to Deksnys and reported on the current situation to him. We answered the necessary letters. We passed on to Deksnys an appeal for support to Lithuanian émigré liberation organizations in the West.

Deksnys gave us some information regarding the West.

We were not able to complete all our assigned tasks at our meeting with Deksnys. He explained to us that the international situation was not in our favor. He was working hard on this issue, but there had been no progress. Deksnys convinced us that for now the best thing would be for us to return. He told us he would come to us in the autumn and would bring necessary supplies with him. We set up instructions for further liaison, said our good-byes, and parted.

We returned to the border, but circumstances did not allow us to make the crossing immediately. We spent ten days in the area. Disguised as local farm workers and carrying farm implements with us, we would often come close to the border zone and carefully observe the Russian soldiers' habits and the newly installed fortifications. We watched as new wooden guard posts were built, as more barbed wire reinforced the border, and as trenches were dug and new bunkers built. After their work was completed, it seemed as though no one would ever get through that border again. Not even a mouse could pass through those reinforcements. Our future looked grim.

Our Lithuanian partisans operating on the Polish side of the border belonged to the Vytautas District. Their main function was to maintain various ties with the West. For a long time their ties with Lithuania were severed. During that time they had joined up with the Polish partisans. When the Polish partisans took advantage of the amnesty and returned to civilian life, our partisans broke away from them and operated independently. Their unit leader was Balandis[15] (Pigeon). We had been given orders by the Vytautas District leader to conduct an investigation of this unit. We questioned the partisans under Balandis's command carefully and learned that he was not liked because he lacked initiative and was irresponsible. I decided to bring him back to Lithuania with me and in his place I left Nykštukas to take over command. We selected Gedgaudas[16] as his second-in-command. The unit's first assignment was to bring Deksnys's package to Lithuania. That would transpire at the end of the summer, towards autumn.

These partisans had a difficult time acquiring food to sustain themselves. The local people were wary of supporting the partisans. The situation was much trickier than in Lithuania, where the partisans had various means of obtaining food.

The previous autumn a partisan unit, led by Tauras,[17] had worn Russian uniforms to go out and collect food from the local people. They had been assigned a mission that would keep them in Poland a month. They had no way of obtaining food, even by trade. They decided that they would have to take it from the local populace that did not sympathize with the fight for freedom. They pretended that they were Russians trying to break through the border to Russia. Tauras would put on a Russian lieutenant's uniform and would go see a farmer on the borderlands. He would tell them that his property now belonged to the Lithuanian Socialist Republic and that a border wall would be set up on his land, cutting his property in half. The Polish farmers were terrified. They feared the "Russian paradise" more than a devil fears the cross. Then Tauras would offer to do the farmer a favor. In exchange for a few sheep or some bacon, he would arrange it so that the border crossed along the edge of his fields, rather than down the

---

15 Antanas Marcinonis, 1914–unknown. He joined the partisans in 1944. He was arrested and sentenced to 25 years in a concentration camp in Siberia. He was released from the concentration camp in 1965. He lived in Kaliningrad and then later in Vilnius. He died in Vilnius.

16 Gediminas Lastauskas, 1923–1992. He joined the partisans in 1944. On August 13, 1947, he was arrested by the Polish Secret Police and was handed over to the Russians. He was sentenced to 25 years in a concentration camp in Siberia. He returned to Lithuania in 1955 and died in 1992.

17 Identity not known, but most likely Antanas Pakruopis, 1909–. In June 1946, he brought Lukša and his comrades to Lithuania. He was arrested on August 13, 1947, by the Polish Secret Police and was handed over to the Russians. He was sentenced to 25 years in a concentration camp in Siberia. He returned to Lithuania in 1956.

middle of his farm, leaving his house on the Polish side of the border. The farmer would be beside himself with joy and declare that there were good men, even among the Russians. Dealing the local Polish farmers in this manner was their main source of a food supply. After some time the locals reported to the Polish Security Police that the Russians were planning to move the border an entire kilometer deeper into Poland. However, both the Polish and Russian authorities were confused by these reports, which created some tension, but the matter was never fully resolved.

A Stormy Return

After all our affairs were in order, we said good-bye to the men who were headed in the opposite direction and traveled towards the border zone. Six of us prepared to make the border crossing into Lithuania. Besides Stumbras, Rimvydas, Rudaitis, Balandis, and myself, we had a fresh partisan in our midst, named Vėjas[18] (Wind). When the Russians had occupied Lithuania he had crossed over the border into Poland and after a while joined with the partisans over there. Nykštukas and Šamas[19] also accompanied us to the border. That same night we reached the Pašešupis Forest, which stretched to the border. Here we planned to spend the day and try our luck crossing the border at night. We decided to spend the night on the edge of the forest close to Lithuania. Moving through the thick underbrush we almost lost our way. We only regained our bearings close to the border. We chose a spot to rest a kilometer and a half's distance from the border. Towards morning there was a deep frost. We kept warm by huddling into small groups. We even dared to start a fire out of dried twigs. We were not in too much danger here. Our earlier experience was that the guard was not too attentive in this area. For that reason, we felt rather relaxed, although we did need to be careful. We considered the situation better than in Lithuania where we were constantly hunted on a daily basis by the Bolsheviks.

The morning of June 5th dawned. It was a Thursday. We broke up into pairs, covered ourselves with branches, and appointed guards. Then we drifted off to

---

18 Antanas Šliaužys, 1927–1951. He escaped the Russian recruitment by crossing over into Poland and finding work with Polish farmers. In June 1947, he returned to Lithuania with Juozas Lukša. In Lithuania he fought with the Vytautas District 43rd Unit. On January 13, 1949, he accompanied a group of partisans to a meeting with the leadership of the Kęstutis District partisans. The group was surrounded by NKVD soldiers. During the fighting that ensued he was wounded and taken prisoner. During interrogations he admitted to fighting against the Soviet occupation as a partisan, but refused to betray any of his comrades. As a result he was brutally tortured. He was sentenced to death and was shot on June 7, 1951, in Vilnius.

19 Antanas Kvedaravičius, 1916–1951. He joined the partisans on the Polish border in 1945. He died in battle in 1951.

sleep. However, once day broke not one of us felt like sleeping any longer. We forgot about discipline and lay on our sides, bathing in the sun. Despite the fact that we were about to return into the kingdom of death, we were all in a good mood. We tried to outdo each other, seeing who could tell the best jokes. In the middle of the day, during prayer time, we did not forget to pray for protection during the coming night's crossing.

A few hours before our crossing was to begin, Stumbras and I went out on reconnaissance. We broke our way through the underbrush to the very edge of the forest and observed the border from under the cover of the bushes. Stumbras explained the situation to me. This area was in between two NKVD border posts—Reketija and Liubava. About 100 border guards were stationed here. Along the border, right under our noses, guards on foot and on horse back, passed by us. We tried to familiarize ourselves with the system of trenches. In several places we noticed hidden trenches. Just before dark the guard changed and reinforcements were brought in. We noticed where the hidden lookout took their positions. After we completed our reconnaissance, we both stared at each other.

"Well, Daumantas,[20] there are a lot of Ivans on the border today. Maybe they got a whiff of us coming?" Stumbras cursed in dialect.

"It doesn't look as though we're going to get across without engaging in battle… Maybe we shouldn't try to cross today. We'll find another spot tomorrow," I said.

But Stumbras disagreed.

"What are we waiting for? If we've made plans, then we should just go through. We'll say one extra Holy Mary for protection. Do you really think there will be less of them elsewhere?"

Reluctantly, I gave in. Only I warned Stumbras not to tell the others about the reinforcements. I did not see the point of panicking them.

"Good, we won't tell them," Stumbras said, "I wouldn't want the new guy to die ahead of his time."

We both laughed and returned to our friends. We found them already prepared to make the crossing. They all surrounded us and wanted to hear what we had learned during reconnaissance. We played down what we'd seen. We didn't tell them we had noticed a few more patrols, that we had located a few secret trenches. Instead, we announced that we knew exactly in what direction we would travel. We marked on our maps and planned to mark the rest of the distance later.

---

[20] One of Juozas Lukša's code names.

I appointed Stumbras to lead us across the border. I warned everyone that in the event of a firefight, they should strictly stick to their orders.

We tightened our backpacks, readied our weapons, and moved in the direction of the areas we had scouted. When we got closer to the forest, I gave Nykštukas and Šamas orders to find a comfortable position and to open fire if we were to engage with the Russians. That would confuse the enemy as to our exact whereabouts and fire power. They both had SVTs. During a battle the sound of these guns came in short bursts. They were to continue shooting after we had escaped from the enemy, so as to give the impression that we had not been able to make the crossing. Afterwards, we kissed and said good-bye to the men who were remaining behind. We moved forwards. Holding our weapons tightly in our hands, we lined up in single file. Before us and to our left was a pine grove in which we had noticed the hidden outposts. Somewhat farther behind them were the guard posts equipped with machine guns. Stumbras took all of this into consideration. As he crossed the frontier zone, he tried to keep more to the right in order to seek out more recessed areas where the guards' machine gun fire might not be able to target us. Without realizing it, he moved too far to the right and drifted into the other outposts.

"Give the password!" a voice shouted in Russian.

We immediately dropped to the ground and answered the Russians with bursts of machine gun fire. A hundred flares illuminated the evening sky as we were fired on him from three directions. Our two comrades, who had remained on the Polish side of the border, opened fire. They did not realize that we had strayed that far to the right and so their bursts passed directly over our heads. The first outpost with which we were fighting was now only a few meters away as we pressed forwards. Enemy fire was intensifying from all directions. I tumbled into the first convenient ditch and with my PPD I greeted a Russian who was shooting past my ears from close range. Because of the thick darkness, I could not shoot with any accuracy. Only when flashes of fire lit up the sky, could I aim my gunfire. Not too far away from me our youngest comrade, Vėjas, was experiencing his baptism by fire. I could hear him struggling to strike back the lock of his rifle. I told him to strike the handle back with his fist. He struggled and swore at his gun.

The gunfire from our closest enemies soon died away. They had either been put out of action or had exhausted their ammunition. In their place other Russians were hurrying and in our direction, discharging flares from time to time. Rapidly, we began to move from the frontier into the depths of Lithuania. I leapt out of the trenches last since I was on the right flank where the enemy's fire was concentrated. I ran to the top of the hill and caught up with my retreating comrades. They had assumed that I was dead and were arguing about how they would collect the documents I had been carrying with me. I called out the password and they replied. We continued our withdrawal together.

We advanced, as had been arranged, through uninhabited countryside that was ravaged with trenches left from the war. There were holes excavated by bombs and wire entanglements. Soon other NKVD border detachments began to fire at us. We hurried to occupy a hillside and when the enemy drew near, we struck back with concentrated fire. The Russians dispersed as we jogged towards the interior. We stopped running only long enough to smear our soles with turpentine to keep the border guards' dogs off of our scent. Meanwhile, the closer enemy detachments had ceased firing. They could only discern the direction of our retreat by firing flares. Hundreds of flares now burst open across the border zone. As soon as they were extinguished, new ones flared up.

After about five miles of swift withdrawal, we stopped to rest. We were exhausted and bathed in sweat. We decided to continue on in the same direction. Masking our footprints and once again smearing the soles of our shoes with turpentine, we began heading in the direction of Liubava, where the Russian's border garrison was located. We calculated that they would not expect us to pass so close past their stronghold.

We approached a brook and took off our boots. We obliterated our tracks by wading through the water. Some of the men's feet were hurting, so they continued walking barefoot. Two of the men had tied their boots to their knapsacks. Stumbras joked, "Men, put on your boots. If the Russians kill us, they'll take us for the *Stribai*. They're still trailing us."

Twice along our way, we took up positions for battle. One of those times amongst horses grazing in a meadow and the second time against a heap of drying peat. After the peat incident, we saw a flare rising into the air very close to our location. We dropped to the ground instantly. We heard the Russians exchange countersigns. It was a meeting of the mounted NKVD. They had completed their ring of encirclement. Fortunately for us, we had succeeded in getting beyond its confines. After the flares had died out, we shouldered our knapsacks and silently moved on. It was clear that the Russians had hoped to keep us within the ring and to beat every inch of the ground in the morning with sizable forces. We were fortunate that we had been able to move quickly and had not gotten caught in the ring.

We headed towards Liubava where we encountered minefields. For some fifteen minutes we had to move very slowly because we were placing our feet inside the tracks of our leader, Stumbras. After passing through the minefields safely, we felt more secure because we did not think the Russians would risk entering them. We sat down again for a short rest. In the border zone it was already fairly quiet. Here and there flares were still rising and isolated bursts of fire could be heard.

When the moon rose and the sky grew lighter, we took stock of our situation. Our losses were very small. Not counting the ammunition used in the fighting, Rimvydas had lost a grenade. I had lost an American pocket flashlight. I thought to myself that the Russian who found it would be alarmed and would assume that the confrontation had involved an American. The Communists hated the West. They believed that we were invulnerable only with foreign help. Our new recruit had suffered the most. While fixing the lock of his gun, he had scraped all of his knuckles. Still, he was pleased that he had gone through his baptism by fire quite honorably. He had even managed to fire thirty shots from his poorly-functioning rifle.

We did not stop here for very long. Dawn was approaching and we still had a couple of kilometers to travel to our hiding place. For our hiding place we had chosen a trench between thickets that were spread over an area of several hundred meters. It was a good place for reconnaissance because all the houses in the area had been razed during the war. We quickly found the family of farmers who had agreed to give us shelter.[21]

The farmer agreed to keep watch. So that he could keep a better eye on the area, he sent out his children to keep watch near by.

Once the watch was in place, we made our sleeping arrangements. One of us stayed alert as additional protection. After the night's sport, we were all drenched in sweat. By dawn we had all caught a chill.

At dawn we received a report from the farmer's son, who had received some news from a policeman in Liubava. While making the crossing, we had shot

---

[21] Since 1946 the farmer, Motiejus Kvietkauskas, had provided his farmstead as a bunker for the Vytautas District IV Division, II Unit. Stumbras and Apuokas belonged to this Unit. The farm was approximately 2–2.5 kilometers from the Polish border. The Kvietkauskas family not only hid partisans safely, they built a well-hidden bunker, provided food, washed the partisans' clothing, and provided them with new clothing and bedding. Their son, Sigitas, acted as a liaison and was a member of the passive resistance. In 1947, he was arrested and interrogated and the location of the bunker was discovered. The parents and son were arrested, but the father was released after the son took full responsibility. Sigitas Kvietkauskas was sentenced to 10 years in a concentration camp in Siberia. On May 22, 1948, both parents and their daughter were exiled to Siberia for materially supporting the partisans. Motiejus Kvietkauskas died in Siberia.

and killed three border guards. All the Soviet Interior Forces of Liubava had moved in the direction of Rekik and Suvalkų Kalvariją (the first direction we had moved in). They were no longer breathing down our necks and we could relax our guard.

I gave the farmer the documents I had brought over from the West and asked him to hide them by burying them somewhere in the fields in an easily recognizable place.

Towards evening it was still quiet in our area. According to the farmer's reconnaissance, all the border forces and the units stationed in Marijampolė were engaged in a large-scale operation over a 50 kilometer area in the direction we had first taken.

We cleaned and oiled our weapons and restocked our ammunition. As the sun went down, we said a short prayer, thanked God for the success we had enjoyed up to this point, ate our dinner, and continued onwards.

Visiting with a Freedom Fighter from Lithuania's First Fight for Independence

The further we traveled from the border, the better prepared we found the fields. We walked spread out in a triangle, so that in the event of attack we would have a wider range from which to defend ourselves. On this march we had to reach the "White House"[22] where our Unit leader Karvelis had set up headquarters.

Along the way we stopped to visit Stumbras's "daughters." A "daughter" is the girlfriend of a partisan. He and his friends had not visited for a very long time. Stumbras led us into the handsomely decorated parlor. Soon the entire family appeared. One of the sons immediately ran out and took up guard. We sat and made conversation with the remaining family members. The oldest daughter and her mother went to cook us a meal on the country stove. We could hear omelets cooking and milk boiling. The father, pleased to have unexpected guests, pulled out a bottle and ceremoniously set it down in the center of the table. Stumbras and Rudaitis "took care of" the prettiest daughter, who had pulled out a guitar and was strumming it, humming the melodies to partisan songs.

"Where are you from?" the farmer asked Rimvydas and I. "I haven't seen you before. You're so new you don't even have uniforms yet."

---

[22] The farmstead of Jonas Pupkas. This was the headquarters of the Vytautas District IV Unit. The bunker was set up underground, beneath the barn. It was discovered by Soviet Interior Forces soldiers on June 12–13, 1947. The partisans Apuokas and Ateitis shot themselves in this bunker and Balandis surrendered. Jonas Pupkas was tried and his family was deported to Siberia.

The support from the civilian society was the single most important factor why the resistance would endure as long as it did. In the picture a number of guerillas are having a good time with a farmer's family in the Vytis military district.

"I'm from far away, from the opposite bank of the Nemunas," Rimvydas said, unable to restrain himself.

"You're from that far away! The Nemunas! What duties brought you here?" the old man asked, completely overcome with curiosity.

Rimvydas smiled.

"You never can know where life takes us, Uncle. We get our orders and we carry them out until we end up spread out in a market square somewhere. If you've made the decision to die for your country, no one asks you on which market grounds you want to leave your corpse for the Bolsheviks to mangle."

The farmer nodded his gray head, sighed deeply, and said:

"It's true, men. Our times are so cursed that even after he dies a man can find no peace. They can't catch you alive, so they vent their anger on your corpses."

The farmer did not even wait for his wife to put the food on the table. He poured everyone a glass and invited them to drink. We did not refuse. The vodka was very strong. Rimvydas, who had never drunk such stuff before, gasped after he swallowed his first shot.

"Well, Uncle, if you're going to treat us this nicely, we'll have to stay a few more days."

"As far as I'm concerned, you may stay. Only, recently there have been a lot of them around. I wouldn't want you to get into a battle. The local Bolsheviks are onto me already."

"That wouldn't be so bad. We'd have a new partisan in our midst," I said.

"Every day my palms itch to show them a lesson. I'd like to get at them before I die. But sorry men, I'm not young anymore. During the fight for Independence[23] I showed them what I had in me."

I watched how the old man's eyes lit up as he reminisced over the past. His eyes flashed around the room, seeing visions of former battles.

Soon the women spread out the food before us. The girls sat down between us and we ate and drank. After all we had been through, we felt happy and relaxed among this family. We forgot about our daily worries. We smiled and flirted with the girls.

An hour and a half later we were on our way again through the night's darkness. We spread out in two columns and moved forwards. It was quiet along the way. No one got in our way and we soon reached Karvelis's headquarters. However, while marching through the fields we drifted to the left. To get our bearings, we stopped at the house of a local farmer. We learned that we had almost passed the place where we were headed. During the day large numbers of Russians had invaded the area, searching for "paratroopers." Although we were now more than thirty kilometers away from the border, we grew more cautious, knowing that at any moment we might stumble onto the Russians. Our suspicions that units were out hunting for us proved to be true. Stumbras began to doubt whether it was worth it for us to report to headquarters that day, because if we engaged with the Russians there we really would not have anywhere to hide when day broke. However, we decided to trust in the good fortune that had protected us thus far. With renewed caution, we decided to take the risk.

Thieves Informing for the NKVD

We walked with vigilance. Suddenly, we noticed two silhouettes dart across our path. Seeing that it was only two people, we should have let them pass, but Stumbras was already too close. He demanded they reveal themselves.

Two civilians crept out of the bushes with their hands raised. They turned out to be two thieves who were looting farms in the neighborhood, taking advantage of

---

[23] From 1918 to 1920 the Soviet Union attacked newly independent Lithuania. Lithuanian volunteer soldiers defended Lithuania's independence successfully at that time.

the situation created by the increased numbers of Soviet troops in the area. Stumbras and Rudaitis recognized them and knew all about their itchy fingers. The looters claimed that they were searching for stray cows, but when one of our men pulled a sack out of the bushes in plain view, they fell to their knees in front of Stumbras and begged his forgiveness. They promised they would never steal again. Stumbras let them off with a warning that the next time he would not be so lenient.

Because of this incident we had to change our direction and walk inside each others' tracks. These particular thieves had themselves recently crossed over the Polish border and might just have a second profession—informing for the NKVD.

Bolshevik Legs over Our Heads

Finally, we reached Unit Headquarters. Four of us made ourselves comfortable, while two went off on reconnaissance. A few minutes later the partisans Ateitis[24] (Future) and Saulė[25] (Sun) came to our assistance. They monitored the area until the sun came up. We had to be careful, because the Russians might spot our footprints at dawn.

We found Ungurys[26] (Eel) at Headquarters. He had participated in the firefight we had heard earlier that night in the distance. As it turned out Rymantas,[27] the Unit leader Karvelis,[28] and he, had walked into a Russian ambush. Karvelis was wounded. He did not know what had happened to Rymantas. Only Ungurys had escaped.

Only now did the local men learn that we had been the source of the excitement at the border. They figured that since the Russians announced that they were looking for "paratroopers" we must have made the crossing safely.

The Headquarter's bunker was of medium size and safety; it had been built for five men. This time there were about fourteen of us crowded into this space. We stripped to our undergarments and stood wedged closely together, filling the entire space.

---

[24] Vincas Gurevičius. He died the night of June 12–13, 1947 when soldiers found the bunker in Jonas Pupkas's farmstead. The bunker was mined, however, it did not explode successfully. Therefore, Gurevičius shot himself.

[25] Identity unknown.

[26] Antanas Murauskas, 1924–1948. In 1945 he was recruited into the Red Army. While on leave he joined the partisans. He was killed in battle February 13, 1948.

[27] Jonas Petras Aleščikas, 1917–1947. He was a lieutenant in the Lithuanian army. In 1944, he joined the underground. He was killed August 2, 1947.

[28] Often confused with F. Čereška who went by the same code name. Sergijus Bendaravičius, 1918–1947. He was a border guard for independent Lithuania. He joined the partisans in 1944. He was betrayed and killed June 10, 1947.

At about ten o'clock we received a report that the entire neighborhood was swarming with Russians. Two groups on foot and on horseback were approaching in our direction. It was obvious that they suspected something. Wearing only our undergarments, we buckled on our belts and began distributing the weapons. Two men with anti-tank grenades took up positions at the entrance to the bunker. Everybody was forbidden to talk, smoke, or even move. If spotted, we intended to make a break through the encirclement. We began to feel the lack of oxygen. The lamp that had been burning was extinguished.

In an effort to ease the tension, we ignored the prohibition against talking and began questioning ourselves and our consciences and wondering out loud whether we had properly said good-bye to our "daughters" and to our wives. We could sense death just around the corner. The company secretary repeatedly requested silence. He had a stack of orders, instructions, and other important documents before him, and was ready to burn all of it before it could fall into enemy hands. Because of our talking he could not concentrate and steady himself for the task ahead of him.

A dog began to bark in the yard. Now we heard footsteps over our heads and heard voices speaking in Russian. Our "guests" had arrived. A deathlike silence prevailed in the bunker. We could hear the farmer arguing with them in Russian. After ten minutes it was quiet. Even the dogs had settled down. Meanwhile, we were rapidly running out of oxygen. We were now breathing heavily, but our bodies were cold and clammy. Time wore on and the air grew thinner. We'd had to block the ventilation opening. After three wretched hours like this, we heard footsteps coming in our direction. From the agreed-upon signal we knew it was the farmer or his wife approaching. Ateitis pushed open the bunker hatch. We saw a woman's face smiling above us.

"They drank the yokes out of all our eggs and moved on. They've probably already left our area. They tried to force us to feed them, but my husband knows how to argue with them," she said.

The oppressive mood soon lifted. We greedily breathed in the fresh air that came wafting through the open hatch. Three of the men climbed out of the bunker. We lit the lamp again. We were all drenched in sweat.

The farmer soon came to the bunker and reported that large Soviet Interior Forces detachments were moving along the highway in the direction of their headquarters. Either they had already finished searching the area or they were going back to change guard. After about an hour we climbed out of the bunker. We ate and went to sleep.

We are Persecuted, but We Continue to Sing

It was quiet in the area until evening. Several hundred Soviet Interior Forces returned to their permanent stations. Karvelis did not show up, so Rymantas, Rimvydas, Stumbras, Kėkštas,[29] and I decided to travel to the bunker[30] in Panėriai. Rymantas led the march.

We did not know the area well. We used maps and a compass and walked across the fields. An hour and a half before dawn we reached the bunker. We were especially careful here because this bunker had been used for a long time and already might be known to Soviet Interior Forces. We crawled the final two hundred meters on our bellies. Once we reached the farmstead, we studied the buildings, searching for Bolsheviks who might be hiding there. There had been recent occurrences where Bolshevik units hid themselves in a farmstead without the farmer knowing it. They would hide in the farm buildings and in the fields and make their appearance after the partisans had showed up. Sometimes Soviet Interior Forces would bury themselves in the hay or in haystacks and hide there for several days waiting. They would wait for the partisans to show up at night. By day they would try to get a sense of the farmer's political leanings. We found Karvelis in the bunker. He had been wounded in the right arm. We also found the Vytautas District leader Skyda.[31]

This day turned out to be somewhat more pleasant for us than the previous day. We shared our stories and did not even notice how the time flew past. We even were able to get some sleep since there had not been any fighting in the area that day. Rymantas, Rimvydas, and Karvelis entertained us with their repertoire of partisan songs. Here I heard a new song for the first time:

Coo-coo bird, this year	*Gegutėle, šį metelį*
Come home early to us.	*Tu anksčiau pas mus parlėk.*
Sing about our suffering,	*Apraudoki mūs vargelį,*
Help us orphans.	*Našlaitėliams mums padėk.*

---

29 Julius Mielkus, 1923–2000. Joined the partisans in 1945. He was betrayed and taken prisoner by Soviet Interior Forces in 1947. He was tortured and interrogated. He was sentenced to 25 years in a concentration camp in Siberia. He returned to Lithuania in 1969.

30 This was the hospital bunker for the Vytautas District. The bunker was located on the farm of Bronius Zavecka and was built into the wood shed. The bunker was used to heal wounded partisans. The nurse Angelė Senkutė tended to the wounded. On June 10, 1947, the whereabouts of the bunker was betrayed to Soviet Interior Forces. Sergijus Bendaravičius, who was recovering from wounds in the bunker at the time, was killed. Julius Mielkus, who was tending to Bendaravičius was wounded and taken alive. Bronius Zaveckas, his wife Marija, and his son Albinas were sentenced to 10 years in a concentration camp in Siberia.

31 Jurgis Vasiliauskas, 1913–1949. He had been a member of the Lithuanian army. He joined the partisans in 1946. He was betrayed and killed on January 20, 1949.

Only when you come home
You won't recognize Lithuania,
You will no longer find the branch
Where you once sat and coo-cooed.

Bet parlėkus nepažinsi
Tu šalelės Lietuvos,
Neatrasi tos šakelės,
Kur kadaise kukavai.

Everything here is destroyed,
Stones and trunks uprooted.
The cities and villages are burned.
Only their foundations are left.

Čia jau viskas sunaikinta,
Riogso akmens ir stuobriai,
Miestai, kaimai sudeginti.
Likę vien pamatai.

A thousand corpses rot,
The wind howls through the fields,
The sun and the moon mourn—
The people exiled from their land.

Tūkstančiai lavonų pūva,
Vėjas kaukia ant laukų,
Rauda saulė ir mėnulis—
Gaila žmonių išvežtų.

Here Mother wrung her hands,
Saying good-bye to her sons.
Here sisters cried bitterly,
Seeing off their brothers.

Čia motulė rankas laužė,
Išleisdama sūnelius,
Čia sesulės gailiai verkė,
Lydėdamas brolelius.

Those streams and springs
Will flow with roses of blood.
Oh, Mother Lithuania,
How much longer must we suffer...

Tie upeliai ir šaltiniai
Kraujo rožėm pražydės.
Ach, Lietuva, motinėle,
Ar ilgai kentėt reikės...

As soon as it was dark we ate dinner and studied the road to reach Vampyras. We washed our joints with cold water to take away the exhaustion of the last few nights' journeys. We felt that we could be a little less vigilant on tonight's journey because the Bolsheviks had not found our tracks. They had veered off in another direction. We were now quite far away from the border. Besides that, a few of our men knew the area. As we came upon a ditch or peat hill, Rymantas would recognize it, and we knew it was not some Russians we had stumbled upon.

The first marches we took that evening were rather pleasant. We set off in the general direction, not holding to any certain road or path. Sometimes we walked through the high rye fields. Rymantas kept the lead, taking large steps, with his weapon ready in case of attack. The rest of us formed a triangle behind him. We walked with our shirts open and our sleeves rolled up. The night was rather warm. The music of the frogs in the surrounding ponds was in dissonance with our energy. After an hour we loosened our ammunition belts. We passed through peat bog, taking frequent rests.

After a few hours of pleasant walking, we approached our destination—Vampyras's headquarters.[32] We spread out so that in the event of danger we would be in good positions. We waited a short while as passwords were exchanged. We passed a few agreed-upon whistles back and forth and crept forwards. One of the farmers[33] was calming the dogs close to the barn.

Inside the bunker we found not just Vampyras and Plunksna[34] (Feather) but a few more partisans who had come by with various business.

"Who do I see here? You certainly disturbed the peace, didn't you?" Vampyras said, firmly pressing Rimvydas's hand. "Our entire kingdom had been quiet recently, but the last few nights neither the Russians nor the *Stribai* have had any rest."

"We didn't want to let you fall asleep on us. We had to conjure up some entertainment for you," Rimvydas shot back, "otherwise life would get boring."

"I never expected you to go across and come back so quickly. Congratulations, Daumantas!" Vampyras continued, now ceremoniously greeting me. "So, tell me, how are things? Did it go well?"

"Thank you, yes, things went well, thank God. How else? We gave the bums a run for their money and came rushing over to see you."

The Report from the West

We were in a good mood as we exchanged stories. We did not even notice how the time flew by. Vampyras set it up so that only four of us remained at headquarters: Vampyras, Plunksna, Rimvydas and I. A few men were selected from those who would be leaving to accompany us on our further journey. We stayed at headquarters and rested and recovered from our journey. As we ate and drank, the day dawned. Then, we thanked everyone for their hospitality and rushed into our hiding place to rest. We decided to sleep a while and then deliver our report about the West. The previous evening had not exhausted us, so we did not sleep for very long.

---

32 Avikiliai Village. The Leonavičius farm.

33 Vincas Leonavičius 1902–unknown. He was arrested September 5, 1947 and sentenced to 10 years in a concentration camp in Siberia.

34 Mykolas Žilionis, 1917–1947. Joined the partisans in 1946. He was university educated. He was betrayed and killed September 4, 1947.

Vampyras especially wanted to shorten the length of our rest. He impatiently waited for information about our future plans. His patience ran out within five hours. I could feel him watching me as I slept. I saw that he was impatient, and so I greeted our "morning," which was already well into the following afternoon. I sat up. Our whispering woke up our other two friends. Each of us sat up on our bedding and we talked. We pulled some of the newspapers we had brought back from the Western free press, some magazines, and some informational brochures from our backpacks. Vampyras took the reading material from us with trembling hands, as though we were handing him a holy relic. His eyes bored into the texts. After he'd finished reading them, nothing could improve his mood.

Through resistance channels we had received an analysis that informed us to expect several more years of difficult fighting. Vampyras and Plunksna grew pensive. We were in the middle of the most difficult time of year for partisans—the summer. It was a season when enemy forces are increased ten-fold. How many people would have to die that summer? Vampyras and Plunksna fell into a deep meditation.

Although activities were curtailed during the summer and consisted mainly of the publication and distribution of our underground press, maintaining contact and concern for civilian welfare and certain operations would demand sacrifices. About two hours or so passed before Vampyras grew weary of searching the pages of the free press for reassuring news.

He collected all the publications together into one neat bundle—Vampyras adored the West—and handed them back to Rimvydas. He buried his face in his hands and wailed out loud:

"They have abandoned us at Yalta and Potsdam! They are making the same mistakes over and over again!"

Then he lapsed into a prolonged silence. No one disturbed him. We all knew that we had a long and terrible bloody road of conflict and death in front of us. No one dared say anything. We all fell into the despair of the moment.

Rimvydas broke the silence by picking up his weapon. He began to clean it. Then I picked up my weapon and began to clean mine. My weapon was rather dirty after recent use. We had not had the time to properly care for our "lovers."

After a few minutes of silence, I dared speak out loud:

"We are powerless to change international events and influence them in our favor. However, what we can do is to continue to fight, using the most effective methods. We must not lose heart. That would only be useful to our enemy. Sooner or later the tenacity of our people's struggle will be recognized and our nation will rise again among other freedom-loving peoples. But for now, we need to think about the best way of reaching our district leader."

"Of course, that would be the best thing we could accomplish today," Rimvydas said, reassembling his automatic.

Plunksna crawled out of our cave and went to see about lunch. He came back and reported that we had spent too much time talking politics. Our lunch was already cold. We hurried off to help the farmer's wife by "taking care of lunch."

Vampyras offered to lead the night march. Besides him we would be accompanied by a few men from the Viesulas Unit and our own Rimvydas. Even Vampyras did not exactly know where our district leader was presently located, since the area had been harassed by the Bolsheviks for quite some time.

The sun was already rising in the east when we made our final trek to the edge of the forest. Along the forest there was a dirt road that we had to cross with particular care. We broke up into three groups. One group held back from the other and we covered our tracks as we crossed the road. Some of us walked backwards, others stepped inside each others' footprints, and still others walked on tiptoe. We did this so that even the smartest Ivan would not be able to figure out how many people had crossed the road. Just before the road and right after it every several dozen steps we would lift our feet as high as possible and then put them down directly from above, so that it would be impossible to tell which direction we had traveled.

We took cover about fifty meters deep inside the forest on high ground. Viesulys took leave of us along with one guide and hurried off to establish contact with Šalmas's[35] Unit, which belonged to Viesulys's company. We all suffered from wet feet. We were hungry and thirsty. Luckily, Viesulys returned quickly and informed us that within an hour Šalmas and a few other men would meet us and that they would have food and water with them. We moved deeper into the forest and waited.

We met Sakalas[36] and Šarūnas[37]—the leader of the Kęstutis Regiment and his adjunct. They too were en route to the district Headquarters. Together with them we made up a rather large group of several dozen men with two machine guns, three anti-tank guns, and several dozen automatic weapons. We felt rather

---

35 Albinas Lazauskas, 1923–1947, a graduate of the Pedagogical Seminary in Marijampole. He joined the partisans in 1946. He was killed in battle October 24, 1947.

36 Kazimieras Grebliklas, 1913–1949. Joined the partisans in 1945. He was betrayed and killed January 20, 1949.

37 Possibly Vincentas Žvingila, 1924–1947. He was a student who joined the partisans in 1946. He was killed in battle July 29, 1947.

secure, despite the fact that Šalmas informed us that after the liquidation of the Marijampolė Communist Party elite, Steponas Bakevičius, preparations were being made for new elections that were scheduled to take place within a few days on June 15th.

The Deputy at the Demonstration

This time the Bolsheviks were extremely cautious—much more cautious than during the January elections. Someone had spread a rumor that the partisans were preparing to pick off the newly appointed deputy before he even got himself "elected." The Communist activists in Marijampolė were worried that they would have to repeat the elections.

In the neighboring village near the forest where we were hiding, by mid-day forty members of the Soviet Interior Forces showed up. They took up positions in the center of the village at the home of a farmer and sat waiting for their comrades to come and begin the demonstrations. The Soviet Interior Officers visited each of the local people and reminded them of their voluntary duty to attend the demonstration. The gathering villagers were carefully monitored by the MGB. They searched the ones who looked suspicious. They were obviously worried that one of the villagers might be an assassin.

The deputy himself made an appearance. He was brought in by the *Stribai*. He took his place at the table. He took off the submachine gun that he was wearing over his shoulder and set it down right in front of him on top of his papers. Then he proceeded to lecture the crowd on the benefits of the most "democratic" elections in the world and the most "democratic" constitution in the world, namely Stalin's constitution. His enthusiasm was outdone only by his fear.

Everything was absolutely crystal clear to everyone present. No one had a single doubt. The villagers warily kept their eyes on the speaker. They knew that if they did not keep up an attentive front, they might not make it home alive. As they stood there obediently listening, they trembled inside, wondering what might be going on in their homes and at their farms as they stood there, powerless to do anything about it. Some of the villagers worried that their very last food reserves were being stolen as they stood there at attention. Some worried that their last few items of clothing were being looted. Still others worried about the safety of their daughters and sisters left behind at home. Because of that fear no one paid attention to a single word their "leader" barked at them. All they knew was that they had to "listen" and then when he was finished speaking, they would have to clap.

As soon as the demonstration was over, they all hurried home to count their losses. The deputy, the *Stribai*, and the NKVD broke up into groups and went "visiting" among the people, demanding food. The group that traveled with the deputy to acquire their lunch was larger than the rest. By this time we had moved to the edge of the forest. We followed their every move. We spoke to the villagers as they passed by. One of the villagers invited us to his home for lunch. He lived close to the forest and felt quite sure that the Bolsheviks would not pay him a visit, as there were only a few hours left before darkness fell. The Bolsheviks knew that the partisans woke up at dusk. The man's farmstead was easily accessible from the forest, even in broad daylight. We set up a few guards and went to the man's farm. By that time the Bolsheviks were already quite drunk. They stole a few horses and carriages and stormed off towards Marijampolė.

"Maybe we should pick one off?" Vampyras joked, watching the retreating wagons through the window.

"Why bother. First you ought to consider the number of lootings that took place today, the robberies, add in the people's fear and then you'll see that it really isn't worth it because they'd only organize new 'elections.' Are we so low as to take down such a poor target? You'll kill them and a few days later the region will be even more terrorized," Rimvydas argued.

I saw that quite a few of the men were itching to kill. No one wanted to let such a perfect opportunity pass. Most of the Bolsheviks were so drunk already that they probably would not be able to roll out of their carriages fast enough.

But, we stood and watched the Bolsheviks escape. Then we returned to the forest. We said good-bye to the men who had accompanied us the previous night. Led by Šalmas, we made it to the edge of the forest where our liaisons were waiting for us.

The Fighters Varnas and Vaidilutė

This entire unit lived in the forest in groups. Varnas (Raven) hid me in a separate bunker, a little further away from the other fighters. This underground room was a meter and thirty centimeters wide, a meter and forty centimeters high, and two meters across. It was lined with pines and thick paper. It was furnished with a few nails and a few shelves and that was all. The most valuable feature of this bunker was that it was so well camouflaged that no one could notice it from outside.

Varnas himself led us to the bunker. Each day, around 11 o'clock in the morning, after he had made careful reconnaissance of the surrounding forest, he would come and wake us. He would signal us with a few agreed-upon knocks, and then we would see his smiling eyes through the breathing hole.

"Have you had enough of lying around underground with the worms?" he'd ask, "I think you must have had enough sleep, gentlemen. Come have some breakfast."

Every day he said those same words.

It took us very little time to get ready. We would sleep in our clothes, only removing our jackets, hats, and boots. We slept with our weapons, belts, and backpacks close by, so that if one morning the enemy showed up instead of Varnas, we would be able to fight. Within a few minutes we would be out of the bunker and shaking Varnas's hand. Then we would go with him to a specified location. There we would find the partisans preparing breakfast. Every day at the same hour we were greeted by a shepherd boy who scouted the local area. We called him "The General".[38] He and a few other shepherd boys kept watch over the local area. Through The General our reconnaissance scouts sent their information about the situation each morning to Varnas. The General was about 15 years old. He was tall and had a quick eye. No matter the weather, he walked around with his shirt sleeves rolled up, his pants legs folded up, his shirt unbuttoned and without a hat. When he approached our grounds, he would crack his whip in the air a few times and wait for an answer. Only after he received a positive answer, would he enter our territory. He did not like to engage in conversation with the individual fighters. He would come and talk to Varnas, and if no one rushed over to offer him a smoke, he would disappear immediately.

We would spend our days together. Within a few days we not only got to know these partisans, but we became friends. The most pleasant man among them was their unit leader, Varnas. He had been an officer in the Lithuanian army. He was a tall man with broad shoulders. He had a dark beard, deep eyes, and red cheeks. He was an unusually gifted soldier. As the unit leader, he never parted company with his machine gun. The Bolsheviks hated him and continually cursed "the one with the beard." As time passed, their hatred for him only grew. He performed his duties with a great deal of attentiveness. Among the partisan fighters he was both a father and an authority figure. His wife[39] and two daughters, who were barely in their teens, lived at the partisan camp with him. Both girls served as liaisons.

---

[38] Liudvikas Kubilius, a boy who lived in the village of Timčiškės, in the county of Kazlų Ruda.

[39] Monika Radvilaitė-Rimienė, 1918–1947. She was a partisan fighter from 1946. She died together with her husband in the headquarters bunker August 19, 1947. After they were surrounded by Soviet Interior Forces, they blew themselves up.

There was a second family that lived at camp as well. That was the Paukšty (Bird) family. Paukštys[40] was a group leader. His father,[41] who had fought for Lithuania's independence as a volunteer, also served together with him. His daughter, Rimgailė,[42] also fought with the partisans.

There was one more incredible fighter in the unit, the liaison-woman Vaidiliutė[43] (Vestal Virgin). Her appearance was not remarkable: she was short, slightly hunched-backed, and had a face that was lined with worry and suffering. Every single partisan deeply respected her for her commitment to the cause and for the many missions she had accomplished. It was nothing to her to walk several hundred kilometers. She was never afraid to take on the most dangerous missions—missions that involved transporting various documents or supplies vital to the underground. Anyone who was lucky enough to have her accept his mission, could rest peacefully that the mission would be accomplished. It took only one day for her to get the partisan underground newspapers into the hands of townspeople in Kaunas or Vilkaviškis. The partisans gave her the sacred code name of a book carrier, or *Knygnešys*.[44] Often, armed only with a single pistol, Vaidiliutė would transport weapons to the partisans. She was a simple field hand, and yet she accomplished some of the most difficult and arduous tasks during this period of fighting.

Partisan Martyrs

During the day most of the partisan fighters in the unit would lie down in the shade along the edges of our territory and would sleep a few hours. Usually, they would come back from their night-time assignments just before dawn. During that time Rimvydas and I got acquainted with the unit's archive, which was made up of several files with orders, instructions, with names of persecuted individuals, and statistics regarding the local agriculture, as well as lists of Lithuanians

---

40 Vytautas Naikelis, 1921–1947. He was a partisan since 1945 in the Varnas Unit. He was killed in battle November 17, 1947.

41 Petras Naikelis, 1897–1947. He was a farmer and had fought as a volunteer for Lithuania's independence. He joined the partisans in 1945. He was killed in battle November 16, 1947 when the location of Varnas's bunker was betrayed.

42 Anelė Naikelytė, 1923–unknown. She was arrested August 20, 1947, and imprisoned in Marijampole and Vilnius. She was sentenced to 10 years hard labor in Siberia and five years in exile. She was released in 1955.

43 Juzefa Petrulionytė, 1920–unknown. She had been a partisan liaison woman since 1945. She was arrested once but escaped. She lived in hiding. On the early morning of September 10, 1947, she was arrested at a farmstead where she was hiding together with the liaison woman Antose Akelaityte-Liepa. She tried to escape from prison, but was severely wounded and died of her wounds.

44 In the nineteenth century the Tsar outlawed Lithuanian books and the use of the Latin alphabet in Lithuania. The book carrier, or *knygnešys*, would secretly carry books and newspapers written in Lithuanian into Lithuania from Prussia.

imprisoned by the Soviets or murdered. There were also accounts of atrocities committed by the Bolsheviks against civilians and partisans.

Because this area was heavily forested, they had functioned well from the very beginning and were quite effective. They also had a fair number of martyrs. The partisan Perkūnas[45] (Thunder) had been sliced into three pieces on a table saw while he was still alive. The unit leader Girininkas[46] (Forester) had horse manure shoved into his mouth, his eyes, and his wounds as he lay dying. The partisan Eumis[47] refused to betray his brothers-in-arms during torture and interrogation. The Soviet Interior Forces cut his tongue out of his mouth. All of these men carried their brother's secrets with them to eternity. A healthy man's imagination can not take in the scope of the torture implemented by the Kremlin's servants.

In the evening the unit leader gave instructions to the groups of partisan fighters. After dinner we prayed for the tortured, for the dead, and for the people who were being tortured now.

* * *

On the night of June 12th I dreamt a horrific dream. I was so tormented by what I had seen in my dream that I woke up and told Rimvydas about my dream. It was day time and I had gone home to my parents' farm. From far away I could see a group of enemy soldiers walking around the farm. The yard, the orchard, the barn were full of soldiers. I pushed my way past them to our cottage. Here I saw a terrible sight. I saw my brother Jurgis in a black coffin in the back of a hearse. He was still barely alive. When he saw me, he pointed weakly at a large wound in his chest that had been made by a series of machine gun bullets. He said that the foreign troops in the area were responsible for his death. Those were his last words. Mournful funeral music was coming from the parlor. All of a sudden I was overwhelmed with rage. I wanted to avenge my brother's death on the soldiers walking around the farmstead, but I felt completely helpless. Tortured by this sense of anger and helplessness, I woke up.

Neither Rimvydas nor I could understand why I had dreamt such a strange dream and what it could possibly mean. Jurgis and I were separated by about a hundred kilometers. We decided that the dream was probably caused by reading the horrific accounts written up in the unit's archive.

---

45 Viktoras Augustinavičius, 1923–1946. He was a partisan in the Vytautas District since 1945. After an ambush on June 4, 1946, he hid in a bunker. He was discovered the following day. Because he was taken alive, Soviet Security Officers brutally tortured and mutilated him. He died from his wounds.

46 Bronius Kvietkauskas, 1911–1947. Joined the partisans in 1945. He died April 9, 1947.

47 Jonas Demikis, 1915–1947. He was a teacher at the Marijampole Gymnasium. He had joined the partisans in the spring of 1945.

A Meeting With the District Leader

Through Vaidiliutė we received news that the district leader was in Neptūnas's (Neptune's)[48] unit and that in four days time we would find him there. Accompanied by a few partisan fighters, we left Varnas's territory and reached Neptūnas's district.

It was dusk. Several dozen partisans were praying around a smoldering fire, led in prayer by the district chaplain. The flickering embers reflected the faces of 56 combatants. Every once in a while the fire would come back to life and a stray flame would be reflected on one of the fighter's weapons. The crackling logs and sputtering embers added their own accompaniment to the prayers.

After the prayer ended, I went to deliver my report to Žvejys. I read the disappointment in his face.

"So you're back," he said flatly.

"Yes, I'm back," I answered.

"The mission failed," he stated blankly, as though testing me.

"How can you say our mission failed if we returned alive," I said in an attempt to disperse his suspicions.

Žvejys was skeptical of our speedy return. For a long time he refused to believe that we had completed even a segment of our mission. Because we were all exhausted, I lay down in one lean-to with Žvejys so that I could talk to him. We talked until midnight and resolved to hold a meeting the following day.

Our arrival had coincided with the arrival of the chaplain. All of the fighters wanted to go to confession and receive communion. The priest held mass at a hastily constructed altar. During mass no one parted company with their weapons. The chaplain's own submachine gun was hanging on a fir branch, close to the altar as he said mass. After mass five new partisans gave their oaths.

After lunch we held our meeting. We exchanged information and decided on a new direction of action. After that meeting, my duties and Rimvydas's duties were considered complete. We received new orders and parted company.

My Dream Becomes Reality

It was a typical partisan evening at the end of June in the forests of Kazlų Rūda. I had handed in my foreign travel warrant, my reports, and the other documents to Žvejys. I was now a rank-and-file partisan fighter again. Everything around us

---

[48] Algimantas Matuzevičius, 1921–1950. He was a teacher who joined the partisans in the winter of 1944. He was betrayed and killed June 22, 1950.

was asleep, only the partisan day was just coming to life. Most of the partisans had already left camp well before sunset, carrying with them lead and paper, and traveling in various directions. The few of us who were left were gathered around a dying fire, sitting on logs.

For some time now in my soul I had felt uneasy. This particular evening I was quite tired. For several days in a row I had been typing. Sitting among us were Žvejas, Šturmas, Naktis, Faustas,[49] Neptūnas, Šaulys,[50] Odisėjas,[51] and a few other regulars from the Unit. We were gathered in small groups talking, about to split up and go off to rest in our lean-tos.

Just before midnight we heard the sound of voices in camp. Three former fighters from Treniotas's[52] unit arrived at our campfire shortly afterwards. They handed me an addressed envelope. I recognized Rimvydas's handwriting. I opened up the envelope and found a letter inside.

Dear Friend,

The dream that woke you up while you were staying with Varnas's Unit turns out to be true. On the morning of June 13th Soviet Interior Forces encircled your family's farmstead. Jurgis was killed. Your mother[53] and your brother[54] have been arrested and taken away.

They tossed Jurgis's body out in the market grounds in Veiveriai.

Please accept my deepest condolences.

Rimvydas

---

49 Aleksandras Gybinas, 1920–1949. He was a teacher who was conscripted into the German army in 1944. After the Germans were defeated, he tried to make it to the American side, but was captured by Russian Soviet Interior Forces and sent back to Lithuania. He lived in hiding and then joined the partisans in June 1945. On September 28, 1949, he was betrayed and lured into an ambush where he was wounded. He shot himself to avoid being taken alive.

50 Antanas Čereškevičius, 1899–1948. He joined the partisans in the spring of 1945. He died in battle June 13, 1948.

51 He was a German who joined the partisans. From December 1946 on he served as the unit doctor. He was betrayed and killed hiding in his bunker September 10, 1947.

52 Identity unknown.

53 Ona Lukšienė was arrested and brought to the Kaunas Prison where she was interrogated and brutally tortured. She proved to be a woman of an iron will. Transcripts of her interrogation reveal that she did not betray anyone under torture or interrogation. Simanas Lukša was torn out of bed and dragged to Jurgis's dead body. The shock caused the eighty-four year old man to lose his mind. He never recovered and died finally on October 13, 1947.

54 Vincas Lukša was arrested and brought to the Kaunas Prison for interrogation and torture. He was accused of supporting the partisans with food and supplies. After his interrogation, Lukša was brought to Vorkuta where he was sentenced on December 20, 1947 to ten years in a concentration camp. All of his wealth was confiscated, including his farm and all his crops.

That was the horrific reality that had taken place a few days ago. It all happened just as in my dream. Jurgis was the first member of our family to sacrifice himself for our country's freedom.

I felt the blood boiling in my veins. Something terrible overcame me. I was in shock. I wanted to absorb that horrific reality, but a thousand thoughts raced through my head and I could not make sense of any of them. I wanted to take revenge against the entire world. The horrors that surrounded us were proof to me that there were no people left on the face of this earth who would help us to save ourselves.

Jurgis and I were closer than any comrades-in-arms or blood brothers could ever possibly be. From the days when we were shepherds in the fields together to when we first entered the University, we were inseparable. Together we suffered through all the hardships that came our way. We had chosen different areas of study, and so for a while at the University our lives parted, but then we were brought together again closer than ever before when we both joined the partisans and our ideals and our work united us.

I did not want to show my suffering to my friends, so I left the camp fire and went to the edge of camp where I could be alone. With every step I took I fought harder and harder to hold back my tears. When I felt as though I was truly alone, I fell down into the moss. I leaned on my beloved submachine gun and I cried like I had never cried before in my life. The only way I could get myself to calm down was by repeating the words of the rosary and the words of the partisan oath—to sacrifice everything once fate had taken me on the road to battle.

I did not even notice when Adjunct Naktis approached me deep in the forest. I gave in to his request that I join our friends beside the camp fire. I tried to calm myself down, but I could not. It was just too hard for me to accept the thought that I would never meet Jurgis alive in this life again. Everything seemed unbearable to me. I felt so small. As small as our nation, tossed aside by the outside world to face all these horrors alone.

In my mind I saw the hundreds of graves where my fellow fighters lay. The trip they took from the battlefield to the closest city streets, market squares, altars, dumps was always the same: their bodies or body parts would be collected from the battlefield, tossed unceremoniously into carts, and brought to the town where they would be tossed out as though they were but banquet food for the Bolsheviks to feed upon. This is when the most ghastly defilement of the dead would begin. The local Bolsheviks would kick the bodies, beat them, drag them around the area tied to horses, cut them into pieces—they would do everything according to their own imagination, which knew no boundaries of decency.[55] Then, afterwards, after the corpses had been defiled, in the dead of night they would toss them into ditches, trenches, dumps, swamps, lakes, or rivers.

This partisan song describes these scenes not as an allusion, but as reality:

Flowing rivers bubble, bloated with tears
Šniokščia sraunios upės, ašarom patvinę
There where blood was spilled, the rye grows…
Kur ištryško kraujas, stiebasi rugys…
Mother has been exiled, Father tortured,
Motiną išvežęs, tėvą nukankinęs,
The Kremlin Horror does not cease.
Nesiliauja siautęs Kremliaus kraugerys

(…)

They spit on you, they kick you, they lay you in the street,
Tave spjaudo, spardo, gatvėse paguldo,
They hide you in a ditch on the edge of town,
Tave uoliai slepia priemiesčio griovy,
As the swallows sing their morning hymn,
Vyturėliui giesmę rytmetinę čiulbant,
They drain you of your very last drop of blood…
Dar lašelio kraujo ieško jie tavy…

After those monstrosities were performed on his body, Jurgis's body was the thirty-sixth (after Kazokas, Kapsas, Papartis, and Aušrelė) to be tossed in a field near the town of Veiveriai. The field once belonged to farmer Raslavičius; it still had trenches in it left from the war. Like everywhere else, after this "funeral" the body was quickly devoured by wild dogs and other wild animals and birds. Usually the Bolsheviks took it upon themselves to toss a few shovelfuls of dirt onto the bodies, but even that was soon washed away by the first rain. Bodies tossed in the field during the winter were not covered at all. Even now passers-by often see

---

55 The Russian soldiers were known to arrange the naked corpses as though they were performing sexual acts.

partisan hands, legs, or skulls poking up out of the ground. Dogs and birds chew on the remains.[56]

Jurgis's body ended up in one of the field's that was least used for these purposes. The neighboring towns—Šilavotas, Sasnava, Gudeliai, Kazlų Rūda, Jūrė, Jankai, Kačerginė, Garliava, and others held far more partisan graves.

One day in the future people will uncover these crimes of the twentieth century. But at that time, even hanging those who committed these crimes against our people will not be enough to wash away the shame of those who allowed it to happen.

The Dainava Headquarters Are Surrounded

After Rimvydas's and my trip to Poland the Lithuanian resistance actively organized new missions. Although it was the most difficult time to complete missions—summer time—nobody even thought about postponing the work that we knew needed to be done and wait for a better time. Every mission demanded sacrifices. At this time large sacrifices were made by the Dainava District partisans.

Rimvydas had barely returned to his district before the Dzūkija partisans organized a meeting of the leadership to discuss new missions. This meeting was discovered by Soviet Interior Forces.

This year in the fight with the partisans Soviet Interior Forces had received orders from their superiors to hunt down and destroy all partisan units. The operative unit leaders were responsible for these initiatives. They were told that if in their estimate their unit could not completely annihilate the local partisans, then they should notify the authorities and request reinforcements from other units. This new Bolshevik tactic was used for the first time when the meeting time and place of the Dainava leadership was uncovered.

It was unfortunate that the partisans were not quite prepared for this new intensity of attack. The Punia Forest for several years already had housed the headquarters of the unit leadership and other important bunkers. The district leader's main bunker was along the edge of a grove where a creek bubbled up from a spring. Here it was convenient to hide tracks during the winter. Only, in the summer was it difficult to hide tracks. The bunker itself was built with two long passage ways leading to well-hidden escape hatches. Both corridors were built in zig-zags, so that if the bunker were attacked the enemy's grenades could not directly reach the

56 In 1988, still during the Soviet occupation, the Raslavičius family, having returned from Siberia, created a memorial to the partisan dead tossed in this mass grave on their land. The memorial is known as *Skausmo Kalnelis* (Hill of Suffering).

people hiding in the bunker. Although the bunker itself was well camouflaged, the fact that it had been used for such a long time made it unsafe. The leadership was well aware of this fact, but they were so busy with such a variety of tasks that they did not have the time to establish a new headquarters and make the move. It was under these circumstances that the Bolsheviks planned their attack.

On the night of August 10-11, 1947, throughout the night 300 American vehicles packed with Soviet Interior Forces arrived in the Punia Forest. These forces were joined by local Soviet Interior Forces. One set of soldiers made a double ring around the forest while the rest combed the forests. At this time only eight partisans were living in the forest: Ąžuolas[57] (Oak), the district reconnaissance leader Senis[58] (Old Man), the district adjutant Linas[59] (Linen), and the other leaders, Lapaitis (Fox), Aras,[60] Patrimpas,[61] Žaibas[62] (Lightening). The district meeting had ended and its participants had already parted.

The massive numbers of Soviet Interior Forces convening in one place was interpreted by the local people in various ways. Many thought a war had begun. No one believed that the Russians would send several thousand troops into the forest to hunt down a handful of partisans. From the Bolshevik point of view the three-year war with the partisans had not been successful. Communist methods that had been developed and tested over a period of thirty years appeared ineffective in subjugating the newly occupied nations. They now were focusing particular attention on the backbone of the resistance—Lithuania's partisans. It was clear to the Bolsheviks that until they had completely stifled the partisan movement all of their attempts to Sovietize the populace would be in vain.

The Soviet Interior Forces Units were armed with long poles. Walking slowly, shoulder to shoulder, they prodded every meter of the earth, until they discovered a partisan bunker. The Bolsheviks surrounded the bunker with three rings of men and set up machine guns pointing at the bunker from various directions. The soldiers closest to the bunker, dug themselves trenches. Then one officer decided to try his luck. For two hours he paced back and forth across the top of the bunker, shouting out a speech in which he invited the partisans to come out and surrender. He personally "guaranteed" their safety. This officer had a lot of patience.

---

57 Dominykas Jėčys.

58 Kostas Šimelevičius, 1923–1947. He died in battle a month after the attack on the Dainava headquarters.

59 Antanas Macevičius, 1916–1949. He was taken alive during the attack on the Dainava headquarters. He was sentenced to 25 years in a concentration camp in Siberia and died there in 1949.

60 Mykolas Petrauskas, 1911–1947. He died in the attack on the Dainava headquarters.

61 Juozas Patraška.

62 Vaclovas Kavaliauskas, 1921–1947. He died in the attack on the Dainava headquarters.

He continued his speech, even as smoke rose from the bunker's ventilation holes. Inside the bunker the partisans were busy destroying documents. He only paused to warn the partisans that by destroying the evidence, they were only making things harder for themselves.

Once the archive had been taken care of, the partisans inside the bunker discussed how they should handle the situation. A few of them, the district leader among them, felt that it was not worth trying to break out because the Soviet Interior Forces were too large for them to realistically break through. They offered to wait a while and then commit suicide. The others, who had more faith in their weaponry, argued that it would be better to break out of the bunker and try to fight their way out of the encirclement. Even if they were to get killed, at least they would take a few Russians down with them on their journey to see Abraham.

After the documents and supplies inside the bunker were destroyed, Ąžuolas pulled out his pistol and shot himself. The other fighters snuck through the passage way and emerged outside. The Soviet Interior Forces were caught off guard when the partisans emerged from underground not at all in the place where they had expected them to. Aras was the first to begin picking off the Bolsheviks closest to him. At first, the Soviet Interior Forces could not even shoot back. They tossed grenades at the partisans who kept coming out of the opening. Three partisans were knocked out before they could even join the fighting. Those who were successful in exiting the bunker tried to break through the three rings. However, in the end the partisan gun fire was just a drop in the ocean compared to the massive forces of Soviets who were literally crawling all over the forest. Only Senis was able to make it through the three rings and find safety by hiding in the bushes. After several hours of talking and waiting, the Soviet Security Officers finally entered the bunker where they found nothing except for the ashes of the burned documents.

After this incident, for the very first time, the Bolsheviks dared to publicly announce through their Soviet press that there was an underground that was disturbing the peace of daily Soviet life. They called the underground a pack of "bandits." This statement was a complete reversal of the position they had held up to this point, namely that opposition did not exist. This time the Soviet newspapers announced that they had successfully liquidated the Dainava District Headquarters, although those same headquarters continued to operate and cause more trouble for the Bolsheviks, only from a different location.

The two partisans who had been knocked out by the grenades woke up. The Bolsheviks took advantage of their situation and in their name wrote a long proclamation in which "they" appealed to their brothers-in-arms to "admit that they are guilty" and that they are going on "the wrong path", claiming that only now had they "opened" their eyes and that they were very "sorry" over the wrongs of their past and "invited" all partisans to finally come to an "understanding" and to turn themselves in to the authorities. These proclamations, including their "authors'" signatures were reproduced in the thousands and circulated throughout the country.

Preparing the Troops

Between August 1–20, 1947, in the forests of Kazlų Rūda, the first partisan training courses took place in the Tauras District. The Žalgiris, Vytautas, and Kęstutis units participated. At the end of the training courses all of the Tauras District leadership was invited together for discussions. We all participated in the farewell party. The courses took place within the region of the Žalgiris Unit. I was accompanied to my assigned spot by the Birutė Unit Leader of Liaison, Aras.[63] After two days march we reached the camp just as the sun was coming up. As we approached, the guard popped out of the bushes and demanded we identify ourselves. A few hundred meters away we saw lean-tos set up in neat rows. In the center of camp stood the largest lean-to. It had a tricolor national flag flying on its post. That was the headquarters of the district leader who oversaw the training himself. The camp guard met us. All of the training participants were still snoring in their lean-tos. The only place where there was any movement was in the northern half of the camp where food was being prepared in steaming pots. We exchanged a few words with the leadership and a few friends and then collapsed in the still-warm lean-tos of the kitchen duty personnel. However, we did not get to sleep for very long. Once the camp knew of our arrival, individual partisans kept sticking their noses into our lean-tos to say hello. Even though we were exhausted from our march, we were too interested in the activities at camp to rest for very long.

There were about seventy combatants in the training camp, including myself. Work continued all day long. In the intervals between maneuverings and tactical drills, there were theoretical lectures. The partisans also learned about statutes and disciplinary regulations.

The following day, as the sun was rising, the last of our awaited guests arrived: Rymantas, Sakalas, the commander of the Kęstutis Unit, Ainis, the commander of the Šarūnas Unit, Uosis, the Geležinis Vilkas Unit commander, and Tautvydas,

[63] Vytautas Mikalauskas, 1925–1948. He was a high school student who left the Gymnasium to join the partisans in the spring of 1945. He was killed February 10, 1948.

The partisans of the Tauras district

the Geležinis Vilkas Unit reconnaissance commander. Vampyras and Šturmas were also at the camp. Almost all of the Tauras District leadership had convened for the first time in a very long time. We glanced around our circle and joked about how if the Bolsheviks had gotten wind of this meeting, they would have sent 50,000 troops after us.

Partisans prepare for an ambush.

Partisans at the training camp

The camp command was always on alert. When the paths leading to camp became worn and obvious, the command ordered the camp to move to another location. Treniotas's Unit had already received orders to find a safe place to move to in case of danger. After the final guests' arrival, the decision was made to move camp. At four o'clock in the afternoon we marched to our new location. All the partisan fighters were divided up into two groups. While marching, everyone was ordered to place their footsteps carefully into the leader's footsteps in order to cover our tracks. By the time darkness fell, we reached the village of Karčiauskynės. Here we stopped at a local farm to ask the farmer if we could drink from his well. The water at camp came from holes that were not dug very deeply. Therefore, the water we drank was either brown or brackish. Five and a half buckets full of clean water quenched our thirst.

We resumed our positions and continued our march. We marched four kilometers and arrived at our newly selected spot. We did not take the risk of setting up camp at night. Instead, we broke up into small groups and went to sleep on the moss. The nights were already cold. By morning our teeth were chattering—especially those of us dressed in summer uniforms.

As soon as the sun came up, we got to work. Again, the whistle woke us and called us to the day's tasks, which this time were different than usual. We had to build the camp. This day was also our final day of training. The District Commander appointed an exam committee, which he himself joined along with Rymantas, the training officer, and Šturmas and Vampyras.

The exams began. Although the training period had not been very long, the results were excellent. Rymantas's program had been fully and thoroughly completed. After two days of exams, the commission announced that they were pleased with all of the fighters' answers. Tauras[64] and Oželis had the highest marks and were both awarded with watches. All passed in accordance with the standards set by the district commander and were promoted. The camp program concluded with a military parade and other entertainment.

A goodbye party was organized for the participants by the kitchen unit. They set up tables and used stumps as chairs in the exam area. The tables were laden with food. The kitchen unit even managed to bake cakes for the occasion. Barrels of beer were brought to the banquet area from some miraculous source. The table was covered with meats, soups, and a variety of delicacies.

The leadership and combatants flocked to the table. Because it was expected that we would be noisier than usual, double the number of men were assigned guard duty and were ordered to take up positions further away from camp.

Before we ate, the district commander thanked the course participants, thanked the instructors, and the unit leaders. He thanked the kitchen unit and everyone who had provided food for the party and wished everyone well.

After three hours of partying, the men quickly assembled into their units, and, after reports were made, displaying strong discipline, they marched with a song to their districts. We, the leadership, remained at camp with the local unit to continue our meeting.

On the second day after we had arrived at camp, the leadership of the Tauras District held a meeting with us. During these meetings the operations of individual detachments and their commanders were critically examined.

On the first day of the meeting we evaluated the activities of the individual units leaders. The individual under consideration would leave the meeting and would wait in the forest, several hundred meters away, until he was called back to the meeting. The meeting was mediated by the district commander. Each participant had to give his evaluation of the individual under consideration. After everyone's words had been considered, a general evaluation would be made.

Only one of the leaders, Vampyras, was deemed not entirely suitable for his

---

[64] Urbantas Dailidė, 1921–1951. He was betrayed and killed February 14 or 15, 1951.

Partisans study for their exams

duties. All the rest of the leadership's activities were praised—some more than others. It had been observed that in Vampyras's area of operation too many combatants were killed. Most of the time these deaths were caused because of a lack of bunkers and a lack of coordination with the local inhabitants. He was criticized for maintaining poor communication with the local citizenry, with his own combatants, and for not providing a strong underground publication. Because of these problems, although he had many successes on the battlefield, it was decided that he should be removed from his responsibilities as a commander.

On the second day of meetings, we discussed expanding the district headquarters. We discussed increasing the activities of the press, information, reconnaissance.

Because of the ever-increasing deportations to Siberia and because of the increasing instances of terror against the local citizenry considerable attention was paid to the section that looked after the welfare of the families of the partisans who had been arrested and deported to Siberia. Plans were made to collect aid for these families. We also discussed how to fight the collectivization of farms. We discussed the problem of colonization. All detachments were ordered to maintain field diaries. We also came to the general agreement that the units had to decentralize the press, so that in the event that one press center was destroyed, another would continue to publish.

Two district leaders raised the question of whether disciplinary methods for combatants should be made more lenient. The current method of moving combatants who had transgressed against Disciplinary Orders to new units where they would be made to feel like new inexperienced partisans was too cumbersome. We decided to use this method only very rarely.

The success of these first training courses prompted the district commander to organize additional courses to be given approximately a month later in districts within the confines of the Birutė Unit, which was under my command. A training program was formulated and candidates were selected from various units.

In the City of Lean-Tos

It was a Sunday. Aras led the prayers at mass. Šarvas's[65] unit had food reserves in their backpacks, which they shared with the rest of us. We marched two more hours and arrived at camp where were met by Kiškis (Rabbit). We quickly divided the area up into sections for trainees, leadership, guards, and the kitchen unit.

There already were signs of our presence around the campsite. On the northern side of camp there were several posts where we hung pots. Twenty meters away Ūkas[66] had tied up a cow that he was trying to protect both from the flies and from the Russians. Our hosts were quite generous and within a half hour they invited us for lunch.

By evening camp activity was regulated by an orderly schedule. All of the participating combatants removed the ranks they had worn up until now and were relieved of their current duties. They were all now equals. You could no longer tell who had earned what rank.

I woke up on the morning of September 9th when Rymantas was already leading the trainees to wash. When I lifted my head, I found two empty places beside me. Rymantas and Šarvas were already at training. The previous evening I had stayed up very late discussing various organizational concerns with Šarvas, Kiškis, and Inžinis.[67] We checked our food reserves and calculated whether there would be enough to feed the combatants during their training period. It seemed

---

65 Jurgis Račyla, 1917–1947. He joined the partisans in autumn 1944. He was killed December 24, 1947. His body was defiled in the Veiveriai market grounds.

66 Povilas Benešiūnas. He joined the partisans in September 1944. On April 23, 1948, his medals were removed for breaking the partisan oath and for maintaining secret ties with the NKVD.

67 Juozas Nėnius, 1908–1949. He joined the partisans in September 1944. He was betrayed and killed.

One of the most remarkable efforts taken by the resistance was the course for non-commissioned officers in Tauras military district in August 1947. The picture was brought by Lukša to the West in 1948.

as though there would be enough. Aras, who had participated in the first training session's farewell party, had already told our unit about what they could expect. It seemed to me that our men were determined to outdo the other men in terms of exam results and in general. The headquarters command was able to obtain the training program from Rymantas along with other necessary literature a few weeks before training. The men had arrived well prepared. Of course, everyone's biggest concern was which unit's men would win first place or second place. After all, it was not just about personal pride, but the pride of the unit. Several of the trainees were students. They were particularly competitive. The men of the Birutė Unit assured me that they would not lose to the men of the Iron Wolf Unit—Tautvydas, Skirgaila, Sakalas,[68] and Šarūnas.

The schedule had to be changed to accommodate the absence of men from the Iron Wolf Unit. A lean-to city emerged on the eastern side of camp. There were various kinds of lean-tos. Some of the lean-tos were rather simple two-sided Russian lean-tos with branches and moss covering the sides and the ends. The tops of the lean-tos were also covered with branches, so that they could not be identified from Bolshevik recon planes. The floors were covered with beds of moss and branches. The rest of the lean-tos were similar. The most interesting looking lean-tos were those built entirely of moss. Their frames were made of branches covered over with a thick layer of moss held together with thin twigs. One opening would be left. These types of lean-tos were the warmest and looked much more attractive than the other type of lean-to. These beautiful multi-colored moss lean-tos decorated the edges of the pathways through camp. The new arrivals to the camp were greeted by this spectacular site when they entered the area.

[68] Vincas Kleiza, 1921–1950. He joined the partisans in March 1945. He died from wounds.

Around ten o'clock half of the Iron Wolf Unit arrived at camp. They were brought there by Čempijonas (Champion).[69] He lined everyone up in front of the camp area and contacted Rymantas. After Čempijonas gave his report, he was assigned a spot to camp. Their region had been overrun by the Bolsheviks. That got in the way of both groups arriving in time for training. According to Čempijonas, the other half of the unit would arrive the following day.

The training leader allowed the new arrivals two hours to rest and get settled in. After lunch they were to join the general training program.

After lunch the trainees set up areas for exercise and dug trenches. Some of them had to join the kitchen unit, as fighters from this unit had been called elsewhere beyond the camp's borders.

During the evening inspection Rymantas announced that the following day's program would proceed according to the prearranged schedule without any changes regardless of the fact that we were still missing some of the trainees. This was also meant to enforce discipline at camp. The trainees were warned that after the whistle blew they had to maintain silence. A patrol and a guard were appointed.

The morning of September 10 dawned in the quiet camp. At exactly seven o'clock the trainees were woken from their sweet sleep by a whistle. Ambo was responsible for the day's schedule. The trainees were divided into three groups and did their morning exercises. The groups were led by Ambo, Čempijonas and Šarvas.

After they ate their breakfast, and after a short break, the men were instructed to assemble the auditorium. A spot was selected along a hill. Two concave enclosures were built complete with a flat surface to write on and backrests. The backrests were constructed out of birch branches firmly dug into the ground and woven with horizontal branches. The birches served as good camouflage from above and at the same time provided shade. We constructed a chair and a lectern for the lecturer in front of the amphitheater. Here we used branches, moss and roots as our building materials. Everything looked quite nice. On two archways, supported by branches, covering a table top, we spread moss in three colors: yellow, green, and red. The chair we constructed could compete in terms of comfort with chairs meant for commissars. We erected a bulletin board beside the chair.

Once the auditorium was completed, our preparatory work was finished. Kariūnas[70] wrote several announcements and sets of instructions on the bulletin board.

---

69 Jonas Valenta, 1914–1949. He joined the partisans in the autumn of 1944. He was betrayed and killed in the headquarters bunker November 14, 1949.

70 Algirdas Šimanskis, 1914–1948. He joined the partisans in the autumn of 1944. He was betrayed and killed November 3, 1948.

At around eleven o'clock our first guard post reported that they had spotted about ten soldiers crossing the road about a kilometer and a half's distance from camp. The guard had not had enough time to discern through his binoculars whether they were Soviets or partisans. They were marching towards camp. Rymantas gave me orders to check out the situation. I took Sargas (Guard),[71] Daina (Song),[72] Audra (Storm),[73] and Jūrelė with me and departed in the direction indicated by the guard. We crept through thick bushes and went in the direction of the lake. Sargas immediately noticed a few men in uniform about a kilometer away. We still could not make out who they were through the binoculars. They had spread out and were creeping forwards. The group seemed to be searching for something. Once the distance between us decreased I recognized Uosis, the commander of the Iron Wolf Unit. Tautyvdas stood beside him and was gazing through the trees. We did not want to break the silence, so we waded through knee deep moss until we got close enough for our friends to spot us.

"What are you doing wandering around here as though you were a peace-time hunter and not a partisan," I said to Uosis, extending my hand.

"These forests of yours are endless," Uosis said, shaking my right hand, "I can't even find a liaison around here."

We all greeted each other. I encouraged the men who did not know each other to introduce themselves. We walked towards camp. I familiarized Uosis with the camp's routine.

"This time the camp does not have liaisons to bring you to us, like last time," I said. "Only Artūras[74] knows about the camp.[75] You are a little late. For two days Vaidila (Shaman)[76] and Tigras (Tiger)[77] waited for you in the places you had agreed upon, but you never showed up. Today we began our full training schedule, so there was no one around to meet you. You had to make due with a rank-and-file liaison. But I don't think you'll be too angry with us. You had a good opportunity to familiarize yourselves with our forests. They are much bigger than the ones you are used to."

---

71 Petras Ašmona, 1913–1947. He joined the partisans in 1944. He was killed in 1947 on September 12th when the Soviet Interior Forces attacked the partisan training camp in the forests of Kazlų Rūda. He died while covering his retreating comrades.

72 Bronius Jankūnas. He was betrayed and killed September 23, 1947.

73 Juozas Grajauskas, 1923–1949. He was killed in battle June 7, 1949.

74 Identity unknown.

75 To this day no one knows where the camp exactly took place.

76 Stasys Mačiūta, 1926–1947. He was killed September 24, 1947 in the headquarters bunker.

77 Bronius Kazakevičius, 1922–1951. He was killed in battle May 18, 1951.

"Yes, you can boast about the size of your forests, but we don't think much of them. You probably couldn't even catch a lame rabbit in these sandy parts," Tautvydas joked.

"Just rustle around in the bushes and you'll find yourself a rabbit the size of a dog," Audra said, defending our territory.

As we exchanged banter, we came upon the camp. I presented the "captured" men to Rymantas. We led them to an empty area of the camp to get settled in. They hurried to assemble lean-tos for themselves, so that they could get integrated into camp life. Although they were exhausted from their journey, they did not even think about going to sleep. We gave them some provisions, but only enough to arouse their appetites for lunch.

Rymantas brought the older trainees from the auditorium. After a few minutes rest, the whistle invited everyone to lunch. The last men from the Iron Wolf Unit lined up with the rest. With this lunch the full training program at camp began. Inžinas walked among this family of forty men, stopping from time to time to make conversation.

When everyone heard the whistle blow after lunch, they hurried off to their assigned clearing. Anbo gave the disorderly group of trainees instructions on how to line up. Until this time the two units had lined up separately. From here on in Anbo mixed them all up and lined them up according to height. He acquainted them with the general rules of lining up—how to quickly find their place in line, how to keep quiet, what to do if they were late and so on. They were also instructed on what to do in the event of an attack.

Normal camp life began. Not one combatant had free time. Inžinas, Tigras, Liepsnabarzdis (Fire Beard),[78] Urėdas,[79] Ūkas and Jonas[80] worked like ants in the kitchen. Every evening Sargas rotated the guard to the four guard posts, never forgetting to test the guards' attentiveness. The camp guard patrolled the camp up and down, carefully watching for anything out of order. Only our training leader, the lecturer, Uosis, and I were not tied down to any schedule and could show up anywhere at any time.

Around five o'clock Uosis and I went to the training region where we observed the trainees practicing greetings, delivering reports, saluting, practicing handling a weapon, fighting without a weapon, in groups, or individually. They were cov-

---

78 Jonas Kazakevičius, 1922–1951. He was killed in battle May 18, 1951.

79 Jonas Stankus. He joined the partisans in 1944. He and four of his comrades were killed in a bunker when they were betrayed.

80 Jonas Račiukaitis died in battle February 2, 1951.

ered in dust; the moss around the area had been trampled. Their faces were covered in dust, but they still were not satisfied with their results. Rymantas spotted us and could not help himself. He commented:

"You see what a run we're giving them for their money. Their faces are as hot as though they'd just gotten out of the sauna. Give them one more hour and they'll be in perfect shape. Only the wounded are having a hard time."

Among the partisans there was a general feeling of freedom and camaraderie. They had a much easier time dealing with tasks during the training sessions that they had encountered already many times out in the field. Their understanding, even of theoretical weapons, out-matched the limits of the program.

The day's exhaustion relieved us of night-time guard duty. After the whistle blew for quiet, there was a deathly stillness in the area of camp where the trainees lived. The moment they lay down on their moss beds, they were asleep. Uosis and I snuck around camp in vain, trying to catch the trainees who dared break the peace. Besides the sound of snoring, we did not hear a thing.

We heard an owl hooting and a rabbit whistling and the grasshoppers chirping.

Uosis and I decided to go to bed.

The following morning I awoke earlier than usual. The camp was absolutely quiet. The only sound came from the kitchen unit. Every once in a while I could hear the footsteps of the patrol or guard returning to camp. After seven o'clock the silence ended and everyone rose with the whistle for the day's activities.

After breakfast the weapons were thoroughly inspected.

Not Everyone Arrived Safely

Uosis told us that not all the partisans who should have arrived with him had made it. A few days previous Šarūnas, along with five other men, had been killed. Using dogs, Soviet Interior Forces had discovered the bunker where Šarūnas and his comrades were hiding. The bunker was completely surrounded. There was no chance of escape. Šarūnas shot each of his men in the temple and then shot himself.

Besides the loss of these men, the unit had lost Ramunė (Daisy),[81] a liaison woman. She had been hiding with neighbors nearby and was arrested. She was tortured mercilessly. During interrogations the Soviet's crushed Ramunė's fingers and wrist joints by slamming doors shut on them.

---

[81] Elena Sabastijauskaitė, 1923–. She was a liaison woman who lived in Kaunas. July 26, 1947 she was arrested, imprisoned in Kaunas, and then deported for ten years of hard labor in Siberia. She returned to Lithuania in 1955.

The Soviet Interior Forces tossed the bodies of the six dead partisans into a cart and then tied Ramunė's arms to the back of the cart. They dragged her behind the cart as they drove to town. Each time Ramunė collapsed, the Russians clubbed her with the butts of their guns until she stood up again and continued stumbling after the cart. By the time she reached their garrison, her arms hung loosely at her sides. Despite this horrific torture, Ramunė refused to talk and the NKVD learned nothing from her.

Who were Those People who Went to Fight in the Forest

During their free time the partisans read the new issue of *The Freedom Scout*. It was a little different than usual because it was now being edited by the leadership of the nation's resistance.

Together with the newspaper a proclamation published by the partisan leadership was included. This proclamation was an answer to Paleckis's proposed amnesty for the partisans.

That evening Rymantas, Uosis and I decided on details regarding the remainder of the lessons and their conclusion. We reported to the district commander, who had promised to visit us if not during training, then at the farewell party. I also wrote invitations to the neighboring unit leaders, inviting them to join us at the farewell party. The invitations were distributed by the unit combatants Briedis (Moose)[82] and Voveras (Squirrel).[83]

As it grew dark we heard the sound of vehicles coming from the direction of the village of Agurkiškės. The village dogs were barking suspiciously loud. We would send guards there at night and double our patrol to two men.

On the morning of September 12th in the forests of Kazlų Rūda the sun had barely reached the tops of the pine trees when the guard's whistle woke up the camp. One after the other, the men rolled out of their moss lean-tos and lined up in the clearing, listening attentively for their unit commander's orders.

"Attention, ten-hut..."

The faces of forty men in the Tauras Unit froze like granite.

I opened the lean-to flap and saw the faces of these men. In my thoughts I returned to ten years ago and compared these men with the soldiers in training in Independent Lithuania's army at that time. On the surface there was not too much difference. The uniform and clothing was the same, only we favored

---

[82] Juozas Bacevičius, 1925–1948. He died in battle.

[83] Alfonsas Krasnodemskis, 1922–1948. He was betrayed and killed June 15, 1948.

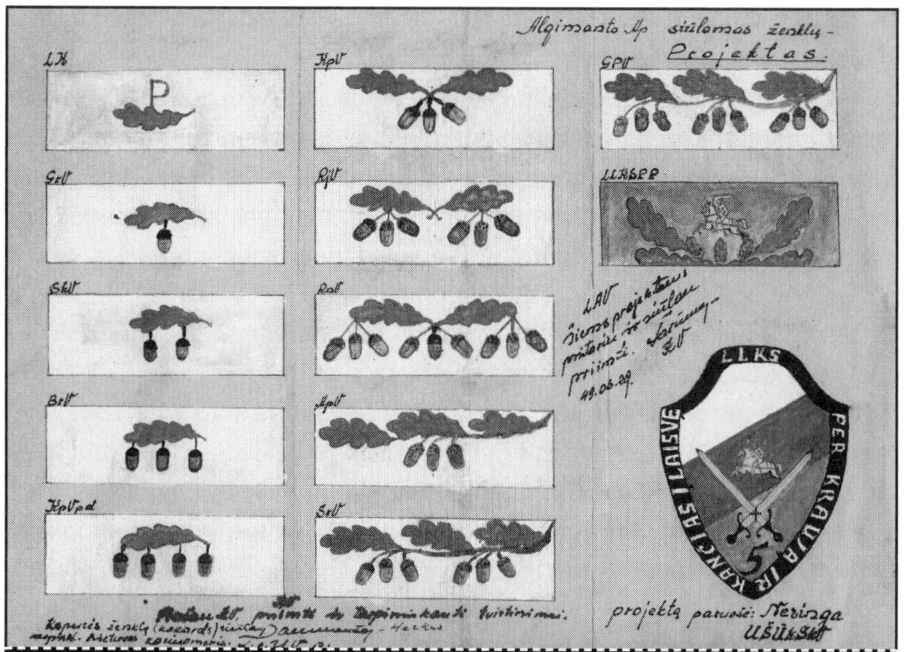

Up to the end of the 1940s the resistance made huge efforts to unite and centralize, something that succeeded in 1949. The strive was to keep up an army-like structure, in terms of uniforms and other insignia. This is an outline for a proposed unified set of ranks, with oak leaves and acorns as the basic symbols.

automatic and semi-automatic weapons. However, if you were to gaze more deeply into the faces of these fighters you would see etched in them the evidence of thousands of days and nights of danger and the experience of living through several dozen harrowing battles and skirmishes. Their well-proportioned bodies often hid the scars of larger or smaller battle wounds. For example, Karys, whose right arm was shorter at the elbow did not lag behind his comrades when cleaning his weapon. Strazdas's[84] both arms were no longer flexible at the joints. Skirgaila could count eight places on his body where he had been wounded. Sakalas had a hard time finding a place on his body that had not been wounded. Bijūnas still could not deliver a report since he had been wounded in the throat a year ago. It would be very difficult to find one man among these forty who was not marked by battle and who had not shed his own blood for his beloved country.

84 Antans Siaurys, 1926–1949. He was betrayed and killed March 9, 1949.

But they were not afraid of these scars. They were not afraid to stain the face of our land with their blood.

The backgrounds of the soldiers were very diverse. Among them were university students, high school students, farmers and laborers. Also among them were priests, older intellectuals, even officers from Independent Lithuania's army. Here you could also find volunteers from the fight for Lithuania's last independence. They were all united with one and the same sense of duty towards their native land and a sense of duty to protect their brothers and sisters from the terror of the Russian barbarian invaders. They felt they had to defend freedom and humanity. They understood perfectly well that to defend their country and their people they would have to sacrifice their own personal lives: That they had only their strength and their alertness to go on. All the while they secretly held onto the hope that finally those who so recently had talked about how to set up life after the War will feel a responsibility towards generations to come and will condemn barbarism, terror, and slavery—the barbarism, terror, and slavery that had taken over the larger part of Europe and Asia. They were also called to arms by the spirit of their ancestors who stood for freedom and independence throughout the ages. These sentiments made blood brothers of the farmer with the student. They stood here, shoulder to shoulder today, hoping to receive the ranks they were working so hard for.

The Liaison Man Artūras

After breakfast one morning, as the trainees were chatting in a group together, the liaison man, Artūras, arrived and reported that in a nearby village the Communists were coercing the farmers into relinquishing grain and other supplies. The men were very upset. Many of them wondered out loud how they and other people in the villages would live through the winter to the next harvest if already they were being stripped of their reserves. Because they were in the training program, they could not leave camp to do anything about the situation.

Artūras saw that the men were worried. He leaned onto his oak staff and inhaled deeply on his pipe:

"We'll get by, somehow, men. As long as God protects us from getting deported to Siberia. Siberia is wide... They are rushing to hoard supplies. First they'll take away our very last bite of bread and then they'll deport us all. All they want is to finish us all off as quickly as possible. Yesterday in the village, the NKVD ran out of butter, so they went and took an entire cow. It doesn't mean anything to them that the cow provided milk and butter for a family with five children."

The shrill camp whistle cut off Artūras's voice. The men stood and left to attend a lecture. Artūras continued his monologue with the men on kitchen duty. Out of his three daughters, two had been deported to Siberia. Only one, Janė, remained. All over Lithuania in every home it was the same story. Only rarely did anyone hear a single word of comfort for their loss. Artūras finished his report and wandered off into the forest. As his bent figure disappeared into the darkness of the pines, he slammed his staff against the trunk of a pine.

I watched him disappear. He was an irreplaceable liaison man and source of information. He was already 67 years old. In spite of his age, he was invaluable to us. He could make it through the tightest encirclement of Soviet Interior Forces with press and orders. Not a single hair on his beard revealed any fear when the Bolsheviks would search through his rags. He would just slam his oak staff against their automatic weapons and say, "What do you think, brothers, I could use one of those to hunt skunks." The Russians never even remotely suspected him of acting as a spy for the "bandits."

Two Women Wander Into Camp

The kitchen duty men looked after preparing our meals and did not attend lectures. One day, four guards were helping with the kitchen work. The previous night they had been caught talking after the quiet whistle had blown and were now peeling potatoes as punishment. An elderly woman and a fifteen-year-old girl were also working in the kitchen. They had been out gathering berries a few days previous and had wandered into camp. The girl's brother was one of the local *Stribai*, so they were both detained in camp for security reasons until we could move to another location. The woman was shocked to see us assembled in the forest.

The woman was from Kačergynė where the armed resistance was not well known. Last year, on September 23, operating on orders from the district commander, several dozen partisans "visited" the town and occupied all the Bolsheviks' strategic points. After they killed those who tried to defend themselves, they took what they needed and left. Before that she had seen the bodies of desecrated partisans in the market square. She could scarcely understand why the Communists had dismembered the men with saws, carved Lithuanian symbols into their chests, and yoked them with rosaries.

Now she was beginning to understand everything. When sixty men lined up for the evening ceremony, she stood leaning against a pine tree watching. Tears rolled down her wrinkled cheeks as she joined us in the words of the evening prayer: "Lord, you who have liberated the people and inspired them with a thirst for freedom, we pray to you, restore the days of freedom to our homeland. Grant us the strength to bear the life of a partisan. Saint Casimir, lead us in battle, as you led our forefathers." When the final words of the prayer died away in the depths of the forest, the woman remained rooted to her spot. She remained there even as the men sat around the campfire singing partisan songs.

During the days the woman lived with us, she carried out the kitchen work entrusted to her diligently and conscientiously. On this particular day she worked harder than usual because she knew we were expecting the district commander and his adjunct.

A Punishment for Unnecessary Brashness

After dinner I had the unpleasant task of questioning and then punishing two combatants—Vaidila and Daina. Some time ago, they had been sent to Kaunas on a mission. While in Kaunas they stopped in at a railway station restaurant and ordered a double shot of vodka each. Vaidila tossed down his drink and became a little light-headed. In the restaurant he approached a policeman seated at the bar and tore off the emblem of Lenin's head from his uniform jacket. He tossed the emblem on the floor and trampled it.

The policeman hurried out of the restaurant and quickly returned with several dozen officials in uniform and in undercover clothing. They jumped on Vaidila. Luckily, Daina was able to draw his "panzer" in time. The Soviet Security Officers reacted by releasing Vaidila, who then drew his "zvezda" pistol. The result of this confrontation was that as the NKVD men ran for cover at their headquarters, the officer raced down the street with the frame of the shattered restaurant window wedged over his shoulders.

Vaidila and Daina carried out their assigned mission. They weren't even wounded. But I still punished them because their actions had put other partisans in danger. Several other partisans were in Kaunas at the same time conducting various missions.

Toward evening the district commander and his adjunct arrived. The district commander was received with full military honors.

Both of our guests had scarcely eaten, so we provided them with a nice meal. Afterwards we inspected the camp, then retired to the "officer's lean-to" for a report of the past three month's activities.

A Sudden Attack

Suddenly we heard gunfire coming from the direction of the eastern end of camp. More gunfire responded from another direction. That was when all hell broke loose. A sentry came running to camp to report that a few hundred yards away several Russians had appeared and an engagement was underway between them and the third section of trainees.

We had anticipated such attacks and were prepared for them. The camp was divided into five battle sections. Each section was responsible for its own trenches and had to hold out until the entire camp was ready for evacuation. We were not prepared to hold out longer because the Russians could bring in fresh reinforcements, causing additional losses for us. In every action our tactics were to deal the enemy a sudden blow, to inflict maximum losses on him, and then to withdraw. This time Rymantas, leader of the training program, assumed command of operations.

The enemy consisted of about sixty men who had approached camp and attacked it from three sides. As the attack began, we had no forces on the right flank of the camp. The trenches there were supposed to be defended by the third section, but that section was now fighting elsewhere. To secure the third flank, the first and second flank went into action. Meanwhile, the enemy was quite close to the right flank. Machine gun bullets splattered near the lean-tos and a group of guards were ordered to retake the captured trenches and to reinforce those threatened by encirclement on the right flank. The group leader, Sargas, began to advance first. Not far behind him, was the sentry Jūrelė. He fired from a German infantry machine gun and with a sudden dash, surged ahead. As he charged forwards he lost his balance and fell with the machine gun on top of him.

"Jūrelė wounded," he called out.

Sargas ran over to the machine gun. Jūrelė pulled out a Russian pistol and crawled backwards, propping himself up against a pine tree. Meanwhile, the other three combatants of the group of sentries managed to reach the trenches and toss grenades at the enemy. Unfortunately, the group leader, Sargas, was shot and could no longer handle the machine gun. Daina then took over the weapon. The sentry group regained control of the trenches. The situation on the right flank was restored.

Meanwhile, the first, second, and third battle stations disengaged themselves from the enemy. The first two sections occupied their own trenches while the third section occupied the trench regained by the sentry group. The kitchen duty group, whose area the enemy had not attacked, received orders to occupy a forest clearing to the west of the camp and secure it until all sections had withdrawn through it.

Still, the Russian offensive did not cease. Blindly carrying out their officers' command, "Forward!" the Russians ran directly into our fire and fell, one after the other, alongside their dogs.

Suddenly Rymantas shouted out across the clatter of automatic gun fire, "I'm wounded! Intensify fire!"

Two enemy bullets had pierced his neck and his right arm. At the same time, on the left flank, enemy crossfire had knocked out Tautvydas, a combatant from the third battle section.

Although their leader had been put out of action, our men did not scatter. With coordinated fire, they mowed down the advancing Russians. In the interim, others collected the camp documents and made preparations for evacuation. They received orders to retreat through the valley. After about half an hour, the enemy's fire started to taper off. The Communist survivors and wounded began to retreat in a panic. Thirty seven of their dead lay in our trenches.

We split into small bands and dispersed. It would have been impossible to continue camp activities since the Bolsheviks would be sure to send in a battalion the next day. We went our separate ways in small groups without significant incident.

Our group encountered a detachment of Russians at one point, but they soon retreated when we opened fire on them. That evening, when we assembled for evening prayers, we paid tribute to our comrades, Tautvydas and Sargas, who only a few hours before had been taken from our midst. We clutched our "lovers" and lost ourselves in mourning for our brothers.

As night shadows covered the bare forest, we prepared ourselves for the night's march, repeating the words of our oath to ourselves—to persistently continue the battle for truth and justice on this earth and for human rights, those same human rights that are talked about so much in the wider world beyond our borders, but that we must purchase at the price of our own blood.

Even now we still have not secured our human rights…

The Heroes of Raišupis

Softly the oak loom weaves linen,

…Tyliai mėto staklės šeivas ąžuolines,

the linen before me, so white, so white…

Baltos drobės tiesias taip baltai, baltai…

I will weave in the linen the words, "Lithuania,

Rankšluostin įausiu – "Lietuva Tėvyne,

my Homeland, land of Heroes, we are your children."

Tu didvyrių žemė, mes tavo vaikai..."

(a Partisan song)

It was growing light when the footsteps of six exhausted partisans rang through the district of Raišupis. Six silhouettes came into focus against the brightening sky. The partisans Liūtas[85] (Lion), Jovaras[86] (Sycamore), Klevas[87] (Maple), Robinzonas[88] (Robinson), Lakūnas[89] (Pilot), and Turklys[90] stopped and in a huddle discussed their situation in whispers. Their faces were lined with worry and were dripping with sweat. Their backs were weighed down by heavy packs and their boots were steaming.

It was the third day already that they had been chased from one area to the next by the Soviet Interior Forces. It was the third day already that in this area Moscow's servants were carrying out a plan of mass deportations of the local populace to Siberia. It was the third day already that they had hurried from one farmstead to the next, announcing the horrific news to those families that were on the deportation lists for exile to Siberia. After receiving the warning, these families would jump half-naked out of their warm beds, exhausted after the work of the summer's harvest, and rush to hide in the fields and forests. Young and old alike were wracked with terror.

Everywhere trucks were arriving at cottages, threatening the inhabitants with deportation, forcing the people to search for thicker and thicker bushes to hide in. The gangs of Bolsheviks, armed to the teeth, walked like packs of grim reapers from farm to farm, handing out death sentences. When they arrived, all they would find were starving dogs slinking around the fences, because the inhabitants of the houses had already been warned by the partisans and had fled for the forests. Everyone wanted to remain on their native land. Everyone was terrified of Russia's wide expanses where they were destined to suffer from starvation and a longing for their native land.

These worries affected the partisans more than their everyday discomforts. When will the suffering ever end? What will happen to the people being exiled

---

85 Juozas Stanaitis, unknown–1947

86 Viktoras Lelešius, 1922–1947.

87 Jonas Popiera, 1925–1947.

88 Vincas Bridžius, 1910 or 1920–1947.

89 Kazimieras Mykolaitis, unknown–1947.

90 Vytautas Mykolaitis, 1928–1947.

today? Where will they find shelter once hundreds of farms are left deserted without their masters?

The dawning day truly was awful. The partisans decided to go to a farmstead on their left—one with stone out-buildings.

Around noon the partisans noticed several dozen Bolsheviks approaching the farmstead where they were holed up. The group leader, Liūtas, quickly gave the order to retreat in the opposite direction. The partisans thought that by taking cover behind the farm buildings, they could successfully retreat and avoid a skirmish. However, once they got several dozen meters away from the farmstead, they saw a number of Bolsheviks spread out on the other side. It was clear that they were surrounded. The partisans returned to the farmstead and holed themselves up in the stone barn. They set themselves up at the windows and prepared for battle.

All of the partisans were equipped with good weapons. They were the best sharp shooters in the Tauras District. Not even a rabbit could escape them in the forest, even shooting with the poorest quality rifle. Needless to say, many more Bolsheviks had died at their hands than rabbits. This time their hatred for the Bolsheviks knew no bounds. They thirsted to take down as many Russians as they could. They knew that they were surrounded and that there was no hope of surviving the battle. The blood boiled in their veins as they watched the Bolsheviks' every move. The Bolsheviks were in no rush to attack them. They waited as several hundred more reinforcements were brought in. They set up several rings of defense.

About two o'clock that afternoon the stress of waiting was broken. The attack began. The Bolsheviks crawled on their stomachs like spiders towards the farmstead. They hammered the buildings with machine gun and submachine gun fire, especially the barn, which was their epicenter. The partisans defended themselves heroically. They directed precise fire at the Bolsheviks as they came closer and closer. Eventually, the Bolsheviks managed to approach the barn under the cover of the other farm buildings. After two hours of fighting, the partisan fire weakened. Some of them had been killed, others wounded, the rest had run out of ammunition. The Bolsheviks could now reach the barn with grenades. Using the last few rounds of ammunition, the remaining partisans were able to kill off the Bolsheviks in the yard. They broke out of the barn and removed the weapons and ammunition from the dead Bolsheviks. Using the Bolsheviks' weapons, they continued to fight.

However, by that point fresh reinforcements had been brought in. Again they made several rings around the barn and tossed grenades. Whenever they hit a partisan, he would detonate a grenade, sometimes taking a friend with him. The battle quieted down and several Russians broke into the barn. The last partisan left alive, Jovaras, shot the first Russian to enter the barn. This Russian was the 67th Bolshevik to die that day. Among the dead were several officers and the NKVD head of the Prienai region. That was the price the Bolsheviks paid to take a bastion held by six partisans.

That evening the bodies of Liūtas, Jovaras, Lakūnas, Klevas, Robinzonas, and Turklys were desecrated and their blood was spilled in the market square. Their deaths served as a symbol of selfless sacrifice for freedom. The mass deportations to Siberia continued that day. Eye witnesses who saw the battle take place vowed with tears in their eyes that they would continue the struggle for Lithuania's freedom.

The Tragedy at the Bunker of the Birutė Unit Headquarters

Who will ask why my tears are falling?	*Kas paklaus, kodėl gi ašaros man rieda?*
Who will bless me as I weed the rue?	*Kas man ravint rūtą "padėk Diev" sakys?*
Who will gaze into my blue eyes?	*Kas akis manąsias atras lino žiede,*
Who will calm my heart?	*Kas, oi kas gi širdį mano suramys?*
(a Partisan song)	

After the disruption of the second training program, we returned to our every day routines. Meanwhile, the Russians had sent heavy reinforcements to their nearest support forces. Day and night they combed the woods and farms, prodding the ground with two-meter long rods, searching for partisans.

During these treacherous days I met Anbo. I was to transfer my duties as commander of the Birutė Unit to him on September 20th. After briefing him on his duties, I detached my insignia of office and pinned it on his shoulder. Anbo sighed deeply. "These stars feel light on your shoulders, but the responsibility that comes with them weighs more heavily."

We were all feeling depressed. It was a premonition that we only understood four days later. At the time I thought I was feeling sad because I would be leaving my former staff officials, whom I had come to love as though they were my own blood brothers. Under the circumstances, these feelings were normal. Nothing I had asked of them had been too difficult for them. They had carried out all their tasks with diligence and integrity. Because of their devotion and camaraderie, our unit had won first place in the district orders.

When the Soviet forces managed to pin down a bunker the surrounded partisans were forced to either give up or die. Sometimes they chose to blow themselves up.

The pictures are from an operation by internal Soviet troops, on October 30th–November Ist in 1949. Due to betrayal 5 bunkers were located and eliminated, and I9 partisans killed

Intensive house searches were being conducted at the place where I was living now. Because of these searches, my former unit men invited me to go with them. I refused to seek security for myself, leaving my other friends in danger. Moreover, I felt that my submachine gun would surely soften the blow of a crisis in a critical moment. It turned out that this decision I had made proved to be what many would call "luck." Four days later an unspeakable calamity occurred.

The morning of September 24th had barely dawned when enemy forces from Marijampolė stormed the Birutė staff headquarters where the new unit commander Anbo, along with two staff officers and three guests, including the district chaplain, were staying. Soviet Interior Forces troops prowled the neighborhood, then turned into Daunora's farm, crowding together in the house. They seemed indifferent. Their real objective, however, was to make sure that all the partisans would leap into the bunker, guaranteeing that they would all be dealt with in one blow.

The bunker in question, where three or four staff members worked, prayed, and rested was not very safe. It had not been possible to excavate it deep enough because of the ground water level. One of the advantages of this underground shelter was that it was near the small town of Veiveriai where a sizable number of Soviet Interior Forces troops were stationed. For some time the Bolsheviks did not suspect that the staff of an armed resistance detachment could be so close to them. From the shelter, on quiet evenings, we could hear the Bolsheviks shouting, practicing, singing. We could also observe the direction of their movements. The bunker was hidden under a summer kitchen, made of boards.

These headquarters were discovered quite accidentally. One evening two *Stribai* were returning from visiting with their girlfriends. They entered Daunora's farm to steal some food. While they were searching for eggs in a potato storehouse not far from the shelter, they heard the clacking of a typewriter. At the time the entrance to the bunker was open and the *Stribai* could see inside. They hurried back to the Soviet Interior Forces headquarters and reported what they had seen.

The Russians did not attack immediately. Through agents they arranged a watch and waited until the bunker was full. They waited in a room of the farmhouse, pretending to be on a routine mission, to give our combatants time to assemble in the bunker. An hour and a half later additional Soviet Interior Forces detachments arrived at Daunora's farm. At that time those inside the house emerged and set up machine guns around the entire farm. Now the premonition that had caused my feelings of sadness came true.

The Communists seized the owner of the farm, an eighty year old veteran, dragged him to the site of the shelter, and ordered him to dig. At first the old farmer tried to defend himself by insisting that he knew of no bunker on his property. Then the Russians beat him and repeated their command to dig. After several more beatings, the old man reluctantly began to dig.

When the soil began to crumble and cave in, the partisans discharged several rounds of automatic fire. No one would volunteer to dig after that. The Russians proceeded to tear down the boards of the summer kitchen.

The partisans now knew that they were lost. They proceeded to destroy documents and records. They burned the papers and smashed their typewriters and duplicating machines. They even slashed and cut their boots, so that the enemy could not use them.

Meanwhile, not daring to dig any further, the Russians decided to take down the bunker with grenades. They piled the grenades into heaps of seven. Then they would run past the bunker and hurl grenades at it. To avoid injury, they would drop to the ground as they tossed the grenade. At the same time, other soldiers maintained machine gun fire over the top of the bunker to prevent anyone from escaping.

The men inside the bunker prepared themselves for their deaths. They prayed and sang songs and hymns. Their voices were scarcely audible outside over the sound of machine gunfire and Russian curses.

Eventually, the grenades ripped a hole in the surface of the shelter. Amidst dense clouds of smoke and dust, Survila and Vaidila appeared on the shelter surface, firing their submachine guns. Our remaining brothers inside blew themselves up with grenades.

The Russians kept tossing grenades through the hole in the roof of the shelter for another half hour. Finally, when they felt certain that no one inside could possibly still be alive, they forced the old farmer to go down to remove the bodies of the dead and any documents that might still be intact.

After the destruction of the headquarters' bunker, the Russians washed the bodies of the partisans and stitched on their detached parts. They reconstructed the faces and stuffed the bodies into fresh uniforms. The corpses were then photographed and taken to the town of Veivariai where they were left beside the former vicar's hen house.

The Communist activists assembled around the hen house and the "banquet" began. Local people and suspects from the area were rounded up and brought to identify the corpses, so that the Bolsheviks could arrest their relatives. However, even after the stitching, the corpses were not recognizable because some of the heads had been broken into two pieces. Even a father could not recognize his own son under these circumstances.

A month later five of our men visited that dreadful place where the bunker had been destroyed. In place of the summer kitchen, posts and timber ends jutted out of the ground. The earth had been heaped into hillocks by grenades. Bloodstained scraps of paper lay scattered about, mingled with the rusted parts of typewriters and shreds of clothing. Inside the bunker there was similar evidence of devastation. There they found the emblem of the *Vytis*, the Lithuanian State emblem, and pieces of a rosary that the partisans had used that night in their evening prayers.

Implementig a Plan With Percentages

At the end of September we had to carry out an assignment not far from Kaunas. The matter was urgent and we did not have time to notify the local partisan detachment of our presence. For this reason, we had to spend the day without shelter. To escape detection, we sought shelter at a small farmstead. We soon learned that the farmer himself was a Soviet functionary, the regional secretary. Beginning early in the morning, he was continually shuffling through a set of papers. One minute he would be scribbling furiously on them, the next he would erase all his scribbling and begin all over again. If his wife or children happened to wander close by, he would vent his frustration by shouting at them.

Finally, we could not take it anymore and one of us said to him jokingly, "That's not a plow you have there in your hand, but a pencil."

After breakfast the secretary hastily packed some papers into a briefcase and tried to make a get-away. We were not absolutely convinced of his loyalty, so we detained him. We told him that we would be the first to leave.

He fretted and said: "Tomorrow morning I have to deliver the completed sowing plan to the regional agricultural chief. So far, I've only been able to register about a third of the region. I must go or I'll end up behind bars."

"Don't worry," we reassured him, "Give us your papers and let's sit down at the table. In a couple of hours your plan will be complete."

The secretary relaxed. He heaved a sigh of relief. "You probably could save me," he said. "All the farmers have already sown or are sowing whatever grain they can. Most likely nobody in the district will try to verify how much has actually been sown according to these papers."

Skirgaila and I sat down at the table to work. The Secretary explained the requirements to us and answered our questions. We understood now how the plan was to be fulfilled. We decided that we would improve his plan by adding on thirteen percent more than the district had originally counted in its plan.

We were able to locate the necessary figures among the secretary's disorderly papers.

After two hours, the seed corn was registered. We checked the total number of hectares twice, counting on the abacus. Then we handed the completed work back to the secretary.

"Here you go," I said, "take it away. You won't find another plan like it in the entire region. Notice, that this plan has exceeded the previous one by thirteen percent. Only, don't go around telling people how you came up with these numbers and who helped you, or you really will end up behind bars."

The secretary was delighted. He took the papers and stuffed them into his briefcase. Then, he tried to justify himself to us. "I'm still new at this," he explained. "This is only the second month they've included me. Before I never listened to what they were talking about at those meetings. I sowed as much as I could on what available land I had. But now there are hundreds of plans and hundreds of projects. You could drown in the paperwork. According to the way they do things, a hen cannot lay eggs without it being written into the plan."

We understood his annoyance at the mountain of Soviet bureaucracy. In every sphere of life there were innumerable plans. None of those plans had any possibility of realistically being carried out.

Plans were also formulated to bolster Soviet propaganda and to improve the Soviet image in the eyes of the world. Such planning was considered "progress," despite the fact that every branch of production in Lithuania since the pre-war period had declined two-fold to five-fold. And now, we the partisans had found ourselves contributing to the situation by fooling the Russians into registering the farmers' seed corn according to the Communists "sacred" plan.

The Secretary fed us generously and was hospitable with us right up until our departure.

A Trap in Kaunas

Around this same time the resistance in Kaunas and the surrounding environs experienced a shock. Mindaugas,[91] the Birutė staff functionary, had been given the task of confiscating food products from certain food manufacturing concerns. He carried out this operation quite successfully. Then, on September 15th, while waiting for public transit in Rotušė Street, he stumbled upon a "zaseda" or ambush taking place in the apartment of a suspect. Mindaugas was diligent and

91 Kazimieras Pyplys, the legendary fighter of the Marijampole engagement party massacre.

quickly took down five NKVD officials and liberated a dozen arrested partisans. As he was being pursued down unfamiliar streets by a crowd, he cut through several backyards and eventually met up with his comrades. With the help of Vytenis[92] he hurried to warn all the liaison posts that might have any kind of contact with the posts in the apartment in Rotušė Street. In the Žaliakampis neighborhood they came upon another ambush and again had to fight the NKVD. An important NKVD functionary who tried to arrest them was shot and killed.

The officials who had been shot in the incidents were evidently well-known antagonists of the Lithuanian people because they were interred with full pomp and ceremony. Their coffins, draped in red, were escorted by several military bands and a crowd of uniformed Russians. They marched in front of the coffins, bearing the orders of the slain officials on pillows. It turned out that one of the men killed that day was Mayor Kirov, also the deputy chief of the Kaunas NKVD.

After the assassination of these NKVD officials, a huge drag-net investigation of documents and suspected persons in Kaunas began. The Russians were now exceedingly cautious. The secret police would now rarely attempt to interrogate suspicious persons or check their documents until they had first knocked their victims down and had handcuffed them. Cyclists suffered because they would be knocked off of their bicycles.

Despite these massive searches, not a single partisan fell into Russian hands.

Again Tragedy Strikes in the Birutė Unit

On September 23, 1947, a second tragedy occurred for the Birutė Unit. The Soviet Interior Forces managed to find a partisan bunker in the home of Stasys Dovydaitis.[93] There were five partisans in the bunker: the unit commander Vaidotas,[94] Jūragis,[95] Daina, Žaibas, and Urėdas.

The bunker was built inside a barn. The Bolsheviks set the barn on fire. The partisans burned all the documents in the bunker, destroyed their equipment, and committed suicide. The partisans' bodies were dragged out of the bunker by the Bolsheviks. They defiled the bodies and cursed at them. They were furious that the partisans had sliced apart their boots. They expected to get some good boots off the bodies.

92 Vincas Šapoka, 1925–1948. He was arrested and sentenced to 25 years in the concentration camp in Siberia.

93 Jonas Dovydaitis, 1906–1949. He was arrested and sentenced to 25 years in a concentration camp in Siberia.

94 Antanas Rundėnas, unknown–1947

95 Vacys Bamblys.

They took their revenge on the bodies of the dead in the market square of Garliava. Only, before they allowed the bodies to be desecrated, Soviet Security Officers used photos to try to identify them.

Fighting Against the Collectivization of Farms

The farmers of Lithuania felt more and more pressure from the Bolsheviks to join the collective farms. But because of their experiences with the Russians, the farmers were in no hurry to join. They knew the misery of collective farm workers in the Soviet Union. The farmers, therefore, did everything they could to remain on their own farms. According to Communist law, however, those farms now belonged to the State. And the State was using every means at its disposal to drive the people into the collective farms.

Soviet officials burdened the farmers with unbearable obligations of various kinds. They made it impossible for them to buy tools, machinery and fertilizer. In order to psychologically prepare the Lithuanian farmers for life on the collective farm, they set up "communal farms" or *Sovchovs* where farmers could share their work and their lives. These communal farms were provided with everything they needed to function well in addition to other privileges. They were exempted from State taxes and other obligations. They were supplied with fertilizers and seed. Reliable tractors plowed their land for them.

Despite the economic privileges the *Sovchovs* offered and despite pressure from Soviet officials, the Russians failed to break the will of the farmers. By the end of 1947, there still were very few collective farms, or *Kolkhozs*, in Lithuania.

Unable to defeat the farmers using economic pressures, the Russians resorted to other methods. They began massively deporting Lithuanian farmers and their families to Siberia and bringing in colonists from Russia to inhabit their empty farms. This process of collectivization and colonization of Lithuanian agriculture spelled the final phase of the Soviet Union's undeclared war against Lithuania.

The armed resistance movement took up the fight against colonization, especially in the provinces. It was impossible to do this in the towns where a large population of Russians had been brought in and were under the protection of the army and the militia. For this reason, the resistance movement against Lithuanian colonization was fought mostly in the provinces where the conditions for the struggle were more favorable.

In the Tauras District the Aušrutai *Kolkhoz* had already been organized. The idea for its establishment had been prompted by several empty farms that had lost their owners in 1941 when their German owners were repatriated from Lithuania. Later, the Russians exiled or imprisoned the owners of other farms that were to be included in the projected *Kolkhoz.*

After that, fifteen families were brought from Russia to operate the empty farms. Several of these Collective Farm workers had been indoctrinated to the principles of Russian imperialism and Communism. They constituted the regional "authorities" and acted as NKVD representatives who were to help the occupying government in its fight against Lithuanian farmers in the Pilviškis *Kolkhoz.* For these reasons, the armed resistance decided to liquidate this *Kolkhoz.*

The question was raised and discussed at a summer meeting of the Tauras District command. All the commanders agreed that collectivization and colonization had to be inflexibly opposed. Opinion differed only on the measures to be used. It was my view, along with two other combatants, that in this anti-colonization action, force should not be used. Others felt that the operation would be more successful if it was carried out with greater force and speed. Since these were the views of the majority, the majority prevailed.

Liquidation of the colonists' *Kolkhoz* was to take place on November 12th. The operation was to be carried out by Šturmas, the Žalgiris Unit commander, along with the help of seventy men. Two days before this operation an attack had to be made on the State alcohol distillery at the Antanavas *Sovchov.* The primary purpose of this attack was to pin down the Russian forces, so as to make it easier to attack the Aušrutai *Kolkhoz.*

While we were preparing for this assault on the *Kolkhoz* we registered and classified the Russians according to the nature of their work. The decision was made to attack the eight farmsteads where the most malevolent Communist activists were living. From the data collected by our intelligence, it was known that there were about thirty-five armed Russians at the *Kolkhoz* and that they had two machine guns.

The first step was to issue appeals written in both Russian and Lithuanian. In these appeals the command of the Lithuanian armed resistance appealed to the newly settled colonists to remove themselves of their own free will from Lithuania within a month. A simultaneous warning was issued stating that those who refused to obey this order would be punished by the partisans according to partisan law. The order did not apply to Russian people whose activities were not injurious to the Lithuanian people.

On the evening of November 9 about 70 Žalgiris men and several staff combatants led by Šturmas surrounded the alcohol distillery in the Antanavas *Sovchov.*

Some of them blockaded the roads to the estate while the others penetrated its center. In two hours time our men had loaded all the distilled alcohol (200 liters in every keg) into two *Sovchov* trucks, collected a number of cows, and had departed. Since the undistilled alcohol could not be placed in the trucks, it was smashed and spilled out onto the ground. After that the guards were removed and all the partisans fled.

The next day there was not only no alcohol, but a shortage of labor at the *Sovchov*. The workers had obviously taken advantage of the attack and were lying around in their beds dead drunk after an orgy of drinking distilled and raw alcohol. Naturally, a search for the missing goods was launched immediately and lasted for several days.

In the Kazlų Rūda forests dogs, Russians, and the *Stribai* competed with one another on the hunt. Soviet Interior Forces troops scoured the roads, searching for the hidden alcohol. And it was worth the search. Every 200 liter keg cost about 50,000 rubles on the black market. The price for one liter of alcohol was 250 rubles.

Soviet Interior Forces succeeded in locating one leaky keg. At that point the Russian soldiers took advantage of the opportunity and drank perhaps even more than the Antanavas workers had. They barely were able to stumble back to the Jankai Soviet Interior Forces headquarters. Our men now had the perfect situation to attack them, but they held back because they were out for bigger game—the Aušrutai *Kolkhoz.*

On November 11th when the neighboring NKVD detachments were looking for the remaining alcohol in the Kazlų Rūda forests, our men occupied all the roads to the colonists' *Kolkhoz.* In the evening, each of the eight groups surrounded the farms assigned to them. The objective was to disarm the colonists without shedding blood, but at the same time to discourage them to such an extent that the very next day they would not only leave the *Kolkhoz*, but Lithuania.

However, that is not how events turned out. On those eight farms the Russians began to resist and shot at the partisans through the windows. The partisans returned fire, forcing the Russians in the wooden houses to surrender. It was only a matter time before the stone houses from which the Russians had been defending themselves with machine guns were captured. Once the resistance was stifled, the partisans posted warning notices and withdrew.

The next day a number of coffins were carried in the direction of Pilviškis from the Aušrutai *Kolkhoz.* The colonists families loaded their belongings into carts and left before dawn. They asked people along the way to direct them to the safest and fastest roads leading to Russia.

These two missions made such an impression on the Communists that the puppet President of Lithuania, Justas Paleckis, who had come to Šakiai to present Soviet orders of "honor" to the mothers of large families, hastily retreated in three Russian armored cars when he heard a rumor that a hundred partisans were marching in the direction of Šakiai. He forgot to distribute the awards before he ran.

Once More to the West

Preparing for the March

It was a perfect December night. Kardas[96] and I marched through the flat fields of Suvalkija towards our liaison point. On his right shoulder Kardas was carrying a light French infantry machine gun. On his left shoulder he was carrying the ammunition. As usual, I had my PPD submachine gun with me. Both of my belts were weighed down with grenades, pistols, and underground newspapers and other correspondence. We marched towards the southeast. From time to time I checked my compass. We only veered off when we stopped at a farmstead. It didn't matter to us whether the farmstead was inhabited by elderly farmers or if it stood empty. In the first instance we had to watch out for dogs. In the second instance we had to look out for Russians hiding in the abandoned farmsteads who would "bless" us with their lead. Because of these frequent meanderings, we often had to check our compasses.

Occasionally a frightened owl would rise out of the bushes or a startled rabbit would dart past. Somewhere off in the distance we heard Russian machine gun fire. Flares were shot up into the air. We could hear individual shots or barely audible bursts of Russian or German machine gun fire. "Most likely our friends have walked into a Russian ambush," we would quietly say to ourselves and keep on walking.

It was already midnight. We stopped beside some bushes and tried to figure out on which side our unit's men were now fighting. For many of them this night would be their last. We stood and listened for a moment. Then we asked for heaven's blessing for our friends in battle and continued onwards. Within half an hour we were reached the farmstead we had been heading for. Kardas tapped out a prearranged code on the window pane. I stood beside him with my weapon ready in case we were attacked. We heard the awaited response to Kardas's knock. The door opened and we crept inside.

The master of the house had barely had enough time to get in his pants. He pulled a package from his attic. The package had been sent by the district head-

---

[96] Identity not disclosed by Juozas Lukša, but believed to be Vytautas Jundila, 1922–1948.

Visiškai slaptai.
Asmeniškai.

BDPS
Prezidiumas
1947.XII.13.
Nr. 998

Į g a l i o j i m a s.

Šiuo pažymiu,kad laisvės kovotojas S k r a j ū n a s yra įgaliotas BDPS Prezidiumo vardu atlikti uždavinius pagal raštą nr.1002.

Gintautas
BDPS [PREZI]DIUMO
PIRMININKAS

B.D.P.S. PREZIDIUMAS

Authorization from the Partisan leadership for Juozas Lukša
"Secret/Personal. Partisan Leadership Presidium. 1947. 12.13
AUTHORIZATION
With this ID, it is certified that Lithuanian freedom fighter Skrajūnas is authorized in the name of the Partisan Leadership Presidium to perform duties according to document #1002.
Signed: Gintautas"

quarters. Among various papers and documents was the district commander's orders bearing the stamp of the resistance, authorizing me to travel to the West in the name of the resistance to carry out several special tasks. The district commander emphasized in his letter that these tasks had to be carried out during the darkest and longest nights of December. As we were considering the tasks we were to accomplish, the farmer's daughters set the table for us and spread out a lovely dinner. We could not stay long though. We were soon on our way. Our task was difficult; it would be the second time I would be going to be crossing the border. I had been given this mission after the men who had been assigned the task previously were attacked by the Bolsheviks and forced to blow themselves up.

At the same time, only through a different set of liaisons, the district commander had sent orders to Mindaugas, a special officer within the Birutė Unit, to pass on his duties to others and prepare himself for the trip to the West. After three days we met at a pre-arranged place where we sat down to plan our trip. The

Armed resistance occurred in all countries in Eastern Europe affected by the Communists. The largest uprising in total figures was in the Ukraine, where the armed resistance joined itself under the name UPA (Ukrainian Partisan Army). The picture shows a group of Ukrainian partisans in the Carpathian mountains.

district economic unit had provided us with the necessary provisions for our trip. We had to chose volunteers to accompany us and map out the journey. Having presented our plan to the district commander, we received his blessing and said good-bye to our comrades. We still had to receive the documents to be taken to the West from the district headquarters.

We said good-bye the night of December 15 in the Tauras District headquarters region. Among the 36 freedom fighters, Taučius, a member of the resistance's presidium, had arrived. Also present were representatives from the Latvian[97] resistance. We raised toasts to the fruitful brotherly battle, and to the leadership of the resistance.

Late in the night we separated and went on our way. Outdoors wet snow fell. We had to hurry if we wanted to hide our tracks in the snow. The Russians were in

97 Abele Haris, 1921–unknown. He was a Latvian partisan who cooperated with the Tauras District partisans. He was eventually arrested and sentenced to 25 years of hard labor in Siberia.

the habit of hunting partisans after a snowfall. It was just too bad for anyone who was held up and could not move before the snow fell.

Šarūnas led us further away, towards Sintautas. We had to cover 40 kilometers that night. In one area we spotted fresh footsteps left in the snow within the last few minutes. Around 19 Soviet Interior Forces had crossed the road and it would not have taken much for our paths to cross. Then we would have been forced into a skirmish. A few steps further, in a village on the right, we heard the village dogs barking. Then we heard windows breaking and doors being broken in. We listened for a moment and then moved on. When we reached our halfway point, Šarūnas brought us to a farmstead to eat and take a rest. The farmer's son, who was on guard duty, came in and told us that someone was creeping through the yard. It was too late to run through the door. We moved into the other room, opened the window and prepared our weapons. We waited for the suspicious party to come to the door. If the visitors were Russians, we had decided that we would jump through the windows and disappear unnoticed. That would keep our host out of trouble. If we were seen, we had grenades that we would use to make our way out. The suspicious parties began rapping on the windows. We realized that the visitors were some of our own. It was Jaunutis and his friends. He had found our footsteps in the snow and had followed us. He had taken three men with him along on the journey.

Now we were a sizable force. There were seven men and we had two sturmovik (MK/43/1) guns, three PPS (the Russian Pistolet Pylemjot Degtyareva), one automatic rifle (SSV) and one Russian automatic. We marched in a line through the fields of Šakiai. These fields had not been worked for several years and were overgrown with weeds. From time to time we would circle onto the road to confuse our tracks.

Finally, we reached the farmstead where the men of the Žalgiris Unit were to be waiting for us. As soon as we entered, we heard the sounds of commands and reports. The cottage was crammed with armed combatants. A oil lamp burned on the table. The combatants were huddled around the lamp sharing their stories.

The Travelling Through East Prussia

We reached the Šešupė River. We found a row boat in a section of the river that was not yet frozen and crossed over to the other side to Prussian land. Our backs were weighed down with backpacks stuffed with provisions, ammunition, antitank grenades and other supplies, not to mention the package that we had to deliver to the West. On the banks of the Šešupė River we saw the former Noviškis Andriejaitis manor in ruins. There was not a single soul left there. Everything was

Together with documents Lukša brought several photos with him to the West in order to tell about the resistance in Lithuania.

destroyed. Even the window and door frames had been broken out and burned. We looked over the remains of Bolshevik "culture" and continued on our way across the East Prussian fields.

This time we had chosen a path to break through the Iron Curtain through East Prussia. We had figured that the border between East Prussia and Poland would not be as heavily guarded as the border between Lithuania and Poland.

We suspected that larger clashes with greater losses took place here. It was the main route anyone trying to escape the Soviet "paradise" would think to take. Our calculations influenced us to take another route, a route through this no-man's land that was once known as East Prussia. Set out before us were fields that had once been fertile, but now were overgrown with weeds as tall as a man and as thick as a finger. As we walked through the fields the weeds tore at our clothing and scratched our faces. Every once in a while a wild boar or a wild pig that had grown fat in a German farmer's barn would come charging out of the underbrush. There was no other sign of life out on the roads. When it grew dark we did not see a single light. From time to time we would pass the sight where formerly a farm house stood. Now all we could see were the remains of a stone wall or part of a foundation. Broken sign posts lay in the crossroads. The remains of soldiers' camp fires were left alongside the road.

This was a land where death roamed the fields.

We walked several dozen kilometers and then sat down in the snow to rest. Not far from us we spotted sledge tracks in the snow. A few days ago someone had passed through here. We thought that it would not be so bad to find a sledge to travel with ourselves. We did not see one living or moving around us at all. We checked the map and stood up again. We walked through the fields because none of the roads led in the direction we wanted to go. In several places we approached trenches three meters deep that were covered over with a layer of ice. We crossed them by laying planks across. Kariūnas lost his balance on one of those planks and fell into the icy water. He was submerged up to his ears. Mindaugas suggested we stop at the next abandoned farmstead, start a fire, dry out his clothing, and have a bite to eat.

We had to walk another two kilometers before we found a comfortable place to stop. We built ourselves a fire in the cellar of a demolished house. We boiled ourselves some tea from snow and the stalks of dried raspberries—our mothers' recipe to ward off a cold. Mindaugas pulled some lard from his backpack and something hard to drink. We wanted to ward off sleep and exhaustion because we had quite a piece left to travel before daybreak.

After we had eaten, we all felt much more awake. Butautas and I even felt brave enough to sing a song out to the deserted Prussian fields. It felt so good to rest, we worried about freezing in place. We were not able to walk the remaining ten kilometers that night without stopping periodically to rest. Every three kilometers we would fall exhausted into the snow. As the sun rose we reached our location in Viliūnai.[98] It turned out that we had been quite spoiled those last few days in Lithuania. We could not cover very much distance without stopping and resting. By dawn we could barely lift our feet. On the final leg of our journey we came across a set of footprints. We realized it would be dangerous to continue onwards in this direction. It was likely that we might stumble upon some local of this wasteland who would figure out immediately from our clothing that we were not Russians. The most likely scenario was that they would take us for American paratroopers. We reached a crossroads of three roads, turned to the right, and came across some sort of graveyard. We hid close by in the ruins of an old manor.

We decided to spend the day here. We were lucky to find a metal ladder propped up against a chimney. We were able to use the ladder to climb to the top of the chimney to keep watch. We could see very well in all directions. Nothing live could get past us within two kilometers without being spotted. Besides keeping look-out, whoever was on guard had to constantly cook sausages or boil tea and watch that the sleeping men's clothing did not catch fire. In a word, the guard had to take care of the resting men's every wish, whether the request be a bite of sausage or a cup of tea. We found some boards and built walls so that we would not be tormented by the wind. Out in the yard we found a stove the Russians had constructed out of a gasoline barrel. We dragged it inside, attached a chimney pipe, built cots out of boards around the stove, and hugging our "lovers" we fell asleep with our clothing on. The smoke from our fire was hidden by a large oak tree that grew beside the house.

The day passed peacefully. We could hear signs of life coming from the east. We heard a dog barking. We could see smoke rising in two places, but did not see any houses on the horizon. We guessed that the village of Stalupėnis was in that direction. Around three o'clock our guard spotted a truck in the distance with

---

98 This was a village about fourteen kilometers to the west from Kudirka's Naumiestis. The village was not rebuilt after the war.

three passengers inside it. Most likely they were Russians out for the hundredth time searching for loot. Some time later a person slunk past with a gun slung over his back, moving in the same direction as the truck.

In the evening we rose. We were no longer tired. We took a few photos for posterity. We cleaned and inspected our weapons and then set out for the night's march.

This night we had a shorter distance to cover, but it had snowed all day, and that made our route more difficult. We left Stalupėnai on our right. We crossed the highway and descended the slope. Here we came upon a swamp with wide ditches. The ice was very thin. Šarūnas lay down on his stomach and crawled to the opposite bank. The rest of us did the same. A few hundred meters ahead of us again there was an obstacle, only this time it was a stream. Here the ice was even thinner. In places there was open water. Šarūnas again lay on his stomach and crawled towards the other side. This time, however, he was not so lucky. The ice broke and he was submerged completely. He struggled to get back to the surface and crawled his way up onto the bank. Then, he calmly helped us make our crossing. He found several hayracks still set up and stripped them to build a bridge from the boards. We crossed the stream dry footed. Only Šarūnas was drenched. The air had grown cold and bitter. His clothing stiffened with ice and his weapon froze. Because we were very close to a town, it was not safe to stop. We traveled several kilometers down the road until we found a suitable cellar. We built a fire, took off our friend's clothing, and began drying him out.

Russian Collective Farm Workers

Two hours later we set out again. We followed the highway for a good part of the route until we came to a hamlet where we saw houses. Lights were burning inside. We turned left, crossed the railway line and went inside a wrecked building to rest. A cold wind began to blow from the east. We started off again.

At dawn we began looking for a convenient hide-out. We hoped to find a German family, but had no luck. Everywhere all we heard was Russian. We found some large haystacks and decided to spend the day inside them.

We each dug a hole inside a haystack. It was difficult work since the hay had become tightly stuck together and our hands were numb from the biting east wind. We packed the hay into some sort of order and entrenched our hideouts with snow so that nobody would notice. Then we crawled inside our "beds." We made some additional adjustments, leaving small holes in the sides for observation. We decided to remain in the haystacks all day, so that the nearby *Kolkhoz* workers would not spot us. We were not very worried about the enemy here. We expected their forces to be small. If they came upon us, we would be able to deal with them effectively. Yet, we took the precaution of sleeping with our boots on, hugging our weapons close. Our feet were frozen inside our wet shoes, but we did not want to take the risk of jumping into the snow in our bare feet. Our soaked fatigues congealed around our legs and our toes trembled in our boots. When it grew dark, we slipped out of our resting places. Our teeth were chattering from the cold. A piercing wind blew in from the northeast. Each of us set out to repair the holes in our "beds". By the time we had fixed them up, we felt somewhat warmer. Although we had no appetite, we ate a snack and began our night's march. About two kilometers further on we reached the highway. We decided to travel along the highway despite the fact that we saw the tracks of several sledges and vehicles. We took the risk because we had to reach the town of Heidemeude. According to the map it was exactly 23 kilometers in a straight line. We expected to reach it by midnight.

As we approached the Polish border, it became urgent for us to find a German and inquire about the situation at the border. We didn't even really know where the new Russian–Polish border was located.

We noticed a light burning inside a house. We thought that perhaps here we might find a non-Russian family. Four of us hid in a ditch while Šarūnas and I crept up to the house and peered inside through the window. However, there were no Germans or Lithuanians inside. The people inside the house were unkempt and their children were squatting on a dirt floor. This was a family of Russian *Kolkhoz* workers.

We were just about to move away from the window when we heard Mindaugas's voice call out in Russian, "Stop! Where are you going?" It turned out that our other comrades had not been sufficiently observant and had not noticed that Russian workers were approaching and were about to enter the house.

We decided to pretend we were Red Army soldiers. We followed the Russians inside the house. Chatting in a friendly manner, we fished for information about the Polish border. Only three of our group did the talking because the rest of us did not speak Russian fluently enough not to raise suspicion. We learned that the local *Kolkhoz* was called Kirov and that the occupants of this house belonged to that Collective Farm. We also learned that there were other *Kolkhozs* further on. There was even allegedly a cooperative. We feigned interest in the cooperative, explaining that we needed to buy cigarettes.

Although we took a friendly leave of the Russian family, we had to do something to put them off our scent. No matter how dull-witted these serfs of the

Communist system were, they still might have recognized that we were not Russians and might report us to the local militia. Therefore, we retraced our steps about a mile and took advantage of the bushes to hide our footprints. Then we returned, passed the same houses, but veered off far to the West. After traveling on a little further, we came across the center of the Collective Farm. From the trampled snow we assumed that more people were living here, so we turned off the highway and moved towards some forests.

We approached the forest with great caution, advancing in battle formation with our weapons held ready for firing. It was indescribably dark, and snow from the branches of pine and fir trees bent under their weight, dropping snow down onto our collars. We had to constantly protect our eyes with our hands. We did not dare use our flashlights for fear of being seen. We proceeded this way for several kilometers as we pushed ahead into the depths of the forests. Since we had not noticed any human footprints, we ventured to light a fire. Brushing aside the snow, we squatted around the glowing flames for a rest. The warmth of the fire revived our faces, raw from the bitter wind, and our numb fingers. With the help of a map, we had scheduled another area as our stopping off point. That area was beyond the roads shown on the map. We anticipated it was another two kilometers ahead. Again, we set out.

We soon encountered various obstacles left from the war. Our path was impeded by barbed wire entanglements, heaped masses of timber littering the ground, and deep anti-tank ditches that intersected our route. We had to surmount these obstacles inch by inch. Meanwhile, a blizzard raged. We were grateful that the blizzard covered our tracks even though we had no way of taking shelter from the storm. Covering our tracks was increasingly important as we approached the border zone.

The morning of December 21st dawned. It was a Sunday. We all hurried to find kindling and logs for a fire. We tried to use underbrush as much as we could because it did not smoke a lot. We gathered fir branches and made ourselves beds. We had a bite to eat, shoved our backpacks under our heads and, in the embrace of our "lovers", tried to get some sleep. One of us was on constant guard duty. The guard was responsible both for keeping watch and for cooking our food. It was already well past noon when we rose from our bear's dens. Although the time for mass was long over, we said our belated prayers, asking the Lord for his blessing on our march and for our nation.

Since it was a Sunday, we allowed ourselves a fancier lunch. Instead of boiled sausage, our table was graced with cooked sausage, fried on the cover of the camp stove. We also had delicious bacon cooked together with onions. To alleviate our exhaustion, we drank something Mindaugas had brought with him: like all proper men, we took our shot of "medicine." Afterwards, we attended to our weapons. Usually partisans began the work of cleaning their weapons when they anticipated battle. It was a matter of instinct. We asked each other what he had dreamed. Feliksas had had the most vibrant dreams. His dreams did not bode well for us. He dreamt that he was drowning somewhere in a river together with Butautas and Kariūnas. Some sort of strange trees were growing alongside the river and were dripping blood into the water. He saw his friends standing some distance from the river, but they were helpless to do anything for them.

According to our plan, we needed to reach the Rominta River near a town of the same name. Somewhere in that area there was supposed to be the Russian–Polish border.

"May God be with us," I said quietly. Then I asked Mindaugas to lead the march.

A Bloody Trip Across the Rominta River

That afternoon after the blizzard ended a deathly silence rang across the land. The fresh snow covered all human and animal footprints. Here and there, in the forest we came across evidence of the Russians' presence. Stacks of timber were sloppily tossed together into heaps two meters high. Branches littered the path. Luckily, it was a Sunday, a day off for the Russians. That decreased the likelihood of running into them.

We traveled the entire time, placing our feet inside our leader's footprints. That was hard on the men at the end of the line. We covered a few kilometers and then came upon the remains of a former military cemetery. In the snow, among young firs, stood lines of wooden crosses over soldiers' graves. These were the graves of Germans. Russians never put crosses over their graves. The Russians put up screaming red stars.

We passed through the cemetery and turned right and reached the road. Here we came across some tracks. On the road, every few meters, there were posts impaled into the ground. On one of those posts we found a warning posted in Russian: *Danger, these forests are being cut*. We saw the tracks of sleds and trucks on the road. Mindaugas was quite sure that we had arrived in the border zone. The unusual quiet and the sledge tracks in the snow confirmed Mindaugas's suspicion. Yes, we had found ourselves in the border zone. We turned off the road and towards the right, where we knew we would find the Rominta River and the bridge that led across it. We walked through a valley, surrounded on both sides by hills. Within a few hundred meters walk we ended up in front of trenches and barbed wire.

This was the new Russian–Polish border. We arranged ourselves into a double row and prepared to defend ourselves. We were able to leap over the trenches, but we took longer getting through the barbed wire. After we made it through the barbed wire, we found we had wandered too far to the right and were standing before a pond. On the left side there was a path that led across the river. We had to follow along the side of the path and come out only before the bridge that led over the river. It was likely that we would run into the patrol on that path.

We had made a deadly mistake by drifting too far to the right. Bolshevik patrol guards on skis had spotted us. They froze a moment on the horizon line, like statues, and then rushed off, apparently to call in reinforcements. Mindaugas got his bearings on the situation immediately. Holding the map in one hand and his Sturmgewehr in the other, he quickly led us on our way. We rushed towards the bridge. The last man in our column swept away our tracks with a fir branch. We reached the path that led directly to the bridge. The bridge was about a hundred meters distance from us. We saw two guards beside the bridge. Both of them were glancing around uneasily. Because we were well camouflaged, we were able to get quite close to them. The Russians were wearing grungy cotton jackets. One was armed with a submachine gun, the other with a simple rifle. We set our sights on them. The Russians had not spotted us yet, but they must have felt our presence because they were acting nervous.

Instead of a command, my comrades heard the music of my submachine gun. They joined in with their own guns, picking up the melody. The Russians fell backwards onto the ground. We pushed forwards. Mindaugas and I kept about eight meters distance between us as we ran over the bridge. We were met on the bridge by Russians running towards us. Again, our "lovers" let out their music as the Russians fell to their deaths, calling out "Stoy, blat!"[99]

Mindaugas and I made it across the bridge to the opposite bank. We lay down on the road, which was covered by a channel about a meter and a half high and was caused by erosion. The channel provided us with the perfect cover. Feliksas and Kariūnas jumped into the trenches. Šarūnas and Butautas crept across the bridge. They had made it halfway across the bridge when suddenly the Russians opened fire on them from all directions. Mindaugas and I returned fire from one side of

---

99 "Stop, bitch!"

the river and Feliksas and Kariūnas from the other. Our gunfire made a joke out of their unit leader's command, "Forward!" Mindaugas and I fired without stopping as we retreated, so that Šarūnas and Butautas could take over our positions. They fired from the bridge. Feliksas and Kariūnas fired from the trenches. The Russians, with burning eyes, kept running into our fire, even though they saw their comrades falling to their deaths in front of them, one after another.

Butautas did not want to waste any more time on the bridge. He gathered himself into one final effort and made a run for it. He was shot and killed instantly.[100] Šarūnas crawled up to him and checked on him. Several rounds of machine gun fire had hit him in the head and chest. Šarūnas tossed Butautas's submachine gun into the river and crawled across the bridge as gunfire whistled past his ears and over his head. He made it over the bridge.

At this point the Russian fire decreased because we had killed eight of their men. Although we were outnumbered, we felt more confident because we had better weapons. Mindaugas and I had given our positions to Šarūnas. Feliksas and Kariūnas jumped out of the trenches and were now crawling across the bridge.

The depleted Russian force was beginning to slowly retreat when Feliksas and Kariūnas were unexpectedly attacked from behind by fresh reinforcements. Feliksas was carrying an anti-tank mine in his backpack. Because of the mine he was somewhat protected from the gunfire from behind.

Suddenly there was a terrible explosion. Snow and dirt rose in a cloud. Feliksas had not even had time enough to call out. Kariūnas was just a few meters away from him. His weapon was knocked out of his hands. Kariūnas snatched up his weapon and stood up. In a few bounds he made it across the bridge, leaving behind the remains of his friend.

The Russians jumped into the trenches that had been previously occupied by Feliksas and Kariūnas. They shot at us with an accurate series of machine gun fire. At this time we also had taken up advantageous positions, only there was no sense in us staying here any longer. We had achieved our goal of crossing the bridge. We could at this point take out a number of the enemy, but we were not protected

---

100 In a note left behind by Juozas Lukša he wrote: "In this section I did not exactly tell the truth. ... In reality out of the five of us, not one of us was killed that day. Only Kariūnas was injured in the fighting. He made it out of that skirmish alive. His wounds healed within three weeks. I 'falsified' certain facts at the suggestion of Deksnys and Pyplys (Mažytis). At the time we wanted to influence the opinion of the powers interested in our struggle, namely the English, that it was not possible to safely make a crossing the way we had. We reasoned that by making the border crossing seem more difficult than it was we would receive more liaison aid from them. It is true, however, that we had a difficult and strenuous fight crossing the border, but we did not lose any men. If you take away the fictional deaths of Butautas and Feliksas, then all the rest of the details of the battle are accurate."

from behind. We could hear trucks entering the forest. We gathered behind a hillock and decided to pick off the retreating Russians. We looked around anxiously, assessing the situation, while quickly refilling our clips. Soon we saw a group of Russians creeping forwards in our direction with their weapons pointed right at us. However, because of the cover of the hillock, they had not yet seen us. They had followed our footprints. It was clear that they would soon stumble right on top of us. We waited until they were quite close and then we fired at them. We shot a long series at them. Our goal was to take down as many as possible and in this way to discourage their comrades from chasing us. We took down the men closest to us, however, there were more on the right. They could not see us, and so they shot blindly in the direction the gunfire was coming from.

As Kariūnas was making a run for it, he was shot in the leg with an explosive bullet. We heard him call out, "Kariūnas wounded." Two of us ran over to check on him. The wound was bad. The bullet had shredded his calf muscles and had shattered his bones. We dragged him along with us. The Russian fire subsided. Kariūnas was heaving. We left a bloody trail behind us in the white snow. There was no chance of stopping now to tie up his wound because the hillock was surrounded by Russians on all sides. We had to retreat quickly. Kariūnas was severely weakened by the loss of blood. The life was slipping out of him. Realizing this, he asked us to leave him behind.

With deep pain in our hearts, we left him. He wished us good luck and asked us to remember him to his mother. We were all overcome with the horror of the situation. Tears were streaming down our faces. As the Russian machine gun fire drew nearer, we left our friend behind. He prepared a grenade and lifted his hand into the air.

From a distance we heard the explosion of his grenade. That grenade took out not only Kariūnas, but a few Russians who had come up close to him.

It had grown completely dark. We knew that we would have to cross the road along the way. That was the end of the Russian border zone, as marked on the map. Usually this region was less heavily guarded than the area surrounding the border. This zone was three kilometers deep. At this time it was hard for us to judge the distance to the road. We relied on Mindaugas's eyes.

Finally, after marching through half-frozen mud, we reached the road. We crawled across the road, expecting machine gun fire at any moment. We were convinced that this road had to be protected by machine guns. But either we were wrong or we had not been seen under the cover of darkness. On the opposite side of the road we ran into a barbed wire fence over two meters tall. I gathered all my strength and together with Mindaugas tore the bottom portion of the barbed wire fence up from the ground. We created a hole just big enough for all of us to crawl through. Once we had crawled through, we breathed in relief and then ran forwards as fast as we could.

We stopped to rest about three kilometers away from the border. It was now completely dark. We stopped to rest only after we had run three kilometers away from the barbed wire. The moon had not risen and the night was completely black. Only now did we dare reflect on the past few hours. We all managed to say a few words to calm ourselves down. We gazed at each other with haunted eyes, our faces lined with sweat. Every sound we heard in the forest seemed suspicious. Quietly, we prayed. We thanked God for our "good fortune." We managed to say a few words, but no one felt like talking. We could feel the cold now. During the battle we had crawled through snow quite a bit and not only was our outer clothing thoroughly drenched, so were our under garments. As the night grew colder, we began to freeze. Our clothing became sheets of ice.

In this manner we began our march. In the distance, on the border, we heard three gun shots. The guard had only now discovered our footprints and were setting off the alarm.

On Polish Soil

We were exhausted, but we pushed onwards. We had about 40 kilometers more to march that night. We were not too concerned about the Polish Security Forces. They were not true Bolsheviks; they were only slaves to the Bolsheviks. Also, we knew that they were not experienced in fighting up close and usually kept a safe distance in a battle. They were also not typically well-armed. However, we were sure that by the next day the Russians would combine forces with the Poles to hunt us down.

By late that night we were thoroughly exhausted and decided to call on a farmer and ask him for a sledge. We were lucky that at the farm where we first stopped we ran into a Lithuanian from Kaunas. Because of him we were given food and a sledge and two horses.

We traveled around 15 kilometers by sledge and then sent our compatriot back and continued on foot in the direction of Pseroslis. We preferred to travel by sledge however, so we stopped in on another farmer. This farmer turned out to be a village elder. He began a long-winded explanation on the rules and regulations of using a village sledge. We cut him off and told him we had no time for rules. The functionary then surrendered and drove us not only to Pserolis, but beyond it. We passed directly in front of the local militia station as we passed through the town. Before sending the village elder home, we advised him to forget the procedure set up by the authorities and cautioned him not report anything.

Then we called on a third Pole. Here we cooked up our lard and onions and rested. Again, we asked for a sledge. This farmer too began a long-winded explanation of procedure. His wife especially wished to obey the authorities. When we left, we promised the woman that her husband would be home in three hours. After driving towards Fornetka, we said good-bye to the farmer and cautioned him to remain silent.

We now began looking around for another farm where we could stop and rest. The landscape was favorable. A rivulet flowed nearby. The configuration of the ground was overgrown with bushes and was uneven. We chose a farmstead and called there. It was just before dawn. The rooster was crowing in the yard and the horses in the stable were anticipating being fed.

When we knocked at the door, the farmer's wife let us in. We asked permission to rest. She saw how exhausted we were and prepared beds for us in the guest room. We washed and looked after our weapons. My comrades fell into a deep sleep as soon as they lay down. I took guard duty and dried my comrades' shoes and prepared a breakfast out of what was left of our food reserves. The farmer's daughters helped me prepare breakfast.

Around noon I exchanged guard duty with Mindaugas. I had just lain down and Mindaugas was just drying my boots when the farmer's wife hurried inside the house and reported that the Suvalki commandant had telephoned orders to the Rutka, Vyžoniai, and Pseroslis militia and the Polish Security Forces that armed men had broken through the East Prussian border and were headed in the direction of Fornetka. Several sledges filled with militia and Polish Security Police were patrolling the neighborhood.

We prepared for our journey and asked the farmer to get some horses ready for us at once. We hid our outer garments in the sledge and dressed in clothing provided by the farmer. We headed in the one direction that was not being searched, Smolnikai.

We drove slowly, so dusk would fall, and arrived in Smolnikai around four o'clock. The driver refused to accept the dollars we offered him as payment. He said that he also had fought against the Communists as a partisan in Poland and that he considered it his duty to help us.

We had difficulty obtaining a sledge in Smolnikai. Most of the people we encountered were afraid of us. Also, it was a few days before Christmas and many people had taken their horses and sledges into town to prepare for the holidays.

After some bargaining, we obtained a sledge. We started off and after we had driven for some time in an easterly direction, we saw three sledges approaching us. We hurried to cover our badges and emblems and weapons, hoping to pass them without incident. But as we passed them, one of them stood and called out "Stop" in Russian. Then another one fired.

Instantly, we were in a ditch and shooting them down one after another. The horses reared and then collapsed in the road. Only one of them managed to escape with his life by running away across the fields. At this point we realized that we were right—the Poles had no combat experience. But we also realized that we going to encounter these types of patrols at every crossroads.

Following the clash with the first sledge, we now encountered a second. Some of the men leapt from the sledge and ran for cover in a neighboring farm house. The others tried to bar our path. A lieutenant crept out from behind a tree and leveled his submachine gun at me. "Who's there?" he shouted.

I knocked his gun from his hands, rammed my gun into his stomach, and ordered, "Hands in the air!" I took the Pole's gun and slung it over my shoulder. Mindaugas slapped him across the ear and said in Polish, "Go to hell, Mr. Lieutenant!"

We could not tell if the Pole was terrified by us or overjoyed at the opportunity of escaping with his life because he hastily saluted us, did a quick turn, and with military precision ran off across the fields in the direction of the destroyed sledge.

The other men shot at us from the neighboring house. The hovels and stables they used for cover were not adequate against our fire. Soon they made a disorderly retreat. Twenty Poles retreated running across the snow-covered slope.

We took stock of our losses. Fortunately, they were slight. Šarūnas lost his backpack in the sledge, but the backpack contained nothing more than the remnants of our food reserves. He also found a few holes in his great coat. Mindaugas and I were more fortunate. Our package to the West was still intact and we did not have a single tear in our clothing.

We continued on our way. Traveling down the road we spotted a sledge bearing a Santa Claus coming towards us, loaded with food and gifts. This Santa Claus was taking his load to the Rutka cooperative. We decided that since he would now have a few less mouths to feed, we could appropriate a one-hundredth of his load. We inspected his load and took a liter of vodka, a pocketful of Christmas candy each, and a kilogram of smoked meats. We wished the driver a Merry Christmas and resumed our journey. Santa Claus lifted his cap to us, grateful to us for not cleaning him out completely.

We decided not to attempt to continue traveling by sledge. We turned off the road and made our way on foot across the snow-covered fields. We finally settled into a deserted sauna. We covered over the windows, lit a fire, and sat down around it, happily feasting on our Christmas treats.

I was worried that we had meandered back towards the border zone. In the skirmish I had lost my detailed map and so we truly did not have our bearings. We decided to visit a farm and find out where we were.

After we left the sauna, we called on a farmer and learned that we were in the village of Kiciolki. As I had suspected, we were indeed very close to the border again. We had to leave this zone as quickly as possible. We asked the farmer to harness a horse for us. He seemed affable enough and made pleasant conversation with us, but just as soon as the horse and sledge were prepared he rushed off to inform on us to the local militia.

We hurried to cover as much distance as possible. Concealing our tracks as best we could, we quickly reached the Cypliškiai–Seiniai highway. Here we ran into a man driving a sledge who told us that a half hour ago he had been ordered to drive Polish Security Officers and border guards. Since he was known in the area for transporting the military in his sledge, we decided to take a risk and ride with him. He drove us to Cypliškiai. We walked some distance to avoid detection and later lay in the straw in the sledge, with one of us seated beside the driver to ensure his loyalty. In this manner, we arrived at the village of V. We gave the driver our vodka as payment and dismissed him.

A Christmas Miracle in the Manger

Everywhere people were preparing for Christmas. Women were cleaning their homes, tidying them up to the last detail and decorating for Christmas Eve. We were exhausted. Our faces were gaunt and spotted with sores caused by constant exposure to the harsh weather. We wanted nothing more than to sleep. Our exhaustion caused our minds to race.

We stopped at a farm. Seeing our exhaustion, the farmer showed us to a back room where we collapsed and slept. One of us took the bed, another a chair, I leaned against the stove, resting on my gun. We did not undress, although our clothing was drenched. We slept with our weapons cocked and loaded and close by. The farmer noticed this and it made him anxious. We did not worry him more by telling him we were wanted men.

During the day Polish Security troops were carrying out searches throughout the area. With machine guns set up in their sledges, they swept through one village after another, ransacking houses and barns. They were searching for the Lithuanian partisans. One of the theories was that the partisans had broken through the border from Lithuania to take revenge. Throughout this period Lithuanians had escaped the Bolsheviks by coming across the border and working as farm hands for Poles. Recently the Poles had grown suspicious of these "refugees" and had begun dealing with them accordingly.

At midday the Polish Security Forces showed up at the farm where we were hiding. We were sleeping so deeply we did not hear them arrive. Our host saw them arrive and almost collapsed in fright. The search began so quickly he had no time to warn us. The Polish Security Forces ransacked his house and outbuildings, searching the barn and stables, going down into the cellars. We slept through it all. By some miracle they did not enter the room where we were sleeping. We think it was perhaps because the farmer's wife had pasted over the door and wall with decorative Christmas paper. Because of her wallpaper job, the door blended in with the wall and was indistinguishable from the wall. The Polish Communists simply did not realize that there was one more room in the house that they had left unsearched.

Once the Polish Security Forces drove off, our host burst into our room and woke us. He kissed our hands and made the sign of the cross and explained what had happened. He declared the incident was a miracle, a true Christmas miracle.

Nevertheless, when night fell, rather than joining the family at their Christmas Eve table, we crept out to the barn and buried ourselves in the hay. There was barely enough hay to cover us and not enough to protect us from the wind blowing in between the chinks in the boards. Lying in the hay in the barn like this on Christmas Eve, we reasoned that we were celebrating Christmas Eve in the purest way. We were in the position of Christ in the manger.

Again, the Polish Security Forces and border guards called on our host. They demanded food and transportation. From their talk, our host understood that more would be passing through. The Polish Security Officers and the border guards spat and cursed because they were frustrated. They could not figure out our whereabouts. Only yesterday at dawn we had been at Kociolki and half an hour later we had disappeared. It was as though the ground had swallowed us up.

This talk and these visits terrified our host, who was timid enough to begin with. We did not dare come out of the barn and join him and his family at their Christmas Eve table. We lay in the straw and thought about the Christian world, exhausted as it was by war and by the chaos of the post-war period. We thought of the people who nevertheless were trying to restore normalcy to their lives by celebrating Christmas as in peace time, as a family.

But war was still waging in our country. As we lay there we thought about our people. How many of them had died in the last few weeks at the hands of the Bolsheviks? How many more had been deported to Siberia? How many more would be deported? Even as we were leaving, the Communists were organizing a new round of mass deportations.

And we remembered our thousands of partisan brothers who had died, tortured, with disjointed limbs, shattered ribs, twisted fingers, their skulls smashed in and their skin burned. We thought of our brothers who took their own lives rather than be taken alive.

Thinking these thoughts we drifted off to an uneasy sleep. In the morning the farmer brought us a plate of leftovers from his Christmas table. Then we shared our Christmas meal in the barn, dug deep into the straw.

Afterword

A Journey into the Heart: A Post-War Love Story

Laima Vincė

> *I dreamt last night I was hiking across a muddy field with my comrades. We were armed and anticipating an attack. As we walked our feet sank deeper and deeper into the mud. We reached a little house beside the forest and I saw an enormous rose bush growing alongside one of its walls. I thought to myself, "Now I'll pick some roses for Nijolė, enough to fill three vases." I dropped my weapon and began gathering armfuls of roses. With my arms overflowing with roses, I followed my comrades into the forest. My mother crossed my path. "Son," she said, "what are you doing? Drop those roses and pick up your gun."*
>
> Juozas Lukša, February 7, 1949

Eleonora Labanauskienė stood waiting on the front stoop to her yellow brick farmhouse. She was wearing her Sunday dress—dark blue with white polka dots. A blue silk scarf was knotted loosely across the front. Her neatly combed wavy gray hair blew about in the light breeze. Eleonora was eighty-eight.

Dahlias and Black-eyed Susans spilled over onto the concrete steps around her feet. The flowers provided a burst of color against the flat grassy plains that stretched towards a line of pine forests in the distance. The sky was blue, yet heavy clouds tinged with gray hung low, close to the horizon line, the threat of rain ever constant.

Lithuanian farm houses like Eleonora's, if they escaped being leveled during the Stalin-era collectivization of farms, look the same now as when they were originally built in the 1930s. The typical lay-out consists of a few small rooms with an old-fashioned brick oven dominating the center of the house. Eleonora and her husband, Vincas, built this house together in 1939 shortly after their elopement. At the age of seventeen, the head-strong Eleonora ran across the fields in the dead of night to marry Vincas, a poor farmer who owned only four hectares of land. Eleonora's parents did not approve of the match. They were wealthy farmers who had made their money in America and, like many Lithuanian-Americans of their generation, had returned to a newly independent Lithuania to put down roots.

After the Soviets occupied Lithuania, Eleonora's parents were exiled to Siberia because of their wealth. They both died there.

Our mini van pulled into Eleonora's yard. Eighty-two year old Nijolė Bražėnaitė-Lukšienė-Paronetto sat anxiously perched on the edge of the front seat. She had flown half-way across the world to meet Eleonora.

Nijolė saw Eleonora first. She did not wait for introductions. She opened the front passenger door of the mini van and walked resolutely towards Eleonora. The two women fell into a tight embrace. Nijolė lay her head on Eleonora's shoulder. They both cried. They stood like that for a good fifteen minutes.

"I saw you on the news on Thursday," Eleonora said finally. "When I realized it was you, I got down on my knees. My daughter, Vanda, came running into the room and said, 'Mama, what's wrong, get up.' I told her I'd just seen you on television. You spoke beautifully."

"They asked me to tell them about Juozas," Nijolė said. "What could I tell them? Fifty-five years have gone by and it still feels like yesterday when he left. Every day when I awake my first thoughts are about him."

"It still feels like yesterday for me too," Eleonora said. "He left my house and walked to his death," Eleonora said. "When I lay down to sleep at night, my head is filled with thoughts of the time when he and Ramanauskas-Vanagas hid in the bunker in my house."

* * *

On the night of October 3–4, 1950, just as United Nations troops were crossing the 38th parallel into North Korea, the CIA flew Juozas Lukša and two of his Lithuanian comrades, Trumpys and Širvys, out of Wiesbaden, under the radar, in an unmarked Dakota C-47 painted black and dropped them behind the Iron Curtain to conduct an information-gathering mission. Lukša's orders were to mobilize the resistance for reconnaissance throughout Lithuania in order to discern whether the Soviets were making preparations for an attack on the West. Lukša carried with him a letter from Mykolas Krupavičius, the head of the Committee for the Restoration of an Independent Lithuania, addressed to the partisans of Lithuania, outlining the current political situation abroad and appealing to the partisans to desist from any form of action that might lead to justifications for further deportations and genocide. Lukša also had with him medical supplies, printing supplies, dollars, rubles, zlotys, gold-plated Swiss watches and a radio transmitter. Each paratrooper carried with him an automatic weapon with cartridges, a pistol with cartridges, ten watches, 2,000 US dollars, and 6,000 rubles.

They were dressed in loose American pants and leather jackets. Each of them had a cyanide capsule sewn into the collar of their jackets.

During the post-war era the CIA had set up a training camp in Kaufbeuren, West Germany as part of a CIA sponsored Cold War espionage effort. During 1950–51 the CIA trained resistance fighters from Soviet-occupied East European countries to infiltrate the Soviet Union to gather information in the event of another war with the Soviet Union. CIA-trained East European operatives were flown back into the Soviet Union under the radar with C-47 Dakotas manned by former RAF Czech pilots. Several such airdrops were done in the Baltics and in the Ukraine. These operations in the end were only moderately successful, mainly because of infiltrations by Soviet counter-intelligence.

Antanas Lukša stands beside the bunker, where his brother, Juozas Lukša, and Alfonsas Romanauskas-Vanagas hid for six months in 1950–1951

Lukša and his East European comrades saw the CIA espionage training as an opportunity to enlist the Americans' help in their nations' struggles while the Americans used these resistance fighters' dedication to freedom in their homelands to gain access to information from behind the Iron Curtain.

Nijolė Bražėnaitė met Juozas Lukša in Paris in 1948 not long after Lukša had broken through the Iron Curtain between the postwar Russian Kaliningrad enclave and Poland. Lukša had been appointed as a special representative for the armed resistance in Lithuania and was sent to meet with contacts in Western Europe to describe the resistance's efforts to fight Soviet oppression in Lithuania and to awaken the consciousness of the democratic world. He carried with him a number of documents and testimonials, including a message in French to the United Nations and a letter in Latin to Pope Pius XII describing the mass deportations of the civilian populace to Siberia and asking for the support of the Catholic Church. Neither of these documents received any significant attention.

Not being able to catch the attention of either the United Nations or the Vatican, Lukša instead turned to various intelligence services in Western Europe seeking special military training. Eventually he was approached by the CIA and invited to participate in the special espionage training sessions taking place in the West German town of Kaufbeuren.

A friend of Nijolė's, Julijonas Butėnas, also a member of the resistance, introduced her to Lukša. At their first meeting Lukša called himself by a code name that tipped Nijolė off not to ask any questions. They became friends and Nijolė showed Lukša around Paris a few times.

Nijolė Bražėnaitė had recently completed her degree in medicine when she met Juozas Lukša. She had managed to complete her studies, dodging the allied bombings of Germany, as she and her twin sister, Vida, traveled from one German city to the next, enrolling in universities and studying in them until the bombings would force the university to close.

Towards the end of the war Vida became ill with pulmonary tuberculosis. Nijolė practically carried Vida in her arms across Germany as it was being bombed by the allies, eventually reaching Austria. By that time Vida was barely alive. It was winter. Nijolė climbed a mountain during a snowstorm to reach a sanatorium hoping they would accept her sister. When she got there she found every bed occupied. She dropped to her knees and begged the head doctor to take Vida in. He did and Vida eventually recovered. Vida married and emigrated with her new husband to Australia. Meanwhile, in 1948 Nijolė traveled to Paris, where she found work as a lab assistant.

The damp Parisian autumn of 1948 and the meager living conditions for war refugees contributed to Nijolė contracting tuberculosis. Nijolė spent 1948 through 1950 in French hospitals and sanatoriums convalescing. Her life was often in danger. War time conditions left the French hospitals undersupplied and understaffed. Nijolė would lie for months on blood-caked sheets. Only when friends took her bed linens home and washed them did she get any relief from the grime.

During that time Lukša remained in Paris illegally, living in hiding in an ever-changing series of garrets and rooming houses, registering under aliases. He spent his days alternately writing his memoir or looking for a means to return to the invisible war being fought in Lithuania. During his time in Paris Lukša had to dodge the NKVD and Lithuanian displaced persons who might recognize him. Because he was in hiding, Lukša could visit Nijolė in the hospital very rarely. That is how their correspondence began.

From 1948 through 1950 Juozas and Nijolė wrote to each other almost every day. Juozas's letters kept Nijolė going during her long illness and Nijolė's letters helped Juozas Lukša cope with his feelings of desperation and loss. Both had lost brothers in the war and both had lost their parents. Both had seen their homes destroyed by Soviet occupying forces and both longed to one day return to their country and to the peaceful life they'd known before the war. Both also strongly believed in the necessity of fighting for Lithuania's freedom.

In 1950 a friend who'd been released from the sanatorium left Nijolė a fish bowl with three gold fish. Lukša admired the gold fish on one of his rare visits. Afterwards, the couple wrote a few lines about the gold fish in each of their letters, playfully referring to the gold fish as their "children." They gave them names, discussed their educations and upbringing. Soon, in their letters they both began writing about how it seemed inevitable that they must marry. They planned their wedding, knowing that Lukša was resolved to return to Soviet-occupied Lithuania to carry out his assigned mission, knowing that he might never return. Nijolė supported him in his decision. It never even occurred to her to ask him to stay; in fact, had she been able, she would have volunteered to fight herself. Nijolė wrote to Juozas in one of her letters, "I envy your opportunity to fight for our country."

Juozas Lukša and Nijolė Bražėnaitė were married June 23, 1950. They lived together as a married couple for only one week. After their honeymoon in the mountains of Treifelberg near Tübingen, Germany, Lukša returned to the CIA training camp in Kaufbeuren. On June 25, two days after their wedding, the Korean War began. The Cold War was escalating and the men receiving training at the camp at Kaufbeuren would have to put their personal lives on hold. Lukša completed his training and shortly afterwards returned to the Invisible War in Lithuania.

* * *

Eleonora and Nijolė waited 55 years to meet and it might never have happened if not for a chance conversation in a café in Kernavė, Lithuania in 2006. I was in Lithuania working on a Literary Translation Fellowship and was invited by friends to participate in a hike through the countryside with a group of ethnographers and archeologists. We stopped for lunch in a café. A man named Rimas, who was seated at my table began telling me about how a year ago he and his three teenage sons had traveled across Lithuania on bicycles searching for "bunkers."

A bunker, or "bunkeris" in Lithuanian, derived from the German World War II term "bunker," means a secret hiding place for the underground resistance. A bunker can be a dug-out in the forest, as was usually the case, or it could be an attic or a root cellar in someone's house. It could also be a barn, an empty well, an abandoned building or any other hidden place.

Rimas told me he'd met a woman named Eleonora Labanauskiene in southern Lithuania in the village of Alendarne who had told him that November 1950 through May 1951 she had hidden two leaders of the resistance, Juozas Lukša and Alfonsas Ramanauskas-Vanagas, in a bunker under the floorboards of her home.

That day in Kernavė I understood immediately that any information provided by Eleonora Labanauskienė regarding the return of Juozas Lukša would be of extreme interest not only to researchers, but also to his widow, Nijolė Bražėnaitė-Lukšienė-Parronetto, a close family friend. Sitting that day at the long wooden table in the café in Kernavė under recast copper coats of arms and racks of moose antlers, it was clear to both me and to Rimas that we had to bring Eleonora and Nijolė together—that these two women would have something to share with each other. Both had aided him as he fought a David and Goliath battle against Soviet Interior Forces.

Our first try to connect the two women was through a laptop. However, that attempt failed. Neither would even try. Eleonora was nearly deaf and Nijolė has macular degeneration with very limited eye sight. But more importantly, both women were of the generation where no technology could replace the bond of human contact. They would not compromise. They had to meet and speak to each other face to face.

When I returned to the United States in June, 2006, I went to visit Nijolė. She was determined to go to Lithuania to meet Eleonora. September 4, 2006 marked the fifty-fifth anniversary of the death of Juozas Lukša. Nijolė wanted to travel to Lithuania to participate in a series of war memorials that would be held that week to commemorate her first husband's death. She also planned to travel to the backwaters of Lithuania to the tiny brick farm house where Lukša had hidden under the floorboards while Soviet Interior Forces and local home-grown Soviet militia informants scoured the countryside searching for him.

The only problem was that someone had to take her and that someone was me. It was my fate my Lithuanian friends told me. Lithuanians are firm believers in fate—a type of fate believed to be woven at birth and to have mystical and logic-defying properties.

And so, I found myself on a plane seated beside my eighty-two year old travel companion, taking a transatlantic flight into a journey of the heart.

No map could lead us to Eleonora. No stranger could get us inside her door. But Rimas knew the way to reach Eleonora. We drove out of the city of Vilnius, leaving behind that oasis of East European post-modernity and descended into a maze of unmarked dirt roads that Rimas knew like the back of his hand. We drove through kilometers of fields that a decade ago had been farmed but now lay fallow. We drove past abandoned villages where almost every resident had packed up and left for Ireland or the United Kingdom, searching for work and a higher standard of living after Lithuania joined the European Union in 2004. We drove past cows tethered to wooden stakes in the ground. We drove past elderly farmers bringing their goods to the market grounds in rough wooden carts hitched to work-worn horses. We were on a journey of the heart.

* * *

Eleonora's husband, Vincas Labanauskas, had a brother who was friends with a partisan who went by the code name Lakštingala (Nightingale). Lakštingala and the Dzūkija Dainava District Partisan Commander Adolfas Ramanauskas-Vanagas (Hawk) approached Vincas Labanauskas in 1950 and asked him if he would agree to allow the local Dzūkija Dainava District partisans to build a bunker in his home. Ramanauskas-Vanagas was one of the resistance's most brilliant strategists and most colorful personages. He was an American-born school teacher who left the classroom to fight in the forest, bringing along with him almost his entire high school class. Vanagas was given the code name "hawk" because he'd trained a large black hawk to perch on his shoulder.

Vincas Labanauskas had not owned a lot of land during the period of independence. Ramanauskas-Vanagas reasoned that being a small farmer made him a "proletariat" in the eyes of the Bolsheviks, assuming his loyalty. Vanagas advised Labanauskas to accept the position of Director of the local collective farm. Then, Labanauskas would be less likely to be suspected of harboring "bandits."

Eleonora and Vincas agreed to allow the partisans to dig the bunker underneath their bedroom. They were both patriots and both believed in a free and independent Lithuania. They felt duty-bound to do what they could to aid the resistance.

It took two nights for three partisans—Lakštingala, Vanagas, and Tauras to dig the bunker. They constructed an underground chamber two meters by two meters wide. The bunker was accessible through a trap door built into the wooden floorboards of the couple's bedroom. The trapdoor was covered with a rug and a bed on top of the rug. The bunker contained two wooden benches, a wooden cot, and a shelf built into the wall. The shelf held a typewriter, grenades, weapons, and ammunition. Eleonora gave the partisans a blanket and a pillow for the bunker.

Nijole and Eleonora

Ramanauskas-Vanagas gave Eleonora a code name—Varna (Crow). He typed up a Certificate of Loyalty and instructed her to hold onto it until Lithuania was independent. He also gave her a gun, a *dešimtukas*,[1] and taught her how to load it, clean it, and shoot it. He instructed her to shoot herself in the left temple if Soviet Interior Forces surrounded the house. Vanagas impressed upon Eleonora that she should not allow them to take her alive. Eleonora kept the pistol in a glass canning jug buried in her flower garden.

Ramanauskas-Vanagas asked Eleonora if she agreed to allow a bomb the size of a bowling ball into her home. If the bunker were surrounded by Soviet Interior Forces, the charge would be detonated, exploding the house and killing all its occupants. Eleonora agreed. She understood that she was sacrificing not only her own life and her husband's life, but the lives of her three small daughters: Vanda (9), Janina (7), and Natalia (5).

Eleonora taught her three daughters to never say a word in school about the "uncles" who visited their home and who disappeared under the floorboards. The girls were good as gold. They kept their parents' secret.

---

1 Tokarev SVT 40.

Eleonora Labanauskienė and Antanas Lukša meet for the first time at Eleonora's home in Alendarnė, Lithuania. Before Lithuania's independence in 1991, it was dangerous for these two former members of the resistance to communicate with each other

Eleonora cooked, cleaned, and provided fresh laundry for the partisans in the bunker. "Vanagas used to say that I would kill him with my cleanliness," Eleonora said, "Because I was a stickler. I made sure every man in the bunker had fresh undergarments every other day."

One day Ramanauskas-Vanagas told Eleonora he was bringing a man from abroad to live in the bunker. When this man arrived, he introduced himself simply as "Mikas" (Juozas Lukša).

"He didn't tell me anything about where he was from, not even his real name," Eleonora recalls. "He was very disciplined and strict, but at the same time very warm and sincere."

Eleonora also recalls that Mikas gave her a watch, but instructed her "not to wear it."

Mikas quickly melded into the daily rhythms of the Labanauskas household. He helped Eleonora peel potatoes and cook. He would read the girls bedtime stories at night or keep them entertained by playing with them during the day. Meanwhile, he dutifully carried out the mission assigned to him by the American CIA.

Together with Ramanauskas-Vanagas, Lukša drafted a set of espionage instructions to be carried out by the Dainava District partisans. Dated November 25, 1950, this document begins with the following statement:

> In the interest of an independent Lithuania and in the interest of the current international community, the Lithuanian underground is hereby asked to quickly provide answers to the following questions, pertaining to all spheres of life in Soviet Lithuania. The underground is asked to exert all of their efforts collecting the following information and to send it to the leadership.

Lukša in Paris

The six-page typewritten document was broken into six sections: Politics, Economics, Administration, Transportation, Education and Religion, and Military. The Political Section concerns itself with finding the number and proportion of Communist Russians sent to infiltrate Soviet Lithuanian government, education, and factories and also with recording the names and numbers of Lithuanians exiled to Siberia. The Military Section covers all aspects of the Soviet Military on Lithuanian soil. Many of the instructions are quite detailed: "How much leeway does the Lithuanian Soviet Socialist Republic have to draft laws" or "How many Lithuanians are recruited into the Soviet Army? Where are they housed? How are they armed?" or "Since Soviet Interior Forces control the coastline and ports, how carefully do they control fishing boats?"

In 1953, two years after Lukša was lured out of hiding and walked to his death along the edge of a Lithuanian forest in Pažėriai, his comrade, Adolfas Ramanauskas-Vanagas, was captured and tortured in the bowels of the KGB prisons in Kaunas and in Vilnius. Allegedly the KGB traced a hundred dollar bill back to him on the black market. It was Lukša's hundred dollar bill. He'd given it to Ramanauskas-Vanagas. When he returned to Lithuania, the CIA had provided Lukša with 2,000 US dollars in crisp new hundred dollar bills. One of those bills came back to betray Ramanauskas-Vanagas in the end.

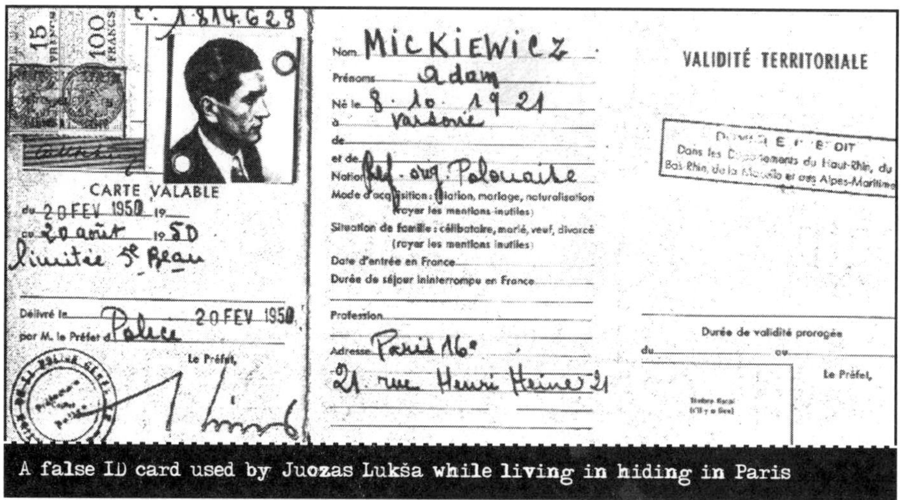

15 FRANCS
100 FRANCS
CARTE VALABLE
du 20 FEV 1950 19
au 20 août 1950
Délivré le 20 FEV 1950
par M. le Préfet de Police
Le Préfet,

Nom MICKIEWICZ
Prénoms Adam
Né le 8 . 10 . 1921
à Varsovie
de
et de
Nationalité
Mode d'acquisition : filiation, mariage, naturalisation (rayer les mentions inutiles)
Situation de famille : célibataire, marié, veuf, divorcé (rayer les mentions inutiles)
Date d'entrée en France
Durée de séjour ininterrompu en France
Profession
Adresse Paris 16e
21 rue Henri Heine 21

VALIDITÉ TERRITORIALE
Durée de validité prorogée
du au
Le Préfet,

A false ID card used by Juozas Lukša while living in hiding in Paris

"Vanagas's misfortune," said Juozas Lukša's brother, Antanas Lukša, "was that he didn't have enough time to kill himself before they took him."

Under intense torture, Ramanauskas-Vanagas revealed that he and Juozas Lukša had hidden in a bunker in the Labanauskas home. Vincas Labanauskas was arrested March 4, 1953, on the Feast Day of Saint Casimir. He was tortured, interrogated, and exiled to hard labor in Siberia for fifteen years. Eleonora was arrested March 14, 1953. She was tortured and interrogated in the KGB prison in Vilnius from March 14, 1953 to August 10, 1953.

"They'd put a noose around my neck and yank it," Eleonora told us.

She was also subjected to the water cell where, badly beaten and sleep-deprived, prisoners were made to stand on a small metal disk submerged in cold water. When sleep overcame them, they'd slip and fall into the cold rat-infested water.

One of the most cruel tortures that Eleonora recalls was when the interrogator would shove her into a toilet stall the size of a telephone booth and then let fifty white rats loose out of a cage into the stall. The interrogator would lock the door shut, leaving Eleonora for hours crammed inside the small space covered by gnawing hungry rats.

Eleonora refused to collaborate and at one point was beaten so badly on her backside, that for a week she had to crawl around on her hands and knees. Then she got the idea to play-act that she was schizophrenic. As a schizophrenic she was of no use as an informant.

"The entire time they tortured me," Eleonora said, "all I could think about was my family, about protecting my family, so they wouldn't be destroyed."

At her trial, Eleonora was offered a lawyer to represent her, for a fee. She refused. "I have a tongue, I can speak for myself," she said.

Eleonora Labanauskiene was sentenced to five years in Siberia, but in the end she was released home to her children because they were minors and there was no one who could care for them. When Eleonora returned home she found that all of her possessions and all of her furniture, including the bed they all slept in, had been confiscated by the local Communists. She was told she would have to buy back her possessions, piece by piece. Eleonora borrowed money from her brother and began rebuilding her life, although she was constantly harassed by the local Communist authorities. None of Eleonora's daughters were allowed by Communist authorities to advance their education beyond high school. The punishments for harboring "bandits" were far reaching and intergenerational under the Soviet system.

I asked Eleonora if she had to make the choice again, knowing what she knew now, would she work for the resistance. Without hesitating, Eleonora nodded and said firmly, "Yes."

* * *

Eleonora took Nijolė by the arm and the two women walked inside the house. The rest of us followed. Eleonora's daughter, Vanda, rushed out of the kitchen, saying "Please, come, sit down at the table."

Vanda led us through the tiny front sitting room and into a small dining room. The walls were plaster and covered with pale green wallpaper. The wooden floorboards were covered with linoleum tiles. A tall row of dark wooden wardrobes separated the dining room from Eleonora's tiny bedroom. A picture of Holy Mary hung on one of the walls above the table. The single window in the room was covered with a curtain knit in intricate patterns from white linen yarn.

"Now you must sit and eat," Vanda said.

We all took our places around the table. Nijolė sat beside Eleonora. The table was covered with a white table cloth. In the Lithuanian tradition a white table cloth is used to cover the table at Christmas Eve dinner or for important guests. There were so many platters of different varieties of meats, salads, breads, compotes, and baked goods that I could barely find a place to set down the bottle of cognac I'd brought and the large box of chocolates.

"We celebrated Christmas Eve and Easter together with Mikas and Vanagas, here at this table," Eleonora said, patting the table. "Times were hard then. It wasn't like now where you can buy everything in the store. We had to raise

Wedding photograph of Nijolė Bražėnaitė and Juozas Lukša. June 23, 1950. Nijolė is wearing the traditional Lithuanian national costume.

our own animals and all of our food. It was hard work."

Vanda picked up a plate of herring, cooked in a sauce of onions and peppers, and offered it to Nijolė. Janina picked up a bowl of beet salad and began heaping generous portions into everyone's plates.

Eleonora took Nijolė's hand in hers and said, "We'd sit here in this room, Mikas and I, and we'd face each other and talk from the depths of our souls." Eleonora paused and then said, "And I'll tell you what he said, 'Oh Eleonora, how sorry I am that I left my young wife, Nijolė, behind. But what could I do? It was my mission. I had to carry out my mission. He did not know if he'd ever see you again."

Juozas Lukša and Nijolė Bražėnaitė dance together during their honeymoon in the Treifelberg mountains in Germany. June 1950

Juozas Lukša and Nijolė Bražėnaitė on their honeymoon. June 1950, Treifelberg, Germany.

Nijole gazed back at Eleonora and said, "In one of his letters he wrote to me, 'Nijolė, you must know that you have competition and that competition is my first love and my first wife and her name is Lithuania.' That was competition I could never overcome. I knew from the beginning that he would go back and fight. That it was his duty. And I accepted it."

* * *

After he was air-dropped into Lithuania, Lukša became one of the most wanted men on the Kremlin's list of spies and saboteurs. The NKVD quickly learned of Lukša's return and initiated a series of large-scale manhunts, combing the forests and raiding farmsteads. There are several documented instances in which men were shot on the spot because of their physical resemblance to Lukša—a handsome man with thick dark brown curly hair, large blue eyes, a ready smile, and an athletic build.

Orders were to hunt down Lukša and to take him alive. In the final stages of the manhunts some of the most prominent Soviet security senior officials, such as Leonid Ejtingon and Lavrenty Beria, were involved in the search for Lukša.

According to KGB archives, between January 11, 1951 and Lukša's death in an ambush September 5, 1951, roughly 50 manhunts were initiated and carried out by Soviet Security forces. On average 1041 troops participated in each manhunt.

1950 rugpjūti.

Mano brangus Aukel,

Dvidešimt su kaupu dienų skiria šią dieną nuo anų mudviejų laimės [illegible] prisiminimų. Dažnai, išniręs iš mano „pirmosios žmonos" glėbio, aš paskęstu kaip niekuomet brangiuos prisiminimuos; svajoju apie savo brangiausią ir taip pasijuntu laimingu, kad, rodos, nesumatai mano laimei konkurentų. Deja, nuolat aš privalau, kaip ir Tu, tenkintis tik tos išsvajotos, jei numirusios laimės prisiminimais.

Kai kartais mūsų [illegible] [illegible] mane Tavęs [illegible], „Išdūsta ir ..." aš tylau, [illegible], kalbėti su Tavim... ...mažiau kalo tu buvai laimingas ir kukliai supranti, kaip tu dabar gali [illegible] tai pergyventi..."

O vistik mudu [illegible] savyje „ai" [illegible] Tavimą ir [illegible] įgrožimus mano „pirmosios žmonos". Aš jį nau, Nijoliuk, kad šalia aš jau gimiaus ne dėl savo vieno, bet dėl mudviejų gerovės, kurie Tu, Brangioji, lydėsi mane savais pergyvenimais ir sava malda. Tikiu, kad mudviejų bendri jausmai, neapvils mūsų ir po trumpo laikotarpio mudu vėl svajosime nei kiek nepavirsti [illegible] laime, kurią svajojom ar ir buvom gyvenom.

O jei kartais likimui patiktų mane fiziniai sunaikint, kai Tu, Nijoliuk, žadėk padaryti mane niekur [illegible] laimingu, [illegible] savo vėl laimingą gyvenimą. Nėra negalima, kad aš ne pavirsčia mūsų tėvolio kovinos žinios dulkinos, nors dabartiniai mano

Lukša's letter to Nijolė

Nijolė Braženaitė Lukšienė Paronetto in 1950

Nijolė Braženaitė Lukšienė Paronetto in 2006

On one occasion a manhunt that took place on May 8, 1951 involved 2316 troops. But, the agreed radio call "5-5-5" in the event of finding Lukša was never broadcast. At the time Lukša was hiding in the bunker under the floorboards of Vincas and Eleonora Labanauskas's home.

In the process of these manhunts 26 partisans were apprehended and killed and 10 were arrested. One Soviet Security lieutenant was killed. Although Lukša himself eluded Soviet Security forces and the NKVD for eleven months, bunkers were raided and necessary supplies and documents were confiscated. The archives provide an impressive list of confiscated items: two typewriters, two radios, documents, printing supplies, two parachutes, a camera, a generator, boots, pants, topographical maps, anti-Soviet pamphlets, one submachine gun, sleeping bags, a compass, ammunition, gloves, Lukša's watch, newspapers, chocolate, 3,600 rubles, 2000 zlotys, a box containing 285 bullets, several pistols, a grenade.

* * *

Before he departed for Lithuania in 1950, Juozas Lukša instructed Nijole to burn the letters he'd written her. She couldn't bring herself to do it. She hid them instead.

I don't think any woman could resist a man who wrote like Lukša or forget him even half a century later:

The warmth that emanates from your letters bewitches me. I'd like it if every time you were overcome with loneliness, with longing for me, I could be with you and give you happiness, a happiness that you've never before known. But, what obstacles get in our way! The God of Fate is cruel. Carefully, with the patience and lovingness of an ant, you build yourself a palace in the future and He comes and knocks it all down with one sweep of his hand, leaving you only with pain and longing and with the mirage of happiness.

May 10, 1949

When Lithuania regained its independence in 1991 an editor coaxed the letters out of Nijolė. It was difficult for her to make the letters public, but in the end she did, for the sake of history. They were published in Lithuania as a collection called *Letters to my Loved One (Laiškai Mylimosioms)*. The publication of the letters led to Nijolė making more and more public appearances in which she was asked to talk about Lukša and their time together in Paris.

Juozas Lukša told Nijolė that he too would burn the letters she'd written him. Only, he too couldn't bring himself to do it. Instead, before boarding the plane that would airdrop him back into Lithuania, he tucked the letters into a brown envelope and with a crayon wrote across the front of the envelope: *Noli tangere circulos meos.*

Those were Archimedes' last words before he was killed by an invading Roman soldier: *Do not disturb my circles*. The legend goes that Archimedes was sketching circles in the sand, too busy with his calculations to notice that the enemy had entered the city. Lukša handed the letters and a circumference to a CIA secretary and instructed her to return them to Nijolė.

Fifty six years later Nijolė entrusted those letters to me.

The letters reveal that the young couple's relationship had been built on a longing for their native country and also on an understanding that Lukša would return to Lithuania to continue fighting in the resistance and that Nijolė would wait for him. In a later dated February 19, 1949 Nijolė wrote:

I believe you know the thoughts I send after you, after your visits, the thought that I so want, together with you, to kiss the land we both haven't seen for such a long time. You'd come to me tonight thinking about how we won't see each other again and we'd both talked about everything, but not about that which is most holy and most painful to us. Maybe it's better that way? After all, nothing is certain either for you or for me. Only it hurts me to think that you thought that I'd placed our happiness above the fight for free-

dom. No, Juozas, I'd never dare ask you to change your position, and I know that you'd never change it. And for that I love you even more. I don't think I'd change anything either if I had the fortune of being in your position.

Lukša replied to Nijolė's letter with the humor that so many people later remembered him for: "I see that you are a woman in the style of the Greek antiquity, 'Either come home with a sword, or don't come home at all." But then in a more serious tone, Lukša wrote in the same letter, "Knowing you, the way I do, makes me proud, and gives me the strength I need to face critical situations."

And yet there were moments when Lukša allowed himself to dream. On March 3, 1949 Lukša wrote, "Oh, wouldn't it be wonderful if after everything were over—everything that is yet to pass—that we could drink in all our happiness."

A few days later, on March 8, 1949, Lukša wrote:

You must agree that happiness doesn't simply hang around at any one time or any one place, but that it is found only very rarely and under the most trying circumstances—that it's hidden and only rarely shows itself. Maybe that's why for us earthly creatures happiness is so dear—because it occurs so seldom and because it takes so much effort to attain it.

Sometimes Lukša railed against Fate. On June 6, 1949 Lukša wrote:

Often, Nijolė, when I am drowning in my longing for you, I cannot understand why Fate has been so cruel to us. First it bound our spirits, and then it separated us just when our days are numbered. Maybe that is alright, but I worry that rather than make us stronger, the result will be that it will destroy us morally. Fate will make us despair of the existence of happiness at all.

Despite his love for Nijolė, Lukša placed his commitment to the resistance above his personal life. In a letter written in August, 1950, just two months after their wedding, Lukša wrote to Nijolė:

...And, after all, the two of us have given up the insistence of "me" and have given ourselves up to the demands of my "first wife." I know, Nijolė, that from now on I won't be fighting just for my own honor, but for our honor, and that you will be there with me in your prayers. I believe that the feelings we share for each other will not disappoint us and one day we will be together again in that joy we dream so much of and in which we both live.

The equipment that the paratroopers would take with them when they were flown back into the Soviet Union to gather information for the American CIA. This is the equipment of Julijonas Butėnas. Among the equipment is the radio transmitter used to send information from Soviet-occupied Lithuania to the West.

Just ten days before their wedding, on June 10, 1950, Nijolė had written to Lukša:

I don't know how to express to you how I feel now that our dreams are coming true. I know that all of it will be very different from how things usually are in life. But all the same, every minute that we are physically separated will make our spiritual bond only stronger, and together we will sacrifice everything for your (and for my) first love.

Perhaps Nijolė's understanding of Juozas's mission stemmed from her own experiences as a participant in the resistance to the Nazi occupation of Lithuania in 1941. As teenagers she and her twin sister printed anti-Nazi proclamations on a printing press hidden along with weapons in their family's garden shed at their house in Kaunas. Nijolė's younger brother, Mindaugas, was conscripted at the age of eighteen into the German Luftwaffe. He used his German uniform to smuggle Jewish children out of the Kaunas ghetto and deliver them to his mother, Konstancija Braženienė, who would hide them in her home, feed and clothe them, and raise them as her own until they could be smuggled safely out of the country.

For her efforts Konstancija Braženienė was exiled by the Soviets to ten years hard labor in Siberia. In the late forties and early fifties the Soviets would exile to Siberia people who had resisted the Nazis on the principal that if they had resisted one regime they could not be trusted not to resist another.

After Lukša returned to Lithuania in October, 1950, Nijolė's friend Julijonas Butėnas handed Nijolė Lukša's final letter to her, written that August.

> *A little more than 20 days separates me from the memories of the happiness we shared in Treifelberg. Often, when I wrench myself out of my "first wife's" grip, I drown in memories of us. I dream of you, Dear One. I feel so happy that it doesn't seem possible that you could find anyone who could compete with my happiness. It is sad that these days, like you, I must rely on satisfying myself with the memory of that happiness I'd so dreamed of, so longed for.*

At the same time, they were both young and felt invincible. "Somehow, we believed everything would work out," Nijolė recalls. "We believed Juozas would complete his mission and return safely."

* * *

When Lukša and his team landed, they encountered their first setback. They'd lost one of the containers, holding warm clothing, rain gear, part of the radio transmitter, medicine, ammunition, food, money, and anti-Soviet literature. Lukša decided not to take the time to search for the container because he reasoned that they did not have much time before the Soviet Interior Forces would arrive. He was certain that they would have noticed that an unidentified plane had entered their airspace. They searched for the container half an hour and then moved on, taking turns carrying the heavy radio transmitter equipment on their backs.

The second obstacle they experienced was that they had been dropped five days walk from their area of operation, the Tauras District. The night had been rainy and foggy and the pilot could not turn on his navigational equipment because it would have been detected on the Soviets' radars. He dropped Lukša and the radio men at the first opportune spot, which turned out to be the Žemaityja region—unfamiliar territory.

They buried their parachutes and continued onwards to their meeting place. The Tyrelis Forest, where they'd been dropped, was mostly swamp, and they were soon thoroughly drenched. It had been raining when they were dropped in Lithuania and it continued to rain heavily during the entire trek. They stopped at a farm in the Dabrupinė Village and went to sleep in the hay barn. The farmer's wife discovered them when she went out to the barn. She invited them indoors. She quickly covered all the windows and rushed to prepare a meal. From her reaction, the paratroopers knew she was accustomed to hiding partisans on her farm. After they ate, they set out towards the Nemunas River. They walked at night and hid in the forest during the day. They ate at farms along the way. Trumpys developed bad blisters from his new boots, so he had to make the trip on foot in his socks.

After three uneventful days' journey, they reached the swollen Nemunas River.

They found a row boat and rowed towards the opposite bank. They could see the lights of Jurbarkas on the opposite shore. A strong current caught the boat and carried them too far downstream. As they cut their way back through dense undergrowth, they lost one of their submachine guns. On the evening of October 10th they reached the Skirkiškis Village where Lukša had some close friends, the Vaitkevičius family. The family was shocked to see that Lukša had returned from the West. They could not believe that he would chose to return to a certain death. They told him that all the partisans who had accompanied him on his trip to cross the border to the West were dead.

The KGB archives in Vilnius reveal that on September 8, 1951, three days after Lukša's death, during interrogation, Marcelė Vaitkevičius said the following:

> In the fall of 1950 Skirmantas (one of Lukša's code names) and two friends arrived. They were armed and were wearing sports clothing. Each of them had a small backpack. They said they'd returned from the West, where they had received training at an espionage school. A plane had brought them back and they'd been parachuted into Lithuania to conduct reconnaissance. They were dropped in the Klaipėda region. They came to us on foot. They hid their parachutes in the forest. After dinner Skirmantas gave me a watch and gave my husband 30 US dollars. He asked if we were in contact with the partisans. He said he wanted to meet up with them. The next day he asked us to bring him to Zavadskis. One kilometer away from Zavadskis's farm I got out and walked. I asked him to come and fix a broken wheel on my cart. When Zavadskis came out into the yard alone, I told him that Skirmantas and his friends were waiting for him. Once they'd met, I returned home.

After this initial contact was made with partisan liaisons, Lukša and the remaining partisans in the Tauras District experienced set back after set back. Several former partisans had joined forces with the NKVD and had infiltrated

Jonas Kukauskas in the CIA training camp in Germany in 1950. Kukauskas betrayed his close friend and comrade Juozas Lukša, leading to Lukša's ambush and death on the night of September 4–5, 1951.

partisan ranks, wearing authentic uniforms and carrying authentic weapons. Because of the deft work of these traitors, called *Smogikai*, partisan ranks in the Tauras District were thinned considerably. Remarkably, Lukša managed to evade detection under those circumstances for eleven months.

Although Lukša managed to remain alive and operate undetected for nearly a year, the intelligence that he gathered now made *him* suspicious to the CIA. Through reconnaissance missions Lukša found that the Soviets *were not* mobilizing to invade the West. In fact, he found that the opposite was true—that the Soviet Union was fortifying its defenses against a perceived attack from the West. Lukša radioed this information to his CIA contacts in Germany. The CIA's reaction was to suspect Lukša of counter-espionage and purposefully sending misleading information. He was dropped from the program and radio contact with him ceased. A second group of spies were parachuted into Lithuania to carry out the same mission. Lukša's friend and comrade, Jonas Kukauskas, was sent on this mission.

By the early fifties, after six years of warfare, the armed resistance in Lithuania was falling apart. By 1951 the resistance's numbers had dwindled considerably. Most of its members had either been killed, arrested and executed, or deported to Siberia. The civilian populace that had provided practical and logistical support had also been mostly deported to Siberia or rounded up onto collective farms and terrorized into submission. As is typical of any prolonged war, order began to fall apart among the ranks. Occasionally, raids on innocent villagers and abuses took place, causing the resistance to lose civilian support and credibility.

Lukša began to plead the case for a civil resistance, but no one in Lithuania at the time was ready to lead it. He argued that small pockets of the resistance imbedded within civilian life could have more of an effect undermining the Soviet system from within. Once it became clear that Lukša had done all he could, he resolved to return to Nijolė and to the West.

In 1951 one of Lukša's comrades, a partisan who went by the code name, Lakštingala (Nightingale), had a friend who had been fighting at the Eastern front for the Russians as a reconnaissance pilot. After the war he had returned home to Lithuania. Lukša talked to Lakštingala about possible alternatives for traveling to the West and Lakštingala talked to his friend about using his Antonov-2 (the so called *Kukuruznik*, or crop duster) to escape across the Baltic Sea to Gotland, Sweden. At the time Sweden was no longer returning refugees. They would have flown at night, possibly in bad weather. The men made an agreement and everything was settled. The only remaining problem was to procure fuel. In the meantime, Lukša was invited to the secret meeting that would end his life.

On the night of September 5, 1951 Lukša was lured out of hiding by his fellow resistance fighter and close friend, Jonas Kukauskas. Kukauskas had lived together with Lukša in Paris and had trained together with him at the CIA camp in Kaufbeuren. Previous to their training with the CIA, they also both trained with French intelligence and would swim together in the River Seine during breaks in their training routine. Kukauskas, nicknamed "Dzikas," was mentioned often and with great affection in Nijolė and Lukša's letters. Almost every letter from Nijolė ended with the line, "Pass on my regards to Dzikas…"

Kukauskas had been parachuted back into Lithuania when the second airdrop was made. Kukauskas and his comrade, another paratrooper who had arrived with him, Julijonas Butėnas, were holed up in a bunker when they were ambushed. Butėnas was wounded in a firefight with Soviet Interior Forces as they tried to exit the bunker. Butėnas and Kukauskas returned to the bunker and Butėnas reached for a grenade to commit suicide together with Kukauskas—standard procedure for partisans surrounded in an ambush. Kukauskas, however, surprised Butėnas by shooting him in the back and killing him. Kukauskas then climbed out of the bunker and surrendered to Nachman Dushansky, the Soviet Security Officer leading the operation. Dushansky used Kukauskas to lure Lukša into a rendezvous where they intended to take him alive. Kukauskas sent a series of encoded messages to Lukša with the intention of arranging a secret meeting. Over the course of several days Lukša and Kukauskas corresponded through a liaison, sending encoded messages that tested each other's intentions. Because Kukauskas had lived together with Lukša in Paris, he was able to answer each of Lukša's questions correctly, ensuring his identity. Although Lukša confided to others before the fated meeting that he had doubts about Kukauskas's loyalty, he decided to go to the meeting because the resistance was in desperate need of supplies and a radio transmitter to contact the West.

Kukauskas instructed Lukša to meet him at a secret location near the village of Pabartupis. Meanwhile, Soviet Security Forces set up an extensive ambush and lay in waiting for Lukša's arrival. Apparently, Kukauskas hesitated and fumbled the answer when Lukša asked the password. Lukša realized instantly he'd been lured into a trap and reached for his gun. A soldier hiding in the bushes close by panicked and shot at Lukša, although orders had been to take him alive. Lukša returned fire, but he was outnumbered. Lukša was killed. Some eye witnesses claim that Lukša, realizing he was surrounded, shot himself in the head to avoid being taken alive. How Lukša died remains unclear because soon after the ambush his body disappeared and was never recovered. Recently, a former *Smogikas* who had participated in the operation to capture Lukša came forward with information regarding the place where his body was secretly buried and attempts have been made to locate his remains. Unfortunately those attempts thus far have failed.

* * *

Nijolė remained alone in Europe for another six years, working for the Supreme Committee for the Liberation of Lithuania. She chose not to board one of the ships filled with war refuges bound for America. She waited in Europe for news of her husband. But news never came.

In 1956 Congressman Charles Kerston, Chairman of the Select Committee on Communist Aggression, traveled to Europe to interview refugees from Eastern Europe on the atrocities committed under the Soviets. Because Nijolė was fluent in several European languages, she was asked by Kerston to accompany him as a translator on his fact-finding mission. While visiting refugee camps in Germany, Kerston pieced together the story of Lukša's death. He broke the news to Nijolė and urged her to move on with her life. With the help of Kerston's family, Nijolė emigrated to America.

In America Nijolė was able to put her medical diploma to use and passed the necessary certification to become a pathologist. She became the department head of the pathology department at Saint Joseph's Medical Center in New York. She remarried, marrying a colleague, the medical doctor Fiorenzo Paronetto. They had two daughters and settled in New York.

Juozas Lukša had known that going back to fight in the invisible war in Lithuania could end his life. In his final letter to Nijolė, written in August 1950, he wrote "If it should happen that fate dictates that I be physically destroyed, then

Eleonora as a young woman

Eleonora in 2008

you, my Nijolė, make me happy, wherever I am, by creating a happy life for yourself once again." Because of these words, Nijolė felt that Juozas had given her his blessing to remarry.

* * *

Nijolė knew that Juozas could not have lived with himself if he had not returned to his comrades and to his beloved nation. In public appearances Nijolė often quotes this passage from a letter written by Juozas dated February 16, 1949, Lithuania's prewar Independence Day:

> *I search and search and cannot find someone to blame nor can I find an answer as to why I am here today and not there where I ought to be. A year has gone by and the not-knowing eats away at my conscience. It's been a year since my footsteps led me away from the blood-soaked soil of my homeland. It's been a year since I've watched the crucifixion of my beloved country. It's been a year since I've heard my people's wails of pain. It's been a year and so many of my friends have passed into death. It's been a year since I've fought together with my fellow Lithuanians in a battle of life and death. I think of all the graves of the past five years, I think of the long lines of my friends marked for death, and I want to live, but at the same time I hunger to see my bones beside the bones of my crucified friends.*

* * *

"Times were horrible," Eleonora said, her face growing dark, "I remember the heaps of corpses the Soviet Interior Forces would bring out of the forests after a battle. They'd dump them in the market square and make everyone walk past and look. If you reacted, they'd take you in for questioning. And the worst was that some of our own village men would join the NKVD and turn on us."

"I don't understand it," Nijolė said, shaking her head, "it seems that the schools were good when we were growing up in independent Lithuania. People were civil. There was law and order. Where did this barbarism come from?"

"War," Eleonora said and gave a firm nod, "war will do it."

"To the Russians, they were terrorists, you know," Rimas said.

"It all depended on what side you were on," Nijolė said, "to the Russians he was a terrorist. To us he was a hero."

"When I was here in the spring," I said to Eleonora, "you told me that Juozas would say you looked like Nijolė. So tell me now, does she look like you?"

Eleonora squeezed Nijolė's hand and beamed. She didn't answer. For me, the answer was obvious. The two women looked like sisters. Both were around the same height, had gray wavy hair that had once been a dark blond, and determined steel blue eyes. Both also had high cheekbones and angular faces, but those features were typical for Lithuanians. Lithuania was a tiny country with a small gene pool, so there was a strong likelihood that these two women might resemble each other.

Yet Nijolė and Eleonora's resemblance went beyond the physical; their resemblance was something of the spirit. Both possessed the resolve and determination it took to stand up to a totalitarian regime and to pay the price—Nijole by losing her husband after only a week of marriage—Eleonora by losing her husband to fifteen years of hard labor in Siberia and by being tortured herself for six months. And both women had the strength of character to come out of the experience just as determined as when they first made the decision to knowingly risk their lives for freedom, for democracy, and for their nation's independence.

"Mikas believed we would be independent again," Eleonora said, "he would say, 'The Russians won't last long.'"

"I remember how Lukša and Vanagas used to teach us how to write our letters," Vanda said, bustling in from the kitchen with another steaming platter of pork chops. "Vanagas would give each of us sisters a stick of chalk and we'd go outside and he'd write the letters across the saw horse and we'd copy them."

"Ah, and do you remember," Eleonora's other daughter, Janina, said, "how Mikas would wrap me in a bolt of Mother's woven fabric and put me up high on top of the shelf. Then he'd tell you to go and find me."

"And of course I never could because it would never occur to me to look for you wrapped in a bolt of fabric and up high on the shelf!" Vanda laughed.

Only years later, when the girls were grown women, did Eleonora explain to them that the man who'd wrapped them in bolts of fabric and who told them bed-time stories was the legendary leader of the resistance, Juozas Lukša.

"One day I was walking to the store when I saw a column of military trucks heading towards our farm," Eleonora said. "A cold chill went through me, but I just kept walking calmly. I went to the store, bought what I needed, and went back home. The NKVD had surrounded our house and was doing a raid. They had four machine guns set up at all four corners of the house. Eighteen of them decided to spend the night in our house, to keep watch."

The memory made Eleonora's blood pressure rise. Her cheeks grew red and she fanned her face. Vanda put her hands on Eleonora's shoulders and offered to take her to bed, but Eleonora shook her away. Determined to tell her story, Eleonora continued:

"Lucky for us, they were all hiding down in the bunker. Night came. Vanagas fell asleep down there in the bunker and he started to snore. He was snoring so loud the NKVD officer burst into our bedroom and began poking around. My husband understood immediately what was going on, so he started to snore in a loud, obnoxious manner. The NKVD officer turned around and walked out. The next day they left. That was a close call."

This story leads Eleonora to another story. The memories come back to her in a rush.

"We'd be peeling potatoes in the kitchen, Mikas and I," Eleonora said, "and he'd pick up the edge of the curtain and curse in Russian and say, 'Are those the Russians coming?' And then he'd laugh when he saw my reaction."

"Could we see the bunker?" Rimas asked, standing up.

Eleonora led us outside, through the flower garden, and around to the side of the house.

"It's all different now," Vanda said, walking behind us, "after it was all over, we turned the bunker into a root cellar."

We opened the door to the bunker. The door was built years later, when Vincas Labanauskas returned from prison camp and busied himself working on the house. A set of narrow wooden steps lead down to a dark closed space. The women have rows of canning jars set on the shelf that once held Vanagas's typewriter and the mens' guns, grenades, and ammunition.

"This is where they had to live, the three of them, Lukša, Vanagas, and his wife, Birutė" Eleonora said. "They spent many long hours down here. It would be humid and then it would be cold, but that was how they lived.

Nijolė stood beside Eleonora and took her hand in hers. They peered down at the dark, dank hole in the ground where Nijolė's husband had lain in hiding, through all sorts of weather, for many long hours, while Soviet Interior Forces scoured the countryside looking for him.

"You had heartache," Eleonora said to Nijolė, staring down into the dark, "but we lived through hell."

Sources

Interview with Labanauskas Family, May 25, 2008, Alendarne, Lithuania. Interview conducted by Laina Vincė Srioginis.

Interview with Labanauskas Family, May 28, 2006, Alendarne, Lithuania. Interview conducted by Laina Vincė Srioginis.

Interview with Eleonora Labanauskienė, September 10, 2006, Alendarne, Lithuania. Interview conducted by Laina Vincė Srioginis.

Interview with Nijolė Bražėnaitė-Lukšienė-Parronetto, June 15, 2007, New York, U.S.A. Interview conducted by Laina Vincė Srioginis.

Daumantas, Juozas. *Laiškai Mylimosioms,* Chicago: Draugas, 1993

Kasparas, Kestutis and Vitkauskas, Vidmantas. *Sugrįžimas (The Return),* Lietuvos Politinių Kalinių ir Tremtinių Sąjunga ir Lietuvos Gyventojų Genocido ir Rezistencijos Tyrimo Centras, Kaunas, 2005

Likviduoti Skirmantą (Liquidating Skirmantas), Birutė Pečiokaitė-Adomėnienė, Kaunas: Atmintis, 2002

Lithuanian Special Archive, Vilnius, Lithuania

An Account from the Post-War Borderlands

A Review of Western Intelligence Reports Regarding the Lithuanian Resistance

Jonas Öhman

Both literally and figuratively, the Lithuanian resistance leader Juozas Lukša's account of the Lithuanian post-war resistance against the Soviet Union is a testimony from the borderlands of post-war European history. Efforts to understand and evaluate this period have only recently begun. Lukša's work is a valuable contribution. For decades *Forest Brothers* was one of the few primary sources regarding the Lithuanian post-war resistance available in the West.[1] Although more than half a century has passed since the book was written, it continues to prove itself to be a valuable resource.

However, there is another formerly practically unknown account of the resistance that appeared in quite a different format: the reports brought by Lukša to Western intelligence services. These reports speak of the situation in Lithuania, and of the Lithuanian resistance, in a manner that *Forest Brothers*, for various reasons, could not. They also shed light on the very complicated post-war international relationships. In some ways, the reports are helpful in understanding the complex nature of the Lithuanian post-war resistance.

As one of the most devoted and capable of the Lithuanian partisans, Juozas Lukša accomplished several assignments of high importance. The most crucial task of all was to establish a connection with the West. As noted in his book, he accomplished this twice, at the beginning of June, 1947, and during Christmas of the same year. This information, indeed, caught the attention of Western Intelligence.

---

1 See for instance the interesting work of Kestutis Girnius, *Partizanu kovos Lietuvoje* (The partisan war in Lithuania), Vilnius, Mokslas, 1990, where *Forest Brothers* is used as a primary source of information.

It is problematic that relevant archives have been classified for a long time, and to some extent this is still the case. For instance, the CIA, to this day has revealed only a small portion of information regarding its involvement in the infiltration of spies into the Soviet Union around 1950. This is especially the case when speaking of the individuals involved.[2] Some reports have been made partially available, giving some idea of the level of comprehension.

Another country that somewhat reluctantly involved itself in intelligence activities at the time was Sweden. The Swedish intelligence was the first to establish contact with Lukša. After his escape to Poland, Lukša arrived on February 2, 1948 at the port in Trelleborg from Gdynia in Poland, together with a certain Jonas Deksnys.[3] Deksnys was the representative for the Lithuanian resistance in the West and resided at that point in Stockholm. He had met Lukša earlier, after his first escape, in Poland. At the time he had brought Lukša's intelligence material to Stockholm, where he presented it to the so-called *T-kontoret* ("T-office"), at the time a newly established intelligence agency responsible for Eastern Europe.[4]

Intelligence reports from the forties, which have been recently released from Swedish archives,[5] provide an idea of the scope and content of the information provided first-hand by the Lithuanian resistance to the West.[6] The direct source of the information is not given in the reports; however, knowing the circumstances, it is safe to claim that the main bulk of available information was brought to the West by or through Juozas Lukša.[7]

---

2 An example is a letter to the widow of Juozas Lukša, Nijole Bražėnaite-Paronetto (later re-married), where she requests information about her former husband. The answer, dated August 9, 2007, states that "No" information can be given, with reference to section 6 of the CIA act of 1949 (CIA reference F-2007-01568)."

3 Swedish Immigration archives, Jonas Deksnys' personal file. So far not a single mention of Juozas Lukša (or his companion Kazimieras Pyplys) has been established in any Swedish records. Other available sources, however, such as Soviet security protocols from interrogations with Deksnys in 1949, confirm that Deksnys and Lukša arrived together to Sweden.

4 For more reading about the rather dramatic life and fate of Jonas Deksnys, see the book *Pavargęs herojus* (Exhausted Hero) by Liūtas Mockūnas (Vilnius, Baltos Lankos, 1997).

5 The fate of some of these archives provide an idea of the peculiar circumstances related to these matters, not only in Eastern Europe. For a long time it was assumed that the records of the so called T-kontoret, the Swedish intelligence agency of the time, had been destroyed. In 1997, however, the then commander-in-chief of the Swedish defence forces, Stig Synnergren, unexpectedly presented the archive in the form of micro-fiches. From the perspective of the (Swedish) author of this article, this act could be perceived as almost symbolic in terms of the official attitude in Sweden towards its post-war history.

6 The cooperation between intelligence agencies in the West did at this time rapidly develop. Sweden, with its geographical location, was an interesting partner for cooperation. One may assume that any information of this kind, perceived as interesting, was relayed to, for instance, the British.

7 According to the Swedish system for estimation of accuracy and reliability of the information, the reports for July 1947 are marked "D3," implying an unfamiliar source providing good information. The reports from February are marked "C3", which indicates an unfamiliar source with high credibility, providing

Anyone with any experience of military intelligence knows that often limited available information in combination with a number of possible errors, misunderstandings, false assumptions, language problems, prejudices, political necessities and other factors, can easily lead to false or distorted conclusions. Further, the information may include deliberate flaws, omissions, and outright disinformation related to the hidden agendas of the source, or of the mediator, of the information. This makes accurate intelligence analysis, even with the context of historical retrospection, very complicated.

The available material will need a more thorough review than is possible to accomplish in this setting. Nevertheless, a brief presentation and analysis of intelligence material may add to the understanding of the topic and provide some background to the material provided in Lukša's book. This material has been abbreviated to its essentials.

One of the reports dating from July 1947 regarding the situation of the Lithuanian resistance[8] is rather detailed:

> The strength of the Lithuanian resistance in the middle of 1947 is stated as 6,200 men under arms, a figure that can be doubled to 12,000 in a few hours by mobilizing the so-called reservists, that is, guerillas living a legal life as civilians but ready to mobilize at short notice. A plan for full mobilization is available, including about 100,000 men of all ages. There are only arms available for about 75,000 of these men. Guns are retrieved by stealing them and by buying them. Russian soldiers and officers are willing to trade guns and ammunition for US dollars.[9]

These numbers are interesting for a number of reasons. They give the impression of a small, but very well organized, underground movement. What is most interesting, in terms of intelligence information of foreign interest, is the mention of the existence of a system for mobilization. In the event of war, a well-organized, locally supported guerilla can create extreme problems for the enemy. This

good information. Having in mind that Deksnys allegedly arrived in Sweden after his trip to Poland and provided the report in June 1947 and that Lukša arrived in February 1948, it is safe to assume that the reports indeed are linked to the information provided through this channel.

8 Report No 82, August 22, 1947, Swedish intelligence agency T-kontoret, Swedish war archives.

9 The sale of guns and ammunition by Russian forces to insurgents has been an issue in all conflicts after World War II. There are for instance several reports of how Chechnyan fighters were able to buy or trade weapons from Russian forces during the conflict in Chechnya (see, for instance, Stasys Knezys and Romanas Sedlickas's book *The War in Chechnya*. Texas A&M University Press, 1999) This detail gives an idea of the "dynamics" in the relationships between a motivated insurgency and a less motivated occupation force.

is especially true if the guerilla in turn can count on tactical and logistical support from the outside.

The numbers of active resistance fighters in the report seem somewhat exaggerated. Estimations by Nijolė Gaškaitė in her book *Pasipriešinimo istorija 1944–1953*[10] suggest that there were about 3,500 armed partisans in the spring of 1947.

The numbers for potential mobilization are no doubt exaggerated. The partisans indeed made up plans for a general mobilization. There were, for instance, staff officers responsible for these matters. Such a large number of potential mobilized guerillas, however, seem extremely high. The purely administrative task of managing such large numbers seems like an impossible task, having in mind the conditions of the resistance. Another circumstance concerns the relatively low level of centralization of the Lithuanian resistance during the period.[11]

All of this information suggests that the numbers (knowing that they would be almost impossible to check) may have been provided in order mainly to make an impact on the receiver rather than to give a real indication of the circumstances. Possibly, this may have been done as a means of drawing attention to the situation in Lithuania.

The report continues:

> Direct confrontation with Soviet army units is avoided. ...The armed activities of the resistance are aimed exclusively against Lithuanian Communists.[12] Occasionally Russian settlers and members of the Soviet secret services are killed as a result of these actions.

Avoiding confrontation with regular Soviet forces was standard tactics for the partisans. The vast superiority of the Soviets in terms of numbers, equipment, training, communications and intelligence made any confrontation very dangerous. An interesting detail, though, is the ambiguity of the report. It is not clear

---

10 Gaškaitė, Nijolė, *Pasipriešinimo istorija 1944–1953* (A history of the resistance 1944–1953), Vilnius, Aidai, 1997.

11 In 1947 only a partial centralization was achieved, only in 1949 a formal centralization of the resistance was fully accomplished. Here one may mention the effort by the MGB to create a fictive organization in 1946 in order to eliminate the leadership with a decisive blow at the beginning of 1947. Thanks to Lukša, who was appointed by his military district to this organization, the plan was revealed in time. The whole story is described by Lukša in his report *MGB pinklės resistancijoje* (The dragnets of MGB within the resistance), *Partizanai* (The partisans) part VII, Kaunas: Association of political prisoners and deportees and Genocide and resistance center of Lithuania, 2005.

12 The wording of the report in Swedish on this point is very harsh, suggesting that the Communists are "ruthlessly exterminated," a rather colorful expression for an intelligence report.

whether the reference includes the Red Army, that is, the regular armed forces, or whether it only refers to the so-called interior forces, meaning, the armed forces of the NKVD (later MGB, or, the Soviet Security. During the post-war period these troops were used extensively against the partisans, for instance for ambushes, search parties and raids against partisan bunkers. The report does not mention the Interior Forces at all. Whether the lack of mention is a misunderstanding, lack of competence, or a deliberate omission, is hard to tell. The tactical and strategic importance of the Interior Forces among the measures undertaken to "Sovietize" incorporated territories cannot be underestimated.[13] This detail may suggest that the information behind the report is provided with a limited understanding of the real situation.

The wording regarding actions aimed at "Lithuanian Communists" provides a straightforward picture of the essence of a partisan war. An outnumbered insurgency facing a well-trained and well-equipped occupation force, over time turns to other targets. The Lithuanian resistance case was no exception in this respect. According to available statistics, the resistance killed at least two civilians for every armed individual (soldier, local militia and others). [14] This is not to say that a guerilla war necessarily breeds only cruelty and chaos, but such a type of conflict over time with necessity results in sufferings for the civil population.[15] [16]

---

13 Juozas Starkauskas has in his book *Čekistinė kariuomenė Lietuvoje 1944-1953* (The Chekist forces in Lithuania 1944-1953), Vilnius: The Center for Research on Genocide and Resistance in Lithuania, 1998, provided an extensive analysis of the activities of the Interior troops during the post-war period.

14 Anušauskas, Arvydas. *Lietuvos išnaikinimas ir tautos kova*, (The annihilation of Lithuania and the fight of its people), Vilnius: VAGA, 1999, p. 575. According to the available information, about 4,000 Soviet troops, local militia, and other armed Soviet officials were killed by the partisans, whereas about 8,000 civilians were killed, making a total number of about 12,000 dead. Fresh statistics from the Centre of Genocide and Resistance Research in Vilnius, suggest that as many as 33,000 civilians in total were killed during the conflict. This numbers are only tentative for a number of reasons but still provide an idea of how much research is left to do in order to fully see the picture. Still, ironic as it may seem, the conflict was nevertheless rather "military" for a guerilla war. Compare for instance to the killing rates in Soviet war in Afghanistan for foreign military personnel vs civilians (about 1–90) and the US war in Vietnam (about 1–30).

15 See for instance the CIA, Intelligence memorandum No. 250, 5 April 1950, p. 2, about the latter phase of the conflict: "(The partisans) have become very cruel and in their turn are killing everyone whom they suspect of being Communist or of favoring the Bolshevists. As a result, many innocent persons have perished, according to source."

16 In the case of Lukša, there is an interesting, personal touch to this matter. In *Forest Brothers* he emphasizes the unity of the resistance and its common goals. There is, however, one case where Lukša lets the reader understand that he was not totally in agreement with the other leaders about certain tactics used. This is where the partisan leaders meet to decide what to do in order to deal with the Russian settlers (p. 348). "All the commanders agreed that collectivization and colonization had to be inflexibly opposed. Opinion differed only on the measures to be used. It was my view, along with two other combatants, that in this anti-colonization action force should not be used. Others felt that the operation would be more successful if it was carried out with greater force and speed. Since these were the views of the majority, the majority prevailed."

Back to the report:

> Almost no Russians are to be found in the countryside, the majority are migrating to the cities. The main reason for this is their fear of the partisans.

The idea that the Lithuanian resistance, with actions aimed at settlers from Russia, should have limited the immigration, is widespread and believed by many Lithuanians even today. However, to a large extent, this is a myth. Doubtless, some information about the "nationalist bandits" in Lithuania reached Russia,[17] however, to believe that this information should have caused a decreased migration is rather optimistic, especially within a society like the Soviet Union where more or less forced migration by the State during these years was a common occurrence.[18]

The next report of interest, dating from February, 1948, suggests a much higher level of sophistication in terms of military intelligence.[19]

Thorough attention is given in the report to the location of the Interior troops and other Soviet units involved in the fight with the partisans. This includes a general description of the MGB interior forces structure, revealing considerable knowledge of the organizational structure and size of the units deployed in the Lithuanian countryside. The way this is done suggests accuracy and experience regarding analysis of intelligence information. For example:

The matter regards an operation against a collective farm in Opšrūtai (named Aušrūtai in the book), near the border with Kaliningrad, which took place on the night of September 15th–16th, where 31 settlers were killed.

The more humane position of Juozas Lukša is further developed in an instruction issued by him after his return in 1951 to the resistance regarding prosecution and punishment of collaborators and others, prohibiting punishments of any relatives or similar such persons and mitigation of punishment for minors and elders. Pocius M., *Partisan resistance in Lithuania 1944–1953: The struggle with inhabitants accused of collaboration* (Summary of doctoral dissertation), Klaipeda-Vilnius, LII publishing house, 2005, pp. 20–21.

17 Juozas Starkauskas retells in his book *Čekistinė kariuomenė Lietuvoje 1944–1953* (The Chekist forces in Lithuania 1944–1953) how interior troops wrote home about their experience from Lithuania and sometimes mentioned the clashes with the partisans. Such stories were censored and could lead to disciplinary measures against the individual soldier.

18 Very few Russians and others, coming from outside Lithuania, tried to settle in the countryside, but this was for reasons other than fear. There was simply no need for any additional population in the agrarian areas. Instead, an intensive nation-wide industrialization was initiated, where, besides some immigration, the local population provided the necessary additional labor force. The large rural population of Lithuania, which formed the backbone of the armed resistance, may thus have prevented Russian immigration, but by other means than armed resistance.

19 Reports No 314 and 319, February 16 and 17, 1948, Swedish intelligence agency T-kontoret, Swedish war archives.

The organization of the MGB is strictly territorial. Lithuania is divided into 32 MGB-districts, with the same borders as the civil administration. The district leader is most often a lieutenant colonel. The deputy commander, also in charge of the operations, is normally a major. In every district there are about 10 counties (there are a total of 309 counties in Lithuania) where local MGB forces are deployed, with 10–300 soldiers in every county. At an average the local units consist of 50 soldiers. Based upon this estimation the total number of active MGB-forces in the county could be 15–20,000.[20]

The report deals with other organizations, such as the Soviet militia (*Izstrebitely*)[21] and with the counter espionage units, SMERSH. The report further mentions possibly the most effective and dangerous of all anti-partisan units, the "OBO."[22] This unit engaged in covert operations with small groups, dressed as and posing as partisans. In several cases the members of these groups were captured partisans who were turned by the Soviet security. Especially during the last years of the conflict these units accounted for a very large part of the partisan casualties.[23]

The report has an interesting attachment.[24] It is a complete plan for setting up a network for intelligence work inside of Lithuania by the resistance. Some extracts:

III. Goal and task of the (resistance) intelligence service

22. To investigate and make up lists of the agents of the enemy, MGB, MVD, local police and local commander, as well as secret agents of the party or its administrative facilities

23. To follow and reveal enemies (MGB, MVD, police agents), find out about their whereabouts, communications, working methods and organization and to disarm them.

---

20 An interesting detail is that this estimation of the numbers of local MGB-units, 15–20,000 troops, directly involved in the operations against the partisans, are roughly corresponding to the numbers suggested by Juozas Starkauskas, though for a somewhat earlier period, about 1946.

21 These Soviet local units were called by the population in Lithuania "stribai" or sometimes "skrebai." They were mainly used as local guards, for patrol tasks, and for search raids in the countryside, sometimes for deportations and similar occurrences. This local militia featured very low standards in terms of combat ability, but their local knowledge was invaluable, especially for the use of the Interior troops. This Soviet militia, mainly made up of Lithuanians who for one reason or another agreed to collaborate, is still today one of the most painful features of the post-war conflict in Lithuania.

22 The name is somewhat incorrect, it should be OBB (*Otdel po Borbe s Banditizmom* – Department for Anti-Bandit measures). Later this department was renamed MGB 2N.

23 It was such a unit that finally lured Lukša into an ambush in 195, where he got killed.

24 Report No 82, August 22, 1947, Swedish intelligence agency T-kontoret, Swedish war archives.

When analyzing the intelligence report it is clear that priority is placed on the counter intelligence capacity of the resistance. This is natural, having in mind the dynamics of the conflict and the urgent need for this kind of intelligence information. The main focus of interest for the Swedish intelligence, however, was actually military intelligence.

This field is addressed in the report. The account provides information about the location, size and type of Soviet Red Army troops in and adjacent to Lithuania. This includes information about ammunition depots, commanding officers etc.[25] At some points the type of information is of some strategic interest. For example:

> On the railroad Smolensk–Vilna–Kaunas–Kaliningrad during the time period June–August 1947 field units with about 1,500 armored vehicles were transported. Of the armored vehicles about 40% were light armor, 50% medium armor (T-34 tanks etc) and 10% heavy armor (T-75 tanks etc).[26]

This kind of information was exactly what Western intelligence was looking for. Also, the sender gave an idea about how such information could be gathered in the future. The numbers were of course of certain interest, but the main message was that an independent intelligence-network was functioning inside the Soviet Union. Such a network could provide extremely valuable information in a conflict situation.[27]

Needless to say, the information in these reports, especially in the latter, needs thorough research, in order to provide an accurate idea of the factual intelligence gathering capacity of the Lithuanian resistance. A few preliminary conclusions can, however, be made.

In general, it can be said that the information in the report dating from July, 1947 seems to be somewhat exaggerated. There is little doubt that the information was based on source material provided by Lukša during his first "visit" to Poland. It remains unclear, however, whether the material was provided to the

---

25 Much of this information is not possible to check in an accurate way, due to the present lack of normal access to relevant archives, which are mainly located in Moscow.

26 This, among others, suggests an intelligence organization very much resembling the standards of modern low-tech intelligence gathering "on location," which is very enduring, with low vulnerability and with a potential to provide very accurate information when allowed to function over a longer period of time.

27 A qualified guess is that this report was one of the main reason why the Swedes decided to engage in the infiltration of agents into the Baltics. A complicated matter, but with a potential high return in terms of first class intelligence information.

Swedish intelligence in its "pure" form, or whether the material had been altered and/or extended. Some of the figures and details of the report suggest the latter.

The report from February 1948, was beyond a doubt provided to the Swedes by Lukša himself. The contents are, both in terms of content and in terms of addressing relevant intelligence issues, much more elaborate. This report suggests that at the end of 1947 the Lithuanian resistance had a fairly well-functioning intelligence network, primarily for counter intelligence, but useful also for military intelligence, the main point of interest for the West, having in mind a potential conflict with Soviet Union.

The material available from CIA sources emphasizes this aspect. It does also accomplish a certain analysis of the development and background of the armed post-war resistance. In one of the most extensive reports,[28] the CIA provides a short, but quite adequate, account the history of the Lithuanian guerilla war.[29] The report provides a clear account of the circumstances leading up to the raise of an armed resistance. The forced mobilization, the arrests, the deportations, and the expectation that war was imminent are, correctly, suggested as the main reasons for the formation of partisan units.

If one can speak of gripping lines in an intelligence report, then the following short account,[30] describing the initial massive support to the resistance from the civil population probably is as close one can come an emotional account:

> The population helped them as much as they could; the farms helped with food; the priests aided in whatever way they could; nurses and doctors helped with medical supplies stolen from the hospitals. The partisans were everywhere.[31]

The realization that the partisans alone were not able to liberate the country is reflected early on in the intelligence reports. The Swedish report from July, 1947

---

28 CIA, Information report CD No 308, Date of release, 9 January, 1952.

29 Ibid. The wordings in the report and other circumstances strongly suggest that one of the main sources of the report is Juozas Lukša himself. The report in a way could possibly be perceived as his last words about the post-war conflict, and the situation in Lithuania, and also further having in mind the present situation in Eastern Europe. This especially speaking of the last words of the report: "(The partisans) feel that they need organization, instruction ad leadership; patriotism alone is not enough."

30 Ibid. p. 1.

31 In a guerilla war the by far most important source of effective and enduring resistance, both from a tactical, practical and—not least—moral perspective is the support from, if not on the whole, a considerable part of the civil population. This was for instance one of the main reasons for the massive deportations from Lithuania, especially in 1948. (One may, on a separate note, wonder why the insight about the importance of support from civil society in a guerilla war conflict, seems so difficult to grasp, even in present day conflicts.)

provides a rather realistic estimation from the side of the Lithuanian resistance regarding the perspective for Lithuanian independence.

> The Lithuanian resistance has no intention of initiating any actions to liberate the country. Such actions will only be taken either in conjunction with a major conflict between the East and the West or in the case of a politically instable Russia.[32]

These words reveal the hope for a full-blown conflict between the West and the Soviet Union. The futility of this hope is presented painfully clearly in the 1952 CIA report as is the fact that there was no alternative under the circumstances at the time than to resist.

> Active resistance might have been prevented if the people had known beforehand that there would be no war in the future.[33]
>
> ...
>
> On the other hand, it must be admitted, that the partisan movement was inevitable. ... for many people there was no other alternative than to join the partisans.

Western intelligence services in the West made no serious efforts to support the anti-Soviet resistance movement. Besides the infiltration efforts by the CIA in 1950, some efforts were undertaken via the Baltic Sea, in the years around 1950.[34] The intelligence services were, however, very well aware of the existence of an organized resistance, of its potential for providing intelligence and, not the least, its immense potential in the event of an armed conflict with the Soviet Union.[35]

This is clearly stated in a CIA-memorandum written in order to evaluate the potential underground resistance in the event of war in 1950.

---

32 The most interesting notion here is, possible, the second option. In a sense the latter, a situation with a politically instable Russia, was exactly what happened in the end of the 1980's. The population in Lithuania sensed the instability and took to action, though mainly by peaceful means. The demonstrations and actions of the eighties led in turn to independence in 1991.

33 CIA, Information report CD No 308, Date of release, 9 January, 1952, p 2.

34 Some efforts were made from the British, Swedish and—later—US intelligence to establish an agent system in the Baltic States by secret infiltration of recruited Balts during the years around 1950. These efforts, as far as is known, failed almost totally. Interested parties may read more, see for instance, in Tom Bowers The Red Web: MI6 and the KGB Master Group, Aurum, UK, 1989.

35 The hope for a war leading to the liberation of Lithuania persisted as long as into the early fifties. Almost every single person interviewed by the author of this article talks about how they waited for "the Americans" to come and liberate the country. This "broken promise" is still today a source of some bitterness among Lithuanians.

> In the event of war, the Baltic nationals ... would be a serious menace to Soviet security.
> Their hope of regaining national independence would be stimulated by even a distant prospect of Soviet defeat. Many Baltic nationals would engage in underground resistance, despite intensive Soviet police surveillance, particularly if US aid were available.[36]

When this memorandum was published, Juozas Lukša, together with his comrades, were already in Germany, training and preparing for their return to Lithuania.

Can, finally, any estimation of the ability of the Lithuanian resistance as such be found in the available intelligence material? In a report referring to 1947, the time period best described in detail in Juozas Lukša's book, the Lithuanian armed resistance received a high recognition from the Swedish intelligence:

> The Lithuanian partisans in 1947...were at that time probably the best organized, trained and disciplined of all the anti-Communist guerilla groups (in Eastern Europe).[37]

---

36 CIA, Intelligence memorandum No. 250, 5 April 1950.

37 Report No 722, November 10, 1949, regarding Russian measures against the resistance movement in Lithuania, Swedish intelligence agency T-kontoret, Swedish war archives.

A picture of Lukša together with Lithuanian partisans after returning. His clothing differs radically and after a while Lukša changed his outfit in order not to draw attention to himself. The guns tell even more about the passage of time.
The two partisans are equipped with Russian weapons typically used by the resistance. The partisan, second on the left, carries a sub machinegun PPS (Pistolet Pylemjot Sudajeva). The clip holds 35 bullets, with an effective range of 200 meters. The construction was based upon an American concept, giving it the nickname "Amerikanka". The PPS m/43 is considered one of the best sub machineguns of World War II.
The man in the middle holds a Tokarev SVT-40 (Samozaradnaya Vintovka Tokareva), a semi-automatic infantry rifle with 10 bullets per clip. For this reason it was nicknamed Desyatka, "Ten". Sometimes the guerillas modified the weapon to hold clips of 30 bullets, adapting from the Czech light machinegun ZB 26, used by the pre-war Lithuanian army. This made it one of the first assault rifles in the world.
Lukša's comrade, Benediktas Trumpys, carries a 9 mm Czech sub machinegun Samopal-25, with the clip placed in the handle. One of the advantages of the gun was that it could use Soviet pistol ammunition. Later infiltration teams were given German sub machineguns.

Appendix

From the Lithuanian Special Archive, Vilnius, Lithuania

Signed by A. Vanagas

L.A.V.
November 25, 1950

LLKS
Instructions Nr. 2
(Concerning Espionage)

In the interest of an independent Lithuania and in the interest of the current international community, the Lithuanian underground is hereby asked to promptly provide answers to the following questions, pertaining to all spheres of life in Soviet Lithuania. The underground is asked to exert all of their efforts collecting the following information and to send it to the leadership.

The underground is ordered to put all of its efforts into gathering this information as quickly as possible and passing it on to leadership in the form of written accounts, maps, and diagrams.

In addition to locating this information, the resistance should provide any additional information that could be of interest to the leadership.

I. Politics

1. How much freedom and power does the government of the Lithuanian Soviet Socialist Republic (LSSR) have to pass laws?
2. What is the number of Communists working in educational institutions, in offices, in factories, and in other agencies in the provinces?
3. Provide concrete information about the different levels of support among the local population for the present Bolshevik system of governance.
4. How many Russian colonists are living within the territory of the Soviet Units operations? How many of them have arrived since the second Bolshevik occupation. What is their occupation?

5. Put together lists of names of individuals deported to Russian, including their names, surnames, age, place of origin, profession, and location of their deportation.
6. Register the number of Lithuanians who have returned from Russia. Register the number of Lithuanians who have died in Russian concentration camps starting from 1941.
7. Collect information about living conditions for the deportees. Include the number of the concentration camp, the number of Lithuanians in that camp, and the surnames of the overseers of the camps. If the deported person does not work in the concentration camp, indicate where he or she works.

II.Economics

1. Collect the number of *Solkhovs*, State Farms, and Collective Farms in the district. Calculate the amount of land that belongs to the *Solkhovs* and Collective Farms.
2. Collect the number of livestock in the *Solkhovs* and in the Collective Farms.
3. Name the factories and industrial plants within the zone of partisan operation. Provide diagrams and sketches of the factories and industrial plants and describe their characteristics.
4. Show the progress of reconstruction in towns, villages, and in the provinces. Provide a list of new factories and industries that have come into existence since 1944.
5. Describe the larger factories and industries answering these questions: a) the lay-out of the factory; how buildings are set-up, etc; b) the number of workers; c) the annual production; d) what percentage of the product is consumed by the civilian population; what percentage is consumed by the local military; what percentage is transported to Russia; e) how is the factory protected; f) is the factory surrounded by barbed wire; g) what is the quality of goods produced by the factory; h) what raw materials are used and how are they acquired; j) how is the factory heated.

III. Administration

1. What percentage of the administration is Russian? What percentage is Lithuanian? What other nationalities are represented?
2. Provide a list of names of the leadership of the MGB and MVD (The Soviet Interior Forces).

IV. Transportation

1. Indicate what new roads and railroads have been constructed. Provide measurements of the new roads and describe their surface quality. Indicate the location of and draw a diagram of new roads and railroad bridges.
2. Indicate whether single or double rails are being used and indicate the width: Russian or Western.
3. Provide information about all bridges, indicating what building materials were used to construct them: wood, cement, steel. Indicate their width. Provide photographs if possible.
4. Collect regular bus and train schedules. Provide information about regular bus routes in the cities, indicating their routes using maps. Find out the state prices for passenger transportation.
5. Provide information about airplane travel: flight plans, prices, necessary documents for travel and procedures.
6. Provide information about necessary documents and procedures for traveling through restricted zones.

V. Religion and Education

1. How many non-Lithuanians study in the elementary schools and high schools? Provide percentages.
2. What is the percentage in various educational institutions of teachers who are Communist Party members? How many of the students have joined the Communist Youth and the Pioneers?
3. Provide typical examples of instances where the Bolsheviks prevented teachers, administrators, or students to practice national traditions or participate in religious practices.
4. Name any priests who have been placed in religious positions by the Bolsheviks. Is a national church being formed?

VI. Military

A. The Army

1. How many units of the Red Army are stationed in the districts of partisan operation? Where are they stationed? What is their number? How many are there? How are they armed?
2. Where are the units' headquarters located? Are they located close to the troops? What kind of communications do they use?

3. What lines of defense are planned and implemented?
4. Which units are Lithuanians conscripted into? Provide their number and their location.
5. Report on observed maneuvers, location of the maneuvers, district, what type of weaponry was used? Were any new and different weapons put into use?
6. Provide lists of military leadership, beginning with the majors.
7. Provide the location of the unit in the spring of 1945 and their present location.

B. Aviation

Provide a list of airports with the following information:

a) Their location, providing central coordinates, indicating what maps are being used.
b) Runways, their number, length, width (provide a diagram in the proportions of 1:25,000), quality of the surface.
c) The main axis of the airport, indicating direction, length.
d) What seasons the airport is used?
e) Objects in close proximity (their height and their distance from the edge of the airport.)
f) What is the angle of the airport?
g) Where are the airplanes housed: in hangars or on the green? Provide a diagram in which it is shown where the airplanes are kept.
h) Where are the airport warehouses located? How are they furnished? How many square meters of space do they occupy?
i) How many hangars? How are they set up?
j) Is the airport accessible by road, and if so, how is it approached?
k) Are there repair workshops located close to the airport? How many workers work in the repairshops. Do the repairshops only perform repairs or do they also build aircraft?
l) Are there units of paratroopers associated with the airport? How are they organized? Provide detailed information about their setup.
m) Provide the surnames of the pilots, beginning with the majors, providing their numbers and associations.
n) Provide the number of airplanes housed in the airport and their type. Does the airport house nighttime fighter planes? Do planes fly at night?

o) Does the airport have anti-aircraft missiles? How are they set up? Are they in the airport or close to its radars, projectors, goniometers, pelengators. How are they set up? Provide a diagram.
p) Is there a civil aviation section attached to the airport?
q) Are signal colors used at the airport? Do the airplanes have a color scheme?
r) Provide details about pilot training associated with the airport.
s) Have "V" weapons been observed at the airport?
t) What is the morale of the pilots?

D. Navy
D. Science and Technology
1. Provide details about the Bolsheviks latest discoveries in the fields of science and technology. Provide information on *soman*, *tabun*, new chemistry, new physiological veterinary science, and on microbiology.
2. Are Lithuanian scientists conscripted into conducting research on chemical weapons? Are they kept in Lithuania or are they brought to the Soviet Union?

E. Defense of the Coastlines
1. What is the size of the coastline patrol and what is their schedule?
2. What is the MVD control of the fishing ports. What is the procedure for fishermen to go out and fish?
3. What is the system of the nighttime control of the ports?
4. How are the boat crew controlled and how is their return ensured? What happens to families if fishing crews do not return?
5. What classifies fishermen as fishermen?

Lietuviškos Kolekcinės Monetos
projektas dail. Rūta Ničajienė
Basanavičiaus reljef
1851-1927
2001-11-16